Lewis W. Day

Story of the one hundred and first Ohio infantry

A memorial volume

Lewis W. Day

Story of the one hundred and first Ohio infantry
A memorial volume

ISBN/EAN: 9783744748773

Printed in Europe, USA, Canada, Australia, Japan

Cover: Foto ©ninafisch / pixelio.de

More available books at **www.hansebooks.com**

STORY

OF THE

One Hundred and First Ohio Infantry.

A Grand-daughter of the Regiment.

A Memorial Volume.

BY

L. W. DAY.

CLEVELAND, O.:
THE W. M. BAYNE PRINTING CO.,
1894.

PREFACE.

Surely no apology is needed for putting in permanent form the history of a Regiment which, on many fields of the great Civil War, distinguished itself for gallantry, heroic bravery, and unquestioned patriotism. The recounting of the deeds of such an organization of men can in no way detract from the honor and glory of other great Regiments engaged in the same grand cause and doing equally effective work. The Grand Army of the Nation was a unit, and what inures to the credit of one Regiment or organization, adds to the honor of all. That Grand Army came into being as by magic. Its object was the crushing out of treason and the utter destruction of the great armies in rebellion against the Old Flag. It was in the field to settle forever the permanency of our form of government. In the accomplishment of these great ends, the One Hundred and First Ohio was an important and very active factor. The Regiment was recruited in the counties of Crawford, Wyandot, Seneca, Huron and Erie, under the call of the President, issued in the summer of 1862. There was much enthusiasm, and the required number of men was soon raised. Camp was established a Monroeville, and here, on the 30th of August, 1862, the Regiment was formally mustered into the service of the United States, for three years or during the war.

To give the history of such an organization, engaged in such a stupendous work, is a most difficult task. A book of a thousand pages were too small to give it well. The story related in the unambitious chapters which follow, is a simple narrative, told without attempt at rhetorical effect, by one who marched in the ranks with the boys, and who,

L. W. DAY,
COMPANY E.
From photograph taken in 1893.

with them, endured the hardships, faced the dangers and suffered the privations of the camp, the march and the field of battle. The Old Flag, powder-stained, and shot almost into shreds, has been assigned an honorable place in the Flag Room of the State House at Columbus, from which it is never removed except on the occasions of our reunions, when the boys proundly fall into line and follow it as in years agone. Though it can never again be unfurled, it teaches a lesson of Fraternity, Charity and Loyalty, doubly impressive because of its story. Though the writer was not physically able to remain with the Regiment to the finish, yet the temptation to continue to use the pronoun "we" to the end of the Story was irresistible. The preparation of the manuscript has opened wide the portals of memory and caused the dead past to awake and live again in all its magnificent energy, while the scenes of years long gone go trooping by—a pageant of surpassing interest, premonitory of the strength, power and greatness of a redeemed Nation, the equal of which exists not on the face of the earth.

A number of the Comrades have given valuable assistance in the preparation of this volume. To all these, public acknowledgment is hereby made. Especial thanks are due and are hereby tendered General I. M. Kirby, Surgeon T. M. Cook, Comrades W. R. Davis, Charles R. Green, Captain Benjamin F. Bryant, J. A. Stewart, Dr. J. A. Norton, Joseph Van Nest, C. M. Funk, Benjamin T. Strong, Wallace Stahle, Norman D. Egbert, William Dewalt, and, indeed, many others, for diaries, war correspondence, reminiscences, and many practical suggestions, and to Librarian W. H. Brett, of the Cleveland Public Library, and his assistants, for many favors. The portraits and illustrations are, for the most part, the work of the Climax Photo-Engraving Co., Cleveland, O.

LIST OF ENGRAVINGS.

		PAGE
A Grand-daughter of the Regiment		Title
Portrait of General I. M. Kirby		Frontispiece
"	L. W. Day	6
"	Colonel Leander Stem	16
"	Dr. Thomas M. Cook	23
"	George E. Seney	33
"	General W. P. Carlin	47
"	Captain James M. Roberts	51
"	James A. Stewart	61
"	Joshua B. Davis	65
"	Joseph D. Reese	73
"	Lieutenant-Colonel Moses F. Wooster	79
"	Lieutenant John B. Biddle	85
"	S. B. Anway	89
"	Lewis Lowe	95
"	Dr. James A. Norton	99
"	Lieutenant James R. Homer	103
"	John Dice	107
"	George S. McKee	113
"	Major Daniel H. Fox	119
"	Samuel Sprout	125
"	David E. Hale	133
"	Dr. George S. Yingling	139
"	Andrew J. Schnurr	145
"	Hiram C. Moderwell	149
"	Lieutenant Isaac P. Rule	153
"	George F. Drake	159
"	Lieutenant-Colonel John Messer	163
"	Captain George W. Hale	167

LIST OF ENGRAVINGS.

	PAGE
Portrait of Benjamin F. Strong	171
" John Dougherty	181
" William P. Myers	185
" Major-General D. S. Stanley	191
" Lieutenant-Colonel B. B. McDonald	199
" Captain James I. Neff	205
" Joseph Van Nest	211
" Charles R. Green	217
" John A. Roberts	223
" Ephraim Baker	229
Kenesaw—Limit of our advance	234
Portrait of William N. Ebersole	241
" General Nathan Kimball	247
" Peter J. DeWitt	261
" Captain Lyman Parcher	277
" Lieutenant W. R. Davis	289
" Captain Len. D. Smith	299
The Battle of Nashville	306
Portrait of O. J. Benham	311
" Jesse H. Hall	315
" William A. Kinney	319
" C. W. Cunningham	321
" Jay C. Smith	325
" E. J. Squire	339
The Stem Monument	354
Worn Out in the Service	464

ORGANIZATION.

At the time of muster-in, August 30, 1862, the organization of the Regiment was as follows:

FIELD AND STAFF.

LEANDER STEM..........Colonel. LEN. D. SMITH..........Adjutant
JOHN FRANZ......Lieut. Colonel. GEO. S. YINGLING....Asst. Surg.
MOSES F. WOOSTER........Major. WALTER CASWELL....Asst. Surg.
THOMAS M. COOK........Surgeon. O. J. BENHAM....Q. M. Sergeant
GEO. E. SENEY...Quartermaster. W. N. BEER.....Sergeant Major
OLIVER H. KENNEDY...Chaplain.   WM. PIERCE......Com. Sergeant
            J. E. MATHEWS....Hospital Steward.

COMPANY ORGANIZATION.

COMPANY A—Captain, Charles C. Calligan; Lieutenants, Asa R. Hillyer and Daniel H. Fox, and 88 enlisted men.

COMPANY B—Captain, Thomas C. Fernald; Lieutenants, Steven P. Beckwith and Otis L. Peck, and 92 enlisted men.

COMPANY C—Captain, Bedan B. McDonald; Lieutenants, Isaac Anderson and John B. Biddle, and 90 enlisted men.

COMPANY D—Captain, Henry G. Sheldon; Lieutenants, J. B. Curtis and John M. Latimer, and 95 enlisted men.

COMPANY E—Captain, W. C. Parsons; Lieutenants, Lyman C. Parcher and Robert D. Lord, and 88 enlisted men.

COMPANY F—Captain, Isaac M. Kirby; Lieutenants, Franklin Pope and Jacob Newhard, and 98 enlisted men.

COMPANY G—Captain, John Messer; Lieutenants, John P. Fleming and Horace D. Olds, and 93 enlisted men.

COMPANY H—Captain, Jesse Shriver; Lieutenants, Herbert G. Ogden and James I. Neff, and 97 enlisted men.

COMPANY I—Captain, Newcomb M. Barnes; Lieutenants, Robert Lysle, Jr., and Henry A. Taggert, and 97 enlisted men.

COMPANY K—Captain, Montgomery Noble; Lieutenants, Milton M. Ebersole and Philip F. Clyne, and 101 enlisted men.

The several Companies received recruits at various times as follows: Company A, five; Company B, four; Company D, two; Company E, six; Company G, seventeen; Company H, five; Company I, twenty-five, and Company K, three, a total of sixty-seven.

BRIGADE, DIVISION AND CORPS ORGANIZATIONS.

THE PERRYVILLE CAMPAIGN Carlin's Brigade, Mitchell's Division, Gilbert's Corps. The Brigade was made up of the following Regiments: 101st Ohio, 38th Illinois, 21st Illinois, and 15th Wisconsin.

THE STONE'S RIVER CAMPAIGN—Carlin's Brigade, Davis' Division McCook's Corps. The make-up of the Brigade was not changed. Carlin's, Post's and Woodruff's Brigades composed the Division

THE TULLAHOMA AND CHICKAMAUGA CAMPAIGNS Carlin's Brigade, Davis' Division, McCook's Corps. The make-up of the Brigade remained unchanged. Carlin's, Post's and Heg's Brigades composed the Division.

THE ATLANTA AND SUBSEQUENT CAMPAIGNS — Kirby's Brigade,* Kimball's Division, Stanley's Corps (the Fourth). The make-up of the Brigade was: The 101st and 99th Ohio, 21st and 38th Illinois, 31st and 81st Indiana, 1st and 2nd Kentucky.

---

*General Cruft commanded the Brigade from May 3 to June 10, 1864. General Kimball and General Stanley succeeded to Division and Corps commands on the death of General McPherson, June 22, 1864.

LIST OF BATTLES AND CAMPAIGNS.

The following is a list of the more important battles and campaigns in which the One Hundred and First took an active and honorable part. The list will bear considerable extension:

The Perryville Campaign, October 1-20, 1862.
The Battle of Perryville, Ky., October 8, 1862.
The Murfreesboro' Campaign, December 26, 1862—January 4, 1863.
The Battle of Nolensville, or Knob Gap, December 26, 1862.
The Battle of Stone's River, December 31, 1862—Jan. 1, 2, 1863.
The Tullahoma Campaign, June 24-30, 1863.
Battle of Liberty Gap, Tenn., June 25-27, 1863.
The Chickamauga Campaign, August 17—September 22, 1863.
The Battle of Chickamauga, September 19-20, 1863.
The Atlanta Campaign, May 3—September 6, 1864.
Tunnel Hill, May 8, 1864.
Rocky Face Ridge, May 9-11, 1864.
Buzzard's Roost, May 11, 1864.
Battle of Resaca, May 13-16, 1864.
Kingston, May 18, 1864.
Dallas, May 25-30, 1864.
Siege of Kenesaw, June 10-30, 1864.
Pine Mountain, June 10-15, 1864.
Battle of Bald Knob, June 20-21, 1864.
The Storming of Kenesaw, June 27, 1864.
Chattahoochee River, July 6-10, 1864.
Siege of Atlanta, July 28—August 25, 1864.
To the West and South of Atlanta, August 25—September 30, 1864.
Battle of Jonesboro', August 31—September 1, 1864.
Battle of Lovejoy Station, September 2-6, 1864.
Battle of Franklin, November 30, 1864.
Battle of Nashville, December 15, 16, 1864.
Expedition into North Carolina, March 13—April 12, 1865.

CONTENTS.

CHAPTER I.
In Camp—First Experiences ... 17

CHAPTER II.
At the Front—September, 1862 ... 22

CHAPTER III.
A Brief Retrospect ... 34

CHAPTER IV.
The Advance Upon Perryville ... 39

CHAPTER V.
Battle of Perryville ... 48

CHAPTER VI.
Crab Orchard to Bowling Green ... 59

CHAPTER VII.
Bowling Green to Nashville ... 62

CHAPTER VIII.
Battle of Knob Gap or Nolensville ... 71

CHAPTER IX.
Battle of Stone's River ... 78

CHAPTER X.
In Camp at Murfreesboro' ... 115

CHAPTER XI.
Liberty Gap—Tullahoma Campaign ... 129

CHAPTER XII.
Chickamauga Campaign ... 141

CHAPTER XIII.
Battle of Chickamauga ... 152

CHAPTER XIV.
The Atlanta Campaign—Tunnel Hill ... 190

CHAPTER XV.
Rocky Face ... 196

CHAPTER XVI.
Battle of Resaca ... 203

CHAPTER XVII.
From Resaca to Etowah—Kingston ... 210

CONTENTS.

CHAPTER XVIII.
From the Etowah to Kenesaw—Dallas 213

CHAPTER XIX.
Kenesaw 215

CHAPTER XX.
Bald Knob 222

CHAPTER XXI.
The Storming of Kenesaw 231

CHAPTER XXII.
Crossing the Chattahoochee 237

CHAPTER XXIII.
Atlanta 240

CHAPTER XXIV.
Following Hood 268

CHAPTER XXV.
From Columbia to Franklin 282

CHAPTER XXVI.
The Battle of Franklin 288

CHAPTER XXVII.
The Battle of Nashville 302

CHAPTER XXVIII.
In Camp at Huntsville—Expedition to N. Carolina—Muster-Out. 317

PRISON EXPERIENCES.

I.
Captain George W. Hale 331

II.
Lieutenant E. J. Squire 338

III.
John P. Gestenslager 346

IV.
George Mann 348

V.
John H. Crawford 351

Death of Colonel Stem 353
Death of Lieutenant Colonel Wooster 357
Roster 360

The Story of a Regiment.

COLONEL LEANDER STEM.

Killed at Battle of Stone's River, December 31, 1861.

STORY OF THE
ONE HUNDRED AND FIRST OHIO.

CHAPTER I.

IN CAMP—FIRST EXPERIENCES.

The thirtieth of August, 1862, dawned bright and beautiful, glorious in all that goes to make a perfect day. From early dawn our camp had been astir, for on that day we were to lay aside—for a time at least, and many of us forever—the garb of civil life, and, donning the blue, were to become the sworn and active defenders of the old Flag and the Nation which it represented. It was a day and an occasion long to be remembered—an epoch in the lives of us all.

The call of the Government in the hour of National distress and danger for strong arms and willing hearts had been sounded, and the response of the loyal North had been so prompt and generous as to be almost *en masse*. From city, town and country, strong-limbed, able-bodied, determined men left home and kindred and business, and gave themselves to the service of the Nation in such great numbers as to make it almost impossible to equip them. A thousand such men, enthusiastic and true, were assembled at Monroeville under the old flag, ready to follow wherever it might lead, and to carry it wherever duty and loyalty might require. An observer scanning our ranks as we stood in line would readily have seen that our men came from farm and workshop, office and school, store and factory.

The regiment was mustered into the service of the United States as the ONE HUNDRED AND FIRST OHIO VOLUNTEER INFANTRY, at Camp Monroeville, Ohio, on the thirtieth day of August, 1862, by Captain Drake of the Regular Army.

The ceremony of "muster-in" was witnessed by a large number of the friends of the Regiment, including the wives and families of the officers and enlisted men, and others attracted by the novelty of so unusual a scene. The Regiment was assembled without arms, in column, Company front, with space of fifty feet between Companies. As the mustering officer approached, each Company was called to attention, and with bared heads and uplifted right arms we took the oath of allegiance and service.

There were present and in line at time of muster-in 977 officers and enlisted men. During the term of service of the Regiment sixty-seven recruits were received, making a total of 1,044 men to be accounted for. At the time of "muster-out" at Camp Harker, Nashville, Tennessee, June 12th, 1865, there were present and in line only 329 officers and men.

Of the 1,044 men to be accounted for, 86 were either mortally wounded or killed outright in battle; 118 died of disease while in the service; 34, while prisoners of war, died of wounds, disease, ill treatment and exposure, and 11 were missing, concerning whom to this day little or nothing is definitely known, making a total of 249 brave boys who never returned. It has proven an almost impossible task to gather reliable information relative to the death of Comrades since the war. Very many, however, have since died of wounds and disease contracted in the army.

After the close of the war the surviving comrades scattered themselves over the country far and wide, all honest, law-abiding citizens who fully appreciated the value of the

Union for the life of which they sacrificed so much, and who still retain the same inordinate love for the old Flag, "Old Glory" as we called it, beneath whose sacred folds so many deeds of daring and heroism were performed, deeds inspired of intelligent patriotism, sacrifices freely made for home and country.

The scenes in and about camp from day to day, as the various companies arrived, almost beggar description. Many of the men had not been much from home, and to say that they were homesick is to state the fact very mildly. Others, throwing off the restraints of home, acted more like wild colts than anything else. A very large majority were, however, steady, earnest men, as reliable in camp as out of it. Our surroundings were utterly at variance with any experience we had ever had before, and it took time to get our bearings.

Captain Jones of the Regular Army was Commandant of the Post until the Regiment was mustered in, and did all in his power to meet the demands made upon him by the men and officers. True, he was a trifle gruff sometimes, but that was only amusing, for we considered ourselves his equal. We learned better a little later on. None of us, except a few who had "seen service," had any correct idea of what we ought to expect, or what others had a right to expect of us. We wanted everything, wanted it right away, and of the best quality, and plenty of it. The cooking bothered us; but to simplify matters, each Company divided itself up into "messes" of ten or more men each, endeavoring to include in each "mess" some one capable of running the kitchen department. There were a few notable successes, but there were many gloomy failures.

Our time after reaching camp and before muster-in, was principally employed in building barracks, policing quarters, drilling in squads, jawing the cook, asking questions, and breaking guard. We took turns standing guard in order that all might have a chance to break out. On the whole we had a very good time at Monroeville.

On the evening of the 3d of September we were ordered to be ready to leave camp the next day. As a matter of course there was much hurry, bluster and excitement, with not a little confusion. It was an experience positively new to us, but one to which we subsequently became quite accustomed.

"What's up! We certainly are not ready for the field," said a doughty officer, who rightly feared that he himself was not well up in the tactics.

"Why not?" said another. "We surely shall not stay here all summer."

"Certainly not, but we can neither march, handle our guns, nor cook our food." Then he ventured the further suggestion that "We'll make a nice fist of it."

"We can walk if we can't march; we can swing 'round like a gate if we can't wheel, and we can starve if we can't cook. We're all right and shall leave here to-morrow. This is not the only place on earth where we can drill." This seemed to be a settler for the little group.

Many of the men had no faith in the 'order,' but thought it a cute plan to keep them in camp—a game to bring the Regiment under better subjection, or at the most to cause them to put their affairs in better shape, that is, get their traps together. But most of us believed the order to be genuine, and acted accordingly. Many of the noisy fellows sang songs, told stories, played practical jokes, and broke guard as usual. They were in terrible straits next morning.

The eve of our departure was spent by many of the officers and men in camp with their families and friends discussing the proposed movement of the Regiment, the prospects of the war, the welfare of the dear ones to be left at home, and such other matters as the time and circumstances suggested.

"We are to go directly to the front," said Col. Stem, in reply to a query, "to aid in repelling the rebel advance into Kentucky. We shall find plenty of work as soon as we reach the field,—any amount of active service from the word go. We shall not all return," said he, a little later. "Our Regiment is composed of good men and true—men who know for what they are fighting, and when the time comes, the One Hundred and First will give a good account of itself, but in doing this, many must fall—we shall not all return." It has been suggested by some that possibly the Colonel had a presentiment of his own early death in battle. But this is very doubtful. If he had he never for one moment betrayed the slightest hesitation or fear.

The sentiments expressed by Col. Stem seemed to be appreciated and shared by all present. The character of the rank and file of the men composing the Regiment was freely discussed, and highly commended. Each company had been recruited in a comparatively small territory, in consequence of which most of the boys had friends and acquaintances in the ranks.

The company drifted apart into little groups, some discussing one subject, some another. Among the topics thus discussed were the following: The conditon of our army in the East under McClellan and Pope; the movements of Grant and Buell; the position and influence of the Copperhead element in the North; the ability of the North to carry on the war; the bad temper of England, etc.

At length the company broke up never again to be united on this side of the Great River. Many of the good-byes then and there said were forever. But the great screen of the future enabled each to hope that he himself might be permitted to return to his home and kindred after aiding to save his country from the avalanche of treason that seemed ready to engulf it. How little each knew of the immediate future! How few comprehended the situation! How terrible the necessity that compelled law-abiding, peace-loving citizens to make such sacrifices! As we slept that night—our last sleep in the peaceful North for many weary months and years,—the very last for many,—we dreamed of home and comfort and luxury, and of the arts and allurements of peace. Often and often in subsequent months and years, under the most trying and uncomfortable circumstances, we dreamed similar dreams, but they were only dreams—vanishing in thin air with the first dawn of wakefulness. They were delightful while they lasted, and we greedily welcomed them, notwithstanding their well known ephemoral character.

CHAPTER II.

AT THE FRONT—SEPTEMBER, 1862.

Early on the morning of September 4th, 1862, the order to be ready to move at once was repeated, and immediately all set to work in great earnest. At 10 o'clock the order to "fall in" was given, and at 11 o'clock we took the train for Cincinnati amid the cheers of the crowd, and the tears and sobs of our friends. There were many sad partings, many heart-rending farewells, much unutterable sorrow. But our hour had come, and we rolled away toward the field of our future trials and triumphs, pleased to entertain the thought that while we could not all return, each felt that he himself might and would come back.

Nothing of especial importance occurred during the day. We talked and joked and told stories, and sang songs, and had a high time generally.

DR. THOS. M. COOK,
REGIMENTAL AND BRIGADE SURGEON.

From Photograph by Bishop, 1894.

As we were hurried forward, events of the utmost importance were transpiring, not only near the point of our destination, but also in many other sections of our great country—events, the importance of which we did not fully comprehend at the time. Bursting through the mountains of eastern Kentucky, the rebel General Kirby Smith was leading his army across the State, threatening Cincinnati and possibly Louisville. Gen. John Morgan had preceded him, and had inflicted great damage on the various railroad lines upon which Gen. Buell depended for supplies. At the same time Gen. Bragg, emerging from the mountains in the vicinity of Chattanooga, succeeded in eluding the vigilance of Buell's outposts, and started on a rapid march northward, turning Nashville, and making straight for the Ohio, having evidently either Cincinnati or Louisville as his objective point. Buell, as soon as he could recover from his surprise and collect his forces, took to his heels, fully determined to overtake him, whip him and drive him back into his congenial South. But Bragg had the advantage of a splendid start—a lead that was of incalculable advantage to him. Buell's men were good soldiers—they had had great experience—indeed, they were scarcely rested from their long march from Corinth after the fall of that stronghold. The race was beautiful and exciting in the extreme. The rebels had the lead, and they kept it until one of those unexpected, unaccountable events occurred which surprise and astonish us, even to this day. The rebel army was glorying in its success, both present and prospective, when, at Munfordsville, they encountered a little band of determined men. They decided to invest the place, and for this purpose their entire army was halted while certain divisions were set to the work of capturing the little fort. They, of course, succeeded, but they lost a day, a day fully employed by Buell in lessening the distance between his army and that of his antagonist. The game at Munfordsville was not worth the candle—to the Confederates. Bragg seemed to appreciate his mistake, but instead of correcting it he proceeded to make a still more serious one a few days later.

Thus, as we and many others were hurrying southward, Bragg, Smith and Buell were hurrying northward. In the East, the Army of the Potomac had been busy but not successful. The second battle of Bull Run had been fought with disastrous results. Portions of the Army of the Potomac had been engaged elsewhere, but in no instance had an important victory been gained, nor had any movement been made to the decided advantage of the Union cause. In the far South victory hung in the balance, each side was afraid of the other, and the Union cause was making progress very slowly. In Missouri and elsewhere in the West the same state of affairs existed. It is true, the Confederates had scored no great victories. They paid dear for their Bull Run victory, as they did for every other. But they seemed to have the advantage some way—the Union cause seemed to be languishing in the field. Indeed, these were the dark days of '62.

This advance of Bragg, supported, as it was, by Kirby Smith, indicated new life and energy in rebel circles, and was correspondingly depressing on the Union side. In the East, West and South the Confederates seemed to have the Union forces by the throat, while from Tennessee and Kentucky they burst suddenly forth and rushed madly northward, as though they would carry the war into the "Free States."

The foregoing will indicate something of the general state of affairs as we rolled rapidly toward the seat of war that bright September day. As a matter of course, with this ascendency of the Confederate cause, the Copperhead element of the North began to hiss and prepare to strike the defenders of the old flag in the back. But their rejoicing was only for a day. The daring adventure of Bragg was destined to ignominious failure. In other sections the Union armies arose, and, shaking off their lethargy, held the enemy at a respectful distance, ready to fall heavily upon them.

In these dark hours the great loyal North became terribly in earnest. With the gathering darkness came the unwavering determination to roll back the tide of treason that was surging at our very doors, no matter what the cost, nor what the hazard. Regiment after regiment was hurried to the front from every loyal State.

> "We are coming, Father Abraham,
> Three hundred thousand strong."

It was a beautiful picture—a demonstration which could have occurred only in an enlightened, liberty-loving Nation. When all things seemed to be conspiring against the North; when our armies were either defeated in the field or held in check by the insolent foe; when foreign nations seemed anxious to find some pretext for recognizing the "rights" of the South; when darkness, deep and appalling, seemed to be settling down upon our cause, then it was that the loyal North nerved itself not only to the task of holding off the invader, but of hurling him back, crippled and bleeding, to the original haunts of treason. And much more: it would follow him into these same haunts, and there strangle the life out of him and his cause. It was upon just such a mission as this that the One Hundred and First was entering as we rolled onward toward the point at which the shock of contending armies would soon be felt.

We arrived at Cincinnati about sunrise on the morning of September 5th, 1862, partook of a splendid lunch prepared by the loyal ladies of the city, crossed the Ohio on a pontoon bridge, and found ourselves in Dixie shortly before noon. We gave a loud, long, defiant shout as we reached the Southern shore, and at once proceeded to "invade" the sacred soil of Kentucky for the distance of about four miles in a southwesterly direction, going into camp about 3 o'clock in the afternoon, tired and dirty. We had not slept well the night before, so we cheerfully lay down on the ground, which, under the circumstances, seemed much softer than the straw at Monroeville. We remained in this place—Camp Stem—until the 9th, drilling and becoming accustomed to our new mode of life. Of course, being green, we were "put upon" more or less—scared and otherwise toughened to the business in hand. We stood guard for all there was in that kind of soldiering, and we often thought there was a great deal in it. We had all the necessary paraphernalia, even to a guard-house. This guard-house, lock-up, or prison, was not always empty. A "prisoner of war" frequently grinned through the logs and rails, of which it was constructed.

Here we had genuine guns—Austrian muskets—which made themselves "felt" if carried for an hour at a time. These muskets were terrors, and no mistake—second cousins to mountain howitzers. We soon learned to "fall in" in pretty good shape, to mount guard, receive the "grand rounds," etc. Gradually it dawned upon us that the whole thing meant business. It was a difficult thing for us to submit to the commands of our officers, some of whom we knew well knew no more about such matters than we did. We had known them at home and had never thought of being inferior to them, or of submitting to their "orders." To be obedient to these men—officers as they were—was a very hard lesson to learn. But we satisfied ourselves by resolving to lick them as soon as the war should end.

Some very amusing things occurred. On one occasion Captain McDonald of Company C, while making the "grand rounds," came near climbing the Golden Stair. He refused to give the countersign to the man on guard when halted, saying, "Weitz, you know me, you know that I am all right, let me pass."

"Not without the countersign. Advance and give it," bringing his gun to a charge.

"Don't make a fool of yourself, I'm the Officer of the Day, and you know it. Let me pass, I tell you," and McDonald spoke in his most authoritative tones.

"I don't know any man on earth," said the soldier, "and you can't pass without the countersign."

McDonald was greatly pleased at the soldier's knowledge of his duty, but he decided to test him still further. He therefore tried to seize the soldier's gun. In this he was a little too slow, for Weitz, springing back a couple of paces, brought his gun to his face and immediately fired, carefully aiming so as to do no harm, and at the same instant called "Corporal of the Guard!" McDonald was satisfied, but the soldier was not, and the doughty officer was marched back to headquarters under guard. The story of the affair soon got out. Young Weitz was highly complimented for his promptness and sturdiness, but every one grinned when Mc. came around.

At another time the drums beat the long roll just at dusk. Now we had been taught that the long roll meant immediate danger, and that on hearing it at any time, and under any circumstances, every man must at once arm himself and rush to his place in the line and be ready for the worst,—that the long roll would never be sounded unless there was serious danger, etc. On this first occasion we attempted to obey instructions literally. Our line was quickly formed—but such a line! The knees of some of the boys smote powerfully together. Some rushed to the line with their guns only; others with belts and bayonets only; some could find neither guns or belts; others fell over everything and everybody; some got the wrong man's traps, and still others scarcely knew which was the head of the Company.

To the initiated it must have been an amusing sight. The men were affected variously. A few were taken suddenly ill; a few were so excited that they scarcely knew whether they were to walk or ride. One or two, forgetting the direction to 'fall in quickly' started off on an independent expedition of their own—presumably toward the front. But to the credit of the Regiment, be it said, the line was quickly formed, and that it was soon in excellent shape. Had there been occasion for real work the One Hundred and First would have given a good account of itself, even under these circumstances. It would have shown the same pluck and coolness that it exhibited at Perryville and Stone's River a few months later. Of course, the long roll on this occasion was a sell. Some of the boys were hot about it and vowed to whip somebody as soon as circumstances would permit. But they soon got over their huff, and as far as I know, no one was ever whipped on this account.

These occasional scares were a part of our necessary drill. Moreover, our officers were by no means injured by such occurrences. Be it known that the officers were not all among the initiated. Who can recall these exciting scenes and not feel an irresistible desire to smile! We were not sure where the danger lay, nor in what it consisted,— but that there was danger, real, close, and threatening, we green chaps thoroughly believed. We could not imagine where the Johnnies were to come from, but we believed they were coming. And when a few shots—a part of the same game—were fired a short distance in front of us, every man grasped his weapon a little tighter, or if he were one of the suddenly sick, his gripe took him a little more sharply. One poor, trembling Hibernian became so mixed up when the shots were fired that after letting his gun fall once or twice, he finally succeeded in throwing away his powder and ramming the ball down so tight that he spent most of the next day in extracting it. Another poor fellow said to Captain P——

"If I don't come out of this alive—"

"O you'll be all right, just give 'em ———," and then turned away to hide his mirth.

It would be interesting to know the thoughts that must have passed through the minds of those who put up this game, knowing it to be a great farce. How they managed to keep straight faces is a mystery.

But we lived and learned, though our education seemed to come to us rather slowly. Our Company drills were quite awkward at first. If I remember correctly, some of our movements were more like the game of "crack the whip" than military evolutions. But we were kept unmercifully and everlastingly at it. On this point I know my memory is correct. We were marched over logs, through ravines, around stumps, through the woods, over fences, into the mud, until we heartily wished every Johnny in the land would go home and mind his own business—we had enough of such warfare. We really lost our patience sometimes, and vowed to thrash the life out of our tormentors on the first favorable opportunity. Our wrath was short lived. A game or two of muggins or seven-up, put the boys in good humor invariably.

Thus the first few days of our soldiering wore away. On the morning of the 8th of September, we were ordered to be ready to move at a moment's notice. We were on the lookout for scares, and were not able to determine the nature of this order. The camp was full of rumors, according to some of which, there were rebels enough in the vicinity to eat us up. We therefore decided to take our chances and fall in. At nine o'clock next morning we moved camp, being assigned to new quarters near Fort Mitchell. We were impressed with the strength of the Fort, and wondered if we should ever face such great guns in actual combat. We rather hoped not.

While we were thus drilling and gaining necessary experience, the people of Cincinnati and vicinity had been thrown a second time into wild excitement. The first had been occasioned by the presence of the Rebel John Morgan in the preceding July. But that danger had passed, and the people had begun to smile at their fears. Suddenly, however, Kirby Smith at the head of a great army had burst out of the mountains of eastern Kentucky, and was approaching like a tornado across the State toward Cincinnati, carrying everything before him. The city was not ready for the assault which seemed inevitable, and disaster appalling and gigantic, seemed just ahead. At the same time information was received to the effect that Bragg with his entire army was rapidly approaching from the South, with Buell following him as rapidly as he could. All this nearly palsied the people of Cincinnati and other river towns. The Governor called for help, using the telegraph and the daily press for the purpose. The response was overwhelming. It was thought that help would be needed for a few days only, and seemingly the whole State started for the 'front' at Cincinnati. Lew Wallace—true, tried, capable General Lew Wallace, was given the supreme command at the point of danger, and soon organized the forces at his command into working parties, through whose efforts the city was soon surrounded with a system of forts and breastworks that would have been of excellent and sufficient service had the rebels undertaken to capture the city.

The response to Governor Tod's call for special help had been so prompt and so generous that the telegraph had to be called a second time into requisition—this time to stop the sending of troops—many that were on the way had to be turned back. Had the occasion arisen these same Squirrel Hunters would have given a good account of themselves.

Finding himself thus completely shut off from the possibility of capturing Cincinnati, Kirby Smith, after remaining two or three days, withdrew his forces to the vicinity of Lexington and Frankfort, and awaited the coming of his chief. A portion of our Regiment happened to be on picket the morning that Smith's forces arrived. Our line was fired upon by their skirmishers, who were three to our one. We returned the fire and rapidly fell back. It was our first sensation of being fired at, also of firing at any human being. None of us were struck, and I doubt if any of them were.

The Confederate army had retired from our front at Cincinnati; the Squirrel Hunters had been returned to their homes; martial law had been abolished, and a serener state of affairs began to prevail. Many of the troops remained in the vicinity of Cincinnati, picketing and drilling, ready to resist any sudden dash the enemy might care to make, but most of the regiments had been quietly transferred to Louisville, that city being Bragg's evident point of attack. By means of spies, scouts and our cavalry, Generals Wright and Wallace had kept themselves well posted as to rebel movements and intentions.

Our Regiment remained a few days in the vicinity of Fort Mitchell, doing its full share of picketing and camp duty. But on the night of the 23d of September we received orders to proceed to Louisville, then the great military center of the West. We took the train at midnight, coming in from the picket line to do so. Nothing of any unusual interest occurred until we reached the town of North Vernon, Indiana. The ladies of this beautiful little city had prepared a splendid lunch for us, to which we did

GEORGE E. SENEY,
QUARTERMASTER.
From Photograph taken in 1893.

ample justice. It was the last square meal that many of us had for a long, long time. After a short delay, we were again on our way, reaching Jeffersonville shortly before night. We crossed the river next morning, September 25th, and went into camp east of the city, just outside the corporation limits.

The race with Bragg had about ended. Buell's veterans, tired, ragged and disgusted, were just beginning to arrive. Bragg had very kindly stepped aside and taken position at or near Bardstown, thus allowing Buell to enter and occupy Louisville. Why he did this is a mystery to this day.

CHAPTER III.

A BRIEF RETROSPECT.

The Rebel General, Sidney Johnson, had hatched a formidable plan of campaign, by which the war was to be carried into the North, thus relieving the South of a most grievous burden. This was his plan:

He, General Johnson, was to surprise the Union army under Grant at Pittsburg Landing and destroy it, or at least so demoralize it that it would be powerless for a considerable time. With his victorious forces he was then to reclaim the Mississippi, and hold St. Louis, Cairo, and the lower Ohio, including the navigable portions of the Tennessee and Cumberland rivers. Another force was to advance from the vicinity of Chattanooga, upon Louisville, while still another was to be sent from East Tennessee to threaten Cincinnati. Each of these columns was to pick up large numbers of volunteers in the country through which it marched.

These several columns were to move so as to strike the

Ohio at as nearly the same time as possible, so as to confuse and separate the Union forces. By rapid and pre-arranged concentration, the Confederate forces were to unite and force their way across the river and there establish a permanent footing. But nothing could be done until the army under Grant could be forced out of the way. It was a fine scheme, and was by no means impossible. It required Confederate co-operation on a vast scale. Through the authorities at Richmond it was possible to secure this. The weak part of the whole scheme lay in the fact that it presumed entirely too much on the inactivity of the Union forces, or the stupidity of the Northern commanders.

With this gigantic plan in view, and as the initial move in the game, Gen. Johnson assailed the Union army under Grant at Shiloh. How his heart must have swelled with inexpressible satisfaction as he saw our lines doubled up and beaten back in the earlier part of that dreadful struggle. His death on that bloody field, before the tide of Union victory set in, saved him the knowledge of the dire disaster and demoralized flight which on the second day sounded the death knell of the scheme to invade the North, so far as the initial move was concerned.

General Bragg, who was familiar with Johnson's plans, and was subsequently appointed his successor, determined to proceed with the execution of the plan, even with the Cairo part left out. He was determined to "carry the war into the North." And he came entirely too near succeeding. Bragg deliberately threw sand in Buell's eyes and then ran away from him, before Buell could see what was up. It was an exciting time. From the east, pouring out through the mountains came General Kirby Smith, rushing headlong toward Lexington and Frankfort, stumbling over Nelson at Richmond and whipping him, then turning north he sat down for a few days in front of Covington opposite Cincinnati, as has been detailed in the preceding pages. At the same time, General Bragg came rushing up from southeastern Tennessee, aiming straight for Louisville. Buell got himself together instantly and took after him. Bragg was so intoxicated with the greatness of his undertaking, and with the flattering prospects of success, that he did two of the most foolish things that could well be thought of,—two things for which we should not cease to give thanks: 1st—He stopped a whole day to conquer a little handful of brave men at Munfordsville, which enabled Buell to come within menacing and maneuvering distance, and 2nd, he deliberately turned aside and took position near Bardstown, thus allowing Buell to pass him and enter Louisville. Why he thus turned aside, yielding, unforced, all the advantage he had gained, and putting himself on the defensive, when he might have crushed his antagonist, and probably seized the objective point of the campaign, is a question which the Lord only can answer—surely Bragg never could. But it was extremely good of him to do so. The act, however, was that of an idiot. A very similar event occurred later when Hood permitted Schofield to pass within musket-shot of his army, and enter Franklin before him. This was another piece of idiocy, for which we have great reason to be thankful.

As previously stated, Buell's army was just entering Louisville from the South as we entered it from the North. The boys were a sorry looking set—brown, dirty, ragged, long-haired, disgusted—well they surprised us. We assured them that while we had not lost all confidence in them, yet we could not excuse them for letting themselves run down so. They smiled a very bitter smile, hovering between pity and contempt when we informed them that each mess with *us* carried a dust brush, and that *we* should use it. They seemed to take delight in rubbing against us, and especially in turning up their blouse collars and showing us what could there be seen. We were disgusted that the boys who were fighting for the old Flag, for Home and Country, and all that, should allow themselves to be in that plight. But it was not long until we "knew how it was ourselves."

The great race for the North between the armies of Bragg and Buell had ended—the 'invasion' was a failure, and Gen. Sidney Johnson's great scheme for transferring the seat of war into the North was as dead as was the General himself.

The North breathed easier, but figuratively speaking, rolled up its sleeves and resolved that, cost what it would, Bragg should be destroyed, or at least he should be hustled out of Kentucky in the shortest time, and in the most unceremonious manner possible. The brave boys who had marched from Louisville to Nashville, from Nashville to Shiloh, from Shiloh to Corinth, from Corinth to the vicinity of Chattanooga, and from there back to Louisville, were about to begin over again, having a great Confederate army to drive in front of them. On the recent march they had simply tried to follow Bragg, straining every nerve to catch up and if possible whip him. But Bragg did not care to be whipped nor to whip any one else. He was simply going to invade the North. He seemed to have forgotten that Buell's boys would have a vote on that matter.

But our army had a different problem on its hands now—Bragg would have to be destroyed or driven out of the State. The boys as well as the officers seemed to appreciate the difference, and bravely girded themselves for the task. How discouraging it must have seemed to Buell's brave old fellows. The work of a year was apparently undone in a fortnight. We new fellows did not fully appreciate the matter for we could not comprehend at that time what forced marches, half rations and life in the field really meant—though we thought we did. Our practical experience during the months and years that followed, materially differed from the pictures we had drawn. But we were on deck ready to do our best. To a great degree, I am persuaded, we comprehended the situation along the whole line. We knew that Bragg's temporary success had forced our left,—that is, the left of our Western army back to the Ohio, but we also knew that we still held Nashville, that "Old Rosy" (although we knew little of him at that time), was keeping Price and Van Dorn busy, in the vicinity of Iuka, that Grant was immovable at Corinth and Memphis, and that if we could crush the impertinent host under Bragg or force it back into the South, things would be in good shape again. We trusted in Rosecrans and Grant, shouldered our Austrian muskets and were ready to "go for Bragg." We went, but found the going pretty hard.

While Bragg and Buell were racing, Rosecrans had whipped the Confederates in his neighborhood into comparative decency; Grant had secured the absolute control of the Mississippi as far south as Memphis; our army held on to Nashville with a grip that boded only evil to any Confederate force that might care to dispute our ownership, and west of the great River the war had degenerated into contests between bands and commands that were more or less predatory in character. In the East our army was rather more than holding its own, and in the far South we were tightening our grip. In other words we were going at the Confederates from every direction, tooth and nail. Uncle Sam was going in to win. But he had undertaken a very large contract and the goods would be hard to deliver.

In order to unify the work of all the armies, General Halleck, who had been in command at Corinth, was called to Washington, and assigned as Commander-in-Chief. He was a fine soldier on paper and in books, but was of no special use in any other capacity. One great trouble with Halleck was he did not correctly appreciate his own uselessness.

CHAPTER IV.

THE ADVANCE UPON PERRYVILLE.

We remained in camp at Louisville until the morning of the first of October, (1862), when we broke camp and began the long tramp after Bragg. We did but little picketing while here, though we took our turn. But we had what seemed to be a never-ending tussle with the manual of arms. We "ordered arms," "shouldered arms," "presented arms," "reversed arms," and "stacked arms," and then repeated the whole thing until we were ready to "fire" not only our "arms" but our officers and every one else responsible for such disagreeable business. Our "rifles," the Austrian muskets, weighed seemingly, a ton, before the drill was ended. As a respite we were sure to have a dose of "load in seven times—load." Then came practice in firing, sometimes by rank, sometimes by squad, sometimes by company. My shoulders ache yet when I think of it. "Ready——aim——" then the wretch in charge of us would deliberately walk up and down the line, raising the muzzle of one gun, depressing another, correcting the position of this one or that, until our arms and shoulders would ache as though a team of horses had been tugging at them. This drill as frequently conducted was a great outrage. Think of holding an old Austrian musket—a regular 12-pounder, at a steady "aim." It took a good deal of muscle to get the thing out straight even long enough to pull the trigger. There is no denying it—the boys did say bad words sometimes, when this performance was being enacted. Then came the marching, well, we were rapidly coming to be machines. We could fall in in regular order, the Sergeant could call the Company roll without the written list of names, we could get up when the reveille sounded, could go for a "p-i-ll and a p-o-w-der" when the surgeon called, (especially if it were our turn to go on police duty), and we *could* go through with many of the Company evolutions, but we did not like to. However, our dislikes did not go for much. We were exercised in great shape. The only thing about this drill that we enjoyed was to see the officers who drilled us, step into holes and fall over logs as they backed around in order to watch us, and then get mad and charge the whole thing to our mistakes. Ordinarily the drill master was about as badly "blowed" as the boys were, at the end of the seance. I have actually seen the boys so tired that they did not care to play "muggins," and I assure you they were pretty far gone when they had reached that stage. After all, the drilling was all right, and we should have had more of it. But we did not think so at that time. Long before the war ended, we forgave our officers and abandoned the idea of "licking" them on our return home. More than thirty years have rolled into eternity since that time and yet these little insignificant events that took place in our early soldiering seem to stand out almost as clearly on memory's page as do the infinitely greater events that transpired in the later years of the war.

Before entering upon the campaign against Bragg who still remained at and near Bardstown, it became necessary for Buell to reorganize his army so as to include the many new regiments just arrived, in brigades and commands with the old troops. In this reorganization, our Regiment was assigned to Carlin's Brigade, of Mitchell's Division, Gilbert's Corps. The entire army was made up of three corps—the First under the command of Gen. A. McD. McCook, the

BREAKING CAMP.

Second under General Crittenden, and the Third under General Gilbert. General Thomas was announced as second in command. This reorganization had been made in an exceedingly brief time. Buell's last regiments did not reach Louisville until the 29th, and yet he was ready for the field on the 30th. We did not, however, move until the next day.

On the morning of October 1st, we broke camp and took the field against Bragg, advancing in five columns. General Sill with one Division was to move along our left so as to hold Kirby Smith at or near Frankfort, while the remainder of our army assailed Bragg at Bardstown or wherever he should make a stand. It was exceedingly desirable to keep these two rebel commands separated.

General Bragg, leaving his army at Bardstown under the command of General Polk, went on the very day that we left Louisville, across to Lexington for the purpose of assisting in the ceremony of installing a provisional Governor of the State. He seemed to have his heart set on this. Polk had been directed to fall back slowly and in good order to Bryantsville just east of the Kentucky river, distant about 40 miles. General Sill's sudden appearance before Frankfort effectually quieted the installation of the new Govenor. Smith had his hands full to keep Sill out of his camp.

When Bragg discovered that Buell was moving in force, he ordered General Polk to change his line and march into the vicinity of Lexington. But Polk deliberately disobeyed, and held to his original course. This so angered General Bragg that with his staff he rode over to Polk's headquarters and ordered a halt. The new Governor seems to have been forgotten, and was left to shift for himself. By this time Polk's army had reached a point some distance east of Perryville. Bragg ordered him to concentrate his forces at the latter place for battle, though it was probably not his intention to bring on a general engagement, but simply to delay Buell's advance as long as possible, so as to get his trains out of the way. Polk was obliged to obey, and the concentration was affected without further delay. Polk was guilty of another act of disobedience on the morning of the battle.

It is true that our army was separated into five columns in the march from Louisville, but the several columns were always within supporting distance of each other. Bragg supposed them to be nearly sixty miles apart, and when he ordered Polk to march toward Frankfort and Lexington, he thought he might defeat Buell's army in detail—he would crush Sill, then he would fall upon one column after another and finish the work in that way.

The departure of our army on that beautiful first day of October, 1862, must have been a grand sight. In five magnificent columns it poured southward for the express purpose of giving battle to an army equal in size and almost within hearing distance. The enemy's pickets were encountered soon after leaving Louisville and the advance of each column of our army was in the face of the enemy's scouts, and strong parties sent out for the purpose of observation.

Looking back to that time it seems quite strange that we did not more clearly appreciate the fact that our forces would not long remain at Louisville. The prospective movements of the army did not disturb us much, though we discussed the matter to some extent. But when the order came to move, we were not ready for it. We had made some preparations for the future, for we had filled our knapsacks full of blankets, clothing and many other articles that would be convenient about the camp. They were crowded to their utmost capacity. The "old boys" made fun of us. Our officers suggested that we lighten our loads in some way, but we "knew our business," and needed none of their help. A number of old soldiers volunteered and very materially lightened some of our stores before morning. Some of our knapsacks resembled freshly supplied peddler's packs. Fully rigged and ready for the march, we must have presented a very unique appearance. But as long as we were satisfied, it was nobody's business. That's what we told the old boys.

At last we were on our way, and though we marched only six miles that day, many a knapsack wabbled quite a good deal before its carrier reached camp. The day's experience wasn't very funny after all. We slept well and were ready for business next morning. It was slightly funny to see each man standing or leaning at an angle measured by the weight of his knapsack. We trudged across the fields, over fences and through the woods into camp about sixteen miles from Louisville that night. But the boys did not all go in together. They kept coming in till midnight. The old regiments stood the march better for two reasons: they were used to it, and they were marching "light," that is, they carried nothing unnecessary. Each had a rubber blanket, a "poncho," and a woolen blanket. We did not look with favor on such an outfit, but when we went into camp that night we began to discuss the merits of the case. Within a few days we had discarded every superfluous article sending the same back to Louisville for storage. Many of the boys never heard from these bundles again, though some of the companies received them at Bowling Green, Ky., early in November. Relieved of this surplus weight, we were able to maintain our place in the line of march with much greater ease.

On the second or third night out we were so unfortunate as to halt and go into camp where a regiment of Confederates had been encamped a short time before. In the morning we found ourselves fairly alive and swarming with that infernal army pest, the grayback. They were so numerous that it was not necessary to turn up our coat collars to find them. How the old boys did enjoy our discomfiture, and how wrathy we were at them for thinking it so funny. One fellow said he did not mind the bitin' of the pesky things, but he could not spare the blood, unless the government furnished better rations. But the graybacks meant it all right, and stuck to us to the end of our service.

Reveille sounded all too soon next morning, and we were off and away in time for a good day's march. We encamped that night on a slight rise of ground, and had a splendid view of the campfires of our column. It was a beautiful sight, the first we had ever seen of the kind. In spite of orders, the supply of rails was constantly lessened that night. Our fourth day's experience was quite similar to the third, with more of road and less of field to march over. On starting out the boys discovered many sore places and not a few stiff joints. But these were soon forgotten. The march was becoming monotonous. This monotony was slightly relieved the night we encamped on the banks of Salt river. If ever a set of wild boys got loose, the 101st boys were that set. They plunged into the river, they ran into the river, they jumped in, they fell in, they threw each other in, they waded, and swam, and "ducked" and dived, and strangled and kicked and floundered, and yelled continually. In short they had a good time.

The sixth of October marks a date in our history which few of us will ever forget. It was on this day that General Bragg lost his temper, and, riding up to General Polk, ordered him to halt, about face and concentrate for battle. Of course we knew nothing of all this, but those whose business it was to know, knew it and acted accordingly.

General Buell, who marched with our corps, the Third, Gilbert's, saw the necessity of concentrating his army in the best possible position. To this end our Corps, our Division at least, was put in motion by daylight, and moved forward at a rate that seemed to us to border closely on a quickstep for several hours. We were on the road, a Macadamized pike, which leads through Perryville. Considerable cavalry, much artillery and many troops, of the Confederate army, as well as of the Union army, had passed along this road within a few days, so that the limestone with which it had been ballasted had been ground to powder. Moreover, for several weeks a severe drouth had prevailed in this section of the State. The weather was intensely hot. The march of the troops raised the lime dust in great clouds; the merciless sun beat down upon our heads almost baking us, the dust seemed to absorb all the moisture in our bodies, and water was not to be had. Our suffering was intense. From early morning till long after sunset, we kept up our weary march. Scores of our boys fell out of line, and though threatened by the rear guard, refused to go further until they had rested. Out of over 900 men who started in the morning, less than 300 stood in line when we stacked arms that night. And the 300 were exceedingly wabbly. We had marched thirty-two miles. Several cavalry skirmishes had taken place during the day, but they were soon over, and we resumed the dreadful trudge. All in all, it was probably as severe a day's marching as the Regiment ever experienced. Longer marches were made, but taking the heat, the drouth and especially the lime dust into the account, this was probably the worst. Many of the boys who had fallen out during the day came up in the night, but many others never saw the Regiment again.

As we staggered into camp that night, what was the condition of affairs so far as the opposing armies were concerned? Briefly this:

Bragg had ordered Polk to concentrate at Perryville.

He was executing the command, and a large force was already on the ground. Other regiments were hurrying into position. While we were rushing like mad in an easterly direction to gain every possible advantage and compel the rebels to fight, they were countermarching rapidly toward the west, to occupy a strong position deliberately chosen for them by Bragg and his officers. On the supposition that Bragg would fight at Bryantsville or vicinity, General McCook had been sent hurriedly to aid in intercepting Kirby Smith, should he attempt to join Bragg. But when it was learned that Bragg was concentrating at Perryville, he was halted and directed to watch out both ways, that is, to keep an eye on Smith, but on no account to lose sight of Polk, and the main Confederate army. Since leaving Louisville we had encountered considerable resistance, but, by comparatively small bands. At Bardstown a larger force had been met and dispersed. Both artillery and infantry had been necessary to dislodge this force which was the rear guard of the main rebel army. The infantry supports were not engaged to any considerable extent. On the afternoon of the 7th, Gen. Buell learned by actual conflict that the enemy was in his immediate front in considerable number. A good deal of hard fighting was necessary to drive them from certain springs or pools of water which were absolutely necessary for us to have. The enemy was finally crowded back to within a mile of Perryville. Our Brigade had no especial part in this encounter, except to enjoy the water.

GEN. W. P. CARLIN,
OUR FIRST BRIGADE COMMANDER.
From Photograph taken in 1894.

CHAPTER V.

BATTLE OF PERRYVILLE.

We remained in the camp into which we had staggered the night before until about 9 o'clock, (Oct. 7) when we advanced and took a position with the reserves. The slight rise of ground on which we were formed afforded us a fine view of the troops as they lay there awaiting developments. The long lines of battle presented a most imposing aspect. We were quite recovered from the exceeding fatigue of the preceding day, and were ready for whatever might occur. We knew the old boys were anxious to see what we would do under fire. We slept that night on our arms, partly for drill and partly to be ready should occasion require. Nothing especial occurred during the night, except the reading of some Confederate letters found in a rebel knapsack. Oh, my; what gush! We were in line very early the next morning, the 8th.

Having forced the enemy well back toward Perryville, and being fully satisfied that Bragg intended to make a stand here General Buell sent a courier to General McCook, ordering him to march at 3 o'clock on the morning of the 8th, and take his place in line on our left. McCook did not receive the order until 2:30 o'clock in the morning, but 90 minutes later he was on the march.

It is pleasant to note that the Rev. General Polk again disobeyed orders on the morning of the 8th. He had been ordered by General Bragg to take the offensive early in the morning and bring on the fight before the arrival of McCook, who was known to be at Macksville, ten miles away. He deliberately took the order under advisement, and finally decided that he would not take the offensive, but would assume

BATTLE OF PERRYVILLE.   49

a "defensive-offensive" attitude. This was very "offensive" to Bragg, who rebuked him, calling him down to business. But by this time McCook was on the ground ready for the day's work.

Early on the morning of the 8th, a vigorous assault was made by the Confederates to recover the springs and ponds of water which had been taken from them the evening before. In this they were not at all successful. They were repulsed very handsomely and with considerable loss. Our Division was in line as a reserve ready to go in whenever the occasion offered. Our brigade was not needed.

When Bragg heard the noise of this assault he very naturally supposed that General Polk was making the early assault on Gilbert's corps which he had ordered. But when hour after hour passed without anything being done, he became nervous, then excited, then wrathy, and then called on Polk, and was surprised to find that the latter gentleman had no intention to obey the former's order to make a vigorous assault at the first possible moment. Bragg was exasperated and it is said he used bad words. Polk deserved a personal drubbing for his insolent conduct. And this was the second offense on this short campaign. On a subsequent occasion when Rosecrans was trying to get in the rear of Bragg at Chattanooga, this same General Polk deliberately refused, or, at least, neglected to obey orders, which saved a part of our army from a fearful defeat. And yet Polk held his command.

Our commanders, at Perryville were not able to understand why the Confederates did not attack in force on the morning of the 8th; but they were very grateful for the delay which enabled McCook to get into position. Even after General Bragg had called on General Polk and ordered him point blank to attack, the latter General did not do so until General Rouseau, who commanded a division in McCook's corps, advanced his right so as to get water, for which his troops were suffering. In making this advance, Rouseau knocked the chip off Polk's shoulder. Then he *was* mad, and immediately made dispositions for attack.

While we were awaiting the arrival of General McCook's Corps, it was very essential that our Corps should remain as quiet and inoffensive as possible. It should be borne in mind that up to 10 o'clock on the morning of the 8th, Gilbert's Corps was the only one on the field. Crittenden had been obliged to march to Rolling Fork for water, and could not reach the field until after McCook was in line. Our Corps faced the whole Confederate army till 10 o'clock that morning.

Awaiting the arrival of McCook, it was eminently proper that Gilbert should keep quiet, but after the entire line was established, it is very difficult to understand why McCook and a portion of Gilbert's Corps should have been compelled to fight the battle alone. Crittenden's Corps did nothing, though it was on the field in ample time to have done excellent service. Thomas was there nervously anxious to participate. But no. McCook's and a part of Gilbert's corps were in for it. Not even was a demonstration made to call off the hounds that were dogging the feet of McCook. Strange to say, Gilbert was not called upon until the tide of temporary defeat rolled our left back and brought the rebel host into our immediate presence. Not until nearly 4 o'clock in the afternoon was even this assistance given McCook's veterans. The stupidity of this performance, or rather the lack of performance, has never been satisfactorily explained, and for the very best of reasons never will be. The most charitable excuse given is that Buell did not know that a great battle had been fought on our left. He should have known it. McCook was anxious for as much glory as he could get, but it was Buell's busi-

CAPT. JAMES M. ROBERTS,
OUR FIRST COLOR BEARER.
From Photograph taken in 1880.

ness to know everything pertaining to the battle as it progressed. He was with Gilbert's Corps, and might have guessed the magnitude of the conflict from the roar of artillery that continued for hours.

McCook arrived on the ground about 10:30, but the main assault was not made by the enemy until afternoon. They had not been idle. Their forces had been carefully posted. On their extreme right and facing McCook's left, Cheatham's corps, massed at brigade front, was in line. Immemediately on his left was Wood, and on Wood's left, Jones. To the left of Jones was Brown, and on Brown's left was Johnson. Back of Brown, Cleburne, and to the left of Cleburne, Liddell. All of these faced McCook, who had only two divisions. They had orders to destroy him. Further to the left, Adams and Powell faced Gilbert's corps, but these were not to attack until McCook had been crushed. Then they were to fall on our front and flank and finish the work. It was a fine plan and worked well for a time.

The rebel onset fell upon McCook's extreme left, held by General Jackson. The rebels were staggered, fairly blinded by the fire of our troops, but unfortunately our General Jackson was killed, almost at the first onset. This resulted in confusion of which the Confederates took prompt advantage. While gallantly endeavoring to rally our lines, General Terrill was mortally wounded. His brigade—new troops never under fire before—gave way, and fell back in confusion. The experienced troops, however, knew their duty and most gallantly did they perform it. The fall of Generals Jackson and Terrill and the loss of Terrill's brigade, caused the temporary loss of our left. Our boys gave way—slowly, but give way they did. No troops on earth could withstand the infernal pounding that was heaped upon them that afternoon by the concentrated rebel army, 16,000 strong in McCook's front.

Our batteries did most excellent service at the critical moment, covering the retreat of our lines, and inspiring them to renewed effort on the first opportunity.

The turning of our left caused the yielding of McCook's entire line a short distance. This brought the tide of battle very close to Sheridan of our own Division. McCook requested his assistance. He also sent to General Gilbert for help on his left. General Gooding's Brigade was sent. It gave a good account of itself. So close had the Confederate line come to General Sheridan that he found no difficulty in "developing" it. Matters were getting intensely interesting in our own vicinity about this time. The dignified and mysterious roar of battle had quite suddenly developed into the viciously wicked scream and crash of shot and shell. The smoke of the guns could be distinctly seen through the trees; the yells of Sheridan's men as they rushed into the fight, could be heard; the bursting of shells near by added to the horror—indeed the very climax of the contest seemed to be reached uncomfortably near by. Sheridan drove the Confederates a short distance, inch by inch. McCook rallied and at once re-formed his lines. Smarting under the defeat he had just sustained, he sought vengeance on those who had broken his lines. At the moment that Sheridan ordered his assault, we received the order to fall in. We had fallen in many times before, but never under such circumstances.

For hours we had been listening to the majestic roll of the battle which now seemed to be drawing nearer and nearer. We had heard the most dreadful rumors of frightful losses; we had seen troops moving rapidly to the support of McCook; the din was now just over the brow of the hill in our front and to our left; shells had fallen dangerously near us, and now in the midst of it all we were ordered into line for the purpose of taking a hand. It seemed pretty tough.

When the Confederates had forced McCook back so as to expose Sheridan's left, fresh troops under Adams were ordered to assail him, Sheridan. This they did most gallantly, but Sheridan was something of an assailer himself. During the entire battle he had raged with an unutterable rage, at not being permitted to attack the enemy in his front. Now that his time had come, he poured shot and shell and bullet and sword and profanity into the rebel lines in front of him. The fight here, was pretty nearly an even one. Sheridan held his own, but could not advance far on account of his exposed left. It was now our time. Carlin's Brigade advanced on Sheridan's right, driving the enemy back handsomely. McCook's reorganized columns fell heavily upon the enemy and the whole face of affairs was speedily changed. McCook's advance was checked, but he held his ground against all comers. Sheridan carried his line some distance, but was careful not to get too far beyond McCook. From his advanced position he delivered an enfilading artillery fire upon the butternuts who were stopping McCook, resulting in their speedy withdrawal. In our own front we had things pretty much our own way. The Confederates under Powell came up with a rush, but went back pell-mell. We charged them across the fields, down the hill, across the river and into the town. Indeed we acted very unwisely. McCook had been unable to advance very far, Sheridan dared not get much beyond McCook's right, but we,—Carlin's Brigade, especially—had gone far in front of any other part of our line. Our battery opened fire on the town, attracting the fire of a rebel battery posted just south of the village. It was impossible for Carlin to fall back without endangering our line. We therefore hugged the earth until after dark when we withdrew in safety. While thus exposed we were between our own and the rebel battery. The screaming of shells as they flew across the valley was a kind of music to which mortals can never become accustomed, and as the evening deepened, and the darkness came on the sight became very grand. The fire from the guns, and the bursting of shells were to us a new kind of fireworks. The rebel battery gave its whole attention to our battery, which "let us out" in good shape.

Darkness put an end to the struggle, and under the cover of night the Confederates withdrew, leaving their dead and seriously wounded in our hands. It was supposed, however, that Bragg would renew the fight on the following day, and Buell made his plans accordingly. Had the battle been continued on the 9th, Crittenden would have had an important work to do. But a comparatively light rear-guard was all that could be found in the morning, and a few rounds from our batteries soon scattered them. We advanced in line of battle toward the town, but finding nothing we "supported" our battery while it shelled the woods beyond the river.

When we fell back from the perilous position referred to above, we halted for the night near an old house used as a general hospital. We had never seen such a sight before. Surgeons of both armies were very busy, the evidence of their efforts being visible on every hand. Doubtless they were kind-hearted and careful, but to us it seemed like brutality. There were several piles of amputated limbs, to which accessions were being made constantly. Dead and dying men were lying promiscuously around. Others were awaiting their turn to be thrown upon the operating table, an old work-bench, while still others were being bandaged and patched up in various ways and assigned to this hospital or that as the character of the injury might indicate. Some seemed to be resigned, others were cross and snappy. Some prayed, some cursed; some were silent and glum as death; others were noisy and almost violent. The deep heartrending groans now and again heard, betokened suffering beyond expression. Those of us who visited this terrible place came away sick at heart, but thankful that we had escaped unhurt. Efforts had been made to find and bring in all the wounded, and many a stretcher bore its bleeding burden to this good Samaritan retreat. Now and then a deep groan came in a-field, indicating that some one, either Blue or Gray, had been missed. Searching parties immediately sought him, guided to his resting place by his cries.

On the afternoon of the 9th we marched northward almost the entire length of the terrible field. Dead men lay as they fell, though the wounded had been removed. In some places the dead had been collected. I remember seeing thirty-one bodies gathered in one place. At another place there were eighteen, and still at another there were twelve. The Blue and Gray were in separate heaps. In one place we saw six men dead—killed by a shell, as was evident by their position. Many dead were found near the fences where they had sought shelter. Several charges had been made in that part of the line held by Rouseau in the vicinity of the "Burnt Barn," and near the haystacks. Here the dead were numerous. In our march we passed a hospital, an old house near Willson's or Wilkinson's Creek—It was a repetition of the one we had visited the night before and had no attraction for us. We crossed the stream now almost dry and went into camp. The horrors and the scenes of suffering witnessed in our march across the battle field, completely sobered the boys, bringing into prominent view the terrible side of those bloody conflicts. We had drunk deeply of the excitement of the conflict, but here we witnessed a few of the results of the deeds performed in the frenzy of battle.

For hours after we went into camp, but few words were spoken. The boys were sitting here and there busy with their own thoughts or writing letters to parents or friends at home.

The battle had been a severe one. Bragg, in his report of the fight, says: "For the time engaged, it was one of the bloodiest and most hotly contested battles of the war." Buell says the same in substance.

The Union losses were as follows:

```
Number killed............................... 916
Number wounded..............................2943
Number missing.............................. 489
                                            ----
   Total...................................4348
```

The Confederate loss was not less than 4500, making a grand total of 8848 men killed, wounded and missing, the work of one afternoon.

Between the evening of the 8th and the morning of the 9th, Bragg withdrew his entire army from Buell's front, and marched rapidly in the direction of East Tennessee. Indeed he had stopped to fight the battle, only to gain time to move his plunder further out of danger. He paid a terrible price for the time, but he got his train out of the way. While the battle was raging in front to Perryville, Bragg's wagoners were lashing their animals to get as far away as possible. Moreover, Bragg doubtless well knew that if he could not whip McCook, even, who had but two divisions on the field, and a part of Gilbert's Corps, he would stand no chance the next day when Buell would put his whole army into the fight. Under the circumstances he had gained as much time as it was safe for him to try to gain. After a dignified delay, a part of our army, notably Crittenden's corps was sent in pursuit of Bragg's retreating forces, but not in time to intercept or even annoy them. After a rest of two days we resumed our march, advancing quite rapidly in the direction of Camp Dick Robinson. But we soon came to an abrupt halt and immediately began to retrace our steps. We returned to the vicinity of Perryville where we went again into camp at 11 o'clork at night, having gained only three miles by the day's march. The next morning, October 12, we marched at 9 o'clock in the midst of a drizzling rain.

Wild rumors were current to the effect that Bragg was surrounded and that the next day we would capture him and his whole army. Our camping in line of battle that night gave color to this rumor. But we did not capture the rebel army the next day, nor did we even hear from it. Resuming our march early in the morning we continued the pursuit in the same jerky way in which it had thus far been conducted. The country through which we were marching seemed excellent, but the Confederates had stripped it of everything that could be eaten by man or beast. Our own trains were not with us and we were soon on short rations and a little later, no rations at all. Our line of march was along the Danville road, tho' we were marching through the woods and across the fields most of the time. The extreme heat added greatly to our suffering. The march was practically without incident until we reached the vicinity of Lancaster on the 15th.

We had marched very rapidly the day before and finally came up with a portion of the rebel rearguard. They shelled us for a while and showed a brave front, but when we marched to the right of the village for the purpose of gaining their rear, they very promptly withdrew. The firing which had been very noisy, had been quite harmless. Falling into our usual trudge we followed the enemy to within one and a half miles of the village of Crab Orchard, where the pursuit was given over, so far as we were concerned. We remained here in camp until the 21st, suffering greatly from the excessive heat, but especially for a day or two for want of provisions. Our trains reached us on the 16th.

CHAPTER VI.

CRAB ORCHARD TO BOWLING GREEN.

On the morning of October 21st we broke camp and began the long, dreary march toward Nashville, moving by way of Lancaster, Danville, Lebanon and Bowling Green. The notion that we must not destroy private property, nay, more, that we must protect it, still had defenders in some of our officers, but it was impossible to enforce such a rule. In spite of all orders, fences would melt away, chicken roosts would yield their treasures, pantries would disgorge their delicacies, and many sheep and pigs would find their way into camp. Our officers had good fires made of pieces of cedar rails, and we never forgot to share with them, and especially the officer of the day, our delicacies and valuable finds in the line of live stock, cured meats, etc. Whether or not this helped to keep them quiet, they can answer.

Nothing of any considerable importance occurred on the march to Bowling Green. We suffered considerably from thirst, but this was unavoidable on account of the exceedingly dry weather. The water that could be had was frequently wholly unfit for use, and was a fruitful source of disease among the boys. Indeed the horrid water that we were compelled to use during the entire term of service, was a never-ending source of trouble. It was the cause of many more deaths than all the Confederate lead that was fired.

The monotony of our march was slightly broken by our passage over Muldraugh Hills. The scenery was beautiful, the roads excellent. We passed the ruins of several battlements which had been thrown up to defend the pass. It occurred to us that a comparatively small army could hold several times its number in check, as long as the attack was confined to the front. But there are other passes near by, and there is no good chance here for a repetition of Thermopyle. The view from some of the higher portions of the road was magnificent. Added to the natural beauty which in the latter part of October is especially fine, our army could be seen for miles, winding its majestic way over hills, across valleys, around cliffs, through the shade and into the boiling sun.

The passage of Green River, near Greenburg, gave the boys an opportunity to go swimming, which they were not slow to improve. Although it was somewhat difficult to swim with the water only knee deep, yet the boys had a "splendid good" time.

Long before we had reached this point nearly every man in the Regiment had become foot sore, many very seriously so. Our shoes were almost as hard and unyielding as wooden ones, and blisters, the like of which we never saw before nor since became very common. The start after a night's rest was a terrible affair. Many a boy declared that he could not endure the pain, and that he would be —— if he would try. But with the "fall in" and "forward" he was quite sure to find his place. But didn't we growl; and didn't some of the boys say words they never say at home! Some of the boys thoughtlessly cut holes in their shoes to relieve the pressure on the blisters, but this only admitted dust and gravel and made bad matters worse. How these unfortunate ones ever got to Bowling Green is a mystery. They probably practiced the philosophy of the Dutchman in the Mexican war. He said it was so hot they could not stand it, but they had to.

JAS. A. STEWART,
COMPANY F.
FOR MANY YEARS SECRETARY OF THE 101ST ASSOCIATION.

From Photograph taken in 1893.

On the afternoon of November 1st, we marched through Bowling Green and went into camp one and a half miles west of town. We endeavored to spruce up as we marched through the city, and advanced platoon front, our officers really trying to have us keep straight lines. They objected to limping, and were not pleased when we indulged in passing remarks on the general appearance of the place as we passed through the streets. Crossing the bridge over Barren river, just east of the town, the temptation was very strong to jump in and cool our burning feet, but the opportunity was not favorable and we trudged on.

In some way we had come to feel that we should remain at Bowling Green a few days for rest. We had also learned that General Buell would here turn over his command to General Rosecrans. Few of our men were special admirers of Buell, and all were ready for a new man.

CHAPTER VII.

BOWLING GREEN TO NASHVILLE.

We remained in camp at Bowling Green until the morning of November 4th. Our time was devoted to cleaning up our old clothes, drawing new, absolute rest, and just enough camp duty to remind us that we were still in the army.

On every hand there were evidences of ruin and devastation. It will be remembered that the first rebel line of defence extended westerly from Bowling Green through Fort Donelson to Columbus, Kentucky. When Grant turned Columbus, which the rebels had called the Gibralter of the Mississippi, and drove the Confederates from Forts Henry and Donelson, Bowling Green had to be abandoned by them. It was immediately occupied by our troops.

More or less fighting had taken place in and about the town from the very beginning of the war. Bragg in his march to the North had passed through Glasgow about thirty miles to the eastward, but his cavalry, and the frequent raids of Morgan and others kept this part of the State in a stirred up condition all the time. A number of tall chimneys standing stark alone, told of destruction by fire, as plainly as did appearances generally indicate acts of vandalism, for vandalism it surely must have been.

Our band-box appearance that had been so exasperating to the old troops, had most effectually passed away, and we looked seedy enough for the most exacting "Old Vet." While at Bowling Green some of us received our knapsacks and bundles which we had sent back to Louisville for storage, soon after we started on our march. Many of us received letters here that could not be delivered to us on the march. Aside from these letters the next greatest comfort we received was the newspapers. From time to time we had rumors in camp and on the march of what was going on in the outside world, but our information was too vague and meager to afford any satisfaction. Our four days here were employed to the very best possible advantage. We profited greatly by the rest. For nearly two days after passing Muldraugh's Hills, we had been practically without food, and had subsequently been very sparingly supplied until we came into the vicinity of Bowling Green. We were, therefore, in the very best possible condition to enjoy food and rest.

The most notable event that occurred while we lay at Bowling Green was the change of commanders. On the 30th of October General Rosecrans had, by order of the War Department, assumed command of General Buell's army, but he did not reach the field until November 2d. He was gladly received by the men of all arms. He had won a most honorable name, and we were glad to march under his leadership. The army which had fought at Perryville and previously at Pittsburg Landing and elsewhere, and which had been known as the Army of the Ohio, was hereafter to be known as the Army of the Cumberland, or the Fourteenth Army Corps. The territory in which it was to operate was to be conquered from the enemy. We were to occupy and hold Middle and East Tennesee, and the northern half of Georgia and Alabama.

Nearly all this territory was at that time under the control of the enemy. The Army of the Cumberland was to have a Department if it could conquer one. We were immediately to move out of the territory of the Department of Ohio, into our own promised land. But we should find many giants in that country.

On the morning of the 4th of November we broke camp, marched up through the city and took the main road southward to Nashville. We passed through Memphis Junction, near Franklin, and Mitchellville, and finally halted at Edgefield Junction ten miles north of Nashville.

We were a little suspicious of our new division commander, Gen. Jeff. C. Davis. He was the fellow who had shot and killed General Nelson in the Gault House at Louisville, and we had never heard that the matter had been carefully looked into, and his conduct approved. He had the reputation of being a great fighter, which reputation he maintained to the bitter end. We were given to understand that Davis meant business from the word "go," and that if the army ever remained in camp for any particular time, we would be treated as a regiment of cavalry and be rushed about the country accordingly. We found long before the end of the war that this was not all fiction. He was eternally wanting to make a "dash," or to raid something. But we came to like Davis very much, as he seemed to have a

JOSHUA B DAVIS,
COMPANY B.
From Photograph taken in 1894.

warm place for his "Innocents," as he called us, after Knob Gap.

The 101st left sixty boys sick in the hospital at Bowling Green when we began our march to the South. We marched until dark the first day, but had plenty of rations, and water was abundant. On the 5th day of November, the second day out, about three o'clock in the afternoon, we crossed the Tennessee line. A stone had been set up, on one side of which was the name "Kentucky," on the other "Tennesee." Each regiment and nearly every separate company passing this point, raised a vociferous shout. We were at last in Tennessee. We entered the State in a drizzling mist, and the hard rain which came on later in the evening failed to impress us with the far-famed beauty of "Old Tennessee." The night was cold and wretched in every way, and the boys decided the State was not worth fighting for. The sun came out next morning clear and hot. We marched until 4 o'clock, when we went into camp full of the rumor that we were to remain right there for the next three weeks—but we were on the march next morning, soon after sunrise, en route for the next camping place. About 10 o'clock, after one or two of those unaccountable, jerky halts, we heard a cannon-shot about a mile in front. Soon another. How our ranks did "close up," and how the fire came back into the eyes of the boys who were tired and jaded with the long march. Of course a few were taken suddenly ill, but almost every one stepped as lightly as he did the day we left Louisville. Another and another shot succeeded the first two, and we were ordered forward, first at a brisk march, then for a short distance on the double quick. But the cannonading had ceased—the musketry fire had been very light—the scrap was soon over. A small detachment of Morgan's cavalry had made a foolish dash for our Division wagons, and had paid dearly for their temerity. Two or three were wounded, one at least was killed, and the remainder ran away wiser than they came. The dead rebel was the subject of very heartless remarks as he lay there at the side of the road with a chunk of cheese in his mouth. He had been shot while trying to rob a suttler's wagon. Our road lay directly across a narrow valley, in a ravine of which Morgan's men had secreted themselves preparatory to their fatal assault. The incident kept us in gossip all the rest of the afternoon. We advanced very rapidly for about five miles, then slowed down and finally went into camp near Edgefield Junction. A day or two before we marched from Bowling Green, General Rosecrans had hurried troops forward to Gallatin on the Tennessee river, and had a large force of men repairing the railroad to Nashville. A very important bridge at Edgefield Junction had been destroyed by the rebels. Events proved that we were destined for this point, to act as a guard during its reconstruction. It rained and snowed the day we had reached the Junction, and, all in all, it was a miserable time and place. But the next morning was clear and crisp and we forgot our hardships.

Morgan and others were reported as hanging on our flanks for the purpose of creating trouble. Moreover, the railroad was not yet in shape and we were not well supplied with provisions. An expedition was planned for relief. On Sunday morning, the 9th, our Brigade—the 101st in advance—took up its line of march for the mountains, nine miles back toward Mitchellville, where we had the brush with Morgan's men a few days before. With our Brigade in the mountains, the forage wagons of the Division could and did scour the whole country for provisions for both man and beast. Our camp, the first night out, was exceptionally beautiful, occupying a small plateau, just large enough for the Regiment, and nearly a mile in advance of the other regiments of the Brigade.

On the 11th we proceeded into the mountains, a detachment composed of Companies E and H, being sent a few miles across the country to determine the presence or absence of the enemy in that quarter. Capt. Lyman Parcher was in charge of the expedition. No rebels were found. On our way back we struck a little community that had thus far escaped the ravages of war. Our boys soon made the discovery, and for a time nothing but sticks and stones, and clods, and bayonets and ramrods, and chickens and geese and turkeys and guineas and pigs could be seen or heard. "The combat deepened," and not even a goose escaped. As we left that field of carnage, we presented the appearance of "Sherman's Bummers," subsequently so famous. We remained in the mountains until the morning of the 14th, when we broke camp and returned to the Junction. Nothing occurred in camp to break the usual monotony of a soldier's life until the 21st, when we broke camp and took up our march for Edgefield, a small village opposite Nashville.

Since leaving Louisville we had been so constantly on the march, that as soon as any one was taken seriously ill, he was placed in the ambulance and conveyed to the nearest hospital. At Edgefield Junction we remained a number of days, during which time one of our boys, Michael Sherer, of Co. E, was taken sick of typhoid fever. He died in camp and was buried in great solemnity beneath the branches of a young cedar. He was an excellent man, a brave soldier, a Christian hero. His younger brother, Adam, was killed in battle at Stone's River, a few weeks later.

Our camp at Edgefield was about three-fourths of a mile from the Cumberland. By dint of hard work, our quarters were made quite attractive. Barring the amount of drilling to which we were daily subjected, we rather enjoyed our sojourn here. On the 23rd, at 2:30 P. M., we had a grand review of our Division by General Rosecrans. All such reviews are bores, but we were glad to see our new commander. He completely captivated us by his fine bearing, his cheerful smile, and especially by the way he took off his hat to us. He even spoke to us, and promised to look after us, and give us plenty of marching and all the fighting we wanted. He was cheered to the echo.

Our army was being concentrated in the vicinity of Nashville. The defenses of the city were being strengthened and extended. With the opening of the railroad from Louisville, every effort was being put forth to gather the largest possible amount of clothing, provisions and other army supplies, preparatory to an advance upon Bragg, who was supposed to be concentrating in the vicinity of Murfreesboro', about thirty miles away.

As a part of the general preparation, we left camp at Edgefield on the 28th of November, and were assigned our position in the line of defense just south of Nashville, near the Franklin pike, going into camp in what was known as Camp Andy Johnson. We remained here, drilling and doing our full share of picketing until the 10th of December, when we were moved some distance to the left, and placed in camp just to the right of the Nolensville or Edmondson pike, Gen. Phil. Sheridan's Brigade being on our immediate left. We frequently saw the General at Colonel Stem's and General Carlin's headquarters, but I question if any of us guessed that the stubby Chief we saw there would ever prove the dashing cavalry leader he afterwards came to be. But it was "Phil," and no mistake.

Although we were nearing the crisis; although the time at which the two great armies were to come into deadly conflict had almost arrived, yet our daily camp life went right along as though nothing was expected. Rumors were afloat and we boys discussed matters to some extent, and yet as I look back to those days I am surprised at the lack of definiteness that our thoughts and our discussions assumed. I speak of course of the rank and file, to which I belonged. We realized that our army was there for business, that Bragg would dispute our advance, and yet these facts did not impress us. They were a species of historical facts. Our discussions were rather tame affairs about what "they", (the commanding Generals, and the army at large), would do.

Notwithstanding our careless and apparently thoughtless way of looking at these matters, when the decisive moment came and we were ready for the advance, we all realized that stirring times were just ahead of us. We knew that we should strike rebel pickets before two hours, and that our advance would be heralded all over the South at once, and that strong hands would be raised against us. But we did not bother our heads about this, and it was quite as well we did not.

General Thomas, leaving only a garrison at Gallatin, moved his two Divisions, Negley's and Rousseau's with Walker's Brigade of Fry's Division, to Nashville, and was assigned his position in the Center. Thomas' other Division was engaged in guarding our communications, especially the railroad to Louisville. McCook with his three Divisions, Davis', Sheridan's and Johnson's, was on the Right, Crittenden with his three, Rousseau's, Van Cleve's and Negley's, was on the Left. Thus were we posted a few miles south and east of Nashville on Christmas Day, 1862.

Carlin's Brigade, the Second, Davis' Division, was made up as follows:—

    101st Ohio, Col. L. Stem, commanding.
    21st Illinois, Col. W. S. Alexander, commanding.
    38th Illinois, Col. D. H. Gilmer, commanding.
    15th Wisconsin, Lt.-Colonel David McKee, commanding.
    2d Minnesota Battery, Capt. W. A. Hotchkiss, commanding.

CHAPTER VIII.

BATTLE OF KNOB GAP OR NOLENSVILLE.

The morning of December 24, 1862, brought with it a great surprise for all our boys. Bright new Springfield rifles were given us in exchange for the Austrian horrors we had so long carried. We went wild over the change and acted much like little boys with new sleds. At once we became anxious to try our new guns on the enemy—nor had we long to wait.

The two opposing armies lay within thirty miles of each other, armed to the teeth, but both apparently in winter quarters. Bragg was at Murfreesboro', having strong outposts at Nolensville, Lavergne, and Triune. His entire front was well and vigorously picketed.

On Christmas night, a council called by General Rosecrans at his headquarters had been attended by his Corps commanders. A decision was soon reached :—to advance at daylight next morning in full force. The position of the Confederate army indicated that Bragg would fight at Murfreesboro', but if not there, then at Shelbyville, twenty-five miles south of that place. Our advance was to be prompt, vigorous, and decisive. The army was to move in three columns —the Left under Crittenden, by way of the Murfreesboro' pike, with Lavergne as the first objective point; the Center under Thomas, by way of the Franklin pike to Brentwood where a halt was to be made pending further developments, and the Right under McCook, by way of the Nolensville pike and dirt roads, with Nolensville as the first objective point. Each Corps had certain specified work to accomplish that first day, and each practically succeeded. It will be observed that the above arrangement threw Thomas for the time being on the right of McCook. This was done to threaten Bragg's possible retreat upon Shelbyville. Should the Confederate general decide to accept battle at Murfreesboro', Thomas could easily move toward the left and take his proper place in line. Our moving columns were to keep in constant communication with one another.

Before daylight on Friday morning, December 26th, our entire army had breakfasted and at sunrise was ready for the field. Our camp had melted away like dew in the summer's sun. Nearly all our regimental wagons were rolling back toward the rear, and only a tent here and there was left standing for the use of the sick until they could be otherwise cared for.

The shrill notes of bugles, the long roll of drums, the commands of officers, the marching of companies and regiments into position, the deserted camp—all indicated even to the dullest of us that a move of very unusual importance was being made. Well did we know, and quite fully did we appreciate that the army was moving forward to engage in a momentous struggle—a struggle which involved the possession of one whole state and half of another—a struggle which we all fondly hoped might go far toward ending the war, but in which we knew many of us must fall.

As regiment after regiment and brigade after brigade filed out of camp, accompanied by its artillery, and took its place in the long line that stretched far down the pike, the scene became one of surpassing beauty and inspiring grandeur—one not soon to be forgotten. Alas! how soon was this great host to be shattered, torn and mangled in dreadful battle, but, withal, victorious.

At the same moment we were filing into the Nolensville pike, Crittenden was moving into the Murfreesboro' pike and Thomas was crossing over to the Franklin pike. Thus, three irresistible columns were to press their way forward

JOSEPH D. REESE,
COMPANY K.
From Photograph taken in 1894.

that day, guided by one master hand, and inspired by one patriotic thought, the utter destruction of the enemy in our front, and the complete overthrow of the cause that army represented. Advancing, our head of column soon fell upon the Confederate pickets, and at once began to skirmish with them, driving them steadily back. At Seven Mile Creek, our Division filed to the right and followed a dirt road which leads south-eastward, passing a mile or so to the south-west of the village of Nolensville. The remainder of the Corps moved straight out the pike. In this advance Carlin's brigade had the lead. The skirmishing soon became quite brisk and interesting. Arriving near the Confederate position, and finding the enemy quite stubborn, our Brigade was thrown into line of battle with Company E, of our Regiment, on the skirmish line. Advancing promptly we crowded the Confederate skirmishers back upon their main position. They did not stand for close work until they had joined the reserve force, and not much harm was here done on either side. The Regiment was hurried forward to the crest of a hill, from which they delivered a volley of musketry upon the rebels some distance in our front. The Johnnies took the hint and moved off rapidly toward the village. One fellow, however, was too brave to run, and was soon cut off—'covered' by many rifles, and compelled to surrender. He was a pompous six-footer, and keenly felt his humiliation. He swore fluently and with great apparent satisfaction, but beyond this he would say nothing, except, 'We'll lick —— out of you fellers before to-morrow night, if you don't git right out of this yere country, —— you.' I should like to meet that chap again—under different circumstances. It was very evident that Hardee, who was in command at Nolensville, intended to show considerable fight. The force against which we had thus far been contending, was guarding the rebel left flank, and had now fallen back to the main line. Our Brigade was at once moved rapidly to our left a short distance, halting in the edge of a dense woods fronting a large open field, beyond which to the eastward lay the village of Nolensville. The moment we emerged from the woods into the open field, a Confederate battery opened upon us to the full extent of its ability, sometimes throwing solid shot, and sometimes shell, many of which came uncomfortably close. Many of us thought we ran considerable risk in advancing under such a protest, but General Carlin and Colonel Stem did not seem to so regard it, and we went right on quite rapidly. Seeing that we were determined to advance, and further, that Pinney's battery was about ready to open on them, these brave butternuts withdrew, and took up a new position nearly a mile south of the town at what was known as Knob Gap, a pass through the hills, easy of defense, except against flankers. By this time we had reached the middle of the large field referred to above, and at once faced our line more to the south, and moved rapidly on the enemy's new position. On either side of the pike and running almost at right angles with it, there was a heavy stone wall or fence, back of which the Confederate dismounted cavalry, in considerable force, had taken position. The prospect was by no means encouraging, but we pushed steadily forward, wading mud in the cornfield ankle-deep. A moment later, the Confederate battery opened again, but our own battery had by this time come into a fine position and replied, even to their very first volley. So accurate and so rapid was the fire of Pinney's gunners, that the rebel artillerists gave their whole attention to them, neglecting us almost entirely. Both batteries were on high ground, while we were laboring along in the low ground between them. The shrieking of shot and shell as they screamed through the air over our heads reminded us of Perryville. It was a very exciting moment. Our line had become irregular and ragged, in consequence of which a brief halt was called to adjust it. We could distinctly see the enemy behind the stone wall, and when a little later, the order was given to fix bayonets, I tell you the situation was becoming quite serious to some of us at least who had never had experience with cold steel. The line moved promptly forward, and in a few moments a charge was ordered. We raised the run, or at least we tried to do so. It had rained hard in the morning and the ground was very soft. The charge was therefore not a beautiful one, the mud was too deep. But we pushed ourselves forward as fast as we possibly could, and before the Johnnies seemed to know it, we were at the foot of the hill from the summit of which the rebel battery was firing. At once they attempted to depress their guns, and rake us with grape and canister. The charge went over our heads in comparative harmlessness. Only a few of our men were injured. Summoning up the very last bit of strength we had left, and using a part of that to yell with, we charged up the side of the hill, over the stone wall and upon the battery still smoking from the volley intended for our utter destruction, capturing two guns and several prisoners. We raised a loud shout as the colors of the 101st were placed between the captured guns. We all understood why the Rebel gunners had neglected us—they had rather more than they could take care of in our own battery, but I have never heard a satisfactory explanation of the harmlessness of the dismounted butternuts behind the stone wall. We found no fault with them, however.

We followed the enemy to the south entrance of the gap, but by this time it was nearly dark, and raining hard. No enemy was in sight, but soon a voice came from the hillside some distance in front : " Here's your mule." We emptied a few of our Springfields at them, but the only response was a repetition of the Southern classic, "Here's your mule." Darkness falling, our picket line was established, and the rest of us, tentless, tired, and wet, rolled ourselves up in our blankets and lay down to soak and sleep.

Speaking of this charge, General Davis says in his official report of the campaign: "Carlin's Brigade charged the battery, carried the heights in his front and captured two guns." General McCook, referring to the same affair said in his report: "The 101st Ohio charged the battery and captured one gun with caisson and teams." *

Long before daylight next morning we were in line ready to renew hostilities. But with the dawn came a dense fog— so dense that we could not distinguish friend from foe at the distance of a few hundred feet. Not until 11 o'clock did this begin to lift. As soon as it was safe the army moved forward toward Triune, the enemy falling slowly and sullenly back toward Murfreesboro'. We encamped in the woods near the town, where we remained over the next day, Sunday, drying out and writing letters.

We had a novel experience here. Quartermaster Seney desiring to reward us for having been such good boys at Knob Gap, issued wheat flower instead of hard-tack. I saw sights the like of which I had never seen before. We knew not what to do with the flour. Our kitchen furniture consisted of one or two spiders to each mess, and a tin cup and canteen apiece. It was Sunday, and we had time to experiment. We poured the flour upon our rubber blankets and then doused it with water till it was wet—if too wet we borrowed and tried to thicken it, or went partnership with some one whose flour was not wet enough. When mixed we tried to bake it. Some wrapped it around ramrods and set it up to roast; some fastened it in a wad at the end of

---

* Two guns were captured.

the ramrod and held it over the blazing fire; some rolled it in paper and put it in the hot ashes; some pegged the stuff to trees near the fire and swore at it. A few henpecked married fellows made passable pancakes, but most of us preferred 'biscuit.' We had lots of fun if we did go hungry.

CHAPTER IX.

BATTLE OF STONE'S RIVER.

If, leaving our biscuit-making for a moment, we could have looked over into the Confederate camp in front of Murfreesboro', we should have been well satisfied that Bragg intended to fight. All that Sunday, (Dec. 28th) he was busy establishing and strengthening his lines, and preparing for our coming. His troops had been called in from Bradyville, Readyville, Shelbyville, and Eagleville—his whole army was going into position.

Early on the morning of the 29th, we took up our line of march toward our left, moving by way of the Bole-Jack road. We knew immediately, that we were headed for Murfreesboro'—Speculation ran high among the boys as to whether Bragg would wait for us. On the whole we rather thought he would. The recent rains had rendered this road almost impassable in some places, and many a time we were obliged to put our shoulders to the wheel and help the artillery out of the mud. At length, after a toilsome day's march we went into camp quite late. Our advance had met with considerable resistance, especially for an hour or two before dark. The possession of the bridge over Overall's Creek had cost a severe struggle, but it remained with us. We went into camp Monday night between Overall's Creek and the Rebel line of battle, Woodruff's Brigade guarding the

LIEUT. COL. MOSES F. WOOSTER,
Killed at Battle of Stone's River, December 31, 1862.

the bridge. Johnson's Division was on the right. We had marched across the fields in which our cavalry had assailed and defeated the Confederate cavalry, and rumors of the conflict were confirmed by the generally demolished condition of things. All were agreed by this time that Bragg was going to fight.

About the first thing we did after going into camp, was to "put our houses in order." Many of us went through our knapsacks and removed letters and mementos which we would not wish to have fall into rebel hands, for who could tell what the next day might bring forth. Tired and hungry, we lay down without shelter and waited for the morning.

Reveille did not sound on the morning of the 30th. At three o'clock we were quietly wakened and immediately formed into line. Here we stood in almost dead silence until daylight. We were then allowed very small fires carefully concealed, with which to prepare breakfast. This was soon over, and in a short time we were ordered forward. With the early dawn came the occasional crack of musketry, as pickets exchanged compliments, and now and then the heavy boom of cannon off to our left. We expected trouble the moment we attempted to advance. In front of us was a large open field bordered on the east and south by very dense woods. The trees were large and very close together, admirably adapted for purposes of defense. Before advancing into these woods, a strong skirmish line selected from the 15th Wisconsin, under command of Colonel McKee of that regiment, was sent forward to clear the way. We followed at a proper distance. This skirmish line had hot work of it, before we had gone far. The rebels contested every inch of ground, and fell back only when compelled to do so. It was very evident that we were nearing the position selected by Bragg for his final stand. So exceedingly severe was this skirmish in the woods, that we were ordered to pile our knapsacks, reserving only our overcoats which we wore, and blankets. We never saw nor heard of our knapsacks again. They fell into the hands of the rebels the next morning. Our skirmish line was relieved soon after noon by a fresh detail from the 21st Illinois, under command of Lieutenant Colonel McMackin. As we advanced the resistance increased. Many wounded were carried to the rear borne on stretchers or supported on the arms of comrades. A riderless white horse dripping with blood, came rushing wildly back from the front, and rumors of the most desperate fighting in Sheridan's front reached us constantly. But in the face of it all we steadily advanced. The character of the woods in our front prevented the use of artillery until we had driven the enemy some distance. Along the pike, and on Sheridan's front, cannon were freely used. As we advanced we gradually came into a dense cedar thicket, in which the defending party had all the advantage. Peering through this underbrush, he could generally get the first sight of his opponent. Many an encounter amounting to a hand to hand struggle for life took place in these bushes, the history of which will never be written. The result depended largely on nerve and dexterity after discovery. Such warfare seemed almost like murder. But finally we had them out of the woods, and forced them back far enough to reveal their line of battle. In doing this we had come into the vicinity of the Widow Smith's house, near the Franklin or Triune Road. The road near the house runs through a cut and is otherwise protected by a ridge or bank. Back of this bank and in the cut, a force of rebels had been secreted. When we reached the opening in front of the Smith house these rascals gave us a volley which, for a moment, staggered the 21st Illinois, which received the most of it. As soon as the rebels had been forced out of the thickets, our Second Minnesota battery galloped into position and began to drum the main Confederate line. A rebel battery well posted near the Smith house replied with great vigor, and fearing our artillery might be charged, our Regiment was pushed close up to our battery as support. At Perryville and at Knob Gap, the shells went over our heads; here they came down alarmingly close. We hugged the earth upon which we were lying, and made ourselves as small as possible. Brave Colonel Stem stood his ground, nor flinched. Dear, noble man, he was to fall next morning. At dark we fell back a few hundred feet and took our place in the line of battle which was soon established. It fell to the lot of Company E, Captain Parcher, to picket in front of our Regiment that night. The two armies—their battle lines—were less than fifteen hundred feet apart. It was a very delicate matter to establish and post the pickets, but by the exercise of great care and by going "on all fours" part of the way, we were finally in proper shape. By mutual, though tacit consent, there was no firing during the night.

All night long we could hear the movement of troops and artillery to our right. So serious did this seem to us that we several times sent word to Regimental headquarters calling attention to the fact. Colonel Stem forwarded the report to Brigade, Division and Corps headquarters, but nothing was done about it. Similar reports were sent from other parts of the picket line, but to no effect. To this day it seems strange that no attention was given this matter. The very existence of the army was jeopardized by the failure to do so.

Rosecrans announced his plan of battle for the next day to his Corps commanders who met him about 11 o'clock on the night of the 30th. McCook was to hold the enemy in check, and if necessary, he was to fall slowly back. With our Left, Crittenden was to attack the rebel Right, drive it back from the river, and press them into and through Murfreesboro'. As soon as Crittenden was well started, our Center, under Thomas, was to advance stoutly, and aid in the rout of the enemy. They were to be swung around and cornered between McCook and Overall's Creek. This move was to commence sharply at 7 o'clock. McCook was especially cautioned to look to his lines, as he was depended on to hold the rebel Left, while Crittenden and the rest rolled their Right back in disaster.

The day's developments had convinced the rebel Commander that he could crush our Right, and roll it back in disaster cornering our army between Stone's River and Overall's Creek. This plan was announced to Bragg's Corps commanders about the same hour that Rosecrans announced his. It will be seen that his plan was the exact counterpart of Rosecrans'. But Bragg ordered the assault to be made at daylight. He thus got the start and viciously held it all day. Rosecrans, in order to induce Bragg to weaken his force in front of our Left, ordered McCook to build fires far to our Right, to give the impression that our lines extended further in that direction than they really did. Bragg, in order to have troops in readiness at daylight, to crush our Right sent a large force in that direction, whether fooled by our fires or not, does not appear.

These meetings broke up—the Corps commanders on each side went to their respective headquarters, communicated with their Division commanders, and at daylight, instead of 7 o'clock, the ball was opened by Bragg and not by Rosecrans, though at the appointed hour Crittenden advanced, cleared his front, and was carrying everything before him toward Murfreesboro'. Depending on McCook to hold our Right, Rosecrans saw his plan working like a charm. Our Center was firm, but the sound of heavy fighting far to our right disturbed the Commander-in-Chief. There was too much of it. The roar of artillery seemed to be growing further to the westward and nearer. Soon a messenger brought the news of the crushing of our Right. Our victorious Left had to be recalled, and dispositions instantly made to stem the tide of defeat.

On the Right, matters had indeed taken a most serious turn. The tacit armistice between our pickets and the rebels in our immediate front, was dissolved with the first rays of the morning. Each man took to his tree or his log and warily "looked out" both for himself and his antagonist. The firing was brisk as soon as we could see. The early and vigorous advance of the rebel line made it necessary to recall our picket line—indeed we were unceremoniously driven in, a number of our boys being badly wounded before we reached our place in the line of battle, a few hundred feet back of us. Although the rebel line did not at once assail us—they were awaiting further developments on our right—their sharpshooters and a heavy skirmish line poured a destructive fire into us. Colonel Stem called for volunteers to silence them. Several arose, (we were lying flat on the ground), one of whom, Adam Sherer, was shot and instantly killed, and a number of others were more or less seriously wounded. At the same instant, the rebel main line advanced and opened on us at short range. Their fire was terrible, but ours must have been more so, for we repulsed them in fine shape. But many of our boys were down.

In the few minutes' lull that followed, we could hear all too distinctly the roar of the fight on our right. Knowing that large masses of troops and artillery had been sent in that direction by the enemy during the night, we feared the ominous sounds that rolled up through the woods from that part of the field.

LIEUTENANT JOHN B. BIDDLE,
COMPANY C.
KILLED AT BATTLE OF STONE'S RIVER, DECEMBER 31, 1862.

But the foe in our front was upon us again like demons —and again we sent them back after a half hour's contest. The few minutes' lull that ensued revealed to us the fact that the fighting far to our right was still further to the rear. We realized that Johnson was giving way. The heavy roll of cannon on Crittenden's front came to us, also, from the extreme left of our army.

For some reason we were moved a short distance to our left, not many rods, however. Our new position brought the line of our Regiment across a great flat rock, as level as a floor almost, and flush with the surface of the ground. There were loose rocks also lying around. Before we had fully reached our new position, the rebel lines again advanced, but were rather more respectful—they did not come so close. We opened a galling and to all appearances a very discouraging fire upon them. The affair was exceedingly hot, the firing being almost continuous for what seemed to be a long time.

It was during this terrible assault that Colonel Stem fell at the head of his Regiment, mortally wounded. Brave, unflinching, cool, and determined, his was an example of devotion and daring worthy the emulation of the bravest of the brave. A heroic effort was made to bear him from the field, but he was too badly wounded, and the almost unheard of fierceness of the assault made this impossible.

In one of the few lulls, the roaring of the battle close at hand on our left, under Sheridan, inspired us. Some of us listened for the sounds on the right, but there was an ominous silence in that direction at that moment. The time for such reflections and observations was but momentary, for again the conflict was on in our own front. We held our ground, not yielding one inch until we were assailed on our right flank, and until we were fired upon from the rear. It would be madness to remain longer, and the order was given to fall back. It was during this fierce struggle that Lieutenant Colonel Wooster fell wounded unto death. He was borne some distance to the rear, but the flank movement of the enemy made it impossible to take him far. "Put me down, boys, and rally to the support of the flag," said he. Circumstances which we were powerless to control, made this necessary, and he, too, fell into the hands of the enemy. Comrade Lepper of Company I, who was also wounded, was captured with him, and remained with him until he died.

The history of the disaster to our extreme Right is known to all. With the routing of Johnson, Davis' right was exposed. Post's Brigade, forming the right of Davis' line, fought stubbornly, but was compelled to give way. This exposed Carlin's right, and enabled the rebels to fire upon us almost from the rear. We had all we could take care of directly in front of us, and we would have held that line until now—but assailed in front, flank and rear, we did well to fall back when we did. Woodruff at once followed. All this endangered Sheridan's right, and soon made it necessary for him to readjust his line, throwing his right Brigade considerably back, and facing it more to the south. He was soon compelled to readjust his whole line, pivoting it on his left.

Thus far we had been fighting in the woods. Back of us an eighth of a mile was an open cotton field, extending westerly and northerly to woods that bordered it on these two sides. In the southern edge of this field, just back of a fence which separated it from the woods, we formed our second line. It proved, however, to be as untenable as our former position, and for the same reason. The Confederates were squarely on our flank, and were protected by the fence along the Griscom road, behind which they were sheltering themselves, and from between the rails of which they were deliberately murdering us. We were also followed through the woods by the troops with which we had fought before falling back. As we formed our second line, two of our batteries, the Second Minnesota and Houghtelling's, took position on an eminence on the northern edge of the cotton field. We were soon ordered to fall back to the woods near the batteries. It took a deal of pluck to do this with the enemy on two sides of us, flushed with victory and numbering three to our one at this stage of the game. We reached the other side in good time, and promptly formed our line. Our Brigade was honored at this moment by the presence of Generals Carlin, Davis and McCook. The latter bravely encouraged the boys to hold the line at all hazards—said he had sent for re-enforcements and that we should soon drive the rascals back. Scarcely had he uttered his words of cheer, when a rebel bullet struck his horse's shoulder, causing the blood to spurt over the general's lap and legs. He was a large, fleshy man, slow of motion, but he dismounted as quickly as the lightest trooper a-horse. Our battery pounded the rebels terribly, but on they came, great columns of them still further to our right and rear. They were within easy musket range, but our ammunition was running low. With the falling back of Post's and Carlin's Brigades, Woodruff's lines were doubled up and his position so changed that Carlin's left no longer touched his right. There was serious danger that Carlin might be cut off from the possibility of retreat. Two rebel batteries wheeled into position at this instant near the Griscom road, and raked our lines and hammered our batteries in a terrible way.

Our artillery replied with great spirit, and we gave their infantry the best the range would allow. The rascals in front of us were in no hurry to charge across the open cotton field, and, to tell the truth, we were not at all anxious

S. B. ANWAY,
COMPANY H.
From photograph taken in 1894.

to have them do so. Johnson's whole Division was out of sight; Post had been driven off the field; Carlin was the extreme right of the Union army, and was greatly outnumbered in flank and in front. There was but one thing to do, and we did it—we fell back. We did so in an orderly way—acting deliberately and according to orders. But how or when our trouble would end, we had not the slightest idea. Off to the west of our organized lines, across an open field, we could see bodies of troops which we took to be rebels, as they doubtless were. The fear of a rush by the enemy's cavalry caused considerable excitement at one time, but such a calamity was not added to our misfortunes. The line of our retreat seemed to be guided by the noise of the battle raging in great fury along the center of our army. In view of the terrible experiences of the morning we listened in dismay to the dreadful roar of the conflict that seemed to shake both earth and heaven. In this horrid din, the most horrid of all was the unearthly yelling of charging columns as they rushed upon each other with bayonet and sword. We seemed to have been transported from earth to the very gates of Hell, toward the open portals of which we seemed to be forced by the still greater danger that lurked in the woods and fields to the south and west of us.

Our batteries, of course, retreated when we withdrew from our third position—one of them, Houghtelling's, soon after fell into the hands of the enemy. Our retreat was beset with dangers on every hand, and had to be conducted with great skill and caution. Reaching the Wilkinson Pike, we formed our line of battle, our fourth position, under the shelter of a rail fence, and determined again to give battle to the enemy still crowding us on flank and front. It seemed useless—our line was so short, so light every way. But it was against nature to go one step further without stopping to show our teeth, and if possible check the victorious foe. We knew well, and so did they, that our Right was crushed, that it was all important for them to gain the Nashville Pike, on which were huddled our ammuniiton trains, the destruction of which would most effectually quiet our guns and make us their prisoners. What wonder, then, that they should advance in such force and with such confidence. The final victory seemed to them to be almost within grasp. At the word of command, our line of battle was formed for the fourth time on that dreadful morning. There was no excitement—we were not panic stricken. Each man looked deliberately to his gun and awaited the storm which was sure to fall. Our ammunition was scarce, and we were ordered to fire only at very close range. The sharpshooters and skirmishers soon appeared in view, closely followed by the rebel line of battle. On they came, nor halted until they were within easy range. On their left were other columns, still continuing that flank movement that had proved so eminently successful since daylight. For our light line, consisting of a few hundred men, to attempt to check such a host were madness. The Confederate line was so close that we could distinctly hear the commands of the loud-mouthed colonel conducting the column. He was one of the most profane wretches we had ever heard. Every order was profusely garnished with great, full-grown oaths of pure Southern extraction, even to the accent. We were almost terrified at such language, but every man in his command obeyed as promptly as a whipped spaniel. Seeing the hopelessness of our position, we gave them one deliberate volley, then continued our retreat. Our pace was doubtless somewhat accelerated by the volley which the profane rebel commander was swearing out when we left him.

The line of our retreat carried us in a northerly direction. We were constantly in the presence of the enemy, with more or less skirmishing, usually at long range, until we reached the Nashville Pike. Approaching this, they very properly halted, readjusted their lines and prepared for serious business. Our swearing colonel was not within hearing distance for some little time.

As we emerged from the woods and crossed the pike, a half mile west of the intersection of the pike and the railroad, we felt a sense of relief. Surely we had finally reached the utmost limit to which the Lord would allow us to be driven. Moreover, the most vigorous preparations were being made to check the tide of defeat on our right. We halted between the pike and the railroad, and awaited developments. Of the four hundred brave boys who had stood shoulder to shoulder early in the morning, many were dead, many others were dying, hundreds were wounded or prisoners, scores were missing—only eighteen were with the colors as we stood there, Major Kirby at that hour in command of the regiment, and Adjutant Len D. Smith being of the number. The dear old Regiment had been hammered front and flank and rear, until scarcely a colorguard remained. It was not yet noon.

Almost at the same instant that we crossed the pike Beatty's Brigade of Van Cleve's Division came dashing down from the left at double quick, and formed instantly a few rods south of the pike. Fixing bayonets, they waited, but not long. Our little Regiment—its numbers slowly increasing by the arrival of boys who in retreating had swung too far to the west to keep with the colors—joined Beatty's right, determined to share their fate, come what would. Harker's Brigade had already passed still further to the right. On the left of Beatty's splendid column was the remainder of Van Cleve's Division, and on Van Cleve's left was Rouseau. The new line thus quickly formed was destined soon to engage in some of the severest fighting of that bloody day. The crushing of our Right had so exposed Sheridan that he was compelled to face almost south, instead of east as at the beginning. Indeed his extreme right faced the west, and the movements of the enemy soon made even this position untenable. He established a new line still further back, facing almost south, and nearly at right angles with Thomas' line, to meet which, the Center was thrown considerably back.

The genius of Rosecrans was nowhere more conspicuously displayed than in the establishment of his new line in the face of the most desperate fighting, and in spite of a victorious foe. Rouseau first flying into the face of the enemy and staggering him, fell quickly into his new position; the Left under Crittenden adjusted itself to its shortened line, and sent Harker's Brigade and Van Cleve's Division to the right, as detailed above.

The new lines thus hastily but most splendidly formed, had not long to wait. Cleburne's Division, fresh and confident, was in position and ready for assault. To his right and facing Rouseau's left was McCown's Division flushed with victory and ready for the final and crowning assault. Soon after noon the storm broke. With a wild yell, the enemy debouched from the cedar thickets in our front, forming as they came. The left of their line charged first, the assault falling upon Harker. His command was ready and waiting. Then Beatty, with words more forcible than elegant, encouraged and threatened his men. Not a man was to fire until he gave the command. He who disobeyed would instantly die. An officer who would permit disobedience would suffer the same fate. On came the same insolent foe that had driven us all the morning. Beatty's men stood at a "ready" and although many of them were falling, not a man discharged a musket. The enemy was alarmingly near, when the order to fire was given. The aim had been deliberate and deadly, and great numbers of the enemy bit the dust when the volley was delivered.

"Forward—Charge!" and the splendid line leaped forward, the remnants of our own good Regiment, joining their right. The Confederate line halted—it looked surprised, but fought viciously. The officers made great efforts to move them forward. With a yell as unearthly as ever escaped from human throats, Beatty rushed upon them with the bayonet. Not even our swearing rebel Colonel could hold his men. The line broke and fled in confusion—Beatty at their heels at every jump.

At the same time that Beatty so effectually astonished that part of Cleburn's line, which came at him on the pike, the troops both to the right and left of him, assailed the enemy with equal force, and immediately the rebel advance came to an end—indeed they were rolled back in considerable haste and not a little confusion. It was a critical moment and the Union boys fought like tigers; the Confederates understood it too, and fought most desperately. There was no straggling, no hesitation. It was cold blooded pluck and irresistible dash with bayonet and sword. But victory rested with the Stars and Stripes, and the hateful rebel rag finally went down on our Right. Thank God, a remnant of the 101st was in at the death.

Later in the afternoon Breckinridge attempting to advance his lines, got into trouble, was whipped, and fell back into his old position near the redout. It was now night, and the troops of both armies slept in line without fires. The night was cold and clear, and we suffered quite severely. Our number had increased so that we had by this time about one hundred and fifty men in line.

Immediately after the repulse referred to above, General Rosecrans sought to further improve his line of battle. It

LEWIS LOWE,
COMPANY E.
KILLED AT BATTLE OF STONE'S RIVER, DECEMBER 31, 1862.
Engraved from photograph.

was therefore moved forward until it extended around the base of a slight eminence, and from the railroad on the right, around to a point about 250 yards in rear of the position held by Thomas during the day. From here the line extended northerly to the river, with strong guards at the fords. This arrangement greatly concentrated the Union lines, and made it possible to use the artillery to excellent advantage. The fighting on the right had been largely in the woods where artillery could not be used to any great extent.

A large Confederate force, had made itself very objectionable in the rear of our army. These rascals had deliberately ridden around our flank and had struck the line of our communication with Nashville, spreading consternation among the teamsters, and the small guards accompanying the different sections of the train. Charging, they easily captured a portion of the train, burning many wagons and destroying many supplies, among which were the rations of the 101st for the next three days. The rebel victory here was, however, of short duration, for our own cavalry happened that way and entered so urgent a protest that our friends, the enemy, were glad to get away alive—they did not all succeed even in that. Quite a number of our boys, who had been captured, were very fortunately for them, recaptured. The rebels had, however, done great damage before they had been driven off. I have since made the personal acquaintance of one of the Captains of the Confederate cavalry, engaged in this piece of business, and find him to be a most generous and refined gentleman, far above doing such things now days.

Our hearts were filled with great sadness as we looked up and down the shortened line that cold evening. Each man contributed his item of information as to the cause of this one's and that one's absence from the ranks. We could account for many, but not for all. Colonels Stem and Wooster, and Lieutenants Biddle and Hillyear, and many, very many of the boys were dead or mortally wounded, scores were reported as being more or less seriously wounded, or captured. Many were in hospital, and not a few were missing.

Our Division—a shadow of its former self—occupied the extreme right of our new line.

The night was bitter cold—we could have no fires, but for that matter the Johnnies couldn't either. Some of our boys thought to have a small one—and gathering closely around the spot selected, started it. General McCook happened to be passing that way, saw the blaze, and rode up to make a fuss about it. He ordered it out instantly and threatened the arrest of every man engaged in the affair.

At the same instant a rebel shell came sailing up out of the darkness, and gave decided emphasis to the General's orders. The fire went out and we continued to shake with the cold. Another little company was more successful about 2 o'clock in the morning. We were almost stiff with the cold. Digging a hole in the ground about eighteen inches deep and two feet square, we started a fire in it, taking as much care to guard it from the eyes of our own officers as from the rebel gunners. It was not very satisfactory, but was very much better than nothing. Captain Parcher told us how the thing had once been done by some soldiers who ought to have been sent to the guard-house for it. He called several times to order the fire out, stopping each time long enough to toast his shins and warm his hands.

"I'll be back again after a little, boys, and if this fire is not out——" with threatening tones.

"All right, Captain, we'll always have a place for you. But don't tell any one."

Sure enough, he came in a short time, shivering with the cold but trying to glower at us.

"Did I not order you to put the fire out?" said he, standing astride the "furnace" and rubbing his hands at the same time.

"Tell us about the Battle of Pea Ridge and your fighting mit Siegel," said some thoughtful soul among us. This started him and our fire was safe. Shortly before daylight, he aided us to put out the fire and fill the hole. We hadn't slept much, but we had kept comparatively warm, and better yet, we had broken a positive order.

The night had not been entirely without incident. Occasionally a crazy rebel gunner would send a shell over our way, and occasionally a shot or two would be sent their way. Around toward our center there was a little musketry at one time, but nothing especially came of it. Between the lines lay a few wounded men whose cries, as their bloody wounds stiffened in the cold, excited our sympathy. We tried to relieve them, but were fired upon, and had to give it up. After daylight tacit consent was given by both sides, and the poor fellows were cared for. In the afternoon a portion of the Regiment was sent off toward the left, to strengthen the picket-skirmish line in that quarter. The boys on post did their whole duty, but those at the picket station worked hard to keep warm around a little fire in a great chimney in a log hut. Some climbed into the loft, kicked a hole through the sticks of which the chimney was built, and with their feet and legs hanging [down in the smoke, lay back and slept until after roll-call next morning. The entire day, New Year's, had been comparatively quiet, although Bragg had been "trying" our lines to satisfy himself that Rosecrans was really present in force. Thomas, and our Right responded in such a manner as to satisfy him, for the time being, at least.

DR. JAMES A. NORTON,
COMPANY K.

After aiding most gloriously in repelling the Confederate assault on our Right, Wednesday afternoon, Harker and Van Cleve were returned to the Left, their places being taken by Starkweather and Walker, who had been doing duty in the rear.

Crittenden was ordered on Thursday, January 1st, to send Van Cleve's Division, now under the command of Colonel Samuel Beatty, across the river to occupy a crest near the lower ford, from which, if in the hands of the enemy, great damage might be done our Left. To the surprise of all, this movement and occupation was effected without opposition on the part of the enemy. Indeed, the enemy were not aware of the change of our line until several hours after it had been made.

The next morning, January 2nd, Bragg detemined to ascertain again, whether Rosecrans were present in force, or whether after all, he were not playing a huge bluff. When the Reverend General Polk organized his force to see whether Thomas was there or not, the latter General proved to be so much there that the Reverend General could not even get his assaulting column out of the woods. He reported to Bragg that he thought Thomas was still there. Cleburn and McCown were able to make the same report concerning our Right. Bragg was now fully satisfied that Rosecrans had not even tried to run away. What he was to do under the circumstances, was a conundrum. He must do something, and that right away. He had driven our Right terribly on Wednesday morning, but aside from that and since that time he had accomplished not one thing. He at once decided to assail our Left. To insure success he would make as much noise as possible along our Center and Right, so as to hold our present forces there, whi'e with all the troops he could possibly gather, he would fall upon Crittenden, crush our Left, fall upon our rear, and finish us up in great shape. Just what the Union army was to do while he was accomplishing all this we were not informed by the Confederate Commander.

It was arranged that Breckinridge, who was on the east side of the river, facing our Left, whose Corps had not been very seriously engaged in battle thus far, although they had done some marching, was to undertake the great movement referred to, that of crushing Crittenden. Fearing that Rosecrans might attempt to assume the aggressive and carry out his original plan of battle, Bragg had as early as Wednesday night, the 31st, ordered two Divisions over to his right to strengthen Breckinridge in that quarter. On the afternoon of the 2nd, he ordered several other Brigades to the same part of the field, preparatory to the grand assault set for the afternoon. As an initiatory step, the Confederate cavalry was sent off to our extreme Left for the purpose of threatening something or somebody. It went so far as to be entirely out of the way. While making this move, some of the officers discovered Beatty's Division in line on the east side of Stone's River. This was immediately reported to Bragg, who is said to have become quite excited over the affair. The surface of the country in Breckinridge's vicinity was such that he could not hide his movements. His purposes were at once divined by Rosecrans and vigorous steps were taken to match him. Rosecrans, possessing this information, was not alarmed at the feints of Polk and McCown later on when Breckinridge was ready to move. Indeed these feints were a notice to him that the Confederate column was ready to storm our position. In the midst of the bluster in our own front he had no hesitation in ordering Davis' Division over to the Left on double quick. We arrived there in time to take an important part in the great game.

Breckinridge formed his assaulting column in two lines

—the first in a strip of woods, the second a few hundred feet back of the first. Both lines moved to the assault in this relative position. This charging column was made up mostly of men who were fresh and eager. They expected to win. They were harangued by their officers, who pointed out the very great importance of the move, and the glory and honor of success. It was to be the greatest military charge of modern times. Battery after battery wheeled into position, and still others were there to take advanced positions as the column cleared the way. A cavalry force was sent around to their right to keep Van Cleve's men and others from running off in that direction.

While all these arrangements were being made by the Confederates, General Rosecrans was also busy. Van Cleve's Division under Beatty was across the river. It must stay there, even if it had to face the whole Confederate charging column. It was impossible to send over to the east bank of the river and post a sufficient force to meet and defeat the great assault that was being prepared. Near the lower ford, in the space between the river and the road which here crosses the stream, is a crest which overlooks the open field across which Breckinridge must pass in falling upon Van Cleve, or in attempting to reach the ford, both of which he would undoubtedly attempt. Every cannon belonging to our Left, and several of those belonging to the Center was hurried to this elevation and rapidly placed in position. Fifty-eight guns were thus trained upon the fatal field. Each gun was loaded with grape, canister, shot or shell, as its position or range would best indicate. A clump of trees in the bend of the river effectually hid these guns and these important preparations from rebel sight and sense.

With delight, Breckinridge saw only one poor Division in his front. On the preceding afternoon he had massed

LIEUTENANT JAMES R. HOMER,
COMPANY E.

From Photograph taken in 1894.

a large force in plain sight, and Rosecrans had paid no attention to it. He flattered himself that the same game was working this afternoon, and that an easy victory awaited him. He would brush away the slight force, and then crossing the river he would take our army in reverse and soon end the agony. It was a grand scheme and Breckinridge was glad that he was alive on that immortal afternoon.

At length the order was given and the charging column moved forward. The moment it was absolutely certain that Breckinridge would attempt the assault, our Division—Davis'—was hurried off on double quick, to the left, to aid in repelling the charge. As soon as Breckinridge's lines had debouched from the woods, Van Cleve's batteries opened a rapid and accurate fire. The infantry fire was held for closer work. Beatty and all the men in Van Cleve's command knew that unless our battery on the crest could hold the enemy, defeat and destruction were surely theirs. But not a man flinched. The Confederate force came steadily on, neither hurrying nor hesitating. With the opening of Van Cleve's accurate artillery fire, they staggered for a moment, then came on like an avalanche. A little further and they saw the line of iron and brass that fringed the crest of the hill on the west bank of the river, each gun of which seemed to grin with malicious satisfaction and self-complacency. The sight astonished them and filled them with horror and dismay. But it was too late to change the plan or direction of assault; the river was between them and the battery, making it impossible for them to charge and silence it—they must go straight on or beat a cowardly retreat. Everybody saw that the lines would be enfiladed, and the officers knew perfectly well that the only way to hold the men and prevent a stampede was to order a charge at once, including both columns. With the giving of this order there straightway arose a yell uttered by no living creatures save a charging column of Confederate soldiers. Our own yell was an awful thing, born low down in Hell, but theirs was a hundred fold worse, especially when they had a desperate job on hand with the odds against them. Their yelling lines came madly on. Van Cleve's men cowered before the impending storm, yet flinched not.

Our guns on the heights were still silent. Crazed by their yelling and made hideously frantic by it, the rebel host rushed on. The rest of the army seemed to be holding its breath—operations elsewhere seemed to be suspended for the moment. Both lines of the assaulting host were now free from the woods and charging forward across the open cornfield. Van Cleve's artillery cut great swaths in their lines, as was attested by the numerous dead and wounded that marked the way back to the woods. Every gap was instantly closed, and no attention paid to dead or wounded.

A moment later and the very heavens seemed to burst with an awful explosion, as every gun in that vast battery poured its contents directly upon the Confederate mass as it rushed upon Van Cleve. Such slaughter! Every gun had been definitely trained upon a particular mass of men, and the great number of dead and dying, wounded and fleeing, told only too plainly how accurate had been the aim. The column of course staggered—it halted a moment, amazed and stricken. Van Cleve poured volley after volley into the writhing mass. The Confederate officers by almost superhuman efforts moved the column forward to the assault. By this time our Battery on the crest was again ready for action, and again it poured its contents upon the yelling mass below. Hundreds more went down, but the lines rushed on, feeling sure that the greatest safety was in close contact with our line, under which circumstances the great battery could not play. It was impossible for Van Cleve's men to stand against such a host and such a rush. They broke and fled toward the ford, closely followed by Breckinridge, over-anxious to get out of range of our batteries. He followed our troops across the river, where he halted for only a partial re-formation of his lines, then rushed on up the hill with visions of victory ever brightening.

General Negley's Division, for the time under the command of Colonel Miller, was stationed just at the top of the hill to the north of our great Battery. He ordered his men down upon their faces that the Confederates might not see them. Van Cleve's men were permitted to pass hurriedly through. By this time Breckinridge's line was rushing rapidly up the hill, or rather bank, when the Division at Miller's command arose and, at short range, poured a terribly destructive volley into their very faces. It was too much. They recoiled, fled, rushing upon their companions who were vainly trying to pass the ford. Miller threw his Division upon the confused mass and put them into a panic. At this moment our Division—Davis'—came upon the ground and immediately took a hand. We plunged into and across the river, and charged the enemy. No sooner had they gained the open field than our great battery on the crest gave them another terrific tempest of iron, sending many hundreds to their long home. But our charging columns were so close upon them that the battery could do no more. The chase was kept up until they had reached the woods in which they had so proudly and so confidently formed for the assault an hour and a half before.

General Cleburne had been rushed from Bragg's extreme Left over to their extreme Right, to assist in staying the flood of disaster that had overtaken Breckinridge. He arrived there in time only to form in front of their used-up columns and protect them from further pursuit.

JOHN DICE,
COMPANY E.
From Photograph taken in 1894.

We halted in the open field before reaching the woods, and, as we did so we demolished every fence in the vicinity, using the rails for protection. These frail breastworks stopped many a bullet.

No sooner had Cleburne taken his position than he arranged to attack us. His officers harangued their men—we could hear them, but could not distinguish their words. All this resulted in a night attack, for it was now dark. Our batteries had been well posted and double shotted. Every man in our line knew the range, and just what to do if the rebels should attempt to come at us, as we imagined they would. When Cleburne made his foolish night attack, his men raised the yell which told our gunners and the rest of us just where they were. Our batteries raked them dreadfully. The infantry firing was deafening for a few moments, but the enemy soon found it impossible to handle us, and retired into the woods. There was a great deal of random firing during the night, on both sides, but no especial harm was done anyone so far as I know. It began to rain in the night, which soon rendered the cornfield across which our lines extended almost impassable. The mud was ankle deep everywhere. It was soft enough, but a little too plentiful to sleep in, though many of the boys tried it.

The field over which we had charged in following Breckinridge was very thickly strewn with his dead and wounded, so much so that we really had to pick our way at times to avoid treading upon the poor fellows.

The morning—Saturday, the 3rd—found us literally stuck in the mud; we hugged our little sections of rail fence and lay flat upon the muddy ground to be as safe as possible from Cleburne's sharpshooters. Our batteries soon shelled the woods and taught them to respect us by keeping further away.

BATTLE OF STONE'S RIVER.

About 8 o'clock in the morning, a portion at least of the 101st was sent off to the left and front to act as a sort of picket-skirmish line. The drizzling rain continued to fall and the day was dark and lowering. There was little heavy fighting on our part of the field, though Bragg frequently tested our lines to see whether Rosecrans were really still in front. The responses that he received finally convinced him and his generals that our lines were strongest everywhere, and weakest nowhere.

We found our picket-skirmish line a most exciting affair. We were in the woods near the small stream that flows into the river further north. The ground was strewn with guns, and bayonets, and clothing, and knapsacks, and even haversacks. But behind every large tree there seemed to lurk a vicious rebel, but we finally reached our trees, running the gauntlet of many a bullet in doing so. The trees were close together and the runs were short.

Off to our left on the edge of a little stream there was an old cotton shed. This was at first held by the Johnnies, but we found time to send so many bullets into it that they left it. A stirring incident occurred at the picket reserve, just at dark. The men were cold and wet, and wanted something warm. They had been ordered not to have a fire under any circumstances. They huddled closely together, however, and decided to boil a cup of coffee. Very thoughtlessly one of them left his place just as the coffee began to boil. Instantly a rebel bullet struck the fire, overturned the coffee and scattered the boys in great shape. The officer in command found relief in profanity, and darkness again prevailed.

We were relieved about this time, and as we went back to our place in the line we witnessed an assault made by the enemy, probably to cover his withdrawal from our front. We had a kind of enfilading view of the conflict. The flashing of several thousand muskets on either side, and a broadside or two of our artillery, made it a much pleasanter affair to look at than to be in. The Johnnies soon fell back to the cover of the woods, and comparative silence again prevailed, broken only by the nervous rattle along the picket line.

About 2 o'clock in the morning we recrossed the river which was considerably swollen by the recent rains, and wading through the mud in many places actually knee deep, went into camp on our extreme right, just back of the railroad. It seemed an unspeakable relief to get our harness off. We had worn our belts almost incessantly since the opening of the fight, and had scarcely dared to put our guns out of our hands. We sprawled out on the wet ground and slept until daylight, then waded into a pond near by, washed up and lay around to dry. The noise of the conflict had ceased. Bragg had retreated and Rosecrans was in possession of the field.

Our regimental losses were heavy. Out of four hundred and twenty men who stood in line at daylight on the 31st, two hundred and twelve were either dead, mortally wounded, or captured. Nearly all this occurred on the first day. The following list of those who were either killed outright or mortally wounded, tells a sad story, but only a part of it. The boys were mangled and torn in every conceivable way. Death came instantly to many, and many others lingered in awful torture. Many of those who were captured endured suffering which can never be described. Andersonville, Columbia, Florence and Libby, received them into their horrors, and gloated over their miseries.

Under cover of darkness the once great Confederate army, no longer able to defend itself against our sturdy lines of blue, sought safety in flight, nor halted until the shelter of Duck River had been reached.

BATTLE OF STONE'S RIVER.

List of those who were killed or mortally wounded:

Col. Leander Stem, Commanding Regiment..............
Lieut. Col. Moses F. Wooster, 2nd in Command.........
Lieut. John B. Biddle..........................Company C.
Lieut. Asa R. Hillyear.........................Company A.
Comrade Cyrus B. Prosser.......................Company A.
Comrade Edwin Runyan ....Company A.
Comrade Simon Huntington.......................Company B.
Comrade Henry Kile ....Company C.
Comrade John J. Moore..........................Company C.
Comrade Charles Pickens........................Company D.
Comrade Isaac Farnsworth ....Company E.
Comrade Lewis Lowe.............................Company E.
Comrade Peter Snyder ....Company E.
Comrade Adam Sherer ....Company E.
Comrade Oliver Bolander........................Company F.
Comrade Alfred J. DeWitt ....Company F.
Comrade Thomas Hollenshead.....................Company F.
Comrade John A. Kerr ....Company F.
Comrade Samuel Martin..........................Company F.
Comrade David Miller...........................Company F.
Comrade Aaron C. Shively.......................Company F.
Comrade John Scott.............................Company F.
Comrade Francis M. Sterling....................Company F.
Comrade Garrett Taylor.........................Company F.
Comrade George Hewitt..........................Company G.
Comrade Curtis B. Mullenix.....................Company G.
Comrade Andrew Meikle ....Company G.
Comrade James S. Ames..........................Company H.
Comrade Dallas W. Hade ....Company H.
Comrade Samuel F. Arndt........................Company I.
Camrade Anthony Dellgeit ....Company I.
Comrade Frederick Franks.......................Company I.
Comrade George W. Gittenger....................Company I.
Comrade Robert McMeen..........................Company I.
Comrade Sylvester Beatty.......................Company K.
Comrade George W. Hulett.......................Company K.
Comrade David K. Newhouse......................Company K.
Comrade Moses Parkhurst ....Company K.
Comrade Samuel Strayer ....Company K.

A large part of Sunday was spent in gathering and compiling information relative to our dead, wounded and missing, and in writing letters home. In the afternoon we received mail—the first since leaving Nashville, December 26th. On Monday morning, January 5th, a detail of two men from each company was made to bury our dead. The field of the first day's conflict, had remained in the hands of the enemy until Sunday morning. The Confederates had gathered, with but little care, most of our dead and placed them in heaps, in some instances building a rail pen around them to protect them from possible roving swine, belonging to some of the residents of the vicinity. Before leaving camp, our little burying party had a full list of the dead.

Many of the boys made donations of blankets, in which to wrap the bodies of their friends and comrades, feeling sure that relatives and friends would desire to remove the remains to their peaceful homes in the North as soon as circumstances would allow. No caskets were to be had—not even rough boxes.

Arriving upon the field we selected our fallen comrades from the several piles, found one or two where they fell, carried a strange dead comrade or two to heaps of other dead, and then began the excavation of the trench, selecting a beautiful location beneath the boughs of a great tree, just within the edge of the woods near the cotton field where we formed our second line of battle on the 31st. We dug a trench six feet wide, five feet deep and long enough to contain all the bodies lying side by side. Then wrapping each poor boy in the blanket donated him by a comrade friend, we reverently lowered the bodies into the trench, and having covered each with branches cut from the adjacent cotton bushes, to break in appearance at least, the fall of the ground upon their bodies, we buried them in unbroken silence. Many a stout heart that had not for a moment

GEORGE S. McKEE,
COMPANY E.
Engraved from a crayon.

quailed before the presence of the destroying enemy, broke down entirely in the presence of this sad sight. Deep but not loud were the imprecations heaped upon the heads of the responsible leaders of the rebellion which made such sacrifices necessary.

While the trench was being dug, a few of us passed on through the woods to the place where our lines had been formed on the morning of the 31st. Everywhere there were unmistakable evidences of the fierceness of the struggle. Broken guns, bayonets, swords, sabers, belts and accouterments of all kinds belonging to both armies, lay scattered about in great abundance. Worn out articles of clothing, pieces of knapsacks, haversacks, tin cups and spiders, fragments of shells, solid shot and unexploded shells, dead horses and broken cannon carriages, drums and worthless stretchers, slight depressions in the ground marking the place where many heroes had fallen and lain for days, great splotches of blood showing where the lives of many patriots had slowly ebbed away in the terrible silence that succeeded the rush of the whirlwind, broken branches and splintered trees, shells buried deep in the trunks of the giants of the forest—all this and a thousand things beside bore indubitable marks of the desperate nature of the conflict.

Placing a rude board on which was carved his name and the number of our Regiment, at the head of each buried comrade, we returned in the afternoon to find that the Regiment, during our absence, had marched across the river, up through the town and out the Shelbyville Pike a couple of miles. We immediately followed, passing down the railroad and over the bridge which the rebels had attempted to destroy. The whole town was a hospital and we gladly hurried through into the country beyond. We experienced little difficulty in finding the Regiment, and were soon as busy as the rest arranging for the night.

Within a day or two we were moved in the midst of a blinding snow storm to a new and permanent position near the river which gives its name to the great battle out of the smoke and chaos of which we had just come.

CHAPTER X.

IN CAMP AT MURFREESBORO'.

The great battle had been fought, and victory rested with us. Bragg retreated from our front on Saturday night, leaving us in full possession of the battlefield for which we had contended nine days. He left with us also his sick and badly wounded to the number of 2,500. On Sunday, the 4th, Rosecrans made some weak attempts to follow the retreating Confederates, not so much to bring Bragg again to battle, as to find out where he was going. The rebel General was not going far, only to Shelbyville and Tullahoma. He had decided to make Duck River his line of defense, and for that purpose he had erected strong earthworks at both these places, apparently for permanent occupation. He established strong outposts both of cavalry and infantry at Manchester, Wartrace and Columbia, and sought to dispute with us the possession of Franklin. Rosecrans' headquarters were at Murfreesboro', Bragg's at Shelbyville, about 25 miles away. Scouting and raiding between the two lines were quite common—and were frequently interesting. Versailles, Eagleville and Franklin became especially familiar to us in January and March, 1863. Bragg felt quite safe in his new quarters, for he well knew that we had been so severely knocked around in the recent battle that we would be glad to let him alone for a time, and we felt about the same way concerning their condition.

But Bragg had one great advantage—he was near his base of supplies. During the Battle of Stone's River, and for some weeks preceding and following that event, Gen. John Morgan had succeeded in almost destroying our railroad communications with Louisville. The road was so badly wrecked that instead of accumulating supplies at Murfreesboro' preparatory to an early advance, we were put upon half rations for several weeks. The ration was a very limited affair. The country was overrun in every direction, and everything seized that could be used.

Just how Bragg smoothed things over so as to satisfy his superiors that his retreat was the proper thing, I am not able to say. It must have required quite as much sophistry as did his explanation of affairs at Perryville. The loss of Stone's River carried with it the loss of the State of Kentucky and most of Middle and East Tennessee, though the latter section held out until the fall of Chattanooga in September following. Nashville had forever passed out of the possession of the Confederate army. Treason, instead of invading the North, was being crowded back into the very nest of the viper of Secession. The Lord's hand was in it.

Succeeding the great battle there came a great lull, lasting for months. With the coming of pleasant weather in the Spring, the Commanding General was anxious to advance, but could not do so for want of supplies, and especially for want of a suitable cavalry force to cope with that of the enemy and protect our flanks and rear. General Halleck at Washington wildly urged Rosecrans to advance. Rosecrans showed his generalship, pluck and good sense in refusing to do so until there were some prospects of success. The two armies faced each other from the 4th of January to the 24th of June, at a distance of about twenty-five miles, each making faces at each other and occasionally making harmless passes. Many an innocent bluff was attempted, but neither dared call the other. Less than four months before, the rebel army, with banners and music and high hopes, had turned Buell's Left at McMinnville, and with the tread of conquerors had attempted to carry the war into the North. The attempt had ignominiously failed. Bragg was practically whipped on his own ground at Perryville, and most decidedly was he defeated at Stone's River in a position of his own selection. We had great reason to rejoice. But the roll-call of the several commands revealed the fact that the victory had cost us dear in the lives of our comrades. There were great breaks in the lists of names— vacancies that could never be filled. On dress parade, our line was but a ghost of its former self. We were soldiers, but many a sigh and many a tear were bestowed upon the memory of our fallen associates and comrades. As the wounded and captured, one by one, returned to us, we gave them a royal welcome.

Our Division Commander, Gen. Jeff. C. Davis, soon tired of the routine of camp life and longed to roam around the country in search of an enemy. We fully sympathized with him in the matter of camp routine, but not in the roaming. In the latter part of January the Confederate cavalry under Wheeler occupied Triune and Franklin. This made our Division General wild. He asked and received permission to take his command out that way to act in conjunction with our cavalry and a small force to be sent down from Nashville for the capture of this impertinent rebel force.

On the evening of the 29th of January we received orders to march at 5 o'clock next morning. Each man was to take three days' rations and forty rounds of ammunition with him. Of course it began to rain before we started, and when, just at daylight next morning, we filed out of camp, it fairly poured. It was one of those cold, drizzling, disagreeable, discouraging, unsatisfactory mornings so common to this climate and section. We soon passed the picket station, said good-bye to the videttes, and bore off toward Versailles, marching rapidly through the slippery mud until near nightfall, when we went into camp near the last mentioned place. It was a dreary, homesick night. We were tired, wet, muddy and ill-natured, but fires were permitted and we were soon in better humor. Two Brigades of cavalry under Colonel Minty accompanied us on the expedition. At this point the two forces were to separate—the cavalry going almost directly south from Versailles some six miles to gain the rear of the rebel force at Triune, while we (Davis' Division) were to advance directly upon the latter place. It was thought that Wheeler would immediately retreat when he discovered the strength of the infantry force sent against him. Moreover, while our two forces were executing these movements, General Steedman, who had advanced from Nashville with a neat little force, was to take position at Nolensville, a few miles north of Triune. Thus hemmed in on three sides, Wheeler had but two alternatives—he must either surrender, or continue his march to the west and north. He was not a man given to much surrendering, consequently he continued his march. Our command arrived at Eagleville on the evening of February 1st, and went into camp for the night. Colonel Minty in the meantime had captured a rebel regiment of 350 men near Unionville, but the grand prize had eluded us. Early next morning we resumed our march at a very rapid rate toward the northwest, finally bringing up at Franklin. But Wheeler had the start of us and soon appeared before Fort Donelson. Failing in the capture of this place and being hotly pursued, he returned, bearing far to the west to avoid General Davis, who had received a large cavalry reinforcement. It had been a fruitless though exciting raid for the rebel.

MAJOR DANIEL H. FOX.
From Photograph.

An amusing incident occurred at Versailles the first evening out. General Davis, with a portion of his staff, was riding about rather rashly, as was his custom, and finally got outside our lines before our pickets were fairly established. He was halted, of course, when he attempted to come in.

"Who comes there?" said the sentinel.

"Federals," replied Davis. But the soldier on duty understood the answer to be "Confederates," and the night being very dark and rainy, he fired, as did one or two guards with him. Explanations were soon made and General Davis was admitted, but he was "hot." He was so angry he nearly had a fit. He couldn't get over it. He always carried with him a large and carefully selected vocabulary of "swear words," but the list was not sufficient for this occasion.

Although we were in the midst of a stirring campaign, nothing of especial interest occurred to break the monotony of the dreary tramp. We crossed the Harpeth river at Franklin, marched up through the town and went into camp just south of the village, on the very ground on which the great battle of Franklin was fought a year and a half later.

We settled down as though we were to stay awhile. It turned very cold and snowed and "blowed" furiously. This seemed greatly to satisfy many of the citizens, who were Sesech through and through.

"You'ns are going to freeze if you stay here," with a sardonic smile which revealed the actual state of mind within and which we well understood. "You'ns 'll freeze dead, sure."

"Not a bit of it. We have this kind of weather the year round at home. But if it should get cold, we'll call on you fellows for blankets, or maybe beds," said some of our boys. But the citizens thought perhaps it would not get much colder.

We had no shelter with us except our pup tents, which, in a storm, were little better than nothing. In pleasant, or even moderate weather they were very good. Especially did we find them excellent on picket duty. They would at least keep the dew off, and would indicate "headquarters." In a storm a pup tent stood no show.

We remained at Franklin, picketing and scouting, until February 12th, when we returned to our old quarters at Murfreesboro'. While at Franklin the boys raided several old tobacco dry-houses, and returned well laden with great burdens of half-dried leaves. These were carefully concealed under blouses and overcoats, fearing the wrath of the Division Commander, but still more the confiscation of their property.

By order of the War Department dated January 9, 1863, the Army of the Cumberland was reorganized, though its main features remained unchanged. General McCook's command was denominated the Twentieth Corps or Right Wing; General Thomas' the Fourteenth Corps or Center; and General Crittenden's the Twenth-first Corps or Left Wing. It will be observed that no change was ordered in Corps Commanders. Our Corps, the Twentieth, occupied the line in front of Murfreesboro' from the river south of the town to the Shelbyville Pike, covering also the Salem Pike. General Thomas' Command occupied that part of the line extending from the Shelbyville Pike to the Woodbury Road ; and Crittenden, from Thomas' left to the river north of the town. It was very evident that, on the advance of the army, Murfreesboro' must be used as a great base of supplies. But it could not be left in the weak condition in which Forrest found it the summer preceding. Elaborate fortifications were therefore planned and completed during our stay. In all this work we did our full share when not off scouting. The railroad and pike from

Nashville were prime necessities. Both were protected by strong works commanding all important bridges and approaches to the river. All these forts swept the country for long distances toward the front and flank. Upon the high ground north of the town immense works were thrown up, seemingly impregnable, and upon the elevated ground further to the east and front, other strong works were erected. Most, if not all these forts were protected by abatti and ditches. Long lines of breastworks extending from fort to fort, along the base, summit, and sides of the hills and elevations, were thrown up and made strong. Many of the breastworks were enfiladed by the forts, and each fort in front had a vulnerable side to the rear, commanded by one or more of the other forts, so that should an enemy force his way into one of them, the others could at once open fire upon them with effect, and should a portion of the breastworks be captured, a number of forts could enfilade their lines. But when our army finally advanced, it crowded the enemy back so vigorously that he had neither time nor occasion to test the strength of our works at Murfreesboro'. His attention was fully occupied at the front.

It must not be supposed that everything else was neglected until these fortifications were completed. Not at all. Rosecrans had determined to keep Bragg south of Duck River. Whenever a force came north of that little stream, it was to be looked after at once, and inasmuch as most of these raids were made westward of the Shelbyville pike, it seemed to fall to McCook to run them down and hustle them back. Our own Division did the lion's share of all of this work. The expedition to Franklin, already noticed, was one of these.

Notwithstanding our drilling, fort-building, and so on, time hung heavily on the hands of some of us, and a movement was set on foot for the purchase of some suitable reading matter. Colonel Kirby very kindly offered to provide transportation for our library as the Regiment moved from point to point, if we succeeded in securing one. The matter was taken up quite enthusiastically, and in a short time a sufficient sum was raised to purchase quite a number of books. A committee duly appointed, made a selection of books we wanted, the list was handed to the agent of the Christian Commission, through whose kindness the purchase was made, and in due time the books delivered. It was an excellent undertaking—productive of much good. Some of these books were, of course, lost, but many of them accompanied the Regiment on its long and wearisome marches and were brought home well worn with much reading.

About the same time, or possibly a little earlier, a kindred enterprise was set on foot, fostered, and carried to success by the same persons who were interested in the library scheme. This was the formation of a society for moral and religious instruction—a society whose influence should be used to stay, as far as possible, the evil influences incident to a soldier's life. This little association was quite successful, and much good was accomplished. Our Chaplain, Rev. Oliver Kennedy, was the prime mover in the enterprise. On several occasions while we lay at Murfreesboro', Chaplains of other regiments addressed us. The memory of some of these meetings is exceedingly delightful, especially of those held near the battle-field. Our good Chaplain soon after resigned, to enter the Christian Commission. He was a good man, earnest and devoted, jolly, but true and tried. He was held in profound respect by all, even the roughest of our boys. He returned to enjoy many years of peaceful life, but died March 23, 1889, at Bellefontaine, Ohio; loved, honored, and respected by all who knew him. And when after long marches, many hardships, and much severe fighting, it became wise to reorganize the little society, our new Chaplain, the Rev. E. M. Crevath, now President of Fisk University, Nashville, was earnest, successful, and efficient in re-establishing the organization on the same broad principles of universal evangelical toleration which characterized the first.

Belief in God, in Jesus Christ, and in the validity of the Holy Scriptures were the only requirements. On long marches our meetings were necessarily dispensed with. But when the occasions were favorable, we met in some secluded spot or nook, or under some old tree, or in the edge of the forest. Many of these meetings were delightful in the extreme, reminding us of former days at home, of present duties and responsibilities, and bidding us look forward to a joyous reunion with those whom we loved, probably on this side of the Dark River, but if not, surely beyond. The influence of some of these meetings still lasts.

Bragg's pickets and videttes kept us so closely in sight that it became necessary for us to do a great deal of picketing. To relieve, and at the same time to simplify matters, our picketing was done by Brigades—the entire force remaining out several days at a time. We were able to make ourselves much more comfortable in this way, and at the same time do much more effective work, should occasion require.

General Rosecrans had been making every possible effort to get into shape for an early advance. He must have supplies, and he must have cavalry. He pleaded and implored, stormed and fumed—but to little purpose. Halleck was still fighting battles on paper. He thought cavalry cost too much. That man Halleck was a mystery.

The enemy in our front was becoming bold. General Rosecrans determined, early in March, to ascertain more definitely where he was and in what force. To do this he sent out three columns, with one of which Davis' Division,

SAMUEL SPROUT,
COMPANY K.
From Photograph taken in 1894.

of course, marched. The three expeditions moved the same day, one from Murfreesboro' under General Sheridan, one from Nolensville under Steedman, and one from Franklin under Gilbert. Sheridan's cavalry attacked Roddy's rebel cavalry a few miles south of Eagleville, drove it back upon a larger force near Unionville, and then chased the whole command on the keen run back to Shelbyville. This was done by Colonel Minty, assisted by our friends and comrades, the Third Ohio Cavalry. Minty then joined Sheridan at Eaglesville. He had waked up the rebel force along the line of Duck River in great shape.

Gilbert's expedition from Franklin was not so successful. The first day's fight was all right, but the enemy fell back to Spring Hill, was largely reinforced, and on the following day drove the Union force back with considerable loss, many being killed and more than a thousand captured. The thing was not well managed on our side, for a force of 2,800 was compelled to go into battle against an enemy having 14,000 men under arms.

The expedition under Steedman from Nolensville succeeded in driving the enemy across Duck River, capturing a number of prisoners and stirring up the natives badly. He fell back to Triune and Sheridan moved up toward Franklin to help Gilbert. This left Steedman considerably exposed at Triune, and at once a force of 6,000 rebels set out to gobble him. At this junction of the game, Davis' Division was called in to help the matter along. On the evening of the 8th of March we received orders to move at 5 o'clock next morning, with three days' rations in our haversacks and forty rounds of ammunition in our belts. We were to march as light as possible. On the 9th we halted at Salem, but on the 10th we effected a junction with Steedman at Triune. It was a fearfully wet afternoon—it got dark an hour too soon, a dense fog settling down on all things. Darkness or stupid blundering, or both, caused one of our regiments—not the 101st—to fire on some of Steedman's cavalry. The mistake was instantly noticed. Fortunately no harm was done. We remained near Triune for a day or two, then moved to Eagleville, and then across to Versailles—then back to Murfreesboro' on the 15th. The three expeditions had resulted in no practical good, though Rosecrans learned that the enemy was in fighting quantities in many sections. Cavalry he must and would have. So he began afresh to hammer Halleck.

The rebel cavalry was never idle. They operated both east and west of us, making dashes here and there and causing much damage in many places. Our Division was called out several times to chase them, but we never came into close quarters. On one of these occasions we advanced with considerable caution to Franklin, where we remained two days, when we left very suddenly, being obliged to halt and form lines once or twice before reaching safety. At one time the entire Division was in line across the Salem Pike, a short distance from that village. Our artillery was admirably posted, but the Confederate force, mostly cavalry, ventured only near enough to look at us. We withdrew during the night and resumed our place in line at Murfreesboro', the Confederates having beaten a hasty retreat in the afternoon. Colonel Minty's appearance on their left flank was the immediate occasion of their haste.

On the 4th of June we had an especial shaking up. For some days the enemy's cavalry had been prowling around, and a force was reported to be stationed near the Shelbyville pike, about six miles out. Our Division was in line very early, and was so divided up as to "bag" the enemy if possible. Our ambush was planned, but it did not work, and the troops returned at night tired and worn out. Much firing was indulged in along the line, but no serious damage was done to either side.

A few days after this, Major McDonald, with a small section of the 101st, succeeded in capturing the enemy's picket station on the Shelbyville pike, and then rushing back toward camp, brought in the vidette station also. The remainder of our Regiment was on the pike ready to help him if he should need us. The Major received many compliments, and he "stepped high" for a few days. We had great sport with him one day—Sunday, after inspection. We had marched out to the place where we always discharged our muskets. The Major had a new horse—bran new, and very green. He was a fine fellow, and the Major sat him like a king. On this occasion he had on his best military outfit, including sash and gloves. He had taken the Regiment out in good shape, and we stood in line. "Company A-a-a," sang out the Major in his best voice, "Ready! aim! *fire!!*" Every gun blazed. But the new horse did not understand it. He was off in a twinkling, nor stopped until he reached camp. Some of the boys almost died of merriment. The Major soon quieted the trembling beast, and with much coaxing got him within a few rods of our line, when Company B suddenly, as one man, fired—and away to camp went poor McDonald, his coat-tails flopping wildly in the breeze. He took some time to get the frightened animal back near the line when another Company fired, and for the third time our Major was carried, blue with rage, back to camp. He was finally compelled to leave his horse in camp and walk out to where we were. We received him with a cheer, but Mc. was ready to butcher the whole crowd. He was advised as a matter of safety, to ride his new horse in our next battle. Poor Mc.! If he had followed our advice, he might have avoided the capture which awaited him at Chickamauga.

By this time the railroads had been repaired, we had gathered considerable supplies, had been gathered at Nashville and Murfreesboro', and the time was rapidly approaching when the Army of the Cumberland would take up its march for the heart of the Confederacy. Our cavalry force, although too small, was nevertheless better and larger than it had been before. Our own Regiment was in excellent condition in camp just south of Murfreesboro'. The information gathered on the 4th of June, together with the reports of spies, scouts, and our cavalry, indicated that the hour had at last arrived when our army should move forward. Orders were accordingly issued to that effect, and early on the morning of the 24th of June, 1863, we broke camp for good. The campaign upon which we were just entering was destined to be a most important one in many respects.

CHAPTER XI.

LIBERTY GAP—TULLAHOMA CAMPAIGN.

The Confederate line, at the beginning of the Tullahoma Campaign, extended from Spring Hill, twenty-five miles west to McMinnville, sixty miles southeast of Murfreesboro', passing in a crude semi-circular form through Columbia, Shelbyville, Wartrace, and Manchester, with main base of supplies at Tullahoma, sixteen miles south of Shelbyville, on the Nashville & Chattanooga Railroad. Shelbyville was the main point of defense. Both Shelbyville and Tullahoma, strong by nature, were rendered especially so by the erection of very strong earthworks of almost every description.

To reach the enemy it was necessary for our army to pass through defiles or gaps in the broken and rocky ranges of hills that run almost parallel with Duck River, in front of the position chosen by General Bragg. These gaps were all in possession of the enemy, and were considered so easy of defense that the Confederates neglected to fortify them except by the use of ordinary field artillery, placed at available points. Bragg intended to prevent our passing these defiles, if possible, but should he fail in this, he expected to administer to us a dreadful defeat in front of Shelbyville, and then, hurling us back against the rocky ridge, he would annihilate us in their numerous defiles. A fine scheme! But Rosecrans had a plan of his own, and very different from this.

On the morning of the 23d we received orders to be ready to march at daylight next morning. Our forces at Franklin and Eagleville received these orders a day earlier, in order to be in proper supporting distance when we were ready to strike. We were to go "light," carrying three days' rations and an abundance of ammunition. The rations might have to last us five days. For some weeks we had expected to move at almost any time, and yet there was a great deal of quiet confusion in camp on the morning of the 24th. In one way and another we had gathered more or less "household goods" about us during our stay at Murfreesboro', very much of which must now be left. But little camp equipage was to be taken—only one wagon being allowed to each regiment. At the last moment everything came with a rush and went with a bang. We flung that away, kept this, and grabbing his blanket and pup tent, each man rushed into line at the well-worn order, "fall in!" We marched a few rods, halted, started, stopped, and kept up this sort of business for a half hour, and then led out at a good round pace. We had not gone far until the rain began to fall in that peculiar fashion which indicated that an all-day contract had been taken. Indeed, the rain, which began at 10 o'clock that morning, continued with scarcely a let-up for seventeen days—at least it rained hard every day for that period of time. But the Army of the Cumberland was just entering upon an important campaign, and, rain or shine, that campaign must be successfully completed.

Each corps of our army had a specific work before it for that first day. McCook was to advance upon Liberty Gap; Thomas, upon Hoover's Gap; and Crittenden, leaving Van Cleve's Division to garrison Murfreesboro', was to encamp near Readyville.

Although we had remained nearly six months at Murfreesboro', the place had few attractions for us, and we had no hesitation in leaving it. A feeling of sadness, however, came over us as we thought of our comrades who had sacrificed their lives at Stone's River, whose final resting place we were leaving, probably forever. But these thoughts were soon vanished as we steadily advanced toward the enemy we had so frequently encountered before.

Our line of march was, for a time, by way of the direct Shelbyville pike, but soon after noon we bore off to the left, and about 4 o'clock we encamped near the village of Millersburg, within a mile of Liberty Gap. Sheridan also encamped near us. Johnson's Division, however, advanced and halted in the immediate vicinity of the Gap. A reconnoitering party was sent forward at once, which soon developed the fact that the enemy was present in considerable force in front of the Gap, and that they would dispute our entrance. General Willich's Brigade at once deployed in line of battle and advanced in fine style, forcing the enemy back into the Gap and upon their reserves, which were well posted on the hill-sides commanding the defile. The enemy was too strongly posted to justify a direct assault by the force under General Willich. A portion of Miller's Brigade was therefore brought up, which so extended the Union line as to envelope both flanks of the enemy's position.

This line moved promptly and steadily forward, forcing the enemy back nearly two miles, but not far enough to give us possession of the southern entrance. Johnson encamped that night in the Gap, near its northern entrance.

General Thomas, with the Center, had accomplished his task. He had not only entered Hoover's Gap, but had driven the Confederates entirely out of it, and held the southern entrance. This had not been accomplished without some severe fighting. Rebel General Hardee was in command of the Confederate forces defending both these Gaps.

We were in line very early the next morning, and at once advanced to Johnson's support. It could not be possible that the enemy would surrender a pass so important as this without more serious resistance than he had yet offered. The morning was very foggy, rendering military operations quite out of the question until about noon. There was considerable skirmishing all the forenoon, most of which was quite harmless. The movements of our army had considerably mystified Bragg and his Lieutenants. Could it be possible that Rosecrans was about to ignore his fine forts at Shelbyville and endeavor to flank him out of that stronghold! Hoover's Gap was already gone; we held the northern entrance of Liberty Gap, and Bragg had no sufficient force at McMinnville or Manchester to seriously dispute the Union advance in that direction. He must draw us toward Shelbyville if possible.

Hardee, therefore, took advantage of the dense fog that overhung the hills that forenoon to bring up reinforcements for the purpose of regaining what he had lost during the afternoon of the day before. Fearing something of this kind, Rosecrans had ordered our Division up within easy supporting distance.

With the lifting of the fog the intentions of the enemy

DAVID E. HALE,
COMPANY F.

From photograph taken in 1893.

became apparent, and dispositions were at once made to thwart them. Evidently an assault was to be made upon us at once. Hardee knew the ground and made his dispositions to the best possible advantage. But Johnson's troops were in position, his artillery was well posted, and a strong skirmish line was well out in front. Carlin's Brigade was hurriedly sent to his assistance, just before the rebel assault was made. The enemy's first attempt was on Johnson's center, upon which they fell most savagely, but were vigorously repulsed. Beaten here, they next attempted to gain the hills and attack our flanks. In this they were also foiled. They seemed desperate. Their artillery was used from the four available points, and so was ours. It was very evident that the final struggle would be brief, but fierce. Again and again they tried to find weak places in our line, but our ranks stood firm everywhere. Still threatening our center, they again attempted to flank us and thus force us out of the defile. It was a critical moment, a moment in which the whole question was to be settled. The key to the situation seemed to be in the possession of a hill on our flank and considerably to the front between the lines. Both commanders seemed to discover the importance of this position at the same moment, and each made dispositions for its capture. The 38th Illinois, of our Brigade, was instantly detailed for the important assault. Grandly they advanced, but were soon repulsed, leaving their dead and wounded on the field. By this time a light rebel force had taken possession of the hill, and the most strenuous efforts were being made to bring up artillery with which to defend it.

Immediately on the repulse of the 38th Illinois, General Carlin, who, since Stone's River, entertained an excellent opinion of the 101st, asked Colonel Kirby if he thought he could reach the hill.

BATTLE OF LIBERTY GAP.

"I will try, Sir," said the Colonel, "and if you will promise not to interfere, but to give me my own way, I assure you some of us will go to the top."

General Carlin promised, and kept his word.

The Regiment was immediately deployed at one pace intervals, the men informed what was expected of them, and the Company officers directed to give no orders except those of caution. The line was to be wholly and exclusively under the personal command of the Colonel.

Calling the Color-Bearer, Sergeant James M. Roberts, Colonel Kirby said in the hearing of us all:

"Sergeant, do you see that dead tree just over the hill beyond the enemy's first line?"

"I do," said the Color-Bearer.

"Can you take a step just 28 inches long and keep it up —no more, no less?"

"I can," said Roberts.

"I want you to keep your eye on that tree," said the Colonel, "and I want you to step precisely 28 inches every time, without halt or hesitation, swerving neither to the right nor to the left—I want you to go right there, to that tree."

"I'll do it," said the brave fellow, dipping Old Glory.

We had heard every word, and enthusiasm ran high. We were ready.

"Forward!" and the line moved out in glorious shape. Each man took a 28-inch step and kept himself aligned. In an incredibly short time the 101st was on the hill-top— Old Glory crowned the summit—the crest was ours. The force sent by the rebels to hold it until their artillery could be brought up with the necessary supports had been forced back by our advance. Our supports were near at hand— the Confederates saw the game was up, and fell suddenly back as our supports came hurriedly forward, the very air being full of Union victory.

Colonel Kirby to this day feels proud of that splendid march. He characterizes it as the most remarkable the Regiment ever made. He is not at all sparing of his praises of the Color-Bearer, Sergeant James M. Roberts, for the important part he played in the matter. This work of the 101st really settled the whole conflict for the possession of the Gap—it turned the tide of victory our way.

The enemy retired to the vicinity of Bellbuckle, leaving us in full possession of the field, giving us the command of the Gap, and its approaches at both extremities.

The affair at Liberty Gap is not set down as one of the great events of the war, yet, so far as the Tullahoma campaign is concerned, it was the severest struggle at arms that occurred. Hardee had his troops stationed at Wartrace and in that vicinity, and was slow in bringing them into action. Thomas had assailed Hoover's Gap with such impetuosity that the slight rebel force at its northern entrance was forced back into and through the defile before relief could be brought up. Not quite so at Liberty Gap. Johnson was not quite so impetuous, and the rebel defending force was stronger and more determined.

When the enemy was driven from Hoover's Gap they took possession at Beech Grove, a few miles south and east, and showed signs of fight. Thomas was ordered to attack them, and, if successful, to follow as rapidly as the state of the roads would allow. He employed the day (25th) that we were fighting in Liberty Gap, in preparing for this assault. If Thomas pursued the enemy, then McCook was to guard both the Gaps. We spent the 26th in camp at the southern entrance of Liberty Gap, awaiting the outcome of Thomas' effort. He was successful, but could not pursue the enemy very far. That night, June 26th, his line of battle extended from the vicinity of Fairfield to within five miles of Manchester, with McCook on his right in strong position, and Crittenden on his left. All this was very discouraging to Hardee and others who were charged with the duty of preventing the concentration of our army south of the ridge. Indeed, they had been charged with an impossible task.

Bragg foreseeing danger, fell back upon Tullahoma, but this was not known to the Federal commander at the time. Rosecrans was seeking to draw Bragg out into the open field for battle.

On the next day Thomas moved his line toward the left a short distance and established his headquarters in Manchester, the Confederate force in that vicinity falling back toward Tullahoma and Dichard. General Rosecrans established his headquarters in Manchester the same day, and bent every energy toward the immediate concentration of his army near that place, preparatory to falling upon the enemy at Tullahoma, beyond which it was not thought Bragg would retreat. Rosecrans had fully determined to assail him in this stronghold unless he should retreat still further, in which case he would follow him and entangle him in the passes of the mountains.

A reconnoisance in force was sent out with the result of finding the enemy in fighting numbers on all the roads. It was reported at the same time by a citizen that the Confederates were in full retreat. To further test this matter, and at the same time to cut the railroads in the rear of the Confederate position, a strong cavalry force was sent around from our left. Everything indicated that we were on the eve of a desperate battle. The plan of attack was deliberately made, and at the proper moment announced to the several commanders.

The plan of assault involved the free use of the bayonet from start to finish. Very early on the morning of the 2nd we were on the march directly toward Tullahoma. Our artillery was almost helpless in the mud which seemed endless. Time and again we stacked arms, and putting our shoulders to the wheel, helped to drag the heavy guns from point to point. We were so confident of trouble before night that we were quite willing to aid in this work, believing that we should need the guns at almost any moment. Nothing of any special interest occurred on the march until about 4 o'clock. The rain ceased toward noon, and in the afternoon the sun came out roasting hot. Several of the boys were overcome with the heat, and were not able to go further.

We had marched nearly ten miles, and were in the immediate vicinity of the outer works of the enemy, north of Tullahoma. We were halted and told what the plan of assault was to be. The bayonet was to be relied on, and every man was to do his duty. It was intimated that the enemy might have withdrawn—the assault would determine that matter. When the order came, at the close of the instructions, to "fix bayonets," many of us were thrilled with a peculiar sensation—by no means pleasant. I confess that I never had what might be called a consuming desire to cross bayonets with the enemy. Lead at a hundred yards was as close as I cared to come. We soon fell in and began the march which was to be so important. We doted on the possibility that our bayonets would not be needed until time to make coffee. In a few moments we were in the woods—our line of battle was carefully formed, and we moved forward towards the "slash," which we could see through the woods, and beyond which we could see the rebel works.

Our cavalry, which had been sent out from the left with orders to cut the Confederate lines of communication, soon discovered the fact that the whole Confederate army was in retreat, that nearly the whole of it had passed into and

DR. GEO. S. YINGLING,
ASSISTANT SURGEON.
From Photograph.

through the mountains, and that we were marching upon a deserted town. We discovered the fact the moment we left the woods and entered the slash. We were not fired upon, from which fact we knew that there were no rebels there to fire. We were quickly convinced that we should have had a hard time of it in making our way through that slash if the rebel guns had been sweeping the ground with grape and canister. We moved steadily forward, prepared for action at any instant, and in a short time passed over the deserted rifle pits, and between the forts, on down through the town into camp a mile south of the village. We breathed easier. But the thought at once presented itself, "This means another long march, for these two armies must fight sooner or later." We did not bother our heads greatly over this matter—we were out of it for the present—and the future might take care of itself.

Very early the next morning, July 3rd, we were on the march in pursuit of the fleeing enemy. McCook's Corps was to pick up everything west of the Nashville & Chattanooga Railroad as far forward as to the Mountains, making Winchester our headquarters. The most serious opposition with which we met was the condition of the roads and the swollen rivers and streams we had to cross. Elk River was a seething torrent. The rebels had destroyed all the bridges, and in one or two places small detachments of cavalry were trying to hold the fords. But a few shells, or a volley or two of musketry even at long range, soon sent them toward the mountains. The fording of Elk River caused us considerable trouble, but we finally got over and went into camp near the beautiful little town of Winchester.

The village was indeed most beautifully located. The mountains present a most charming appearance during certain portions of the year. Their blue summits piercing the light, fleecy clouds that lazily drift across them; the occasional showers born among the crags, tumbling headlong down their rough sides; the lifting fog scattered by the rays of the morning sun; the halo of evening resting like a crown of glory on the rugged peaks; the unutterable beauty of the soft moonlight resting in silence on this whole region of chaos, and gilding with silver this expression of nature's wrath—the whole scene filled us with awe and admiration, and inspired a feeling of reverence for Him at whose command not the mountains alone, but the great Earth itself stood forth in glorious majesty.

It was along the base of this mountain range that our army lay at the close of the campaign. Beyond it, the enemy.

CHAPTER XII.

CHICKAMAUGA.

It was the 17th of August, 1863. Orders had been issued the day before for the general advance of the army. We had lain in camp at Winchester since the evening of the 3rd of July, awaiting the repair of the railroads both in our rear and in our front, and the accumulation of at least a reasonable amount of provisions and supplies of all kinds. All this had now been accomplished. Sheridan's Division of our Corps had already gone forward, and with the completion of the repairs on the railroad over the mountains, had occupied Stevenson and Bridgeport, driving the rebel outposts at these places across the river. The enemy was in force at Chattanooga with strong outposts at Harrison's Landing, a few miles above the city, and Hardee's Corps was still in Sequatchie Valley. Bragg did not anticipate an attack on his left by way of Stevenson and Bridgeport, but very confidently looked for Rosecrans to come at him directly in front of Chattanooga, or possibly, further up the river. He felt sure that the Union army would not attempt to cross the Tennessee River, Sand Mountain, Lookout Mountain and Missionary Ridge, while the Confederates held Chattanooga and vicinity. He felt quite secure in that quarter. He therefore waited.

Rosecrans' plan of campaign was, first of all, to maneuver Bragg out of his strong position at Chattanooga, into the open field where the chances would be even. To do this he must close the Tennessee, climb the mountains, and appear in strong force well back on Bragg's flank. It was this move that we were to commence on the morning of August 17th.

The extreme left, under Crittenden, was to advance down Sequatchie Valley, drive Hardee out, and appear before Chattanooga and Harrison with all the confidence possible. The movement was a feint to cover the crossing of the river by our other Corps. Crittenden was to make a great noise and do as much damage as he could. At the same time, Thomas was to advance as quietly as possible, and take position not far from Bridgeport, but was not to show himself more than was necessary.

One Division (Sheridan's) of our Corps, was already at Bridgeport and Stevenson. Johnson's Division was to advance by way of Bellefonte, further to the right, going into camp near the river at that point. Our own Division—Davis'—was to advance by way of Cowan, Mount Top and Crow Creek, encamping near Stevenson. All these movements were so well turned and so promptly executed that everything moved like clock-work.

We encamped the first night near Cowan at the base of the mountains. Very early next morning we were under way. Occasionally we stacked arms and gave the artillery and wagon train a lift, otherwise they would have remained behind. Our camp, that night was on top of the mountain. The scenery from the sides of the mountain and from the town was very fine and full of inspiration. If the mountains from Winchester had presented a scene of surpassing beauty, the river stretched out before us now was equally charming and radically different, entirely out of harmony with the war-like mission in which we were engaged. Reveille sounded at 2 o'clock next morning, and a march of 18 miles brought us to camp near Stevenson. Every Brigade, Division and Corps was on deck and in its place awaiting the next move. The river was carefully reconnoitered for the best crossing places. These were soon determined : Shellmound, Bridgeport, Caperton's and Bellefonte. Caperton's and Bridgeport were the principal crossings. To our Division fell the duty of laying the pontoon across the Tennessee at Caperton's, near Stevenson. As soon as the pontoon train could be brought up we took position on the north or right bank of the river, sending a couple of regiments across to protect that end of the bridge when laid. A small cavalry force of the enemy on the opposite bank showed some signs of interference and were promptly shelled, whereupon they left us in our glory. The 21st and 38th Illinois, of our Brigade, were the first to pass over after the bridge was finished, followed by the artillery of two Brigades. Our own Regiment and the artillery of another Brigade remained over Sunday on the north bank. From the moment the bridge was completed, on Saturday evening, until the Monday night following, troops and trains and artillery were constantly passing over the bridge. The column seemed to be unbroken. A portion of Thomas' troops passed here though most of his men crossed at Bridgeport.

On Monday morning we crossed and took our place in the column. The ascent of Sand Mountain we found to be about as difficult as that of the Cumberland at Cowan.

Here, as there, we were obliged to assist the artillery and trains, but this was done very cheerfully, as we had good reason to believe both would be handy to have around a little later on. Sand Mountain is well named. It has a flat top, about 12 miles wide where we crossed, and is as sterile as the middle of an Ohio State Road. The few people—citizens— that we saw, did not look as though they knew enough to last them through the week, nor did their actions belie their looks. Our camp that evening was near the southern slope of the mountain. Descending next day we went into camp in Will's Valley. This is a long, narrow affair lying between Sand and Lookout mountains, through which Lookout Creek flows into the Tennessee a few miles below Chattanooga. Many small farmers—exceedingly small, some of them, live in this valley. A pig, a patch of potatoes, a pipe and a hunk of pone, are all that are necessary to a cracker's existence. We soon moved our camp across the valley to Winston's, at the entrance to a gap in Lookout Mountain bearing the same name. On the 9th of September several Divisions of the army south of the river having come into supporting distance of each other, we broke camp, and passed across Lookout Mountain into Shinbone Valley—a march of 18 miles. Lookout, like Sand Mountain, is quite flat at this crossing. Near the summit at Winston's Gap is a very beautiful waterfall. The water, plunging over a precipice, strikes the bottom nearly 90 feet below. Some of us discovered this while scouting, but on attempting to return we found that we were within the Confederate line, as was clearly proven by our capturing two of their pickets, belonging to Wheeler's Cavalry Division. About the only information we could get out of these intelligent fellows was that "you'ns 'll git licked like ——— when you git down on the other side of this 'ere mountain." Our "scouting" was an irregular affair—we had been out hunting for peaches, and accidentally stumbled

ANDREW J. SCHNURR,
COMPANY E.
From old photograph.

upon the falls and also the rebel pickets. We were brought up with a round turn for being outside our line. First we received a scoring from our Captains; then we were called before Col. Kirby, who gave it to us pretty straight, and then we were hauled up before Gen. Carlin who poured several broadsides into us. The thing was getting monotonous and tiresome. The more the General talked, the more indignant he became at our "lack of common sense." He subsided very gracefully and promptly when in sheer self-defense we informed him that his younger brother, his own aide, was with us.

I have the old pass yet which permitted me to go and come through our lines at pleasure, without question, but I came near losing it on this occasion. [I was Brigade Topographical Engineer for a time].

Passing down the slope of Lookout into Shinbone Valley, we came near to Alpine, Georgia—the first time we had crossed the line into that State.

From the 10th to the 16th of September, there is no possible explanation of the movements of either army except on the ground that neither commander knew where the other was, nor what he was trying to do. Bragg marched and countermarched, passing sometimes within cannon shot of our isolated Brigades. One of our Divisions—Negley's—marched boldly down a narrow winding mountain gap almost into the very embrace of a whole rebel Corps. But neither side knew it for some time, then Negley whistled for help and actually got away. But his getting away was due more to insubordination in the Confederate lines than to anything else, though he managed well. When Bragg finally learned that Negley was in the cove, McLimore's, he ordered an assault by fully 30,000 men. Poor Negley! and poor Baird who was at the top of the mountain at the entrance to the gap into the cove! Hindman was to slip around and get into Negley's rear and on his flank. Buckner's Division was ordered around to help Hindman—making two Divisions on flank and rear. Moreover, Polk's Corps was to support this brave movement. Cleburne was to attack in front the moment Hindman's guns were heard. Bragg was at the front with Cleburne to see that the thing was well done. But Hindman and Buckner wanted to do it some other way, and Bragg wouldn't let them. They were therefore not enthusiastic. Instead of attacking Negley at daylight, as Hindman had been ordered to do, he took his own time. Poor Bragg waited at Cleburne's headquarters all the forenoon and until 3 o'clock in the afternoon, when Hindman's first gun was heard.

Hindman was so slow that when he did attack he found the cove empty. Negley, discovering his danger, promptly withdrew. For pure, unadulterated bungling, the palm belonged to the Confederates on this occasion. But Bragg was neglecting another opportunity equally favorable. Our Brigade and most of McCook's Corps were in Shinbone valley, not far from Alpine, entirely out of touch with the rest of the army. Bragg gave us no attention, but allowed us to get away in perfect safety.

It should have been stated that as soon as the Confederate commander was satisfied that Rosecrans' main attack would be made on his left flank, he withdrew his army from Chattanooga, and remained more or less on the wing, in the vicinity of Ringold, Gordon's Mills and Lafayette, hoping to catch the Union army as it debouched from the mountains into the open country. His intentions were strictly in accordance with business, but his subordinates were careless, insubordinate, or incompetent. The two incidents given above are in illustration. Another was the case of Crittenden, who entered Chattanooga when Bragg left it, and who had advanced well down toward Gordon's Mills. After vainly trying to catch Negley, Bragg ordered Polk to attack Crittenden in his exposed position, and take him dead or alive. So important did Bragg consider this movement that he sent three separate orders to the Rev. General with positive instructions to attack at once. But Polk simply sat down in what he called an offensive-defensive position, that is, he drew up his army, showed his teeth, growled at long range, but was quite as ready to move backward as forward should prudence get the better of valor.

While these things were transpiring in Crittenden's and Thomas' fronts, our Corps (McCook's) was prowling around in Shinbone Valley, near Alpine.

On the evening of the 12th, our several Corps were located as follows: Crittenden had concentrated his entire force in the vicinity of Gordon's Mills, with Polk not far away; Thomas was in McLimore's Cove, near Cooper's and Stevens' Gaps, and the remainder of the Confederate army was back of Pigeon Mountain, a short distance away, with strong outposts at Dug and Catlett's Gaps. Bragg's headquarters were at Lafayette; McCook was at Alpine, twenty miles southwest of Thomas.

Bragg, utterly disgusted with the inexcusable failure of his attempts to crush our army in detail, gave orders on the 13th for the concentration of his forces on the right, or east bank of Chickamauga, for general battle.

Twenty-four hours before that time, General Rosecrans had sent a messenger in hot haste, ordering McCook to withdraw from his exposed position at Alpine and close on Thomas at the first possible moment. Haste and discipline were everything.

On the morning of the 13th, therefore, at the same hour that orders for the concentration of the Confederate forces on the east bank of the Chickamauga were issued, we began our march back across Lookout for the purpose of taking

HIRAM C. MODERWELL,
COMPANY C.
From photograph taken in 1894.

our position on Thomas' right. We crossed the mountain and encamped the next evening five miles north of Winston's in Will's Valley. Strange as it may seem, we remained here until the middle of the afternoon of the next day, and then marched back to Winston's, ascended the Gap and went into camp a few miles out on a mountain road leading eastward. Reveille sounded very early next morning, and we were off at once. A wearisome march across Lookout in the direction of Stevens' Gap, brought us to the head of that pass just before night. The next morning we descended into the valley—McLimore's Cove—and at once formed line of battle. We confidently expected an assault—certainly by the enemy's cavalry, and possibly by their infantry also, but it did not come, and after a careful reconnoisance we moved to our left and forward several miles, meeting no particular opposition. We encamped that night—the 17th—in line of battle along the road leading from the Cove to Gordon's Mills and Chattanooga. The picket line was doubled, and every precaution was taken to guard against surprise. We were in line at three o'clock next morning, but did not move until 6 o'clock. We—McCook's Corps, and a portion of Thomas'—were separated from the main body of the Confederate army by the narrow ridge of Pigeon mountain. The two armies were from three to five miles apart. Very many of us had quite a correct notion of their relative position.

When Bragg found that he could not defeat our army in detail, he began to wish himself back in Chattanooga behind his fortifications. If General Polk had obeyed orders and assailed Crittenden the moment he arrived in his vicinity, he might have opened the way, but that was not done, and now that the two armies lay confronting each other in a more or less confused and uncertain state, it became evident that a great battle must be fought for the possession of the high road leading to Chattanooga. As the cords began to tighten, and the conditions became more and more intense, Bragg was seized with the notion that he must have posession of the aforesaid road. To accomplish this end he concentrated his forces on the east side of Chickamauga, so that his right should greatly overlap the Union left, as nearly as he could make out where our left was. His intention was to crush Crittenden as he had crushed McCook at Stone's River, and then holding the roads leading to Chattanooga, he would fall upon Thomas and McCook and beat them before they could concentrate for effective defense. His plan was doomed to failure.

It should be noticed that on the 18th and the early morning of the 19th, Bragg received large reinforcements, both from Lee's Army in Virginia and Pemberton's Army, recently paroled at Vickburg. The only assistance Rosecrans received was the sending of Burnside into East Tennessee, but this was in reality no assistance, as it resulted in the sending of Buckner's Division from that quarter to Bragg at Chickamauga. Moreover, Bragg had the advantage of knowing every inch of ground on which the two armies were about to advance.

Bragg's orders, issued on the 13th, for the concentration of his forces on the east bank of the Chickamauga, were being slowly executed, his Corps Commanders feeling that they had plenty of time. With the withdrawal of Bragg's forces from the vicinity of Lafayette, Thomas crept cautiously toward Crittenden, but could not extend his front very much, not knowing just how large a force the enemy had left at Lafayette to look after our right. This concentration of the enemy was well known to Rosecrans, Thomas and Crittenden, and the moment that McCook arrived and fell into line at Stevens' Gap, Thomas moved his two Corps toward the left, encamping on the evening of the 17th at

Pond Spring. He was now well closed up on Crittenden's right—and Rosecrans began to breathe more easily. In the afternoon of the 17th, we followed Thomas toward the left about five miles and encamped for the night.

We were expected to move toward our left as rapidly as possible on the morning of the 18th, so as to get our Division closed well up on Thomas' right. But his trains were in the road to such an extent that we made very slow progress. We were constantly ready to come to a battle front, but had no occasion to do so. On account of Thomas' trains, McCook was obliged to encamp on the evening of the 18th at Pond Spring, six miles southwest of Crawfish Spring, and ten miles by road from Gordon's Mills. A detachment of Mitchell's Cavalry was stationed a short distance in advance of us, and just across the river facing them was Wheeler's Confederate Cavalry. During the night the trains had moved forward and to the left out of the way, so that early in the morning we moved forward, reaching Crawfish Springs between 8 o'clock and 9 o'clock, no especial incident occurring on the way.

CHAPTER XIII.

BATTLE OF CHICKAMAUGA.

It was a beautiful Indian Summer morning, perfect in every respect. We all enjoyed it greatly, but realized that its beautiful serenity would be broken before night in all human probability. We, in the ranks, had gathered sufficient information to cause us to believe that both armies were pushing as rapidly as possible northward toward Chattanooga, and that they were liable to come into collision at any moment. In a general way we were correct.

LIEUTENANT ISAAC P. RULE,
COMPANY I.
KILLED AT BATTLE OF CHICKAMAUGA, SEPTEMBER 20, 1863.

The Battle of Chickamauga is very difficult to describe. It was a sort of running fight for a time, both armies being vigorously engaged in shifting further to the north—on our side, for the purpose of holding more securely the roads leading into Chattanooga, and on the Confederate side, for the purpose of regaining control of these roads so as to shut Rosecrans out of that stronghold and force him back into the mountains, where his army might be destroyed in their rugged defiles.

The general conflict was brought on rather by accident while this movement was in progress, and before either commander was ready. So rapid had been the change of position of Brigades, Divisions and Corps, and so completely had corps lines been broken up by the exigencies of the hour, that neither commander knew the position of the other. Indeed, he did well to know the exact location of his own Brigades and Divisions.

Almost half the Confederate army had crossed over to the west side of Chickamauga, and yet it was reported to General Thomas about 10 o'clock on Saturday morning, the 19th, that a single Confederate Brigade had been seen in the woods near Reed's Bridge, and that inasmuch as that bridge had been captured the night before, the capture of this rebel force would be an easy and proper thing. The fact was that five Divisions, comprising nearly twenty Brigades were across the river ready for business at that moment. Yet all unconscious of this, General Thomas ordered General Brannan to advance and see what he could find. Instead of one Brigade he found the woods full of them. He had advanced so far and pressed his inquiries so closely that he could not fall back without greatly endangering his whole line. Baird's Division was therefore sent to his assistance. The two Divisions were at once assailed by Forrest's Cavalry, by Willson's and Eaton's Brigades, and later by Walker's

Division. After a gallant fight they (Brannan and Baird) were compelled to give way, Baird losing one of his batteries. Thus the great battle was commenced very unexpectedly to both sides. So unready were the Confederates that Brannan, with his single Division, drove the enemy about a half mile before they could get upon their feet. Rallying, they regained their lost ground, and, although supported by Baird, our side was so unready that not a man could be sent to reinforce our driven lines until it was too late.

Shortly after this repulse, Johnson, of McCook's Corps, arrived upon the field, and was sent at once to form on Baird's right, but Baird was not able to do much fighting for awhile. The result was that Johnson was driven back with great loss. By 3 o'clock in the afternoon, through excellent fighting but bad generalship, our lines north of the Vineyard Farm had lost very heavily, had been driven back to the Chattanooga road, and in at least two places across it, and generally the battle was going heavily against us.

As already stated, McCook's Corps, excepting Post's Brigade, which was guarding Stevens' Gap, reached Crawfish Springs about 9 o'clock in the morning.

It was here that we heard the first unmistakable rumblings of the great battle, soon to become general. Filling our canteens at the beautiful spring that gushes in great abundance from the broken rock in the hillside, we were placed in position to guard the crossings of the river, or to move elsewhere, as occasion might require. In our immediate front, near the bridge over Chicamauga, and still further to our right, there was considerable firing—mostly artillery. We rested in line of battle. The beauty and balminess of the glorious morning were wholly lost sight of in the face of the coming storm of battle, indications of which were unmistakable on every hand.

General Rosecrans, with his staff, was at Crawfish Springs

nearly two hours; while we lay there the constant coming and going of officers and orderlies, some of them in hot haste, was evidence that the situation was exceedingly grave, and that events of great importance were already taking place, in widely separated portions of the field. There was no sign of excitement or nervousness about the General, but he was exceedingly prompt and decisive in his issuing of orders. These orders, for a time at least, included a continuance of the "side-step" toward the north, that our whole army, and not simply a few Brigades, might cover the roads leading to Chattanooga—that is, that our left might overlap the enemy's right. This movement was continued, notwithstanding the fact that the hostile forces had already come into collision, and were at that moment engaged in fierce conflict. This was not a notion — it was a necessity — to meet a similar movement on the part of the enemy. Rosecrans seemed consumed with the importance of keeping Bragg off the Chattanooga road. About 11 o'clock, Breckinridge, from the south side of the river near Gordon's Mills, opened up a furious cannonade on Wood, who held our line at that point. It was principally noise, for his batteries were neither well posted nor well served. At the same time a Division crossed the river, but after fifteen or twenty minutes' fighting, was glad to return. Very soon after this, a messenger from General Thomas handed General Rosecrans a dispatch. Instantly an order was issued to General McCook, and a moment later Davis' Division was in line and off at a quick step toward the north. We had been ordered to report to Thomas, and thither we went as fast as we could go, following a dirt road which runs parallel with the Chattanoga road, past the Widow Glenn's house, soon to become General Rosecrans' headquarters.

We had before us a march of something over five miles, the first four of which were made at almost a trot, the last mile or more at a double-quick. The 101st had the lead of our Brigade, although Heg's Brigade led the general line on this march. There was much excitement as we approached the field. Evidently we were coming into the immediate vicinity of the severest of severe fighting. Not a man hesitated. Filing across a corner of a field we were rushed into position in the open fields of the Vineyard Farm, just over the brow of a slight eminence, on the side sloping toward the enemy concealed in the woods. General Heg's Brigade was in the woods on our left. For a short time Carlin's Brigade was the extreme right of our effective front in this part of the field. There was a bad break between Carlin and the troops in the vicinity of Gordon's Mills. Our line, as we came upon the field, was formed under a murderous fire from rebel sharpshooters and skirmishers. The rebel lines were being formed and adjusted under cover of the woods. We were instantly ordered down upon our faces, an order we cheerfully obeyed. We were not permitted to lie there long, for the crisis of the day's battle had arrived, and must be fought to a finish on the Vineyard Farm.

Davis' Division had arrived most opportunely. The message which Rosecrans had received from Thomas and which set our Division in motion, reported the result of Brannan's and Baird's first set-to with the enemy, briefly outlined above. Very soon after this, Johnson of our Corps, reported on the field, and was immediately formed on Baird's right. Palmer, who came upon the field at the same time, was formed on his right, and on Palmer's right, Reynolds. While all this was being done, the Confederates had also been adjusting their lines. Walker's entire Corps was added to the host, and the rebel line was on the point of advancing. As soon as our new line, consisting—from left to right—of Brannan, Baird, Johnson, Palmer and Reynolds, had been formed, it assumed the offensive and bore down on the enemy with such irresistible force as to drive them back in confusion. Brannan recaptured the battery taken from Baird in the first assault. The enemy were crowded back at the point of the bayonet until they reached their original position. At this critical moment, General Bragg ordered Cheatham's whole Corps into line. Crowding Brannan and Baird back, they fell in great force upon Johnson, driving him from his position; then concentrating on Palmer, they forced him back, and also Van Cleve, who was coming to his assistance. This left Reynolds so exposed that he, too, was compelled to yield, but not until he and Van Cleve had hotly contested every inch of the way. But the Confederates were victorious along our entire left and well down toward the center. Disaster seemed to attend our efforts at every point. The second epoch in the battle had been decided against the Union Army.

It was at this stage of the battle that our Division arrived on the ground, as stated above. Indeed, the roar of the musketry and artillery on our immediate left as we formed in line, was still in full cry, it being the supreme effort of the enemy to crush Palmer, Reynolds and Van Cleve. Very soon after we came into position, they were successful, the Union lines being crowded back to and, in one or two instances, across the road. The National line, though shattered and badly broken, was at once reformed along the Chattanooga road, ready for the best work possible. But the scene of conflict was to be moved to the Vineyard Farm and its immediate vicinity.

No member of the 101st who was present on that afternoon when we went into line, will forget the scene. Coming upon the field, as we did, on the double-quick, we were glad to lie down as soon as we came into position. The fighting at that time was almost wholly on our left. Near

GEORGE F. DRAKE,
COMPANY D.
From photograph taken in 1894.

us, in that direction, the roar of musketry seemed to be almost constant, sometimes rolling off further to the left, then surging back toward us until it seemed to be at our very elbows, while frequently the crash of cannon by single piece, section, or entire battery, hammered and pounded and shook the very earth, filling the air with shot and sharpnell and bursting shell. The unearthly music to which we listened as we lay there was greatly intensified by the frequency of battle yells as charging columns met their equals in countercharge, and by the further knowledge that Death and Destruction were then and there reaping an abundant harvest. In the midst of all this we were ordered to our feet and into the woods directly in front of us. Carlin was to lead, followed by Heg further to the left, in such a way that by means of a half-wheel our entire battle line might be formed as soon as the enemy's left should be struck. Without hesitation on the part of any, the order to advance was obeyed with alacrity. We had but little difficulty in clearing our front of skirmishers and sharp-shooters. Advancing cautiously, but steadily, through the dense woods, we soon struck a strong rebel force advancing obliquely across our front toward our left. Instantly the two lines became engaged in a most desperate conflict. But little artillery could be used on account of the density of the woods. Our Division Artillery had been posted on the slight eminence in front of which we had formed on coming upon the field. Hearing the din of battle in Carlin's front, Colonel Heg hurried his Brigade forward into line in time to receive a severe assault made by the left of the Confederate line that had just crushed Reynolds and Van Cleve. He made a vigorous though fruitless stand. Colonel Heg was killed very early in the conflict, and his Brigade became demoralized and soon fell back in considerable confusion. They retreated through the woods toward the Chattanooga road, near the point at which we had crossed it on entering the field. The enemy followed them closely, taking many prisoners.

About noon, General Wood, in command of a Division at Gordon's Mills, and General Barnes, in command of one of Van Cleve's Brigades near the same place, had been ordered further to the left. Wood reached the field at the moment that Heg's broken columns reached the road. Forming one of his Brigades at the entrance to the woods, and the other in the open fields just back of the crest and to the left of our Division Artillery, he allowed the stragglers to pass through and then poured shot and shell and musketry into the advancing force until they were glad to stop. In addition to this, two batteries a little further to our left, opened on them with terrible effect. During this time Carlin's Brigade was engaged in a most desperate contest in the woods. Our single Brigade was fighting rebel General Johnson's whole Division. With Heg gone from our left, and with no support on our right, we could not maintain our position. We therefore fell back, contesting the ground inch by inch.

In this retreat, however, we lost many men, not a few of them by capture. The assault upon the right of our line was viciously maintained. A number of our men were cut off. The tenacity with which our troops held to their position, and their unwillingness to retreat, are accountable for most of the captures. The Brigade fell back in fairly good condition, to the edge of the woods which we had entered an hour before. The enemy was close upon us on every hand. As we came out of the woods we were delighted to see a Brigade of blue coats rapidly forming just to the right of our Division Artillery in the edge of the woods. It was Barnes' Brigade, of Van Cleve's Division, which had just arrived from Gordon's Mills. This gave us new hope, and again we formed our lines slightly in advance of our first line, across the same open field. The assaults upon our right and our left had been so desperate, and so overwhelming in numbers, that our flanks were of necessity thrown back. Had it not been for the support of Barnes on our right and Wood on our left and rear, Carlin's Brigade would doubtless have been captured. As it was, we were soon ready to give battle again. Our ranks had been greatly thinned—many of the boys were out of line—killed, wounded, or captured. On the left, and considerably back of us, the battle raged in great fury. It was Wood assailing the victorious followers of Heg's retreating men, consisting of a portion of Fulton's command and of Law's Division. The moment was a critical one, and but for the aid of the artillery belonging to Van Cleve's and Reynold's Divisions, which could not be used in the woods in which those Divisions fought, the Confederates must have gained possession of the road. As it was, they were held in check for a time, and severely punished. Our lines, shortened by the conflict in the woods, were formed from near the center of the open field into which we had retreated, extending northerly toward the edge of the woods in which Heg had originally formed. Our left was of necessity thrown back on account of the presence of the enemy in that quarter. Barnes' Brigade was formed to the right and slightly in advance of our Division Artillery, which occupied the elevated position in front of the Vineyard house. Owing to the density of the woods, it was not possible to use our artillery in the conflict, out of which the Brigade had just emerged. Scarcely had our lines been formed, when with a wild rush, the Confederates came out of the woods to assail us, as they supposed, on flank and front. They were not aware of the presence of Barnes, and for a moment they were staggered. They fell upon our front and left most furiously, but with

LIEUTENANT COLONEL JOHN MESSER.

From Photograph.

the assistance of our Division Artillery and one of Woods' batteries near Buell's position, we not only held our ground, but charging their lines we drove them back into the woods, capturing General Gregg, who had been wounded in the charge.

Rallying and extending their lines further to the left, they succeeded in doubling us back to such an extent that it became necessary to retreat or fall into their hands. The latter was not to be thought of. Sullenly, therefore, we fell back. But soon seeing that we were badly flanked on our left, and further that our artillery could not play while we were in front, we hastened, nor waited the "order of our going." Falling back to the edge of the woods, about six hundred feet from the main road, we reformed our lines in good order and awaited the next move. There was not the slightest hint of a panic in our midst. A company of Wilder's seven-shooters was sent to our assistance, but was soon recalled, their services being needed further to the left of our line. During all this time there had been considerable fighting on our left, especially near the extreme left. Bragg made a third attempt to turn Thomas. No sooner had this assault been repulsed than did Thomas send Brannan's Division down toward the Vineyard Farm to aid in repelling the continued assaults that were being made in that part of the field.

Our rest in the edge of the woods to the west of the Vineyard house was destined to be of short duration. The Confederates had not ventured over the brow of the ridge, or rather swell, to the east of the road, but lying flat on their faces they hoped to be able to command and possibly occupy the road. Their lines were hammered most unmercifully by Wood's artillery and by other batteries that had been brought into position for the purpose, until, seeing that they were wavering, a charge was ordered. Instantly our line was in motion. Carlin charging directly across the open field, Buell was on our left and Barnes on our right. Our artillery at every available point poured shot and shell and canister into their ranks. Their line gave way at every point, and was rushing pell-mell for the cover of the woods at the eastern edge of the fields in which we were fighting, when to our horror we beheld a splendid line of fresh Confederates issuing out of the woods facing our left. Maddened rather than palsied by this unexpected sight, our lines stood like stone walls, though our men were falling like leaves in Autumn. Barnes was soon put in a most critical position, and Carlin was forced back a short distance. This column was Triggs' Brigade, which had been sent fresh and unbroken to the rebel General Johnson's assistance. Triggs bore off to our right to aid Robertson, and in doing so fell in the way of our batteries. Half his command fell or ran in a few minutes, and the remainder was used by Robertson for a short time. Most fortunately had General Rosecrans called General Sheridan from Gordon's Mills. He came with rapid strides up the main road, helped Barnes upon his feet as he passed, fell like a withering curse upon Robertson, recaptured a battery that Wood had just lost, and took the offensive at once. With Sheridan's assistance the enemy was soon dislodged from the road at every point near us and was forced back into the woods, though in most places at the point of the bayonet. It was now 5 o'clock. The enemy, defeated at every point, seemed willing to remain quiet in the recesses of the glades and woods into which our last supreme effort had hurled them. The afternoon's work had been such that we surely had no desire to follow them into their fastnesses. The battle ceased suddenly and for the day soon after 5 o'clock. Our line was quietly withdrawn over the brow of the hill, where we lay on our faces, not knowing what the enemy's next move might be. But we were not disturbed. At dusk we were withdrawn to the edge of the woods, our lines carefully adjusted, our cartridge-boxes replenished and everything put in order for a surprise at any moment.

As the several companies fell in for roll-call, there came over the boys a sadness that none save those who have had the actual experience can understand. There were many vacant places. Some of the boys were dead, some were wounded unto death, some were prisoners, some were missing, many were in hospitals, maimed and mangled.

Darkness had settled over the field, and silence deep and pervading had succeeded the roar and din of battle. Floating out upon the solemn stillness would now and then come the heart-burdened cry of some poor fellow, who, falling between the lines, was compelled to lie there unknown and uncared for the live-long night. Some of these heart-broken wails ring in my ears to this day.

Tired and powder-begrimmed, we lay in line of battle that night, too weary even to dream. Our rest, however, was brief.

It was Saturday night, and the day's conflict, though inexpressibly terrible, had not determined the matter. Another battle must be fought, the preparations for which were immediately begun on both sides. The change of front forward toward the left and toward Bragg's right had resulted in mixing up Divisions and Corps to a wonderful degree. All this was more or less demoralizing. But the exigencies of Saturday's battle made it necessary.

The solemn stillness of the night succeeding the battle was broken here and there by the stealthy movement of troops on both sides going into position in the new lines, preparatory to a renewal of the conflict with the coming dawn. Snarles and misplacements of troops were corrected;

CAPTAIN GEORGE W. HALE,
COMPANY F.

From photograph taken in 1893.

rations and ammunition were distributed; broken and disorganized detachments were combined, and everything possible was done to insure success in the coming battle.

Sheridan, who occupied the extreme right of our line, was ordered by General McCook to go into position near the Widow Glenn's house. To do this in safety he moved his right Brigade back and along the rear of his other two Brigades, which remained in line and came into position on their left; then taking his next Brigade he moved it back and to the left in the same manner, always keeping two Brigades in line. He thus reached his new position in safety. While doing this, he left his picket-skirmish line undisturbed. As soon as Sheridan had moved, General Barnes, who was between him and Davis, moved to the left and came under Wood's command. This left our Division on the extreme Union right. Soon after midnight, we were quietly aroused from our slumbers and very noiselessly moved toward our left and rear. We had not the remotest idea as to where we were going, and there was not a little growling at being called up at that time of night. Colonel Martin was in command of Heg's Brigade. After the usual jerky halts, we came into position, called the roll, and lay down to finish our nap. With the dawn, a half hour later, we fell in, but were soon permitted to stack arms and lounge in the immediate vicinity.

Our front extended along the crest of one of the spurs or foot-hills of Mission Ridge. Through the thin woods we could look out over the plain on which the armies had so fiercely contended the previous day, lying there in all the beauty and charm of a perfect September morning.

In front of us, at a distance of nearly five miles, we could distinctly see the line of fog or mist that overhung the Chickamauga, extending from Gordon's Mills, four miles south of us, away northward toward the Tennessee. The fog was neither dense enough nor near enough to prevent the opening of a battle. What caused the delay we were not able to make out. It was not Rosecrans' purpose to make the attack. He was on the defensive, and yet it must be admitted that daylight found him not quite ready for the fight. The four hours' delay granted by the Reverend General Polk, through his stupid neglect, was industriously used by General Rosecrans in rectifying his lines and correcting the errors made during the darkness of the night. Daylight found Thomas' command parted as follows: On the extreme left, Baird, then Johnson of McCook's Corps, then Palmer of Crittenden's Corps, Reynolds, Brannan and Van Cleve. On Thomas' right under Crittenden were Negley of Thomas' Corps, and Wood, and on Crittenden's right were Davis with two Brigades and Sheridan.

At daylight it was observed that Thomas's left did not cover the Reed's Bridge Road. General Negley was at once ordered from his position under Crittenden to fill out this part of the line. His reserve Brigade was sent at once, and he was about to follow with the remainder when a noisy assault was made on our skirmish line, causing him, on Rosecrans' order, to delay. By this time, nearly 10 o'clock, the assault had opened furiously on the left. Negley was hurried off on double quick. Upon the withdrawal of Negley, Wood was moved into his place. This drew him away from Davis, and when Davis followed him a few minutes later, a gap was made between our right and Sheridan's left. Our two Brigades were stretched out as much as possible to fill this gap, but Sheridan, under orders, remained near the Glenn House with Wilder's Cavalry.

Bragg's plan of assault was to begin on his right, and then follow in regular succession toward his left, until the whole line should become engaged. The assault was to have been made **at daylight**.

General Polk was in command of Bragg's Right, and General Longstreet of his Left. Polk had been ordered to open the battle very early in the morning, but as late as 8 o'clock he had not reached the field. He had slept on the east side of the Chickamauga, and, it seems, took a nap or two too many on Sunday morning. At all events, Bragg, becoming weary and irritated with waiting, went to that part of the field in person, and, not finding Polk there, ordered the assault. This was shortly after 10 o'clock. Steadily and quite rapidly the noise of the conflict came nearer to where we were. There was difficulty in establishing our line—Davis could not touch Sheridan. It was at this time, about 11 o'clock, that a most unfortunate order was given to General Wood by General Rosecrans. A dispatch from Thomas led him to believe that a serious gap existed between Wood's left and Reynold's right. This was not true, however, and Wood knew it at the time. The order was positive, directing Wood to close up on Brannan's right. This order could not be obeyed, as there was no gap. Brannan was in his proper place. Wood was in the dumps about something—mad at Crittenden for one thing— and, putting the order in his pocket for future use, as he said, immediately withdrew his Division from the line, and moved to the support of Reynolds, this being his interpretation of the order. This left a gap on the left of our Division. Until reinforced by Negley and Van Cleve, Thomas had hard work to protect his left flank. But with these reinforcements and his splendidly posted lines around the crest of an elevation, which runs parallel with the Chattanooga road, he was able to hold his ground against all comers. Rosecrans' reserves, under Granger, were guarding the gap through Mission Ridge at Rossville. Of course, we, who were in the ranks, knew nothing of Wood's fool move, nor of the fact that Sheridan was not up to us on our

BENJ. T. STRONG,
COMPANY A.

From photograph taken in 1894.

right. We were looking toward the front, and soon found more than we could manage.

Steadily and most majestically the tread of battle came our way. It found us in position, back of some slight barricades fixed up by Negley's men early in the morning.

We had been in line waiting for them some minutes, many of the boys using the time in strengthening the slight protection in front of them. As the minie balls of the sharpshooters began to drop in upon us, each snugged himself close up to his rail, or chunk, or stone, or log, or tree, determined to drop the first butternut that dared to show himself. All thought of joking and frivolity now ceased, and every man, knitting his brows, gave all of himself to the work in hand. We were soon in the midst of that period of murder which precedes almost every battle—the contest between the skirmishers—in which deliberate and deadly aim is taken upon particular individuals. Many a rebel bit the dust in consequence of coming within the range of our guns, rested on our rude breastworks. Our firing at this stage of the battle was not rapid, but it was exceedingly effective. Their skirmish line, deployed at a distance of about one pace, as I remember it, made a rush, to determine whether we were there in force, and received in their faces such a volley as sent them in great confusion to the rear. They left many dead and wounded in the open space over which they had foolishly charged. Their main line, however, was just back of them, and we were given only a few moments' breathing spell.

It seems strange, nevertheless it is a fact, that General Longstreet, becoming tired of Polk's long delay in opening the battle on our left, determined to send forward as a single assaulting line his whole force. To avoid pitfalls and surprises, he ordered a very strong skirmish line. It was this skirmish line that struck us and was repulsed, as stated above. On Davis's right and left, however, this line met with no obstructions. The fatal breaks in the Union line of battle were thus discovered, and instant arrangements made by the Confederates to force their way through. In the meantime, the rebel line in our immediate front rushed upon us. In an instant the battle was on in all its fury. We had the advantage of an open field in our front. The rebels hesitated to attempt to cross it, and for a short time we fought at decent range. But the Confederates were desperate, and attempted to cross. A moment before doing so, they had halted to adjust their lines. We reserved our fire and waited for them, snugging ourselves into the smallest possible space. With a yell, and firing as they ran, they debouched into the field. With deliberate and deadly aim we emptied our guns into their ranks not two hundred feet away. They staggered, halted, hesitated, and before they were aware of it received another volley, which sent them flying to the cover of the woods. Many of our boys had been wounded, and some killed, but the Confederate loss in our immediate front must have been, at this time, ten to our one. If our lines had been continuous, the history of the next two hours would have been different. We should have held our ground.

Massing their forces, the enemy passed through these fatal gaps in our lines and assailed us on both flanks, while, at the same instant, with double line, they assaulted us again in front. No pen of mine can describe the scene at this state of the battle. On our left, in Thomas' front, the conflict was at its height. Great numbers of cannon were in full roar on either side. In our own front and on both flanks the contest raged most furiously, but was confined to infantry on account of the woods. What with the deafening roar of the musketry, the yells of charging columns, and the pounding of Thomas' artillery, it was a scene that can neither be described nor forgotten. When the Confederate ranks, with wild yells, rushed across the open field in our front, we gave them the contents of our guns, and many scores went down, but other scores took their places, and the line rushed on. Springing from our slight protection, we determined to meet them cold steel to cold steel, and for a short time the combat was furious. The flank movement of the enemy had, however, settled the question. We were rapidly being surrounded. The order to fall back was given.

Under the circumstances, it was impossible to preserve company or even regimental lines. Emerging from the woods into the open fields, we discovered long lines of Confederate troops hurrying toward our rear, and others advancing directly upon us. At the same time we saw a Union column advancing on the double quick. They halted, formed, charged, were dashed into pieces, and hurled back in confusion. It was a portion of Wilder's command. Sheridan made a determined stand, but was completely overpowered and forced to fall back. General Carlin attempted to re-form our lines near the Dry Valley road, but found it impossible. The 101st was well represented in this new line. The defeat of Sheridan and our whole Right wing, and the rolling back of the Center, under Crittenden, made this position utterly untenable. Our retreat was continued in great confusion, though we were not again disturbed by the enemy. Our position, near the Dry Valley road, was abandoned on the approach of the enemy in force.

How we reached Rossville that evening is a difficult question to answer—indeed, we did not all reach it. A remnant of the Regiment kept with the colors all the time. When we went into camp that night we stacked fifty-nine guns, but this number was considerably increased before morning. The fugitives divided near where we had made our last stand, many passing through Mission Ridge by way of McFarland's Gap, and many—probably most—moved through the fields and woods along the base of the Ridge to the Gap at Rossville, five or six miles away, toward Chattanooga. Those of us who were last found well beaten paths leading across the fields, through the woods, over hills and along valleys, all leading in the right direction. During all this dreadful march to the rear we could hear the incessant pounding of artillery off in the direction of Thomas' position. The sensations we experienced were novel and by no means pleasant. A sense of duty called us back in the direction of the cannonading, but we were disorganized; without leaders, concert of action was impossible, and we continued to drift rearward.

It was upon the defeat of our Division and the rolling up of Sheridan, which carried with it our entire Right, and the doubling back of the Center, that General Rosecrans left the front, proceeding to Chattanooga to select a proper position to which he might conduct his army. But Thomas remained and saved the day. It would be interesting to follow the great battle on this part of the line, but we had no hand in it that day. Suffice it to say that the stubbornness of Thomas made it possible for us to reach Rossville that night—to reorganize, and finally to march in good condition to Chattanooga. So far as Davis' Division was concerned, the crushing of our Right, as faintly outlined above, ended our connection with the Battle of Chickamauga.

Reaching Rossville in detachments, squads and singly, we were assigned a position in a new line, which we at once set about strengthening. What front we might be able to present was very uncertain. Indeed, so few were present that but little preparation was even attempted until the next morning, the 21st, by which time quite a large number of stragglers had put in an appearance. At dusk Sunday evening less than seventy-five of the 101st men were present.

Many had been wounded, many captured; a large number had become entangled with other commands, and were not able, at once, to find our position. Some who passed through McFarland's Gap bore too far to the west, and, for a time, lost their way. With daylight next morning many returned to the Regiment.

Our losses in the terrible conflict through which we had come, were heavy. The several contests on the Vineyard farm told on us terribly, and again on Sunday, when we were almost surrounded in the woods, we lost heavily, especially in captured and wounded. In all these struggles the boys showed true and lasting courage and did their full duty to the last moment.

The state of affairs at Rossville that Sunday evening was by no means re-assuring. With wonderful rapidity affairs assumed a presentable shape, and we were ready early on Monday morning to do some service. Our lines, however, were very thin. By noon Monday all were in their places that would be there for some time. The Union soldiers captured at Chickamauga had hard lots in rebel prisons. They were subjected to the most inhuman treatment from beginning to end. One's blood boils to think of it, even after the lapse of thirty years.

During Sunday night and early Monday morning, General Thomas withdrew his army from the second battlefield of Chickamauga and took position at Rossville. There were a number of false alarms during Monday, each of which showed that we were still somewhat nervous. About 9 o'clock in the morning the enemy appeared in force in Thomas' front, on the Ringold Road, but they made no serious attack. Their cavalry, and several detachments of infantry, showed themselves in Chattanooga Valley in our own front, but they were satisfied to look at us at long range, and we were entirely satisfied to have them do so.

Our commanders had no thought of holding Rossville for a longer time than was necessary to arrange matters at Chattanooga. This was all accomplished on Monday, the 21st, and at 9 o'clock that evening the army began its march to that city. To cover this movement, General Brannan's Division was posted, early in the evening, about half-way between Rossville and Chattanooga. General Baird was to remain at Rossville until the other troops had all been moved. Very strong picket lines had been established, and these, with the cavalry, were to remain until morning. It came our time to fall in and take up the march soon after 10 o'clock. Our fires were left burning, and every indication possible was left to convince the enemy that we were still there. Soon after daylight we reached the suburbs of Chattanooga, and when we learned that we were not to cross the Tennessee, a wild shout went up and we took cheerfully to the work of building breastworks and fortifications. This was commenced immediately—we had scarcely time to prepare breakfast. The morning was delightfully pleasant, a light haze hung like a crown over Lookout, and every thing, notwithstanding our recent disasters, put on a cheerful and encouraging aspect. This cheerful and good-natured outside did not prevent terrible havoc before night, among the houses and barns, in our vicinity, whether constructed of wood, stone, or brick. Everything available was used in the construction of our earthworks. Not only so, but every building in our front that stood in the way of a clear field, was devoted to the torch, unless it could be used as stated above. Toward sundown great columns of black smoke floated lazily heavenward, and hung like a menacing cloud, an unmistakable evidence of ruin and devastation. The sight of their burning houses must have been gall and wormwood to the Confederates, who were already going into position on Mission Ridge and Lookout Mountain.

Willing hands and strong arms had accomplished much during the day. Though as yet incomplete, our line of earthworks was strong and durable, and we felt ready for the foe whenever an assault might be attempted.

But Bragg was in no hurry to attack. Though he had driven Rosecrans from the field of Chickamauga, the Union army still held the grand prize—the possession of Chattanooga, the key to East Tennessee and North Georgia.

Sad, sad were our hearts when we remembered that many of our boys were left dead and dying on the battlefield; that many others were in the hands of the enemy, destined to the horrors of the infamous rebel prison, and that many others were torn and mangled, maimed, perchance, for life.

The following list includes the names of those who were killed or mortally wounded:—

Comrade Captain William H. Kilmer, Commanding Company F.

Comrade Lieutenant Charles McGraw, Commanding Company E.

Comrade Lieutenant Isaac P. Rule, Commanding Company I. Died September 20, of wounds received September 19.

Comrade Abram Inman, Company A. Died a prisoner, on field of battle, of wounds received Sept. 20.

Comrade George Lameraux, Company A. Killed in battle, Sept. 19.

Comrade William L. McPherson, Company A. Died October 13, of wounds received September 19.

Comrade Samuel Wilson, Company A. Died in the hands of the enemy, of wounds received September 19, at Chicamauga.

Comrade Milton C. Dodge, Company B. Killed in battle, Sept. 20.

Comrade Michael Dise, Company C. Killed in battle, September 19.

Comrade Peter Eicher, Company C. Killed in battle, September 19.

Comrade Joseph Hund, Company C. Killed in battle, September 19.

Comrade Felix Kimmick, Company C. Died September 23, of wounds received September 19.

Comrade Henry W. Miller, Company C. Mortally wounded, Sept. 19. Died in hands of the enemy.

OUR KILLED AND MORTALLY WOUNDED.

Comrade Tilley E. Quaintance, Company C. Killed in battle, September 19.
Comrade John D. Blair, Company D. Killed in battle, September 19.
Comrade Flavel B. Jones, Company D. Killed in battle, Sept. 20.
Comrade David Hilficker, Company E. Killed in battle, Sept. 20.
Comrade Sovereign Brown, Company F. Killed in battle, Sept. 19.
Comrade Christian H. Gleser, Company F. Killed in battle, September 19.
Comrade George Lawrence, Company F. Killed in battle, Sept. 19.
Comrade Isaac C. Cassen, Company G. Killed in battle, Sept. 20.
Comrade James M. Garmon, Company G. Killed in battle, Sept. 19.
Comrade Frederick Dibble, Company H. Died in Andersonville prison, November 9, 1864, of wounds received at Chickamauga.
Comrade Joseph Keller, Company H. Died in Camp Dennison, of wounds received in Battle of Chickamauga.
Comrade Aden W. Miller, Company I. Killed in battle, Sept. 19.
Comrade William Moore, Company I. Killed in battle, Sept. 20.
Comrade Daniel Wagaman, Company I. Killed in battle, Sept. 20.
Comrade William F. Bacher, Company K. Killed in battle, Sept. 19.
Comrade Louis Columbus, Company K. Killed in battle, Sept. 19.
Comrade Luke A. Long, Company K. Died September 22, of wounds received September 19.
Comrade Jeremiah Nichols, Company K. Died December 25, 1863, at Chattanooga, of wounds received in Battle of Chickamauga.

The merits of our fallen comrades were freely discussed, and many a letter sent to the mourning ones at home.

The Regiment was under the command of Lieutenant Colonel John Messer* until he was wounded about 4 o'clock on the afternoon of the 19th. His wounds were serious, compelling him to go to the rear. The command then fell upon Major Bedan B. McDonald until he was captured, while gallantly leading the Regiment. Adjutant Len D. Smith being next in rank, assumed command during the remain-

---
*Colonel Kirby was absent on leave, but hurried forward on hearing that the army had moved. He rejoined the Regiment at Rossville, September 21.

der of the battle and the retreat to Rossville and Chattanooga.

The Old Flag seemed to be the center upon which the rebels converged their fire. At one time, not only the color-bearer, but every color-guard, was dead or wounded. Seeing the colors in the hands of a badly-wounded man, Colonel Messer seized them, but was remonstrated with by Lieutenant Bryant and others. In that moment's hurried conversation, Messer was twice wounded—once in the arm and once in the side. Comrade Abel Knapp, of Company A, bravely took the colors and valiantly carried them through the remainder of the battle. On Sunday morning, Comrade Christian M. Funk was detailed as color-guard.

In shutting himself up in Chattanooga, as General Rosecrans had done, he surrendered not only Missionary Ridge, but Lookout Mountain also, the latter carrying with it the control of the railroad and wagon roads back to Bridgeport and Stevenson. The only wagon routes between Chattanooga and Stevenson ran close along the bank of the river on the north side, but as the Confederates held the south bank, these roads were not at our command. The result was that all our supplies of every kind had to be hauled by a very circuitous route extending from Stevenson across and up Sequatchie valley, over Waldron's Ridge and down the valley on the east side of this Ridge—a distance of over seventy miles. The route was bad at the best, and when the Fall rains set in they soon became almost impassable. We were almost out of rations when we reached Chattanooga, for, during the battle, it was not possible for our supplies to reach us. It was as much as ever that our ammunition train could be kept within reach. We were soon put on half rations, and the ration itself reduced in variety. Later even this was reduced. In some instances actual suffering followed. Corn intended for the animals

JOHN DOUGHERTY,
COMPANY I.
From photograph taken in 1892.

of the command was stolen in more instances than one, and greedily devoured by the boys. The arrival of the "Cracker Train" from Stevenson was always hailed with delight, but had to be guarded. The roughness and muddiness of the road soon made it impossible for the trains to deliver even a half load at a time. The route over the mountains, and even in the valleys, soon became lined with dead animals, and many a train had to be abandoned on account of insufficient means to move it. As the cracker boxes were unloaded more or less crumbs would sift out and fall into the mud. These the hungry boys would pick up greedily, even with strife sometimes, and washing them in the river, would devour them with great relish. Rebel cavalry made several dashes upon our trains and succeeded in doing much damage. Attempts were made upon our railroad communications beyond Stevenson, but no great success attended these raids. Our communication with the north or right bank of the river at Chattanooga was effected by means of a pontoon bridge. This bridge the Confederates tried hard to destroy by sending down stream, from various points above the city, huge rafts of logs. In one way and another this calamity was averted. Our Field Hospital was located across the river, and was under the efficient care of our Surgeon, Dr. Thomas M. Cook, and his corps of assistants. It should be remembered that the Confederates held the entire space in our front, extending from the river at the base of Lookout on our right around by way of Missionary Ridge to the river on our left, not far from the mouth of the Chickamauga. All this, with the river and mountains back of us, put us practically in a state of siege. We were hemmed in completely, and were rapidly approaching the starving point.

Immediately upon the retirement of our army to Chattanooga, the authorities at Washington began to bestir themselves to provide the necessary assistance to preserve and extricate Rosecrans from his perilous position. Rosecrans had called long and loud for assistance and reinforcements before leaving Winchester, but they were not forthcoming. Instead of sending a portion of Grant's army, all of which had been relieved of active duty by the annihilation of Pemberton's army and the dispersing of Johnson's, it had been scattered by sending a corps here and another there, but not a man to Rosecrans. Of all the useless military men on this earth, Halleck was the chief. When too late he sent two dispatches to Grant to send forward certain forces. But these dispatches did not reach Grant until after the Battle of Chickamauga. The instant they were received they were acted upon, and the forces reached Chattanooga in time for the Battle of Missionary Ridge, before which time Grant had succeeded to the chief command.

Troops were also hurried from the east by way of Cincinnati to Bridgeport, for the relief of the beleaguered army, but all this was after the disaster, if it were a disaster, at Chickamauga. These reinforcements from the east were under the command of "Fighting Joe Hooker," and did excellent work in breaking the Confederate line on our extreme Right and thus opening up the cracker line. Arrangements for this movement were in preparation when General Rosecrans was relieved of his command. The Army of the Cumberland under Thomas, the Army of the Ohio under Burnside at Knoxville, and the Army of the Tennessee, Grant's old army at Vicksburg, were consolidated, and the latter General placed in supreme command. The change was made on the 19th of October,

In the meantime many minor changes had taken place. The army had been reorganized. The four Corps— Granger's, McCook's, Crittenden's and Thomas'—had been reduced to two, the Fourteenth and Fourth. Generals Mc-

Cook, Crittenden and Negley had been relieved and were awaiting investigation of their actions at Chickamauga; Van Cleve had been assigned to the command of Murfreesboro'; Johnson and Steedman had been assigned to other commands; General Brannan had been placed in command of the artillery, and General Reynolds went upon General Thomas' Staff as Chief. Very many other minor changes were made. General Carlin was promoted and given the command of the First Division of the Fourteenth Corps, but took with him none of his old regiments. General Davis was placed in command of the Second Division of the same corps, but had none of his former Brigades.

The 101st was assigned to General Craft's Brigade of Palmer's Division of the Fourteenth Corps. Our Brigade consisted of the 101st Ohio, 21st Illinois, 38th Illinois, 81st Indiana, 29th Indiana, 31st Indiana, 1st Kentucky, 2nd Kentucky, and 90th Ohio. This was the organization as announced October 20, '63.

Picket firing, important skirmishes and artillery duels were sufficiently frequent to keep us alive and watchful. We were frequently aroused at night by a rattling fire on the picket line.

The difficulty was, that we were liable to an assault at any time, and no one could tell what was coming when these "feelers" were thrown out, especially when they came just before daylight. There was much artillery firing on both sides. If our fire did no more harm than theirs, but few were badly hurt. Out of 230 shots fired by the Confederates one afternoon, from the point of Lookout, into our camp, or as near to it as they could strike, only two casualties occurred—one man wounded in the foot and the fifth wheel was knocked off one of the battery carriages, and yet some of their shells and solid shot fell well down toward the city. Very many of their shells exploded before reaching

WM. P. MYERS,
COMPANY H.
From photograph taken in 1894.

our lines. Our batteries returned the fire, doubtless with equal effect. One morning, just after daylight, their batteries facing our left, set up a great noise and sent much iron our way, but most of it fell short. Our batteries, as usual, responded leisurely. Nothing came of the affair. On one occasion there had been great activity along the rebel front, and it looked very much as though an assault was to be made at once. Their long lines were clearly visible. Preparations were at once made to receive them. Shells were planted so close to their lines that the puff of smoke accompanying the explosion often revealed the heels of a number of fleeing Johnnies. For some reason they never made an earnest assault.

One noisy afternoon, when everybody was under arms, and when we really expected an assault, General Carlin was sitting on his horse just in front of our line, when a solid shot, or a shell that failed to explode, came from Lookout, bounding along the ground, striking just under the horse and covering everything with dirt and dust. The shell found the General the very picture of soldierly manliness; it left him hatless, speechless, blind, and sputtering. His horse was wild, but the General managed him. When we saw that he was not injured, we sent up a shout that was, as usual, carried along most of our line. It was an amusing affair.

The scenes in our hospitals were too terrible to bear description—they were Perryville repeated and exaggerated. There, the poor fellows received attention at once. Here, they lay on the ground for some time, many of them, before they could be cared for, and then, if able, they were conveyed in wagons and ambulances to Chattanooga, a distance of ten or twelve miles. Bones broken and partially knitted, had to be re-set; wounds that had never been even washed, had to be torn open afresh; limbs that might have been saved if taken in time, had to be amputated ; strong bodies had been rendered weak by the loss of unstaunched blood. I remember one poor fellow who called, in his delirium, for his wife and children, appealing to them by name and crying with pain in his feet. Poor fellow! both legs had been amputated at the thigh two days before. His cries gradually became weaker, his pains less acute—he died before morning. I cannot allow myself to think of these sights and scenes, even now, almost a third of a century later.

General Grant arrived at Chattanooga on the evening of the 23d of October. Within a few hours after his arrival, the plans originated by General Rosecrans and his Chief of Engineers, General W. F. Smith, for re-victualing the army, had been examined and approved. They were ordered into instant execution. General Hooker, who, with his entire command, was at Bridgeport and immediate vicinity, was ordered to cross the river and advance in the direction of Chattanooga, by way of Shellmound, Whitesides, and Wauhatchie. At the same time a strong force was to be sent from Chattanooga toward Bridgeport, by way of Brown's Ferry. The two forces were to meet in Will's Valley, near the northern end of Lookout. It was not believed that this could be accomplished without a severe struggle. Hooker was fully advised of the character and importance of the move, and directed to act with the utmost precision and promptness. With the advance of Hooker it became necessary to assign other troops for the protection of his rear. A portion of this work was assigned to General Palmer. Our Brigade and one other were to guard the Tennessee from Bridgeport to Shellmound. On the very day that Hooker crossed the Tennessee to carry out his part in this great movement, our Brigade crossed the river at Chattanooga on the pontoon bridge, and marching rapidly over mountains and through valleys, reached Rankin's Ferry, near Shellmound, at the moment Hooker was ready to fall upon the enemy at Wauhatchie. On crossing the river, we relieved his men who had been stationed there as guard. We took up our position and for a time did guard duty—the first experience of the kind we had ever had. For awhile there was exciting work. General Hooker punished the Confederates who attempted to impede his march toward Brown's Ferry, inflicting a severe defeat at Wauhatchie, on the night of October 30th.

This movement forced the Confederates out of Will's Valley and established railroad and wagon communication with Bridgeport and thence northerly to the civilized world. On Monday, the 2d of November, Colonel Kirby was directed to take four regiments and march at once to Bridgeport for the purpose of guarding the railroad bridge over the Tennessee at that point. The four regiments selected were the 101st Ohio, 31st Indiana, 29th Indiana, and 21st Illinois. These regiments remained here doing guard and picket duty most of the time until the 26th of January, 1864. On that date we again went to the front, moving by way of Shellmound Point of Lookout, Chattanooga, and across Missionary Ridge to Tyner's Station, where we remained, doing picket and scout duty, until February 9th, when we moved to Ooltewah. We remained here without special incident until the opening of the Atlanta campaign, May 3d, 1864.

REORGANIZATION—The reorganization of the Army of the Cumberland for the Atlanta Campaign, was announced in April, 1864, as follows:—

GENERAL GEORGE H. THOMAS, Commanding.
FOURTH CORPS.
GENERAL O. O. HOWARD, Commanding.

ORGANIZATION.

FIRST DIVISION.
GENERAL D. S. STANLEY, Commanding.

FIRST BRIGADE.
GENERAL CHARLES CRUFT, Commanding until June 3, 1864.
COLONEL I. M. KIRBY, Commanding after June 3, 1864.

101st Ohio.	21st Illinois.
90th Ohio.	38th Illinois.
31st Indiana.	1st Kentucky.
81st Indiana.	2nd Kentucky.

SECOND BRIGADE.
GENERAL W. C. WHITAKER.

THIRD BRIGADE.
COLONEL WILLIAM GROSE.

ARTILLERY—5th Indiana, and Battery B, Independent Pennsylvania.

SECOND DIVISION.
GENERAL JOHN NEWTON.

FIRST BRIGADE.
COLONEL F. T. SHERMAN.

SECOND BRIGADE.
GENERAL G. D. WAGNER.

THIRD BRIGADE.
COLONEL C. G. HARKER.

ARTILLERY—Battery G, 1st Missouri; and Battery M, 1st Illinois.

THIRD DIVISION.
GENERAL T. J. WOOD.

FIRST BRIGADE.
GENERAL A. WILLICH.

SECOND BRIGADE.
GENERAL W. B. HAZEN.

THIRD BRIGADE.
GENERAL SAMUEL BEATTY.

ARTILLERY—6th Ohio, and Bridge's Illinois Light Battery.

THE FOURTEENTH CORPS.
General John M. Palmer, Commanding.

THE TWENTIETH CORPS.
General Joseph Hooker, Commanding.

CAVALRY.
General W. L. Elliott, Commanding.

CHAPTER XIV.

THE ATLANTA CAMPAIGN—TUNNEL HILL.

When General Grant was called to the supreme command of our armies, he requested that Gen. W. T. Sherman might be assigned as his successor to the command of the Department of the Mississippi. This request was promptly granted, General McPherson succeeding General Sherman as commander of the Army of the Tennessee.

General Sherman soon found himself at the head of an army of nearly 100,000 men, well disciplined and ready for the field. His command consisted of three separate armies:

The Army of the Cumberland, General Thomas, 60,500; the Army of the Ohio, General Schofield, 13,500; the Army of the Tennessee, General McPherson, 24,500; a grand total of 98,500 men.

Opposed to him was a brave, well officered Confederate army of 70,000 men, under the command of Lieut. Gen. J. E. Johnson. The leading or corps commanders of the rebel army were Polk, Hardee and Hood, all of whom we had met in battle before. Bragg had been relieved of his command in the field and was acting as "President" Davis' chief military adviser.

MAJOR-GENERAL D. S. STANLEY,
COMMANDING FOURTH CORPS.
From steel engraving.

Generals Grant and Sherman had arranged to act in concert in the coming campaigns. Each was to press the enemy so hard that he would not be able to reinforce one army from the other, as had been done at Chickamauga. The two campaigns—one from the Rapidan against Richmond, the other from the Tennessee against Atlanta, were to begin at the same time, and were to be conducted without let-up.

The country between Chattanooga and Atlanta is naturally divided into three sections: the first mountainous, the second more open, and the third hilly and broken. The first section extends as far south as Dalton. It is broken by mountains, valleys, gorges, gaps and ravines, many of which are passable only at certain points. This section is traversed by few roads, all of which are narrow, ill-made, winding, and in many places almost impassable. The streams are small, rapid, and generally at the bottom of deep gullies. The country is wooded, with clearings and cultivated patches here and there, with now and then a village consisting principally of a combined smith and wagon-shop, a corner grocery, or "roost" for the loafers, and a grindstone. The railroad from Chattanooga to Atlanta manages to get through this belt in some way. The whole section is an emphatic protest against military operations on any large scale. Sherman was obliged to conquer not only the rebels, but the mountains also, as he advanced. South of Dalton the country is more level and open for about thirty miles, when the mountains are again encountered. The rivers of these several sections offered serious impediments to our advance.

At the beginning of the campaign, the Army of the Tennessee was at Gordon's Mills, the Army of the Ohio at Cleveland, and the Army of the Cumberland at Chattanooga. Our own Regiment was at Ooltewah, half way between Chattanooga and Cleveland. The rebel army was in force at Dalton, ready to dispute our passage southward. Strong detachments of the enemy were posted at various points, all the roads and passes were carefully guarded, and their cavalry and scouts were on the watch near our lines. They had not yet fully recovered from the surprises of Lookout Mountain and Missionary Ridge. They seemed to have a profound respect for Yankee push and pluck. They therefore watched, ready to spring upon us if we should give them the opportunity, or to fall back if we became too much in earnest. We were generally in earnest, and they were generally falling back.

On the afternoon of May 2nd we received our marching orders for the next day. Rations were prepared, cartridge boxes were refilled, and everything put in ship-shape for permanent advance. The campaign would be conducted for the most part in the mountains. Long wagon trains were therefore impossible. Only one wagon was allowed for each regiment, and one pack mule for each company. Every care was taken, however, to have always at hand an abundance of ammunition. The railroad was to be kept in repair up to our front as we advanced so that our wounded might be sent back to Ringold and Chattanooga, and necessary supplies promptly forwarded. It was the balmy month of May and the men marched "light."

At 1 o'clock in the afternoon, May 3rd, we moved out of our camp at Ooltewah and took up our line of march southward, encamping without special incident shortly before night, six miles toward Catoosa Springs. At 5 o'clock next morning we were under way, passing through Catoosa Springs between 10 o'clock and 11 o'clock. Halting and resting here a short time, we went into camp on a ridge nearly a mile south of the Springs. Being in the advance, we struck the enemy, who was in small force, shortly before we went into camp. Our picket lines caused them to retire and be quiet. We remained in camp until the morning of the 7th.

The advance of our Brigade was a part of the forward movement and concentration of our entire army. McPherson was at Gordon's Mills, Schofield at Red Clay, and Thomas near Ringold. Sherman's army presented a front of sixteen miles. May 5th and 6th were spent in completing the concentration of our forces and in many other necessary preliminaries. Everything except fighting men and supplies was sent to the rear. Our army was stripped to the waist; the enemy was in sight; it was time to strike the first blow.

Well aware of Johnson's strong position, and knowing the character of the country in his front, Sherman sought at the very outset of the campaign to weaken the enemy by the boldest kind of a flank movement. While Thomas threatened Johnson's center, and Schofield demonstrated against his right, McPherson struck across the country by way of Dogwood Valley and Snake Creek Gap to the vicinity of Resaca, some miles south of Dalton. But he could not reach this position before the 9th. It was therefore necessary to operate along our front with some vigor, in order to hold the enemy's attention until McPherson could reach his destination.

We were in line very early in the morning of May 7th, and soon after daylight began to advance, our Brigade leading. We soon met the enemy's pickets, and shortly after encountered their skirmish line. The 101st and two companies of the 81st Indiana, were deployed as skirmishers. Advancing, we forced the rebels steadily back until they reached their main line, but not without some severe fighting. The Confederates did not wait for close work, consequently our casualties were not numerous. There seemed to be method in this rebel retreat, for no sooner had we reached the immediate vicinity of Tunnel Hill than it was discovered by our commanding officer, who had ridden forward to an eminence, that a rebel Brigade, was already moving to charge our skirmish line. The situation was exceedingly serious. Seeing the danger, but deciding to hold the position, Colonel Kirby, who commanded the Regiment, looked back for supports, but none were in sight—a gross neglect on the part of the Brigade commander. The next best thing was instantly done—orders were issued to "rally by companies", preparatory to fighting our way to an assembly of the whole. The rebel cavalry were coming over the railroad on a trot, when our old commander, Jeff C. Davis, with his characteristic watchfulness and promptness, appeared on a high range of hills to our right, and quickly placed a battery in position. Opening briskly, he soon broke up the enemy's column and relieved us from our unpleasant situation. Advancing to the foot of Tunnel Hill, General Davis and his staff, galloping forward to meet us, ran into a nest of rebels in the underbrush, and were fired upon, one of his orderlies being killed. Company C, of our Regiment, dashed forward to the relief of the General, and quickly routed the enemy. Davis was profuse with his thanks to his "innocents," as he pleasantly called us since the affair at Knob Gap, in December, 1862.

While we thus held our Brigade front, two of Whitaker's regiments gained the enemy's flank, when, together, we rolled the butternuts down the hill, into the ravines and valleys beyond the crest. In the meantime, Sherman's Grand Army had moved forward—the lines of blue faced those of gray—the giants were about to engage in a conflict which would not end for a hundred days. It was the opening of the Atlanta Campaign.

CHAPTER XV.

ROCKY FACE.

Rocky Face is a long, irregular ridge, extending nearly north and south. Its sides are rough, rocky, and steep—almost impossible of ascent, its top narrow and in places jagged and rocky. To the north of it is Tunnel Hill, from which it is separated by a narrow, wooded ravine; and to the west of it, that is, in front, is Mill Creek Valley, and a gorge leading westward, while to the south is the famous Buzzard Roost Gap. Nature, in one of her spasms in the remote past, seemed to have fixed up this desolate region for Johnson's especial benefit. Had McPherson failed to get through Snake Creek Gap, many more of our boys must have died here in the attempt to dislodge the enemy.

The Confederates were in force along the ridge and at Buzzard Roost, including several knolls in front of the latter. A strong picket line guarded the base of Rocky Face —there seemed no weak point anywhere. We of the rank and file were not reliably posted as to all these details, and yet we managed in some way, how I do not know, to have a pretty fair knowledge of our surroundings. We knew that McPherson was off on a flanking expedition, but we did not know how he was to get out of the mountain tangle, nor where he was to strike. We knew where Schofield was, and readily comprehended his duties. But when our whole army, saving our own Corps, began the movement to the right, we were stumped. We planned many a campaign in which, it must be confessed, we had little regard for roads, rivers, ravines, or ridges. In this campaign we were always greatly interested in all the side movements of our command, and various were the guesses and predictions made by the boys as to destination, and what would occur on arrival.

The next morning after the affair at Tunnel Hill, Sunday the 8th, was cloudless but very smoky. There seemed to have settled a thick haze over all the wild region around us. Generals Howard, Stanley, and Cruft were on Tunnel Hill near us, awaiting the lifting of the fog. The results of the previous day's work had been such as to make prompt and vigorous action necessary. The enemy was very strongly posted, and might on learning of McPherson's movement, detach a sufficient force to crush him. Thomas must therefore strike quickly and as hard as possible, so as to hold Johnson at Dalton. McPherson was to fall suddenly upon the enemy's rear, destroy his communications, and do all the damage possible. Schofield was to hammer them on the east. Notwithstanding all this, Johnson sent three Divisions to look after McPherson, which made it necessary for the Union General to take up a strong defensive position at the mouth of Snake Creek Gap. Two of Johnson's Divisions were then returned to the front. Sherman was disappointed at McPherson's failure, but at once made arrangements to transfer his whole army to the vicinity of Resaca, excepting only our Corps (Howard's) and Stoneman's cavalry. This great movement was successfully executed, and for a time the Fourth Corps alone confronted the enemy north of Dalton. All this required several days. Pending these movements the fight in front of Rocky Face continued. About 9 o'clock on the morning of the 8th, the fog having cleared away, we advanced, passing down the southern slope of Tunnel Hill, into the valley and in front of Rocky Face. Schofield advanced at the same time nearly two miles, when he struck a line of works which prevented further progress. A little later in the day our Division was advanced nearer the Ridge, and at once became sharply engaged with the enemy's skirmish line. The sides of Rocky Face were so steep that as yet the enemy had not succeeded in dragging up any artillery, but from the knolls near Buzzard Roost they kept up an ugly fire. Soon after noon our former commander, Jeff C. Davis, led a force against these knolls, and, assisted by our Division artillery, routed the rebel force stationed there and took possession—finding it necessary to entrench himself at once. This movement developed the position and, apparently, the force of the enemy at the Gap. Remaining within three hundred or four hundred yards of their works at the base of the Ridge, and skirmishing with them all day, we, at dusk, were relieved, and soon after went into camp for the night on Tunnel Hill.

We advanced very early next morning, and soon encountered the enemy's pickets, and an hour later were ordered forward. Under cover of brushwood and trees we forced our way up to the base of the mountain and held it all day. Our nearness to the Ridge was really a protection. Late in the afternoon an unsuccessful assault was made on Buzzard Roost Gap. The assault was gallantly made, but the fire of the enemy, both from the gorge and from the ridge, almost directly overhead, was too much. The Union loss was about sixty, confined to the 96th Illinois and the 84th Indiana.

On the 10th the enemy succeeded in dragging several mountain howitzers to the summit of the ridge, with which they proceeded to shell our lines. Aside from this and vigorous work along the picket line nothing especial occurred. Our own Division was transferred to the Right, relieving General Davis, and taking a position at the danger point. The line along the base of the ridge was simply to be held. Our new position was not only to be held, but, with it as a base, demonstrations against the enemy in Buzzard Roost Gap were to be made. The change meant dangerous work, and much of it. By this time, evening of the 10th, McPherson had reached his destination, and was threatening

LIEUTENANT COLONEL B. B. McDONALD.
From photograph.

Johnson's rear. The Rebel Commander at once detached three Divisions to look after him, as previously stated.

On the 11th it was rumored that the enemy was retreating, and an assault upon Buzzard Roost was ordered to determine the matter. This was a costly affair for our Regiment. A similar assault had been attempted on the 9th with disastrous results.

It was late in the afternoon. The Brigade was moved by the flank along the base of Rocky Face, toward the mouth of the Gap or Gorge, marching rapidly under a sharp fire. As soon as the head of the column reached the front of the Gap an assault was ordered, and the 101st, under Colonel Kirby, was placed in the lead. Without so much as halting to form, the grand old Regiment was deployed forward on double-quick as skirmishers, and pressed right on. Lieutenant Colonel McDonald was sent to the extreme left of the line, with instructions to move as close to the foot of the ridge as possible on that side. The line would continually "guide left." Scarcely had we entered the mouth of the gorge when we met a murderous fire of cannon and musketry from front and both flanks delivered most viciously. Pressing forward, detached forces of the enemy occupying prominent points were speedily driven back. The resistance soon became so strong and determined that we could advance but a few yards at a time, securing some prominent projection or point of rocks and holding on until we could get breath and see another opportunity for a rush. Thus the line was forced forward, till at length we found ourselves immediately in front of the enemy's main line of works stretching across the further opening of the Gap, only a few rods distant, and alive with men. The ground in our rear was so completely swept by continually bursting case shot and canister that it seemed utter destruction to attempt a retrograde movement. It must have been our very impudence that saved us from annihilation. We could advance no further, nor could we retreat. We could only hug the rocks and work our muskets with all the vim that was in us. The situation just at the coming of night, in that dark gorge, with the ground seemingly on fire from bursting artillery missiles all about us, was wierd and awe-inspiring in the extreme.

We had neither seen nor heard anything from the rest of the Brigade, nor from our Brigade Commander, since we first entered the gorge. Adjutant Neff was sent back, going on his hands and knees until he passed the line of fire, and soon after, fearing that Neff could not get through alive, Sergeant-Major Jay Smith was also, in like manner, sent back, to communicate with our Brigade Commander and learn what orders he had for us. Both Neff and Smith succeeded in getting through and returning to us, bringing word that our Commander deemed it useless to attempt to succor us—the sacrifice would evidently be too great—and that we should rely on ourselves to get out as best we could. We, therefore, held on, doubling our diligence and keeping the enemy from any attempt to capture us, until about 9 o'clock at night. When it became so dark that our movements could not be seen, word was passed along the line that we would attempt to withdraw by the center, man by man following his next comrade from right and left as rapidly as possible. All were thus safely withdrawn, nor did any ever desire more experience of that kind.

The Regiment received unstinted praise from General Stanley for our magnificent work on this occasion, and to the end of the war he always manifested a very high regard for us.

At the commencement of the movement no special instructions were given Colonel Kirby as to the object to be accomplished. Consequently he was left with the impression that he was to open the way for a determined effort on the part of the Division and Corps to break through the gap. The officers and many of the men believed that we were going as a sacrifice to accomplish this purpose. But not a man showed the least trepidation nor lost perfect self-control.

Had it been known that this same Buzzard Roost Gap was guarded that very moment by thousands of Confederate soldiers, all under arms, it is not at all likely that our little Regiment would have been flung into it. The very insolence of our advance doubtless convinced the Confederates that they might next day expect an attack somewhere in force. Our losses in this assault were quite severe.

KILLED.

Lieutenant Alex. C. Hosmer, Commanding Company A, was mortally wounded, and died next day on the way to the hospital at Ringold. He had been given every possible attention at the field hospital, under care of Dr. T. M. Cook, our Regimental Surgeon, now in charge of the Brigade Hospital. Brave almost to recklessness, Lieutenant Hosmer fell at his post.

Comrade Frederick Jefferson, Company A.
Comrade Theophilus Gould, Company F.
Comrade Joseph M. Anderson, Company F.

WOUNDED.

Comrade Wm. Meacham, Company B.
Comrade Emanuel Kies, Company C.
Comrade Henry Rupersberger, Company C.
Comrade George H. Sauer, Company D.
Comrade John Otzensperger, Company E.
Comrade James H. Corning, Company F.
Comrade Shipley H. Link, Company F.
Comrade George Somers, Company I.
Comrade Isaiah Solomon, Company K.
Comrade David Good, Company F.
Comrade John S. Miller, of Company B, was accidentally wounded at the same time.

Many others were less severely wounded, of which no record was made at the time. Our losses would have been very much greater had it not been for a slight depression in the ground, of which we took instant advantage, just as the Confederate batteries, double shotted with grape and canister, opened on us. The discharge went a few feet above our heads and did comparatively little harm. Had it come a few minutes earlier it would have played havoc with our men.

Falling back under cover of darkness, as stated above, we took up a strong position and held the entrance to the gorge ready to resist any sortie the enemy might attempt. Considerable firing was kept up along the skirmish line all night, but nothing serious occurred.

From the summit of Buzzard Roost, General Johnston must have observed the general movement of our army toward his left. That he did discover this and rightly divine Sherman's intentions, is clearly shown by the fact that when Sherman debouched into the open country from Snake Creek Gap, he found the Confederate army very strongly entrenched at Resaca waiting for him.

CHAPTER XVI.

BATTLE OF RESACA.

During the night of the 12th, the Confederates withdrew, falling back to Resaca. The pursuit was instantly taken up. Our Division marched at 7 o'clock on the morn- of the 13th, passing through Dalton at 9 o'clock, and encamping at night about nine miles north of Resaca. Our camp was in the woods on a by-road leading to Sugar Creek, and we were by no means sure of the position or strength of the enemy near us. Soon after leaving camp in the morning, we came upon the Confederate rear guard, with which we skirmished all day. They made especial resistance at and near Dalton. A few miles further south, their cavalry became so stubborn that it was necessary to bring artillery to bear on them in order to cause them to move on. Later in the afternoon both cavalry and infantry turned upon us, and the fight became quite spirited. But they were steadily pushed back. Our losses were slight,

We resumed our march next morning at 6 o'clock, and soon fell upon the enemy. Toward noon the action became quite brisk, and for a time it looked as though most of our Corps would be engaged. The Confederates, however, gave way and we pursued them vigorously for some distance. They fell back to their main lines at Resaca, and our Corps halted at about 4 o'clock within a mile of the Confederate main works. General Sherman's army was in line facing the enemy in the following order: On the extreme right, resting on the Oostanaula was the Army of the Tennessee, General McPherson; on his left, the Army of the Cumberland (excepting our Corps), and on the left of this, the Army of the Ohio. Our Corps had halted on the left and in rear of Schofield. As soon as it was learned that General Howard was within supporting distance, Schofield was ordered to make an assault. Indeed, Sherman's entire line stood to arms and was soon engaged. Howard was ordered forward with instructions to join Schofield's left. This we did with great promptness, Kirby's Brigade being at this hour, 4:30 P. M., on the extreme left of Sherman's army. The 101st was ordered forward as skirmishers, as indeed it had been both that day and the day before, every time we came in contact with the enemy. At least half a dozen times on the march the column had been halted, and the 101st passed to the front, until it became a

CAPTAIN JAMES I. NEFF,
COMPANY H.
From photograph.

common saying among the boys of the other regiments: "The rebs are in front; there goes the 101st forward." The skirmishing here was pressed with such vigor over the rough, wooded sides of the broken ridge that it assumed almost the proportions of battle. The enemy was steadily driven back toward their main line. But the Confederates soon perceived that their right greatly overlapped our left, and at once took advantage of this fact, sending against us an overwhelming force.

A full Division, marching in the valley below, passed to our left, then wheeled and assaulted our flank, which was badly in the air. So imminent was the danger at this point, and to our Brigade especially, that to avoid capture, our batteries, under Captain Simonson, were withdrawn and so placed as to rake our present position after we should be driven back. There was practically no support on our immediate left, Sherman's lines in this part of the field not having yet been fully established. Our Brigade held on as long as it was possible to do so, but our assailants were two to our one and we were compelled to give way. Realizing the importance of this part of the line, Sherman at once sent reinforcements. In the meantime our batteries, aided by our own best efforts, had stayed the enemy.

Captain Simonson, 5th Indiana Battery, posted in an open field back of an old peach orchard, supported by the 101st, which had fallen back to that position, repulsed the rebel advance spoken of as moving against and around our left flank. The charging column came almost to the muzzles of Simonson's guns. In the heroic service of those guns the Captain, with bared red head gleaming in the light of his blazing cannon (it was just dusk), constantly reiterated the command: "Load them steel guns to the muzzle." As fast as his men were lost, details were made from the 101st to take their places. So pleased was he with the service of these men that he persistently asked that they might be permanently transferred to him. Of course Colonel Kirby would not part with such men. But so proud was the Captain of a gay boy of Company D that he begged permission to borrow him a few days to ride on one of the artillery carriages. General Hooker came upon this part of the field with one of his Divisions, just at the close of this artillery fighting, and riding up to Captain Simonson and laying his hand on the brave man's shoulder, with glowing countenance, asked what battery it was and whether the Army of the Cumberland had any more like it. The Captain's laconic reply was: "———st battery in the army, General." On the arrival of help, we joined them, and with a wild yell and a still wilder rush, we drove the enemy back into his works, and held our ground against his best efforts to dislodge us. Other Divisions were sent to this danger point, so that before midnight our lines overlapped those of the enemy.

Johnston's plan had been to crush our left, double our lines back, and roll Sherman against the mountains west of the town. The wicked assault upon our own Brigade was the initial move in the great plan. Our stubbornness and the timely arrival of assistance, spoiled his plan. In our immediate front the Confederate position was very strong —hills, ravines, thick woods, forts and earthworks stared us in the face. Further to the right, Camp Creek separated the contending lines. Here, also, the enemy was strongly entrenched on high ground. The problem of dislodging the Confederate army was a very serious one. Great slaughter must follow a direct assault. Johnston had been flanked out of Dalton with comparatively little hard fighting, but this could not be accomplished here—severe fighting seemed necessary. Planning a flank movement, however, Sherman had so disposed his force as to leave a part free, and further, with the advance of our lines, still others would be released by convergence. With these troops he at once began a flank movement that had the desired effect of drawing Johnston out of his works, not for battle, but for escape. The severe fighting during the afternoon had resulted in Sherman's getting a foothold on the east side of Camp Creek, close up to the Confederate line. This, to them, was exceedingly discouraging. Moreover, General Polk, who had command of the rebel left, had lost to McPherson the very strongest position on that part of the Confederate line, and though he tried in very desperation to dislodge the boys in blue, he failed in every attempt, and at last, about 10 o'clock at night, gave it up. This brought the railroad and wagon bridges over the Oostanaula within range of Sherman's guns. Having lost these bridges, Johnston at once ordered the laying of a pontoon further up the river, out of range of McPherson's guns. He was also obliged to cut a new road to this new bridge. In the meantime, Sherman had also caused the laying of a pontoon at Lay's Ferry, a short distance down the river.

Following the repulse of the enemy in our own Division front, noted above, we were treated to heavy artillery firing. The skirmish line was noisy until late at night—there was prospect of a great battle next day. We were rapidly becoming accustomed to being under fire all the time. The "bing" of the minie seemed to be losing many of its terrors, and the boys took narrow escapes as a matter of course. If a comrade were only slightly wounded, he was quite likely to be laughed at. If a shell came unusually close, it was quite sure to be greeted (after it had passed) with a "—— you," or something of that sort. And yet, as Dr. Cook expressed it, "It was hard to get used to being killed."

The night of the 14th passed without special incident, both armies resting in line, ready for work.

Sunday, the 15th, was ushered in by a renewal of skirmish firing along our entire front. Suspecting that Sherman would advance his left, General Hood strengthened his intrenchments and ran a battery forward to hold us in check. But his gunners were soon picked off, and the battery remained between the lines until night, when we brought it in.

Johnston was in trouble. He was hemmed in on the north and west by our troops; on the south by the Oostanaula, the bridges over which were commanded by McPherson's guns; and on the east by the Connasauga. Moreover, Sherman had at least one Division (Sweeney's) of Dodge's, Corps, south of the Oostanaula. Johnston saw clearly that he could not hold Resaca. He therefore decided to withdraw. This he did on the night of the 15th. Under cover of darkness, two-thirds of his army—Polk's and Hardee's Corps—crossed the Oostanaula by the railroad and wagon bridges. These bridges were within cannon range of Sherman's guns, but darkness made it safe for Johnston to use them. The remainder of his army crossed on the new pontoon laid on the night of the 14th. Early on the morning of the 16th, Sherman occupied the town, but immediately put his army in motion. Some crossed at Lay's, some at Resaca, and some still further up the river. Our own Brigade, Division and Corps, crossed at Resaca.

Our regimental losses at Resaca were as follows:

Comrade Joseph C. Lapham, Company H, mortally wounded May 14th; died in hospital at Resaca, May 16th.
Comrade George S. McKee, Company E, wounded.
Comrade David Good, Company F, wounded.
Comrade Cornelins Siberts, Company F, wounded.
Comrade William J. Burns, Company H, wounded.
Comrade Leonard G. Cole, Company H, wounded.
Comrade J. F. Yeager, Company H, wounded.
Comrade Joseph Van Nest, Company I, wounded.

Many others were wounded, but less severely.

CHAPTER XVII.

FROM RESACA TO THE ETOWAH—KINGSTON.

Falling back from Resaca, General Johnston determined not to risk a battle with Sherman in the open country. Halting a day (the 16th) near Calhoun, he again put his army in motion for the hill country south of the Etowah. His retreat was covered by a strong rear guard, which succeeded in causing considerable trouble and not a little delay. Sherman was determined to force Johnston to fight before he could reach the hills. To this end he put his army in rapid motion and pushed vigorously forward. The Army of the Cumberland was considered able to take care of the entire rebel army long enough to allow either Schofield or McPherson to make an extended flank movement. Thomas, therefore, advanced directly upon Johnston wherever he could be found, while McPherson and Schofield, with equal persistence, sought his flanks.

Marching on the 17th, the Confederate Commander took position just south of Adairsville, but not finding it to his liking, soon continued his retreat. His army was kept wonderfully well in hand, and seemed to lose neither its pride nor its spirit in consequence of retreating. Sherman's army was also well in hand and brim full of enthusiasm. Our Brigade encamped near Calhoun on the evening of the 16th. The entire Army of the Cumberland was in our immediate vicinity that night, but Johnston retreated under cover of darkness.

Continuing our pursuit, we left camp at daylight, and soon began skirmishing with the enemy. Cheatham's entire Division and Wheeler's Cavalry were acting as rear guard. Skirmish firing was heavy all day, and especially so in the afternoon.

JOSEPH VAN NEST,
COMPANY I.
From photograph taken in 1893.

Johnston had encamped in line between two hills, but he could not cover his front and flanks to his satisfaction, consequently he continued his retreat. At 8 o'clock next morning, the 18th, we resumed our march southward, passing through Adairsville an hour later, and encamping at night four miles north of Kingston. Aside from the usual skirmishing nothing of especial interest occurred. Our three armies kept well abreast and within easy supporting distance.

Daylight of the 19th found us on the march. A heavy fog hung over all the country. As we neared Kingston the fog lifted and we began skirmishing, our Corps taking a number of prisoners. A few miles south of the town we came upon a body of Confederates who showed fight. We immediately gratified them and soon had them on the run. The affair was quite serious for a short time. Our Regiment, with suitable supports, was deployed, and steadily carried everything before it. Our losses were as follows:

Comrade Charles Scott, of Company D, killed.
Comrade James Campbell, of Company B, wounded.
Comrade Joseph D. Reese, of Company K, wounded.

A number of others were slightly wounded.

We continued our march, skirmishing very heavily at intervals all day, and encamped near Cassville, nearly five miles southeast of Kingston. The enemy held a very strong position here, but on the approach of our army again retreated, passing south of the Etowah River, and leaving us in possession of all north of it.

General Sherman here halted his army for a few days' rest, and for the further purpose of repairing the roads in his rear and accumulating supplies, preparatory to the next stage of our advance. While thus resting, the Army of the Cumberland was at Cassville, the Army of the Tennessee at and near Kingston, and the Army of the Ohio near Cassville Station and the bridge over the Etowah. Our Regiment spent the 20th, 21st and 22d in comparative quiet. It seemed a little strange to spend a whole day without being shot at, and without hearing the music of cannon and musket. It was, however, a variation which we greatly enjoyed.

CHAPTER XVIII.
FROM THE ETOWAH TO KENESAW—DALLAS.

On the afternoon of the 23rd we resumed our march, our Division having been ordered to a position near Dallas. We advanced by way of the Burnt Hickory and Pumpkin Vine Creek roads. We here lay in reserve until the 30th. The Confederate army had taken a strong position at Dallas, and gave every indication of an intention to make a final stand. Our army experienced much trouble in crossing the Etowah, and in getting into position, but all this was accomplished in due time. On the 27th, our Division was placed in line, relieving General Wood, who had been ordered to flank the enemy's right.

On the morning of the 30th our Brigade was ordered to Kingston, as escort for the Corps wagon train. This was a change of duty relished by some of the boys, but not by the majority. Notwithstanding the hardships, exposure, and danger, most of the boys preferred the front. While we were at Kingston, the 21st Illinois, returning from their veteran furlough, rejoined the Brigade, fresh and ready for business. At length, having performed our duty as escort, we rejoined our Division, near Ackworth, June 7th.

Comrade Norman Gregory, of Company A, was killed at Dallas, May 30th, as we were attempting to advance our Division line, only a few hours before we were withdrawn for escort duty.

During our absence the enemy had been hard pressed in the vicinity of Dallas. The position was naturally a very strong one—dangerous and difficult of direct assault. Stanley's Division, excepting our own Brigade, had relieved a portion of Davis' forces, and had come up close to the enemy. The fighting along Sherman's center and left was very severe, the enemy being strongly entrenched. Finding the Confederate position unusually strong, Sherman slowly moved his army to the left, turning Johnston's right and forcing him back upon New Hope Church. On the night of June 4th the Confederate army was withdrawn, moving in the direction of Big Shanty, a few miles north of Kenesaw. General Sherman immediately followed, but did not assume the offensive until the 10th. In the meantime the railroad was repaired as far south as Ackworth, and the army fully supplied with rations and ammunition. It was during this period of rest that our Brigade returned from escort duty. On the 9th of June the 38th Illinois rejoined the Division, having returned from veteran furlough.

On the morning of June 10th, Sherman's entire army was again in line ready for the field. General Cruft, who had commanded our Brigade thus far during the campaign, being seriously ill, was sent back to Chattanooga for treatment. Colonel Kirby was appointed his successor, and remained in command of the Brigade until the close of the war. Such a command was not new to him, for on several occasions, and for a considerable time, he had been in command of detachments consisting of several regiments and charged with duties delicate and responsible. Cool and collected, he had already proven himself reliable under circumstances requiring nerve, decision, and pluck. Indeed, there were few in the army who were clearer headed than he, under fire, or in close quarters of any kind. While we all rejoiced in his well-merited promotion, the 101st boys felt as though they had met with personal loss. Hitherto he had sustained peculiar relations to our Regiment—now he would sustain the same relation to all the regiments of the Brigade. We could no longer be his "peculiar people." Careful and prompt, Colonel Kirby always struck quickly and hard, but he never forgot to look after his men, and his promotion made no change in his bearing toward the boys. He was succeeded in the command of the Regiment by Lieutenant Colonel McDonald, who continued to be our Commander until the close of the war.

CHAPTER XIX.

KENESAW.

Our Brigade, under Colonel Kirby, took advance of our Division in the campaign which ended in the expulsion of the enemy from Kenesaw. Starting at 7 o'clock on the morning of June 10th, we struck the rebel skirmish line within an hour. They were soon forced back upon their main line. The 21st Illinois, and the 31st Indiana, were deployed, and soon became hotly engaged. The enemy were driven about half a mile when our line was halted and strongly barricaded. We were in front of the enemy strongly posted on Pine Mountain. Palmer was on our left and Hooker on our right. Both had been heavily skirmishing. The position held by our Brigade was an exceedingly important one. On the following day we were moved some distance to the left and relieved a portion of Palmer's Corps. We immediately went into line, and were soon ordered to advance the position about five hundred yards. On account of the wariness of the enemy, this could not be done until dark. The night was gloomy and wet—as dark as Erebus. Cautiously feeling our way, we advanced our line and strongly intrenched ourselves, ready for the worst in the morning. The general movements of Sherman's army on the 10th and morning of the 11th had developed the fact that the enemy was in our front in full force, his lines extending from Kenesaw to Pine Mountain, and thence southwesterly to Lost Mountain.

On the discovery of this fact, General Sherman acted with his usual promptness and decision. General McPherson was ordered to advance towards Marietta, moving eastward of the railroad; General Thomas in the center, was to move upon Kenesaw and Pine Mountain, and General Schofield upon Lost Mountain. General Johnston's lines were twelve miles long—much longer than he could properly defend. McPherson's movement to his right made it necessary for the rebel commander to extend his lines still further in that direction.

At about the same time that our Brigade advanced and intrenched its lines (June 11th), our entire army drew nearer the enemy, and was prepared for mortal combat. For two days the rain had fallen almost incessantly, rendering the roads—poor at best—almost impassable. The country in which we were operating was badly cut up with ravines and ridges, rendering the movement of artillery extremely difficult.

General Sherman's plan was to break the Confederate line between Kenesaw and Pine Mountains, then roll it back each way, capturing as much of it as possible and demoralizing the rest.

By this time we had become so accustomed to skirmish firing that unless we were in the line actually participating, we scarcely noticed it. Now and then, when it became unusually severe, the boys would straighten up, make some characteristic remark and then forget all about it. Not so

CHARLES R. GREEN, Company A.
(ANTIQUARIAN.)

with those in the skirmish line. There the quick eye and ready shot were exceedingly necessary to good health and a whole skin. No soldier on either side was so foolish as to stand bolt upright, when a tree, a log, a stump, a stone or a hole in the ground, or anything else, would afford a shelter. Intrenching tools were kept constantly on hand, not only for the regiment in line, but to be used as occasion might require by the skirmishers. Tens of thousands of those skirmish pits were dug both by the blue and the gray.

Heavy skirmishing continued on the 12th, 13th and 14th, our lines having been advanced about fifty yards on the 12th. The enemy's position in our front seemed to be exceedingly strong. Every approach was carefully guarded, and it was worth a skirmisher's life to show his head. Gradually but surely the Armies of the Tennessee and the Ohio were closing in on the Confederate flanks, and Thomas was steadily crowding Johnston's center. The Confederate Commander soon saw that his line was too long and that Sherman's efforts to break his center would sooner or later succeed unless he shortened his front. He decided to abandon Pine Mountain, and defend a line extending from Lost Mountain to Kenesaw. Preparatory to this movement, several Confederate officers, Johnston and Polk among them, were observing the movements of Sherman's army from the fortified summit of Pine Mountain, when a shell from our Division battery, the 5th Indiana, exploded in their midst, instantly killing General Polk. That night Johnston withdrew his lines, abandoning this strong position. Not being aware of this fact, we pressed our lines forward very early next morning and soon found ourselves within their works.

The position of the enemy was soon developed and our lines made to conform to the new order of things. Our own Brigade, formed in two lines, three battalions front, took its place under a galling fire, established its skirmish line and held its ground. Under heavy fire, a portion of our skirmish line extending across an open space, was intrenched. This work was commenced and prosecuted with great bravery by the 31st Indiana and a portion of the 90th Ohio, and completed by the 101st. To accomplish this required the constant exhibition of unadulterated pluck.

This line was established right up to the line of abatis in front of the enemy's works and within clear, short range of their rifles.

It was accomplished by deploying two light lines of skirmishers. Each man in the front line was provided with a short block cut from a pine log, which he could readily handle, and each man in the rear line had a thick brush, with the stick sharpened so as to be easily thrust into the ground. The first man advanced crawling on his stomach and rolling his log before him, his comrade following with his brush as soon as the designated line was reached. The brush was set up in front of the log to obscure the sight of the enemy's riflemen, and the boys lying prostrate fell to scraping out an intrenchment. Thus three regiments were quickly and firmly established under the very noses of the enemy.

Captain Simonson, Chief of Artillery for the Corps, seeing our position, came forward and said he would like to get a battery up there, if possible. Colonel Kirby told him that if he would indicate the position he would like to occupy, he would aid him in preparing it. While standing side by side marking the desired position, a rifle ball struck the Captain in the forehead, killing him instantly. His death caused great grief throughout the entire Corps, as he was recognized as most eminently successful in his department. About this time General Hooker's Adjutant General came up and said that General Hooker had been informed of the position we had gained, but had declared it impossible for any troops to hold it, and had directed his Adjutant to ride forward and make inquiries. Colonel Kirby suggested that he report to General Hooker that there were troops which could gain, occupy and hold just such a position. During the night the Brigade Commander, with Colonel Yoeman, of the 90th Ohio, was constantly on the picket line. Shortly before 3 o'clock in the morning they became satisfied that something unusual was going on within the enemy's lines. They very cautiously moved forward with the picket line into the dense abatis, and, as they advanced, became more and more convinced that a movement of some kind was being made by the enemy. Orders were sent back for the battle line to advance boldly, and at precisely 3 o'clock we were over the enemy's works and on the heels of their retiring lines. We were the first of our force to gain the inside of the rebel works.

The Confederates had again fallen back, still further shortening and strengthening their lines. The stubbornness with which Johnston defended his outposts and the care with which he shortened and strengthened his front, indicated that he had resolved to make this position his last ditch.

During the afternoon our Brigade advanced a mile and a half, taking position on a commanding ridge on the right of General Gross. The enemy's skirmishers had been found and the usual firing resumed. Later in the afternoon we were marched to our left and assigned a position, supporting the right Brigade of General Newton's Division, our vacated position on the ridge being occupied by General Beatty's Brigade.

The general movement of our army on the 14th, which resulted in the enemy's abandonment of Pine Mountain, was such as to cause Johnston much concern. On our extreme left, McPherson pushed hard and with commendable success.

A portion of General Leggett's Division captured a spur of hills, taking many prisoners and securing a position for our artillery, which resulted in the enemy withdrawing a portion of his line to healthier quarters. Our own extreme right, the Army of the Ohio, was pounding vigorously and successfully. The Confederate Commander was still clinging to Lost Mountain, though in doing so he greatly weakened his line between that and Gilgal Church. Leaving Stoneman to look after Lost Mountain—which he did in an admirable manner—General Schofield directed his attention to the weak point of the Confederate line to the west of Gilgal.

On the morning of the 18th, our Division lines were advanced about a half mile, our Brigade supporting General Newton's right, but at 4 o'clock in the afternoon we went into position in the front line, joining General Wood's left. During the night of the 17th, seeing that the persistence of our center and right must soon destroy his left, General Johnston ordered the abandonment of Lost Mountain and the weak lines connecting it with Gilgal Church. This humiliating move must have cost the proud rebel a severe pang. And yet it is said that he took great pride in being able to withdraw without our knowing it. Certainly he was an expert in such matters.

The rebel Commander was in hard luck. Having let go of Lost Mountain, he tried to establish his left behind Noyes Creek. We fought him there on the 18th, while the Army of the Ohio menaced his flank. His left was practically in the air, and he did the only safe thing—he again withdrew on the night of the 18th and took a strong position at Kenesaw. It was now Sherman's chance to make a mistake, which he at once proceeded to do. McPherson was well around to the east of Kenesaw; Thomas was in front of it and in fine condition; Schofield was hard by on Thomas' right; Stoneman was well mounted, and there was no reason why Thomas' suggestion to flank Kenesaw by a movement to our right should not have been adopted. But Sherman was full of fight, and possibly hoped to destroy Johnston and end the campaign right there. At any rate, the flank movement was not to be made.

The heavy down-pour of rain in the afternoon of the 18th made our movements on the morning of the 19th quite difficult. But at that stage of the game nothing short of death or an exceedingly severe wound was accepted as an excuse for not being in line. With the dawn we were in motion, preceeded by a very strong skirmish line. Steadily we pressed forward, driving everything before us until we struck the rebel intrenched lines at Kenesaw. Kirby's Brigade was on the right of our Division front, Whitaker in the center and Gross on the left. The free use of musket and cannon was resorted to on both sides during the entire day, and especially in the afternoon as we neared the enemy's main works. A number of our boys were wounded and the work in hand assumed an unusually important character. It was very evident that a life and death struggle must soon ensue. Our entire Division front was strongly intrenched that night.

CHAPTER XX.

BALD KNOB.

The next morning, Monday, June 20th, brought with it severe work for Kirby's Brigade, and, indeed, for Stanley's entire Division. The hostile main lines were distant from each other about eight hundred yards, each having a strong skirmish line in its front, constantly on the alert to check, and, if possible, prevent, any forward move of the other.

JOHN A. ROBERTS,
COMPANY C.
From photograph taken in 1894.

Between these main lines lay a high hill, conical in shape, almost destitute of timber, and known as Bald Knob. It was directly in front of our Brigade, and was strongly held by the enemy as a most important advanced position. To the left of this, and in Whitaker's front, was a similar hill, though not so high, nor strongly held. Between these hills the ground was low and somewhat swampy.

Our skirmishers were wide awake and hotly engaged. The sullen boom of cannon could be heard to right and left of us as the brave boys of the National line sought closer contact with the enemy. The angry voice of our own Division Artillery screamed and yelled across the intervening space only to wake the noisy dogs of war on the other side. In the afternoon the situation grew still more serious and we stood to arms for desperate work. Whitaker assaulted and carried the hill in his front, and held it against the repeated attempts of the enemy to dislodge him. At the same time, our Brigade skirmish line, commanded by Major Angle of the 90th Ohio, charged recklessly up the side of Bald Knob and actually captured the stronghold. This charge was born of the yells and excitement of Whitaker's men, and had not been ordered by anyone. Before support could be sent them, they were heavily assaulted and compelled to retire. As they fell back they were met by General Kirby in person, who quickly readjusted and reinforced the line, and ordered a second assault upon the hill. Most gallantly and successfully was this assault made. The hill was cleared, the position was ours, for we had twice captured it. But there was no support on our right—Kirby's Brigade being the extreme right of Stanley's Division. Without support on this flank, the position on the summit of Bald Knob could not be held. Constantly from the batteries on the Confederate main line there came up screeching shell and solid shot, while from their driven skirmish line, now reinforced and turned at bay, there rained upon us a fearful storm of binging lead. To most of this we were able to respond most effectively. On the right as our line charged up the hill, a densely wooded ravine was passed, into which the enemy immediately threw a strong force, which at once assaulted our flank and right-rear. This, with the terrific fire in front, rendered our position wholly untenable, and we were obliged to retire.

It should be borne in mind that only our skirmish line had thus far been engaged—the Brigade, as an organization, had not left the main line, and at the close of the action described above our skirmishers resumed the pits, out of which they had madly dashed an hour before. Our Division main line was everywhere intact, and our own Brigade front had not been even slightly endangered. Even the Confederate skirmish line did not venture beyond their rifle pits on the summit of the Knob. The left of our Brigade had been swung slightly forward, in support of Whitaker's advanced position.

General Stanley was with our Brigade during the latter part of the conflict, and had witnessed the struggle of our skirmishers for the possession of the Hill. This was in accordance with his custom. Wherever help was needed, or the fight was thickest, there Stanley, brave, true, generous, big-hearted Stanley was sure to be found. Soon after the affair was all over, General Howard rode up and demanded to know why the hill had not been held. The situation was fully explained to him.

"General," said Kirby, "order troops forward to cover the woods and I will again take and will hold Bald Knob."

"How long will it take you to get ready for the assault?" inquired Howard.

"I am ready now, sir," said Kirby, saluting and motioning with his sword toward his men, who were more than ready for the fray. But for reasons best known to himself, Howard did not act on Kirby's suggestion, and no further assault was made that evening.

Darkness soon falling, the strife ended, and the field of conflict became quiet, broken only by the vigilance of the skirmish-picket line. Keen eyes, and many thousands of them, peered into the darkness from our side along the entire National front, and on the other side, equal thousands peered our way. These faithful sentinels watched and guarded while the main line rested and slept. So sharp was this watchfulness that even apparent danger was sure to wake the musket, and almost instantly shot would answer shot, soon to die away again into silence deep and suggestive of the coming storm.

The night following the first assault on Bald Knob was spent quietly and peacefully as any since we had come under the frown of Kenesaw. Our main line was in splendid shape, well posted, strongly intrenched, confident and brim full of enthusiasm. During the night, however, the Confederates had brought several batteries—at least thirty guns—on their main line to bear on the Knob, hoping to render it absolutely untenable, should we again succeed in capturing it.

At dawn of the 21st the hosts on either side were in line awaiting developments. Detachments of troops were moved here and there; the skirmish line was strengthened almost to the proportions of a battle line; orderlies were sent off in various directions; officers were scanning the front through their field glasses; ammunition was distributed, batteries were stationed to sweep the entire front—in short, everything betokened an important move immediately to be made.

At 11:30 o'clock General Kirby was ordered to prepare to assault the stronghold in his front. He was to drive the enemy from the Knob, fortify and hold it against all comers. The artillery of our own Division and a portion of Wood's was ordered to concentrate their fire upon the enemy in the vicinity of the point to be assaulted. At 12:30 Kirby reported that his Brigade, accompanied by the Pioneer Corps, was ready to advance. Immediately the noisy music began, and for fifteen minutes the very heavens seemed palsied with the roar of cannon and shriek of shell. Responding, the Confederates opened every battery in position, sending us shell for shell and shot for shot.

In the midst of this terrific duel the word was passed along the line,—we were to assault, capture and hold the hill. Steadily but irresistibly we were to push on, no matter who nor how many might fall. The pioneers were to accompany us to build intrenchments, while we with musket and bayonet should keep the enemy out of their way.

Steadily, grandly, the old Brigade, at the command of General Kirby, moved out, with either flank thrown back to accommodate the line to the peculiar formation of the ground. On our right Colonel Nodine of Wood's Division threw forward two Regiments, the 15th and 49th Ohio, to cover our flank, and placed a battery in position to plow the Confederate skirmish line. On our left Whitaker's men were in line and his batteries still in action. In our own front was the hill, crowned with frowning rifle pits and fringed with gleaming steel.

As we moved out and up the hill, the thundering of our artillery ceased, our flanks obliqued into position, and with cheers and yells we pushed for the top, nor stopped till the last rebel had taken to inglorious flight or had fallen into our hands. Our charge had been furious and successful. But instantly we became the target for the concentrated fire of the main line Confederate batteries. A defensive line was immediately chosen, our front made to conform to it, and under the most terrible artillery fire imaginable, our pioneers fortified the position with the utmost gallantry. As an evidence of the severity of this fire, it may be stated that General Kirby was struck five times with pieces of shell within half an hour. One fragment tore the skin from the back of his bridle hand, another tore the clothes from his left side, another tore the left stirrup off and ripped the sole from his boot. How any one escaped death or wounding seems a mystery.

Soon after the summit had been captured, General Howard came up and ordered that every effort be made to hold the position. At General Kirby's request the 5th Indiana Battery, which had been with us in many a severe action, and in which we had unbounded confidence, was sent forward to us and immediately went into effective action. Heavy firing continued all day and during much of the night. The position we now held was a most important one, overlooking a portion of the Confederate works. Our success had enabled Howard to advance his main line nearly 500 yards; Hooker, on Thomas's right, had pushed forward nearly 700 yards, and our left was holding on like grim death, gradually creeping nearer to Marietta and the rear of Kenesaw.

Speaking of the work of the pioneers, General Kirby said: "My pioneers, particularly, won my admiration on this occasion by their almost superhuman efforts and great gallantry."

At 3 o'clock on the morning of the 23d, having held Bald Knob during the 22d, we were relieved and ordered one mile to the right, where, relieving other troops, we went into the front line about daylight and immediately began skirmishing with the enemy. Toward evening we charged them, drove them back and fortified our new position. All this brilliant fighting was dulled by the incessant rain-

EPHRAIM BAKER,
COMPANY C.
From photograph.

fall, the unfathomable mud and the deep gloom that brooded over the desolate region in which we were campaigning.

General Howard, speaking of the assaults of the 20th, wrote as follows to General Thomas:

NEAR KENESAW MOUNTAIN, June 20, '64.

General Thomas: General Stanley succeeded in carrying the hills in his immediate front. Driving the enemy out of his skirmish rifle pits, he advanced close up to the enemy's works and made a cover in Whitaker's front. * * * Colonel Kirby had not established a main line on the hill he took, and his skirmish line was driven back a short distance. This, however, can be easily retaken, as it is under the fire of Wood's batteries.

O. O. HOWARD.

The following congratulatory order, referring to the work of the 21st, was issued by General Stanley. We appreciated it at the time, and certainly do so yet.

HEADQUARTERS 1ST DIVISION 4TH A. C.,
KENESAW MT., GEORGIA, June 21, 1864.

Colonel Kirby: General Thomas has been notified by General Howard of your success in charging and holding the Hill (Bald Knob) in your front to-day, and in a note to General Howard expressed his gratification and thanks to the troops for the work they have done.

Please communicate to your command the thanks of Generals Thomas and Stanley for the success they have achieved.

I am, your obedient servant,
W. H. SINCLAIR, A. A. G.

It was at this stage of the conflict that Sherman was compelled to decide between a direct assault and a flank movement. Fearing that his own army, as well as that of the enemy, might conclude that he would not assail a fortified position, he decided not to flank, but to assault. His lieutenants, notably General Thomas, strongly advised otherwise. But he had reached a conclusion, and the army, always loyal, settled down to business. During the 24th and 25th we continued to hold the ridge which we had captured on the 23d.

CHAPTER XXI.

THE STORMING OF KENESAW.

On the 23rd of June, Sherman issued his final orders for the assault upon Kenesaw. This was to be made at two points—one upon Little Kenesaw by McPherson, the other upon Kenesaw proper by Thomas. These assaults were to be made on Monday the 27th, three days after the orders were issued.

The morning of the 27th dawned clear, bright and warm. Our own Division front had been selected as the point from which Great Kenesaw was to be stormed, but our Division was not to make the attack. We were to act as support, while General Newton's Division assailed. The hour fixed for the assault was 8 A. M. General Gross' Brigade was to hold our breastworks, while Kirby's and Whitaker's Brigades advanced with the charging column. The line of our breastworks was within musket range of the enemy. When, therefore, Newton's Division formed for the assault, it immediately drew down upon itself and us the concentrated fire of the rebels. The whole side of the mountain seemed to burst out in flame and smoke. Many in the assaulting column, and not a few of our own men were struck down while forming. Not a moment was wasted, not a man hesitated. The order to charge was given; the men leaped forward and rushed and clambered and climbed up the sides of the mountain, which seemed to shake and fairly quake beneath the shock of cannon in full roar from base to summit. Bravely our men struggled forward, but the odds were against them from the start. The dense mass of felled trees and brush covering a space at least two hundred yards wide; the very strong line of *chevaux-de-frise* lining the ditches in front of their works; the general entanglement of obstructions, and the fire of the enemy, both front and flank, made success impossible. Our own Brigade followed closely, and participated in the awful contest. Braver men than Newton's never wore the blue; but neither they, nor we, nor any other troops, could succeed under such circumstances. The assault failed, and with thinned and bleeding ranks we fell back to the cover of our breastworks. Our Division loss was one hundred killed and wounded. Newton's much more. But the enemy had been severely punished also. They remained in their works, and showered iron and lead upon us in wonderful abundance. While this assault was being made, our batteries along the entire line, from Schofield's right to McPherson's left, belched and bellowed.

McPherson's assault on Little Kenesaw met with no better success. It was all a great mistake, the responsibility of which Sherman took wholly upon himself.

During the assault on Kenesaw, so heavy and low had been the fire of the enemy's artillery that soon after the close of the awful struggle the leaves and brushwood took fire, seriously endangering our wounded, who lay everywhere from our lines clear up to the enemy's parapets. By one common and humane impulse, hostilities ceased, and the rebels, throwing down their arms, joined our boys in manning the stretchers to bear our wounded to our lines.

Following this unsuccessful assault, we lay comparatively quiet until the morning of the 2nd of July. Even the picket firing was light during this time. Both armies seemed to be resting. On the 28th, by mutual agreement, we buried our dead, who had fallen near the rebel works. The same privilege was granted the enemy, whose loss in front of Hooker, on the afternoon of the 26th, and the morning of the 27th, was quite serious—Hood, with his usual impetuosity, having, on his own responsibility, fallen heavily and unsuccessfully upon our lines in that part of the field. His loss in killed, wounded and prisoners amounted to about one thousand.

The old order of things seemed to be resumed July 2nd; indeed, on the 1st there was much heavy firing. Our army was again bestirring itself. The weather had been fine for several days, and was becoming very hot. On the afternoon of the 2nd we moved some distance to the left and relieved a portion of General Newton's Division.

General Johnston, seeing that he could not break up Sherman's lines that were gradually closing round him, and especially fearing a flank movement on our part that might cut the railroad south of him, decided to fall back. This he accomplished on the night of the 2nd and the morning of the 3rd. Doubtless Johnston had in some manner learned that Sherman had decided to withdraw McPherson from the Left and transfer him to our extreme Right, leaving Thomas where he was, with a view to turn him away from Kenesaw. Indeed, such a movement on the part of our troops was in process of execution, when, on the morning of the 3rd, word was brought that the enemy had fallen back and that our skirmishers (Thomas') were already in possession of their works. If this flank movement had been ordered before the 27th, many precious lives might have been saved. Pursuit was at once ordered, and our Brigade, marching through Marietta, encamped at night near the Confederate lines, five miles south of the town, having skirmished with the rear guard since early morning. Our army took many prisoners—our Brigade its full share.

On the morning of July 4th we advanced in very strong lines, compelling the enemy to give way, and finally driving him out of his skirmish-pits. The Confederates proved so exceedingly stubborn that at night we strongly entrenched ourselves, expecting serious work next morning. In this we were to be happily disappointed.

KENESAW—LIMIT OF OUR ADVANCE.
From photograph.

RUFF'S STATION ABANDONED. 235

Though his present position (near Ruff's Station) was a very strong one and well fortified, yet Johnston decided not to attempt to hold it on account of the ease with which it could be flanked. He therefore decided to withdraw. He was forced to this conclusion by the promptness with which Sherman had followed him from Kenesaw and the closeness with which our lines enveloped him. On the night of July 4th and the morning of the 5th he retired, crossing a large part of his army to the south side of the Chattahoochee river, but strongly holding the northern approaches to the railroad and wagon bridges. The apparent ease with which the Confederate Commander withdrew his forces from the immediate and hostile front of his antagonist, marked him as an expert in such matters.

The campaign, since we crossed the Oostanaula, May 16th to July 5th, had been very severe—quite different, in many respects from any experience we had hitherto had. During the last half the rain had fallen almost incessantly, rendering military operations extremely difficult. But we had managed to keep close up to the enemy, and had been almost constantly under fire. The prolonged rains caused considerable sickness, though, all things considered, the health of the Regiment was quite satisfactory. To Colonel Kirby's good sense, sound judgment and unremitting care, we were indebted on many accounts. Early in the war each commanding officer seemed to measure his own greatness by the length of his list of killed and wounded. Not so later—never so with Colonel Kirby. He was never known to flinch, nor hesitate in obedience of orders—was always ready—but never forgot his "boys," as he still affectionately calls us, and so conducted his movements as to avoid any unnecessary exposure. The boys knew this and honored him for it then—they almost worship him now.

Our losses at Kenesaw are given below:

KILLED.

Comrade Captain Wilton N. Ebersole, Commanding Company K. Mortally wounded in charge upon Kenesaw, June 27; died in Chattanooga, July 12, '64.

Comrade Jotham A. Curtis, Company D. Mortally wounded in charge upon Kenesaw, June 17; died in Nashville, Aug. 15, '64.

Comrade Nicholas Myers, Company G. Instantly killed in front of Kenesaw, June 20, '64.

Comrade Leroy Mullenix, Company G. Mortally wounded July 4, near Ruff's Station; died in field hospital, July 25, '64.

Comrade Edwin C. Pomeroy, Company B. Mortally wounded June 21 in front of Kenesaw; died at Chattanooga, June 30, '64.

Comrade John H. Rickey, Company D. Mortally wounded near Kenesaw, June 20; died at Big Shanty, Georgia, June 22, '64.

Comrade Nicholas Broshire, Company I. Mortally wounded in assault upon Kenesaw, June 27; died at Chattanooga, July 6, '64.

Comrade Jacob Blosser, Company K. Killed on the picket line on Bald Knob, near Kenesaw, June 20, '64.

WOUNDED.

Comrade Gideon D. Webb, Company A. Wounded in assault upon Kenesaw, June 27, '64.

Comrade Dennis Mullen, Company B. Wounded in front of Kenesaw, June 23, '64.

Comrade William Cox, Company E. Wounded in front of Kenesaw, June 23, '64.

Comrade Jeremiah Ritter, Company E. Wounded in assault upon Kenesaw, June 27, '64.

Comrade Henry T. Layman, Company E. Wounded in front of Kenesaw, June 23, '64.

Comrade Chas. C. J. Hilgendorf, Company E. Wounded in front Kenesaw, June 23, '64.

Comrade Michael Stump, Company F. Wounded in assault upon Kenesaw, June 27, '64.

Comrade Daniel Huber, Company I. Wounded in front of Kenesaw, June 20, '64.

Comrade John W. Dicken, Company K. Wounded in assault upon Kenesaw, June 27, '64.

Comrade Rufus H. Slaymaker, Company K. Wounded in assault upon Kenesaw, June 27, '64.

Many others were more or less seriously wounded in the many fights and the almost constant picket firing. But the boys became so accustomed to the presence of danger and to reports of killed and wounded that little attention was paid to slight wounds. Dr. T. M. Cook, originally our Regimental Surgeon, now in charge of the Brigade hospital, labored diligently in season and out to relieve the sick and wounded. Decided, prompt and efficient, he was one of the most valuable officers in the Medical Department of our army. He was always with the Brigade, or as near to it as circumstances would permit. Nor was he among those who used the knife indiscriminately. Were it possible to save a wounded limb, amputation was not permitted. The boys all felt that in Dr. Cook they had a faithful and competent friend.

CHAPTER XXII.

CROSSING THE CHATTAHOOCHEE.

When the Confederate Commander abandoned his line of intrenchments at Ruff's, he threw the larger part of his army across the Chattahoochee, but continued to hold very strongly the northern approaches to the railroad and wagon bridges. There were several ferries in the vicinity which were destroyed as soon as the Confederates had crossed. Our Corps, moving to the left of the railroad, came upon the rebels at Pace's Ferry just as they had finished crossing and had cut the bridge, a portion of which we saved. Our batteries were quickly brought into position and a vigorous fire opened on the enemy on the opposite shore. Palmer, on our right, was not so fortunate, and Johnston established himself at the bridges, as stated above. Still further to our right Hooker had very serious difficulty in crossing the Nickajack Creek, which, indeed, was not effected until the next morning, July 6th. On the evening of the 6th the Army of the Cumberland faced the Chattahoochee— Hooker on our extreme right, Palmer on his left, facing the bridge, and our Corps—Stanley's—on his left, near Pace's Ferry. McPherson, with the Army of the Tennessee, was on Thomas' right, and the Army of the Ohio in reserve back of McPherson and not far from Nickajack Creek. About the same time the Union cavalry seized Power's Ferry, about five miles to the left of our Corps. To the enemy everything indicated that Sherman would endeavor to cross the Chattahoochee in the vicinity of Turner's Ferry, some miles below the railroad bridge.

That Johnston expected this was clearly shown by the disposition of his forces, his main line being posted so as to cover the river in front of Thomas and our right. From his position as reserve, Schofield, with the Army of the Ohio, could be detached without affecting our front and without the enemy's knowledge. The problem of crossing was a puzzling one, requiring boldness of conception and promptness of execution. A plan was at once devised : Schofield was ordered, with his army, to move back of Thomas and to seize the ferry at the mouth of Soap Creek nearly ten miles above the railroad bridge. This movement was brilliantly executed on the 7th, the enemy being completely surprised and easily defeated. At the same time our cavalry, under Garrard, was ordered to seize their important factories at Roswell, still further to our left. This was also accomplished, but Garrard was in danger, and Newton's Division of our Corps was sent to his assistance. No sooner were these important movements well under way, than was the Army of the Tennessee withdrawn from the enemy's front on Thomas' right, and sent by forced march to our extreme left, even to the left of the Army of the Ohio. This left Thomas on our extreme right, with the rebel line extending much further west and south than his, but across the river. It was a critical moment, success depending upon celerity of movement and boldness of front. McPherson was always on time. He crossed the river and went into position. Thus, as early as the 9th of July, Sherman had secured three good crossings—at Roswell, at Soap Creek and at Powers—a pontoon at the latter place having been thrown across by our own Corps. With two of our armies —Schofield's and McPherson's—on the Atlanta side of the river, Johnston saw the game was up, and withdrew to the south side himself, burning the railroad and wagon bridges behind him.

As soon as it was ascertained that he had withdrawn, our Division was ordered to the left. We encamped that night near Schofield's pontoon bridge at Soap Creek Ferry. In order to mislead and distract the enemy as much as possible, our cavalry under Stoneman and Garrard, were sent out on a five days' raid, threatening the rebel Left; General Rouseau was ordered to move with another large cavalry force from Decatur, Alabama, still further to the right and south of Atlanta—all being ordered to destroy railroad and other public property to the utmost. These raids were quite effective, though they did not cut much of a figure in the final result. The weather was intensely hot, and much care was necessary to avoid sunstroke. Both armies needed rest and seemed ready to take it. No vitally important moves were made on either side for several days. Our Corps, however, crossed the bridge at Soap Creek on the 12th, and at once took up an important position on high ground about one mile below the crossing. In the meantime Thomas had extended his lines toward Powers' Ferry preparatory to crossing.

Reviewing the movements of the contending armies, it

seems strange, even at this date (1894), that the Confederate Commander should have left this part of his front so utterly unprotected. Schofield crossed at Soap Creek without difficulty, only a small cavalry outpost with one piece of artillery being on guard, and this within six miles of a crossing held by us. True, Johnston expected Sherman to cross many miles below, but of this he could have no possible assurance. As it was, Sherman was able to cross the river at his leisure, not a score of casualties occurring in the entire passage. Johnston's neglect was most fortunate for us.

Erecting temporary fortifications, we remained in our new position until the morning of the 18th. While the left of our great army was thus comparatively quiet, General Thomas kept up vigorous demonstrations in his front, to give the impression of an intention to cross at any moment.

CHAPTER XXIII.

ATLANTA.

If we could have passed within the rebel lines, we should, about this time, have met our old acquaintance, General Bragg, who was there to look over matters and report to "President" Davis. Neither Bragg nor Davis were friendly to Johnston, and the Confederate Commander need expect no favors. Bragg, who was Davis' Chief of Staff, entered no complaint to Johnston, nor did he seriously criticise him to his face. Forgetting how his own Fabian tactics had led him to flee from Perryville, from Stone River, from Shelbyville and from Tullahoma ; forgetting that he had been deposed from the command of a mighty army, and that he was now only the Chief of Staff of a civilian "President," Bragg nevertheless hurried back to

CAPTAIN WILLIAM N. EBERSOLE,
COMPANY K.
Mortally Wounded at Storming of Kenesaw,
June 27, 1864.

Richmond full of complaints and charges against Johnston, who, during months of almost constant battle, had managed his army in such a masterful manner as always to present a strong front so splendidly posted that Sherman dare not assail him by direct assault, but was compelled to move to the right or left as best he could to turn his position. It was his military skill that enabled him to do so at precisely the right moment, and in such manner as to save every man. He never ran—he never fell back precipitately. Bragg rushed from the line of Duck River before our army had even commenced to converge upon him; he ran from Tullahoma, while we were practically stuck in the mud miles away near Manchester, nor stopped until he had placed not only the mountains, but the Tennessee between him and danger. Not so with Johnston. He stood his ground and fought like a tiger. Not until his position became absolutely untenable did he withdraw, and then, though we seemed to have him by the throat, with his arms and legs ready for binding, he would quietly slip away, and confront us again in a new position well selected and thoroughly fortified. Johnston was a soldier, as much the superior of Bragg as Bragg was of the ordinary officer. And yet this Chief of Staff carried such reports back to his master as resulted in the removal of Johnston and the enthronement of a man— Hood—who, though a good fighter, had less judgment even than Bragg. But he was a rebel in arms against his country. Eternity will not obliterate such a stain.

When the knowledge of this change came to us, all were delighted. We knew well that none among them all could do better than Johnston, and the probabilities were, not so well. Hood had achieved a good reputation for dash in the east, and he had already tried it on Hooker. Assuming authority that did not belong to him, he had fallen impetuously upon "Fighting Joe" and had been most unmercifully

SOUTH OF THE CHATTAHOOCHEE. 243

whipped and driven from the field. He was not invincible, that we knew. We were soon posted as to his methods, and our officers were on the lookout for sudden dashes. General Johnston was relieved on the 17th of July, '64, General Hood at once assuming command.

On the morning of the 17th our great army was early astir. Thomas was that day to cross the Chattahoochee; the Army of the Ohio was to advance toward Decatur; and the Army of the Tennessee was to move out in the direction of the Augusta railroad. A pontoon was thrown across the river at Pace's Ferry, and on this, and at Power's Ferry some distance above, Thomas crossed over and took a strong position.

Our own (Stanley's) Division was already over, and very early on the morning of the 18th we took up our advance with the general movement. The investment of the enemy was to be accomplished by a grand right wheel, pivoting on Thomas' right, though this pivot was, itself, to advance slowly. Nancy's Creek, the first natural barrier, was soon passed, and Thomas' line at night extended from a mile south of the railroad bridge, in an easterly direction, to Buck Head, near which place our Corps encamped. Our Division was not in the lead on the 18th, and had little to do with the heavy skirmishing which continued from early morning. The general advance of the army made it necessary for Thomas to cross Peach Tree Creek on the 19th, and serious opposition was anticipated. Our own Division, and also Wood's, were so far to the left as to bring us in front of the North Branch of Peach Tree Creek.

Advancing from Buck Head very early on the morning of the 19th, we struck the rebels in considerable force soon after 6 o'clock in the morning. Our Brigade was at once placed in the front line on the left of our Division. Wood's Division was thrown into position south of the Buck Head and Atlanta road, at the same time. After a severe brush with the enemy, we drove them from their position, capturing the bridge which they had partially destroyed, and quickly rebuilding it, went into line south of the stream, well satisfied with our success. At the same time, the other two corps of Thomas' army and the other division of our Corps, had been contending with the Confederate skirmishers, and did not cross Peach Tree Creek until in the afternoon. On the night of the 19th, Thomas' line extended parallel with Peach Tree Creek and south of it, to the Buck Head and Atlanta road, along which Stanley's Division was intrenched. The flanking movement of the Armies of the Tennesee and the Ohio had caused a dangerous break or gap in our lines between Thomas and the Army of the Ohio. Into this gap, nearly two miles in extent, our Division, and also Wood's, had been thrown. This accounts for our position on the Buck Head road, and for the break between Wood's and Newton's Divisions. Marching very early on the morning of the 20th, we advanced for some distance along the road, then turned south, and before night had crossed the South Fork of the Peach Tree Creek. In doing this we had met with serious opposition and considerable delay, having to rebuild bridges. In the afternoon the enemy made a determined dash to regain their lost ground, but failed. We drove them back upon their main lines near the Wright house, and ourselves occupied their skirmish pits. In the evening, the 9th Indiana made a vicious attack, and brought away forty-three of the enemy without losing a man.

While we were thus busily employed, the remainder of Thomas' army had been desperately engaged. From our position we could distinctly hear the roar of the battle. The attack had come largely in the nature of a surprise, and was the first serious move of the new Commander, Hood.

Thomas' right and left were able to protect themselves by temporary breastwork, and did not suffer much, but his center—Hooker—was caught in the open fields and pretty badly punished, though he gave six blows in return for every half dozen he received. The attack was characteristic of Hood—assault after assault was made—now upon the left, now upon the center, now upon the right, rushing like demons and yelling like fiends. But our boys stood their ground, nor yeilded a foot of it. They maintained gloriously the fighting name of the Army of the Cumberland. Toward night, weary of their dreary failures, the enemy withdrew. Our loss was very heavy—1,600 killed and wounded—theirs much greater. The Union lines were quickly adjusted, the dead and wounded properly cared for, and everything placed in readiness for either offensive or defensive work.

General Hood was much chagrined at this failure, and resolved to redeem himself at the first favorable moment. Meanwhile, on the 21st, our forces everywhere were crowding in upon him in a most determined way; so much so, that at night he withdrew from the elaborate line of works constructed to prevent our advance after crossing Peach Tree Creek. It cost Hood a struggle to play the Fabian act, but compulsion was upon him. He withdrew his forces into Atlanta, and we promptly closed in upon him. In following him to his new position our entire Division was deployed. Our skirmish line amounted almost to a line of battle, and the fighting became very severe at times. Several vigorous attempts were made to drive us off, but each was repulsed, and at night we intrenched close up to the foe. While these important movements were being made in our front, the Army of the Ohio and the Tennessee were equally busy. Schofield entered Decatur a few miles east of Atlanta, and proceeded along the railroad toward the city—McPherson coming in on his left secured possession of an eminence south of the railroad and so near Atlanta, that the central parts of the city were clearly visible, and within range of his best guns.

General M. D. Leggett, of Blair's Corps, (17th,) was ordered to occupy and hold this hill with his Division, against all comers. Leggett was a fighter, and immediately fortified himself strongly, believing that Hood would not yield so important a point without a severe struggle. General G. A. Smith's Division was posted on his left, and Dodge's was in reserve. On Leggett's right was Logan's Corps, or that part of it not elsewhere engaged. The importance of the position was fully appreciated.

It would be interesting to follow the events of the great Battle of Atlanta which followed, but we had no active part in it, and it is not necessary to our story. In common with our entire army, we deeply mourned the untimely death of General McPherson. Under General Leggett's magnificent leadership the enemy was repulsed on every hand, and finally compelled to seek safety behind the defenses of Atlanta. Again Hood had signally failed.

The death of General McPherson made several changes necessary. General Kimball became our Division Commander, in place of Stanley, who succeeded Howard as Commander of our Corps—the latter having been assigned to the command of the Army of the Tennessee.

While our three armies were closing in around Atlanta, the engineers and pioneers had been putting the railroad and wagon roads in good condition, so that soon after Hood's disastrous assault of the 22nd, cars were running into Thomas' camp, and the army was sure of provisions and other supplies.

Finding the defenses of Atlanta on the east and north to be too strong to warrant direct assault, General Sherman

GENERAL NATHAN KIMBALL,
IN COMMAND OF DIVISION AFTER BATTLE OF ATLANTA.
From photograph.

determined to raise the siege of the city, and, transferring his army to the west and south, to operate against his communications, thus forcing the enemy again into the open field. To this end, the Army of the Tennessee (Howard's) was transferred July 27th, from our extreme left to the extreme right. Learning of this movement, Hood sent General Lee with a strong force to attack Howard before he could intrench himself in his new position. The attack was made with great spirit, but the boys in blue were immovable. From their rail pens, and other barricades hastily constructed, they simply mowed down the rebel columns, and although not less than six assaults were made on some parts of the line, yet not one of them succeeded. This affair, known as the battle of Ezra Church, was exceedingly disastrous to Hood. He did not try his peculiar tactics again until Franklin. Within a day or two the Army of the Ohio (Schofield's) was also withdrawn from Sherman's left and transferred to the right, going into position beyond Howard. This, with the addition of Palmer's Corps, carried Sherman's lines as far south as Eastport. To meet this movement of the Union army, Hood was obliged to extend his lines south, in the direction of Jonesboro'.

For days and weeks Stanley's Corps had held a most important part of our lines on the extreme left, really covering the front formerly held by more than twice his active force. During all this time he had practically bluffed his way, depending largely on the impudence of his skirmish line, but occasionally dashing into the face of the enemy with such viciousness and determination that Hood seemed not to care to test our real strength. True the rebel General was not able to make out just what General Sherman's plans were, and was so deeply absorbed in what was transpiring west of Atlanta that he gave little heed to matters elsewhere. While we watched and bluffed on the left of our line, Schofield and Howard and the remainder of Thomas' army made themselves strong and exceedingly dangerous in their new positions. Poor Hood! He was in hard luck. When he succeeded Johnston it was expected that he would first check the National Army, then whip it, and then either capture it or put it to ignominious flight. His first brilliant sally was at Peach Tree Creek, on which occasion he fell upon our army in the field, and sought by sudden and repeated dashes, by the prodigal use of cannon and musket and bayonet, and by all the arts of war at his command, to break through the National lines and roll our army, decimated and bleeding, back upon the Chattahoochee, an easy prey for other forces ready to seize and destroy it. But like a wall of granite Thomas' veterans stood, dying rather than yield an inch. And though Hood flung Brigade after Brigade against the Union boys in rapid and bewildering succession, it was the gray and not the blue that receded, broken and bleeding. Again, the closing in of our army around Atlanta, the wresting from Hood of one strong line after another, until our best guns actually commanded the city, rendered the Confederate Commander so utterly desperate that he resolved once more to try his chances by fierce and unexpected assault. Under cover of darkness he sent a magnificent army around the Union left and back to our rear, with instructions to slay, to kill, to destroy utterly, and not to stop for blood or human sacrifice, but by all the demons out of hell to loosen the grip which the National Army then had on the very throat of the Confederacy. Bravely, grandly, worthy of a better cause, these Confederate hosts took their stealthy way through the forests, and along by-roads, and when the sun next morning threw light upon the night's transaction, the Southern columns were almost ready to form for the assault. The tactics of Peach Tree Creek were repeated. Column after column, like great, living missiles of death, were hurled upon the flank and rear of McPherson's command, while from the works around Atlanta another great host rushed out to fall upon the front of these same devoted lines. Had this latter movement been better timed, the history of that dreadful day's struggle might have been different. As it was, the National lines under brave General Leggett stood firm, and though fighting the enemy in the rear, on its flank and in front, yet again it was the gray and not the blue that receded, broken and bleeding,

Later, when Hood learned that the extreme left of our army was being transferred to the extreme right, he resolved to fall once more on our columns, this time while they were in motion, with such fierceness and in such numbers that they would be compelled to flee. With cannon and musket and bayonet, and with blind impetuosity, he again and again charged the National lines in the vicinity of Ezra Church. But, with the first notes of the coming storm, the Union boys halted, faced the foe, and with rail, and log, and chunk and stone, built themselves barricades from which they hurled into the faces of the oncoming lines of gray such a storm of lead, and iron, and bursting shell, that first staggering, then halting, then fleeing, the rebel line sought shelter in distance and the cover of friendly woods. Again Hood had been whipped on ground of his own choosing, and at the door of his own citadel—again it was the gray, and not the blue, that receded, broken and bleeding.

No wonder the Confederate commanders seemed paralyzed; no wonder he allowed Stanley to stretch out his lines to twice their proper length; no wonder he was afraid to try the strength of our left. He persuaded himself, finally, that Sherman was putting on a bold front simply to cover his retreat across the Chattahoochee. Indeed, he held to this insane notion until the Union Commander came near cutting the Confederate army in twain on the day of the battle of Jonesboro'.

Finding Hoods works, on the north and west of Atlanta too strong to be taken by direct assault, General Sherman decided to compel the Confederate Commander to come out into the open country, and thus ignore the defenses of the city. To do this he must move his army still further to the south, toward Jonesboro'. This he promptly decided to do, and on Thursday, August 25th, our Corps received orders to withdraw from the position which we had held so long and so successfully, and move to the other flank of our investing lines. The watchfulness of the enemy made this a difficult and a dangerous thing to do. It was not to be thought of in broad daylight. In the evening, however, leaving the skirmish-picket line in position, with instructions to keep the Confederates very busy, one Brigade after another withdrew so quickly that we were gone some time before they were aware of the move. Meanwhile the pickets kept up the usual noise, and the rebel batteries continued to drop an occasional shell over into our empty works. Not until nearly 10 o'clock were the pickets withdrawn. Of course the Confederates attempted to follow us, but they did so with extreme caution, fearing ambush and everything else bad. Later they came closer and were troublesome, whereupon General Kirby turned his Brigade, and entered such a determined protest that they gave up the pursuit and caused us no further trouble. We encamped that night on the south bank of Proctor's Creek, northwest of Atlanta, the remainder of our Corps being on the north bank of the same stream.

Before beginning this movement everything not absolutely necessary to an active campaign, had been sent to the rear—such as surplus wagons, the sick, and the wounded; indeed, we were stripped of everything except the clothes we wore, ten days' rations in the wagons, which would have to last us fifteen days, and an unlimited amount of ammunition. We were decidedly "light" on this march.

The next morning, Friday the 26th, we were in line very early, and soon moved out at a brisk pace for the right of the Fourteenth Corps, in the vicinity of Utoy Creek, which position we reached in safety in the afternoon. As we plodded along, now on the road, now in the woods, and now across the fields, we could hear the sullen boom of cannon off on our left, and now and then the faint echo of bursting shell. The weather was intensely warm—this being the hottest day we had ever experienced. Very great care was taken, but notwithstanding this, many a boy in blue went down, beneath the merciless rays of a Southern sun—many recovered, but not all. Even to this day, not a few of our men suffer seriously from the effects of the almost unheard of heat of the valleys and plains of Georgia.

Weary and almost prostrated by the intense heat, we slept in comparative peace, but with the earliest hints of the morning we were again in line, and after breakfast—a frugal meal quickly despatched—we resumed our march southward. Passing beyond the right of the Fourteenth Corps, we became the advance of the Union army, and the old order of things was soon established—again the everlasting picket firing rang in our ears. At times we encountered cavalry only, then cavalry and light artillery, and not infrequently we had brushes with the infantry. In our own front, only the skirmish line was engaged this day, and at night we went into camp near Mount Gilead Church.

While we had been making this move to the south or right of our investing lines, the Twentieth Corps had concentrated at and near the bridge over the Chattahoochee, prepared to defend our supplies at that point, and to occupy Atlanta the moment Hood should abandon it. Our entire army was working slowly but surely toward the left of the Confederate position, and every day brought us nearer his communications.

Very early on the morning of the 28th we again pressed forward, pushing the enemy back, and compelling him to keep at a respectful distance. At night we were in line near Red Oak. It was at this stage of the great game that Hood made his worst mistake. He persisted in believing that Sherman's object was simply to put on a bold front while his army should cross the Chattahoochee. This accounts for the fact that we met so slight opposition at Red Oak, on one of his main lines of supply. He should have been there in full force before Stanley reached that point. As it was we had reached this important line of railroad without serious opposition, and the next morning a portion of our Brigade set to work with a will to tear up and destroy this road as completely as possible. The railroad wore a most discouraged look when our boys were through with it. Only a few charred ends of ties, and twisted rails galore, were in sight. Wooden structures were burned, stone culverts were blown up and torn out, and the stones, by means of heat, were split and demolished. The next day, the 30th, we pushed on toward the South, but at almost every step we encountered their skirmish line, which was still more stubborn than usual. The hills and highlands in the vicinity of Mud Creek gave them great advantage, of which they fully availed themselves. They were at times too strong to be handled by our skirmish line, and the artillery had to be called in. The outlook was so serious that night that we strongly barricaded our position when we went into camp at Flat Rock, near Mud Creek.

In line very early next morning, we at once struck the enemy, with whom we skirmished during the live-long day. By this time Hood began to realize his mistake and stir around in great shape. Our entire army had gone so far toward the South that his defenses at Atlanta amounted to nothing. He saw that if he remained there, Sherman would cut off his lines of supplies, and that his army must either cut its way through the National lines, starve or surrender. He would not surrender; he could not hope to cut his way out; he, therefore, was compelled to follow Sherman. This would bring him out into the open field, where the Union army felt abundantly able to whip him.

Hood found it exceedingly difficult to believe that Sherman's grand army was actually on his flank, that it was a "condition and not a theory that confronted him." But stern facts soon impressed themselves so deeply on his mind that he seemed dazed and confused. He ordered troops here and there, at times almost at haphazard. Realizing that Sherman's object was to cut and permanently hold the railroad running through Jonesboro', he sent two corps of his army to that place to prevent such a calamity, but in the confusion of the hour, he foolishly ordered one of them back to Atlanta, and before it had reached that destination he changed his mind and ordered it to return to Jonesboro'. But, meanwhile, Sherman had made the best time possible, and was already astride the railroad north of Jonesboro', and Hood's returning corps had to move further to the east, along a new road, to reach the position it had left not many hours before. In the meantime, the Union army had not been idle. On the contrary, every energy had been exerted to the utmost to strike the enemy before he could intrench himself. Our own Corps (Stanley's), after destroying the railroad in the vicinity of Red Oak, as stated above, moved in the direction of Rough-and-Ready, a tumble-down station on the Macon Railroad, about midway between East Point and Jonesboro'. The day was one of stirring incident along our entire front. Every man seemed to know that a great crisis was approaching, and each nerved himself to do his own particular best. Strange how the unity of the great movement seemed to impress itself on the boys. True they knew nothing surely, except that with which they came in contact, and yet all knew that we were many miles south and west of Atlanta—that we had turned the frowning forts and long lines of breastworks and rifle-pits of that city, in which the Confederates had unbounded confidence, and behind which they had taken permanent position, as they supposed, and we felt that one army or the other must now go down.

We were inspired with the notion that it was possible to wind up the campaign in a short time, and this gave zeal and energy and enthusiasm to every move. The lines were kept well closed up—there was little straggling, notwithstanding the intense heat, and every order to advance was obeyed with alacrity. This spirit actuated our entire army, and made it invincible. Not so on the Confederate side. That brave army under Bragg had been driven from Perryville, through Murfreesboro', and out of Chattanooga; under Johnston it had been steadily forced back from Rocky Face, through Dalton, Resaca, and Dallas; from Kenesaw, across the Chattahoochee, where, tired of this Fabian policy, General Hood was placed in command to prevent the further retreat of the army in gray. But even Hood was speedily forced back into the strong defenses of Atlanta, notwithstanding the magnificent fight he made on all sides to prevent such a result. And now, again, that same army in gray was compelled to abandon its strong fortifications and move again into the open country. Doubtless they, too, felt that the game would soon be ended, but their experience had not been such as to give them great hope of success. They knew as well as we did, that when they left Atlanta our troops (the Twentieth Corps) would speedily occupy it, and that once lost they could never regain that city. Though they marched rapidly and promptly to their new positions in the open country, yet their step must have lacked elasticity and confidence, their spirits buoyancy and enthusiasm. But they were soldiers, every man of them, true and tried, for whose prowess and daring we had great respect. They would surely withstand us with undaunted courage and heroic bravery.

The steady on-push of Stanley's Corps on the 31st was splendidly emulated by the other parts of the Grand Army. We went into camp about one mile west of the Macon Railroad, in what was known as the Big Bend; Schofield on Thomas' left, struck the railroad just south of Rough-and-Ready; the army under Howard had forced its way across Flint River, but in doing so had been heavily assailed by the Confederates, who hoped to roll him back in confusion upon and into the Flint River, completely paralyzed and broken. This accomplished, they were to fall upon Schofield near Rough and-Ready, and beat him off in some way. All this was to result in forcing Thomas to flee for his life across the Chattahoochee. But the whole thing was a failure from the Confederate standpoint. Howard, though hard pressed, held his own, and the commanders in gray had all they could do to keep him out of their own works, much less could they drown him in the Flint. They hammered spasmodically at Schofield, but he selected his own camping ground that night, and there was no encouragement for the Confederates in that quarter. Thomas, instead of fleeing as he should have done, according to Hood's program, moved steadily forward until a part of the Fourteenth Corps (Davis') struck the railroad, and the other Corps came close up to it. Sherman's army was badly scattered that day, but in the rattled condition of the Confederate Commander, it made no difference. Barricading our position and throwing out a strong picket line, we slept that night feeling sure that the next day would bring great things to pass, for we had received orders to tear up and utterly destroy the railroad in our front. That the enemy would prevent this if possible, we had no doubt, and if we succeeded we well knew that Hood could not long remain in Atlanta, for he could get no supplies.

The first gray streaks of the morning of September 1st discovered the Union Army in line ready for the arduous work before it. Marching early, our Brigade soon struck the railroad, and turning south, began the work of demolition. Everything that could be burned was committed to the flames; cedar ties proved to be excellent material for heating the rails, and adjacent trees offered solid supports for bending them; a roaring fire of cedar rails soon destroyed the wooden culverts, and a few pounds of powder blew up the stone ones. The railroad was utterly wrecked—nothing was left, except the roadbed, and even that looked exceedingly disconsolate. We continued this destruction until we met other forces on our right engaged in the same business, when, according to instructions, we rested and waited for further orders.

If the railroad presented a dilapidated appearance after receiving our attention, the boys themselves looked and felt little better. The weather was exceedingly warm, and the fires, necessary for the destruction of ties and bridges and the heating of the rails, rendered it hot almost beyond endurance. Perspiring like old soakers, the boys used their blackened and rusty hands to brush the great drops of "sweat" from face and neck and breast, until they were a sight to behold. They looked as though they had been embracing unwashed camp-kettles, frying-pans, and the greasy sides of all the S. B. boxes in the army. Each laughed at the other, and in a little while managed, one way and another, to clean up and look all right. But there remained many streaks of black as broad as your two fingers, and many splotches the size of a silver dollar, as nearly as we could remember how large such a thing was.

We had not rested long before the entire Corps was ordered to move down the railroad toward Jonesboro' and join the left of the Fourteenth Corps. Marching rapidly we soon struck the enemy and gave them our entire attention.

Up to this hour the work of the day had been deliberate, no haste had been enjoined, but now everything was to be rushed. The change had been brought about by the discovery that a portion of the troops that had been in Jonesboro' the day before, and which had assaulted Howard, had been withdrawn, and Sherman determined to attack before it could be returned. To this end he put his entire army in motion. Two Brigades were sent to the south to cut the road in that section; Howard was to batter the rebel lines on our right with artillery; Davis, with the Fourteenth Corps, was to assault on the north of the town; and Stanley was to prolong Davis' lines east of the Macon Railroad, and join in the assault. Davis was already in line, wrathy because he could not at once fly into the faces and clutch the throats of the enemy bristling in his front. Stanley was making Herculean efforts to reach the position assigned him, and so nervous was Sherman that several orders to "hurry up" were sent us.

Arriving at the designated point, not a moment was lost, but the Corps at once formed, with Kirby's Brigade on the right, resting on the railroad; Gross' Brigade on its left, and Taylor's (Whitaker's) in reserve.

The ground in our front was rough and broken and covered with trees of considerable growth, among which grew an almost impenetrable thicket of brush and brier. In and back of this and completely hidden from view was a strong Confederate skirmish line, amounting almost to a line of battle; and back of this was their main line, posted a short distance in front of a strongly fortified position along the crest of a ridge. The force in our immediate front constantly riddled the jungle in which we were struggling, and many a bursting shell forced its unwelcome way into the midst of the thicket. The bushes in our front seemed sometimes fairly to bulge; every rise of ground that overlooked our position was strongly held, and every open space across which we, in our advance, must pass, was completely covered. It seemed an almost impossible task to carry a line of battle through all these entanglements, even if no enemy had been on guard to prevent it. But with a vigilant and determined foe added to these obstructions, our progress was necessarily slow. Indeed, some of the regiments found it necessary to abandon the attempt to preserve a regular line, and marched in column, company front, in order to make any progress at all. Without hesitation we pushed our way steadily forward with all the energy possible, and although murderously assailed by an unseen foe, though contending against odds that seemed overwhelming, we drove the enemy out of the jungle, and halting in the edge of the thicket to adjust our line, the Brigade fell upon the Confederates and forced them back into their works along the crest of the hill, and but for the coming of night this position also would have been assailed.

The Brigade on Kirby's left (General Cross') had advanced under similar embarrassments, and was ready for the assault soon after Kirby cleared his front, as was also Colonel Taylor's (Whitaker's), but it was too late—darkness prevented further hostilities except along the skirmish line. Orders were received for a vigorous assault at dawn next morning. But this was not to be made, the Confederates withdrawing during the night.

However, anticipating a severe battle next morning, we strongly barricaded and intrenched our position and lay down to rest—all except the poor fellows who had to go on picket. It rained, it almost poured, but nothing was neglected on this account. In line before dawn of the 2nd, we waited the revelation of the light, and were not a little surprised to find the strong works in our front held only by a light picket line, which was soon driven off.

It was about 8 o'clock in the morning, September 2nd, when we began our march down the railroad, through Jonesboro', in pursuit of the retreating enemy, whom we found strongly posted along the crest of a ridge about one mile north of Lovejoy Station. We had not moved far that morning until we passed between the hills on the right where Carlin had so bravely and so successfully assailed the Confederate position, and the ridge on the left, which we at that very hour would doubtless have been assaulting had the enemy remained. We found it much more agreeable to pass in columns down the railroad than it would have been to fly into the teeth of the foe in line of battle. The rifle-pits along the brow of the ridge, reinforced by head-logs, rocks, etc., looked lonely. They were uninviting, even in the absence of their gray defenders. Without stopping for close examination, we pushed on as rapidly as possible and soon came upon the enemy as stated above. Stanley's Corps held the left front, his right resting on the railroad.

As we neared Lovejoy Station, we could see the boys in gray working like beavers to fortify their new position. Doubtless they were greatly discouraged, but no one would have thought so to see with what magic their new position was fortified. Breastworks soon crowned the ridge. In many places head-logs, rocks and everything else that could contribute to make the position strong were brought into use. While this was being done by the infantry, their

PETER J. DeWITT,
COMPANY I.
From photograph taken in 1890.

artillery was wheeled into position and immediately began shelling our lines. Our troops were being deployed as rapidly as possible along our entire front, and could not afford to be fooled with by the enemy's batteries. Schofield threw two or three sections into line, and so did Stanley, and the Confederate gunners soon had enough of it for the time. Kirby's Brigade came into line on the left of our Division under very discouraging circumstances. Along the entire front of the Confederate position the country was open and exposed to the sweeping fire of three batteries posted in a most admirable manner. Not only so, but the ground itself was against us. Bogs, pools of water, deep trenches that might almost be dignified as ravines, seemed to lie everywhere, and to advance we must climb and clamber, wade and jump, and face the rebel artillery at the same time. The prospect was not encouraging. Barricading our position for temporary protection, we waited the movement of Howard's men, our orders being to move forward with them. It was the middle of the afternoon before he was ready to attack. Even then, his extreme left moved slowly and only a short distance. Stanley's right charged forward, but was held back by the lack of support on the right of the railroad. Our own Brigade made a dash to the front, drove the enemy back upon his main works, but on account of the enfilading fire of the enemy's batteries, we were obliged to retire a short distance and protect ourselves as best we could by the natural formation of the ground.

The fight here was an ugly one, in every sense of the word. The Confederates hid behind their strong works, and poured a murderous fire upon everything within range, employing both artillery and infantry. Their batteries swept their entire front with shot and shell, grape and canister. On our side we gave them the very best we had, and sought constantly to come to a closer embrace. But all things seemed to be against us. The rain fell in torrents, flooding the whole country; the ground was rough and rocky, ridged and full of pools, swamps and swollen streams. Notwithstanding all this, we succeeded in keeping the boys in gray well down out of sight behind their breastworks. Several of our batteries were well posted and splendidly served. More than one rebel gun was knocked out so completely that it had to be abandoned as useless, and many a bad breach was made in their main works. A gallant charge was made by some of General Woods' men, of our Corps, and we also were under orders to assault. Wood, though he gained the enemy's works, was unable to hold the position, and a little later our order to charge was countermanded. Thus the bitter contest continued until darkness put an end to the struggle. We had gradually worked our way nearer and nearer to the enemy, until we were in position to assault their stronghold, but here, as at Jonesboro' the afternoon before, the coming of night ended the deadly strife. At dusk, the rumor, well authenticated, was circulated that Hood had abandoned Atlanta and that our Twentieth Corps (Slocum's) had occupied it. No one, unless he had been present, participating in the long, wearisome struggle that began at Tunnel Hill and was still raging at Lovejoy, can fully understand the thrill of joy, pride, and satisfaction, that filled the hearts of the boys in blue at the announcement of this glorious news. No wonder they cheered. No wonder some of the rougher ones accompanied the next ounce of lead they sent screeching into the Confederate works, with, "There, take that——you, and be quiet," and that others, under the excitement of the moment, should become reckless in their attempts to "lay out" the foe still bidding us defiance. Nor is it any wonder that many of us cherished the belief that the end might be near, while still others, inspired by this fond hope, fairly embraced each other, even while the air was filled with rebel iron and lead. "To-morrow," said one, "we'll lick the life out of old Hood, and next day I'm going home." Every countenance, every word, and every act showed clearly the intense enthusiasm of the hour. Without becoming careless, each man doubled his diligence, watched his chance, and did his best. Though doomed to disappointment; though more long months must drag their weary length into eternity before we should be permitted to go home, yet many a powder-stained boy in blue that night dreamed of home and friends, and peace and quiet, even amid screeching shot and bursting shell.

Without shelter, with little supper, and with no comforts at all, we spent the long, wet night in the front line, ready on the instant for any duty the occasion might demand.

Early next morning, the 3rd, we were relieved, and placed in the second line as reserves to the Second and Third Brigades. The day was spent in comparative quiet, neither Commander feeling inclined to assault the other with any degree of vigor. The skirmishers, of course, shot at each other all day, and frequently made a great deal of noise; the artillery used up more or less ammunition, and the two armies stood like tin giants stripped for battle, but seemed satisfied to glare and frown, and dare the other to come on. The 4th and 5th were spent similarly. Each army needed rest, and each Commander needed time to answer the question "What next?" Hoods' problem was to devise some way to prevent Sherman's further advance into the heart of the Confederacy; and Sherman's was to devise the best possible move by which to break up and annihilate Hoods' army. Hood was greatly at sea and needed time. He was therefore glad to see that Sherman was in no hurry to assail him in his present quarters. Moreover, he doubtless read correctly the thought or purpose in Sherman's mind when he began the destruction of railroads. He did not believe Sherman would go much further south unless he should effect a junction with other Union forces at Mobile or Savannah. But he was very uncertain, and remained strictly in position and keenly on the alert as long as Sherman showed fight. Sherman, on the contrary, knew well that the army which he had driven from Dalton to Lovejoy was in no condition to take the offensive, and that it was aching to be let alone for awhile. He therefore felt entirely safe in ordering the withdrawal of his forces from Lovejoy and in retiring to Atlanta. Accordingly, on the 5th of August the order was given, and the same evening the National army, "of its own free will and accord," began its movement toward the rear. The Confederates offered scarcely enough objection to this to be polite. True, they did send a small escort; they did honor us with a few shells, but not enough to be interesting. They were glad to be rid of us.

Kirby's Brigade began its movement to the rear just before night on the 5th, in the midst of a most terrific thunderstorm, and a perfect avalanche of rain. Considerable difficulty was experienced in moving the hospitals. The night was intensely dark, the roads fearfully muddy and greatly cut up, and the rain discouraging in the extreme. Halting just north of Jonesboro', our Brigade and Division went into camp about daylight, near the battle-ground of September 1st. Everyone was in good spirits. We were not retreating—we all knew that—for we had whipped the enemy, had driven him into the country, twenty miles south of Atlanta, and were now going back to rest and recuperate. Remaining near Jonesboro' until the 7th, ready to accommodate the enemy should they demand any more fighting, we, in the forenoon of that day, withdrew still further, halting, at night, seven miles south of Atlanta, and soon after noon next day, September 8th, went into camp east of the city, near the Augusta Railroad. Sherman's entire army was soon concentrated in and around the former capital of western rebeldom, but strong pickets were stationed on all the avenues leading into the city, and so close a watch set that it was impossible that a surprise should occur. We did our full share of picket duty while here, as we had always done since the day we left Monroeville, and as we continued to do as long as there was a foe in the field.

The change from the tremendously active campaign at the front, to the quiet of the camp, was so marked that it took us several days to become accustomed to our new surroundings—not that any of us hankered particularly for "life at the front," but we had been in the immediate presence of the enemy so long that it seemed a little strange that comparative silence should reign from morning till night. But we managed to get used to it. The boys spent their time variously. They soon learned the state of affairs in the East, and were more than ever convinced that the war was approaching a speedy end. Some were sure that we should not again be called into action. They felt that Hood had been completely whipped, and that Grant had Lee so effectually by the throat that he too must yield. Awaiting developments, we borrowed little trouble about the future, and spent our time as boys in camp usually do.

The fall of Atlanta was looked upon by thinking people everywhere throughout the North as a sure omen of the triumph of our cause. Great joy filled all loyal hearts, while feelings of despondency and discouragement took possession of the enemies of the Old Flag. The victory was, indeed, a glorious one, but it had been expensive, not only in treasure, but in human life and sacrifice. The Army of the Cumberland alone lost in the campaign beginning near Tunnel Hill, early in May, and ending with Lovejoy, as follows: One hundred and ninety-six officers and two thousand eight hundred and forty-five enlisted men were killed, a total of three thousand and forty-one; eight hundred and ten officers, and fourteen thousand nine hundred and seventy-three men were wounded; one hundred and four officers and two thousand six hundred and three men captured, making a total loss of twenty-one thousand five hundred and thirty-one.

During the stay of our army at Atlanta, especial attention was given our sick and wounded, many being sent North for better treatment. Those who remained received every possible attention. Our Brigade Surgeon and his able assistants devoted every energy to the relief of the suffering. For months the hospital had been transported from point to point, from field to field, as the army advanced. Few of us, I fear, fully comprehended the difficulties with which this important branch of the service was constantly beset. Nor did we begin to comprehend the difficulties against which the Quartermaster's Department had continually to contend, especially during an active campaign. To Seney, and Benham, and their assistants, we were under deepest obligations. Only an unwavering perseverance and an unconquerable determination could win under many of the conditions that confronted the army.

We were "at ease" in a marvellously short time after going into camp near Atlanta. The mail came regularly from the North, and daily a large packet of letters left our camp for northern homes, accompanied by many blessings on the loved ones to whom they were addressed. Time wore rapidly on without especial incident until the beginning of October.

Meanwhile, great thoughts found lodgement in General Hood's fertile brain. The necessity of doing something, and of doing it right away, was upon him. After due consultation with the "President," and with Beauregard, who had been placed in general command, Hood seized the bull by the horns and attempted to move his army toward the north. In this he succeeded—that is, he marched north. His intention was to force Sherman back to the Ohio. This would be a much greater thing than Bragg had accomplished when he compelled Buell to retreat from Chattanooga to the Ohio, or than Sherman had done in forcing the Confederates from Dalton to Lovejoy. Success was by no means sure, but there was a possibility, and he decided to take his chances.

Sherman, in the meantime, had been in communication with General Grant with reference to a movement across the State of Georgia to the sea. He really contemplated ignoring Hood, in large part; that is, Hood might follow him if he thought it safe, or he might try his luck further north if he could get there. Of course, ample provisions were to be made to prevent his doing any great harm, but the theater of war was to be changed. This whole matter was involved in so much uncertainty, and fraught with so many dangers, that a decision was hard to reach. General Hood kindly came to the rescue, removed the difficulties, and made the march to the sea possible.

CHAPTER XXIV.

FOLLOWING HOOD.

We remained in camp at Atlanta, quietly resting and recuperating—but doing our full share of picketing and scouting—until the 3rd of October, when we again "fell in" for a new campaign. From the very day we went into camp to the day we left it, rumors of this and that were more or less current. According to some, Hood was about to move eastward so as to aid Lee at Richmond; according to others he would go westward and threaten Nashville; still others had it that he would stay where he was till Sherman moved; and yet others reported Hood as getting ready to throw his entire army on Sherman's communications, but the latter was not credited even by the most experienced bluffers in the Union camp. When, about the 20th of September, the Confederate Commander moved his camp and went into a new position covering the West Point Railroad, there was considerable excitement among our leaders until the new position was developed. Hood's left now rested on the Chattahoochee, and he lost no time in throwing a pontoon across and sending his cavalry over. Sherman's cavalry was also on that side, and the two forces had constant trouble. While we boys played muggins, and seven up, and smoked, and lolled and slept, Sherman and his Corps Commanders spent sleepless nights on Hood's account, and in determining what they should do if Hood should do nothing until they were ready to move. On the 29th and 30th Hood crossed the river and headed northward. The duty of the Union army was at once manifest, and it immediately rose to its feet ready for business. Not until the 2nd of October were Hood's intentions sufficiently revealed to enable Sherman to take the field except with his cavalry.

Rebel General Wheeler had been causing so much trouble in Tennessee that Sherman had deemed it wise to send reinforcements back to Chattanooga and Bridgeport, to take the places of other troops sent to Nashville, and on the 28th of September, Thomas himself was ordered back to the latter city to collect and organize a force sufficient to preserve peace in that section.

At daylight on the morning of the 3rd, we moved out of camp, our Division leading, and passed directly through the city, now a vast military depot, encamping that night in the old rebel works, on the Smyrna camp ground, within five miles of Marietta, savage old Kenesaw looming up to the northwest of us. So far as the rank and file were corcerned, the march had been without incident, but when we went into line about 4 o'clock that afternoon, the situation became suggestive, to say the least. We had been ordered to take ten days' rations in our wagons, and the whole outfit reminded us of the recent Atlanta campaign, only we were headed the wrong way. Stanley was ordered to develop " Hood's plans," but this was a difficult thing to do until Hood could be found, and to some extent interviewed. Every effort was made by Stanley, now in command of the Army of the Cumberland, in Thomas' absence, but without definite results. Slocum's Twentieth Corps was left to hold Atlanta, but all other troops in the vicinity were under marching orders. The Confederate army was in camp that night near Powder Springs, ten miles west of us. We were in line early next morning, but lounged near the butts of our muskets for many hours. A signal message from the top of Kenesaw reported the rebels in the vicinity of Big Shanty tearing up and destroying the railroad. A half hour later our cavalry was reported as forming to attack them. Still later, the bugler sounded "forward," and with old-time alacrity the boys took their places ready for any emergency. Passing through Marietta, we went into camp near Little Kenesaw. Ten wagon loads of ammunition and ten ambulances to each Division indicated the character of work we might expect. In addition to this each regiment had one wagon. The Confederate assault on Big Shanty was successful, and later in the day Ackworth fell also. General Stanley was ordered to make a feint against Pine Mountain on the morning of the 5th, to prevent, if possible, the rebel assault on Alatoona. which was evidently being planned. This movement was promptly made, but the Confederates gave us but little heed until much later in the day, and made a most vicious though unsuccessful attack on Allatoona. A vigorous effort was made to cut off the Confederates now falling back from Allatoona along the Dallas road to the main rebel army now near New Hope Church. The effort failed, but only by a scratch, and night found each of the opposing armies apparently ready for the other.

The sight of old Kenesaw called up many sad recollections. It was here that many of our brave boys had fallen; here that many a brave deed had been performed; here many a terrible sacrifice had been made. It seemed, indeed, strange after three months to find ourselves back in this historic section, and especially to be occupying the same lines then held by the enemy, and looking for them in the same direction they then looked for us.

A cold, misty rain set in next morning, and we shivered around camp all day, no move having been ordered. General Sherman spent most of the day on the top of Pine Mountain, from which a most beautiful view of all the country can be had. Hoods' main army was now at Dalton, only twelve miles west of us, quite as uncertain of the Union position as Sherman was of the Confederates.

Shortly before sunset we witnessed a most beautiful sight, which many of the boys probably still remember. The day had been wet and gloomy, disagreeable and uninteresting every way. But just as the sun was sinking behind the mountain wall that bordered the western horizon, the sky took on a deep leaden hue which soon changed to a much lighter haze, and this becoming more and more transparent, seemed almost to dance upon hill and mountain top, then changed rapidly into deeper and brighter shades and colors, until finally all the wild region seemed bathed in a sea of crimson and gold. Even stern old Kenesaw relaxed his savage features and looked glad, while the lesser hills and valleys beamed with radiance. In the midst of this indescribable scene, the great sun sank reluctantly into his grave behind the hills, buried in a halo of ineffable glory. It was all a vision of surpassing beauty, utterly at variance with the warlike preparations seen on every hand.

The movements of Hoods' army were so completely hidden by the cloud of Confederate cavalry kept constantly between him and Sherman, that the Union general was kept guessing an uncomfortably long time. Sherman was exasperated, and bent every possible energy to gain reliable information. Our cavalry, under Elliott and Kilpatrick, ceased not day nor night to patrol the whole country, and to inform General Sherman of every possible piece of news that could be picked up. Corps and Divisions of the rebel army would lean off well toward our lines, and sometimes make bold, dangerous breaks. The capture of Big Shanty and Ackworth, and the assault upon Allatoona, were examples. Another such plan was now hatching. The Confederate main army was to push on rapidly, threatening Kingston, and especially Rome, while another strong force was to rush rapidly forward and seize Resaca and Dalton, and utterly destroy the railroad between these two places. A corps of infantry was to assist the cavalry in this matter. The plan worked well, though Resaca was not taken, but Hood could not hold his gains. While the rebel army was thus pushing northward, Sherman was equally busy, but could not move so rapidly at first, the rebel scheme not being developed. On the afternoon of October 8th, however, reliable information of the Confederate plans having been received, we were put in motion, and camped that night one mile from Ackworth, in the same place we occupied before the siege of Kenesaw. On the afternoon of the 10th, assembly was sounded from Division Headquarters, and in half an hour we were off in good shape, passing through Allatoona at sunset, and crossing the Etowah at 9 o'clock the same evening. Two hours later we went into camp near Cartersville. The march upon which we were just entering north of the Etowah, proved a wearisome one. The Confederates had the start of us, were keeping it, and by bold dashes here and there by their cavalry and detached bodies of infantry, kept their plans quite to themselves; so much so, indeed, that when on the 11th we came into the vicinity of Kingston, General Sherman ordered our Corps to remain there until something definite should develop. But before midnight, General Stanley had orders to move at daylight next morning. A strong force of infantry and cavalry was reported as marching upon Resaca, directly in our front, and later it was stated that the place had been captured. This was an error, but it spurred us on just as though it were true. On the 12th, when we heard cannonading off in the direction of Rome, we made up our minds that we should soon have a chance to measure strength again with the enemy, but this was also a mistake. It was only a blind—Hood crossed the river a dozen miles west of Rome, but he did send a force to capture Resaca and Dalton. Our marching much of this time was through the woods and brush, over fields and fences, along ravines and around the hills, with little to break the monotony. Thus the Fourth and Fourteenth Corps pushed steadily on until our Division and Brigade went into camp about noon on the 14th, on the old battle-field north of Resaca. The march had been a very severe one, but not a man fell out by the way, nor flinched from duty.

In the meantime the Confederate army had pushed steadily northward, and had gone into camp in Snake Creek Gap the day before we reached Resaca. Throwing out a strong force, both of infantry and cavalry, they made short work of the little garrison at Dalton. The railroad between this place and Resaca was utterly destroyed. The move was a brave one, though it was of no permanent benefit to the Confederate cause. The force engaged had to run for camp to avoid capture by our troops rapidly arriving. Hood did not attempt to hold the road, nor even the strong passes at Tunnel Hill and Buzzard Roost, in which we had had a most uncomfortable experience on the evening of May 11.

By this time the Confederate whereabouts were better known, and Sherman decided to fall heavily and suddenly upon Hood's army as it lay divided in Snake Creek Gap and west of that, and, if possible, capture that part which occupied the Gap. To this end we were called into line very early on the morning of the 15th. Leaving the old battlefield we moved out in great haste, marching directly westward for a time; then, turning more to the north, we struck the "hill," and were ordered to move directly over into Snake Creek Valley and prevent the escape of the Confederates in that direction. It was an awful "climb." There was practically no road; we could take no wagon, no artillery, not even an ambulance. The mountain was rough—very rough and steep. In time of peace we should have said that it was utterly impassable, but in war nothing is impossible, and we finally got over, but the enemy had fled, and we descended in peace. The Gap was greatly obstructed by fallen trees, rocks, etc., most of which had to be removed before the artillery and trains could be brought forward. General Hood moved his headquarters that day from Villanow to Cross Roads, nine miles south of Lafayette, and our Division went into camp in Snake Creek Valley. Our entire army was near at hand, but had not succeeded in capturing any part of the rebel army, not even in compelling Hood to stop and fight. Soon after noon next day, Oct. 16, we marched a short distance and went into camp in the more open country beyond the Gap.

Sherman was greatly exasperated. He had expected to bring Hood to battle before this time, but that event seemed quite as remote as it did the day we left Atlanta. The Confederate Commander had good reason for not stopping to offer battle. His officers were unanimously opposed to it—not one of them believed it a safe thing to do, for the Confederate rank and file still had the same respect for Yankee push and bullets they had on the Atlanta campaign, and would not stand. Hood says he wanted to fight at or near Lafayette, but was overruled. The entire host was over-anxious to get away from Sherman—Hood therefore decided to move his army still further west, and cross the Tennessee at Florence. Sherman decided not to follow him further. He would reinforce Thomas and let that General look after the Confederate army.

Having thus decided, he made immediate preparations to return to Atlanta with a large portion of his army, when he would organize the long cherished campaign to the sea. Hood was tardy in revealing his intentions, so that it was the 20th before Sherman felt it safe to take definite action. In the meantime, Stanley's Corps had received orders to reduce to the lowest practicable point all baggage, materials and trains. This, we all knew, meant rapid marching, and probably short rations. All surplus material was sent to Chattanooga. The Corps changed camp two or three times, going into quarters on the 20th near Galesburg, where we remained for some days living on the "fat of the land."

We remained in camp near Galesburg until the morning of the 27th. Nothing of especial importance occurred, though the camp was full of all manner of rumors. One of them had it that we were to return at once to Atlanta; another that we were to go to Chattanooga; another that we were to continue to follow wherever Hood might lead; another that our Corps was to go to Nashville and come at

Hood from that side, etc. No great amount of sleep was lost by the boys over these rumors.

At last Hood's movements indicated clearly that it was his intention to cross to the north side of the Tennessee river, and further, that he would make this crossing much further west than Guntersville, which common rumor had fixed as the probable place. This being settled, Sherman at once set about arranging his plans. He would follow Hood no further, but would leave him in the care of Thomas. He himself, with four Corps, would return to Atlanta and prepare for the march to the sea. That Thomas might have an army sufficient to defeat Hood in pitched battle, Stanley's Corps, and, a few days later, the 23d Corps, were sent, mostly by rail, to Athens and Pulaski. It must have set the Confederate Chieftain a-thinking when he learned that Sherman with four great army corps, was deliberately moving back toward Atlanta and the other two corps were going off in a still different direction. Though Hood did not like to be ignored, yet the temper of his forces was such as to make him want to be "let alone." Indeed, if we had "let him alone" at Columbia, Franklin and Nashville, I think he would have been still better satisfied. He tells us he was in doubt what to do, but finally decided to "go north." That other genius, Beauregard, was with him at this time, and probably helped him to come to this brilliant decision. At any rate, he would play his hand out, take Nashville, and then see what to do next.

We had remained idle in camp for a number of days, the entire Corps being in reserve to the 14th and 23rd, but on the evening of the 26th we received orders to march to Alpine next day. The Regiment had been there before, in September, 1863, when Rosecrans was maneuvering for position at Chickamauga. The march to this place next day was uneventful, as was also that of the following day to

CAPT. LYMAN PARCHER.
COMPANY E.
From photograph.

Lafayette. We were to move to Chattanooga and be subject to Thomas. All were in the best of spirits, and confident of final victory. From Chattanooga the Corps was to be transported by rail—which, to the 101st, would be a novel experience. From Lafayette we moved directly toward Chattanooga, passing Gordon's Mills about 1 P.M., and encamped at Rossville about 5 o'clock. The very name of the stream, Chickamauga, which we crossed at the Mills, carried us back to the fall of '63. As we marched across that famous battle-field, memory was busy with the events of those two dreadful September days. The old Vinyard House, in front of which our Division Artillery roared and thundered; on the right of which reinforcements came to our relief, dealing terrible vengeance upon the boys in gray, wild with temporary success, and back of which we rallied more than once; the rolling ground to the right of us, in front of which our lines were first formed, and for the possession of which we fought so long and for which so many of our boys died; the dense woods beyond, into which we drove the strong line of the enemy, and out of which they drove us; the woods to the left of us, in the edge of which we readjusted our lines, and leaped again upon the foe; the ditch just to the left of the road, now almost obliterated, but then filled with dead and wounded; the woods beyond the opening, in which Colonel Heg died while leading his Brigade—these, and a hundred other sights, recalled the events of that bloody day. Not a man in the ranks that had not lost a friend in that great battle. Further to the left were the woods that skirted our position the next morning, and when on that awful Sunday, so many more of our boys went down to death and life-long suffering. A little further on we passed that part of the field which gave to Thomas the sobriquet of Rock of Chickamauga. So busy was memory, that much of the time we marched in silence. Even the camp at Rossville had its dreadful memories. Here, after the battle, we gathered our shattered forces, counted our dead, and cared for our wounded. We were glad next morning to leave the place and march for Chattanooga, going into camp not far from the foot of Lookout. Here again memory was busy. Visions of the day on which we reached this same ground after Chickamauga, came before us, and again we saw the loyal boys in blue busy as nailers intrenching against the foe surging along the crest of Mission Ridge.

To our intense dissatisfaction, we here learned that we were not to be taken by rail to our new field of operations, but that Kirby's Brigade had been detailed to conduct our long and very valuable train over the mountains to Pulaski. This was work that we abhorred, but the 101st always obeyed orders and so did Kirby's Brigade. We started at 2 P. M. next day, October 31st, having in charge a train fully four miles long. Our course lay through Shellmound, Bridgeport, Stevenson, up Crow Creek Valley, and over the mountains to Cowan, and through Winchester to Athens, and thence to Pulaski. The march was made in the quickest time possible, and was wholly without interest or spice, unless rain and mud, and rut, and swollen streams, and mountains, and broken bridges, and braying mules, and swearing drivers, constitute interesting events. But General Kirby delivered the train on time and in good shape, and felt like a free man when, with his command, he found himself again in the front lines.

It was now Saturday, November 12. Thomas had exerted every energy to collect his army and organize for defense. It was not possible to undertake offensive movements, but Stanley and Schofield, with their two Corps, must hold the enemy in check as long as possible, yielding ground only on compulsion. As we filed into camp that afternoon at Pulaski, what was the state of affairs? Briefly, as follows:

General Hood's entire army was at and near Florence, on the Tennessee; one Division of infantry, and a large part of his cavalry, were north of the river, and the remainder of his army was ready to cross. Our cavalry, under General Garrard, had made it exceedingly lively for them, and Hood was in the dark as to what force was actually in front of him. Thomas, at Nashville, was rapidly organizing the new troops, calling in such posts and garrisons as could be spared, and planning to meet every probable move that Hood would make. That Nashville was the rebel objective point, no one doubted. Stanley's and Schofield's Corps were at Pulaski and near by, and so disposed as to watch Hood to the best advantage. General Granger, with a small force, was at Decatur. Our force was not sufficient to prevent a flank movement, which would doubtless be undertaken. Picket and scouting duties here were very severe.

From the 14th to the 22d nothing especial occurred except that we continued to strengthen our position, for we knew that Hood's army was very much stronger than ours, and that we could not hope to beat him in the open field. All had great confidence, however, in Thomas, and believed that he would in some way bring us out all right. Hood was not far away, and was making great efforts to get his army across the Tennessee. Our cavalry force was very small, but was very effective, and gave him much trouble, and kept General Schofield, who was in command at Pulaski, well informed of rebel operations and intentions. It rained almost incessantly while we were at Pulaski, culminating on the 21st in a driving snow storm, followed by bitter cold weather. It froze, but not hard enough to bear up a wagon. As a slight protection, many of our boys constructed shanties or huts, certain houses in the vicinity furnishing the necessary material.

Hood at length succeeded in getting across the river at

Florence, and early on the morning of the 21st, in the midst of the snow storm referred to above, began his march north. Before starting, however, he prepared the following address to his troops:

"SOLDIERS: You march to-day to redeem by your valor and your arms one of the finest portions of our Confederacy. This can only be achieved by battle and by a victory. Summon up in behalf of a consummation so glorious all the elements of soldiership, and all the instincts of manhood, and you will render the campaign before you full of auspicious fruit to your country, and lasting renown to yourselves."

Wet clothing, tenacious mud, driving snow and whistling winds chilled the enthusiasm of the boys in gray, as with chattering teeth they listened to the reading of this address, and sullenly moved forward wading the November mud ankle deep. They encamped that night twelve miles north of Florence, and at 5 o'clock next morning resumed the march.

Knowledge of these movements was at once communicated to General Schofield, and as soon as it was certain that Hood would not turn easterly and attack Pulaski, our army was put in rapid motion, that we might reach Columbia in advance of the Confederate army. The race, though not a rapid one, was full of excitement and hard work. On the 22d our army began the march, one Division being sent forward to Linnville, half way to Columbia, and the remainder of the army put in marching order. The forenoon of the 23d was spent in loading all available railroad cars with provisions and other material to lighten as much as possible our wagon train. At 12:30 Kimball's Division in advance moved out, going into camp at 11 P. M. just south of Linnville. The roads were simply dreadful—in time of peace they would have been considered utterly impassable. The poor animals, under lash and oath, dragged the heavy artillery and ponderous army wagons through mud which, in places, was more than hub deep. We in the ranks picked our way as best we could, but kept well together. The line of gray a few miles to the west of us on the Mt. Pleasant road was doing precisely the same thing. Thus on and on, hour after hour, the rain falling incessantly, the roads becoming worse continually. But Yankee pluck won the day, and we went into line in front of Columbia before the Confederates could reach the place. The 23d Corps on the right, Stanley's on the left, our Division on the extreme left. We immediately began to intrench.

CHAPTER XXV.

FROM COLUMBIA TO FRANKLIN.

General Hood, with his entire army, had made a brave and vigorous effort to reach the line of Duck River at Columbia in advance of the National army, but he had failed, and our line of retreat upon Nashville was still open. It was expected that the Confederate General would at once offer battle, and as our army was then situated, Schofield would have been compelled to fight, even at great odds, for the bridges and their approaches on both sides were in such condition that not even our train could cross, much less our army, in the face of an active enemy. But Hood contented himself with skirmishing along our entire front, but did not attack in force. The situation did not warrant this comparative quiet, and our leaders at once came to the conclusion that plans for a flank movement were being devised by Hood. Even we in the ranks were not a little surprised at the tameness of the struggle, though we were by no means anxious to see the oncoming Confederate lines, which we hourly expected.

Our cavalry was constantly on the alert, and soon

SPRING HILL.

brought word that the enemy were preparing to cross the river some miles east of us. So probable was this report that on the evening of the 27th the entire Union army was withdrawn to the north side of the river, to be in readiness to prevent the success of such a movement, and to continue our retreat if necessary. Stanley's Corps was placed in position some distance back of the town, while the Twenty-third Corps, under Cox, was stationed near the river to guard the bridges. The enemy soon followed to the river, and the skirmish contest continued with the stream between the opposing lines. The fight waxed very warm at different times, artillery being freely used on both sides, but at no time did the conflict rise to the dignity and stateliness of battle. Thus through the 28th. Early on the morning of the 29th reliable information was received that Hood was crossing the river in force at Huey's Mills, about eight miles east of Columbia, on the main road to Spring Hill; that his cavalry was already over and a full corps of infantry (Cheatham's) would immediately follow; that the head of the column would reach Spring Hill about noon, thus cutting off our line of retreat to Franklin. The situation was becoming very grave. The Confederate plan was to fall heavily and very suddenly upon our communications at Spring Hill, gain our rear, and crush our little army by the sheer force of numbers. To accomplish this, General Cheatham advanced in very strong force, followed by a large part of Stewart's Corps, the whole being preceded by a cloud of cavalry that completely hid the infantry columns. Hood, Forrest, Cheatham and others were on the ground to urge the greatest promptness of action and celerity of movement. It was the opportunity of Hood's life, and he resolved to rise in his might and crush utterly the fragment of the National army that had dared to interpose itself between him and his Northern goal.

Without drum or bugle, or ostentation of any kind; with long, steady strides well sustained; with victory, and glory, and immortal renown in plain sight, as they thought, the boys in butternut and gray gave their whole attention to the work before them. At noon on the 29th this magnificent force was in the vicinity of Spring Hill. The cavalry, in strong force, was forming for assault, and to all appearances, the town, the little force defending it, and our line of retreat to Franklin and Nashville, were at the mercy of the foe.

But at 8 o'clock that same morning, General Stanley had taken two of his Divisions, Wagner's and Kimball's, and started in hot haste, bound also for Spring Hill, though he was not informed as to the force of the enemy against which he would have to operate. We, too, got down to our very best long-distance gait, and without waiting for drum or bugle, or any other accessories, led out toward the point of greatest danger, determined to reach Spring Hill first. Seven miles out from Columbia we crossed Rutherford Creek, and learning here that a strong force of the enemy was marching upon this point, our Division was halted to defend the place against anything and everything in gray or butternut that might come that way, while Stanley, with the other Division, marched rapidly on. Our lines were quickly established east of the pike, pickets were thrown well out, and our position strongly barricaded. Here we remained during the rest of the day, practically inactive. Back of us, at Columbia, we could hear the familiar boom of cannon, and to the left of us, at Spring Hill, from noon on, borne on the heavy air came the sullen groan of distant artillery. The situation was grave and very dangerous. But here, as on one or two other occasions, the very insolence of our movements brought success out of threatened disaster. To General Stanley and the brave boys with him, is due great credit for the work done that afternoon in saving our line of retreat and the vast wagon train upon it. He reached Spring Hill just in time to bring to nought Forrest's assault upon the place. So admirably did he handle his little force, so splendidly did he post his artillery, and so quickly did he transfer this brigade and that regiment, that he fully convinced the Confederate leaders that not only was a very large part of Schofield's army present, but that in some way Thomas had sent reinforcements from Nashville. The uneven contest lasted till night, and when the Confederate army went into camp, they did not dare advance their lines so as even to cover the pike, much less to occupy it, believing, as stated above, that a large part of the National Army was in their front. The whole thing seems like a piece of fiction.

The day seemed endlessly long as we lay at Rutherford Creek. The distant thump of cannon to the right and left of us; the anxious looks and nervous movements of our Brigade and Division Commanders; the mysterious woods and the silent hills in front of us; our own knowledge of the actual state of affairs, all conspired to give to the time and place a sense of oppression which my pen is utterly inadequate to describe. We seemed to be standing at the very mouth of a volcano; its deep rumblings could be heard on all sides; the dread eruption must soon come, but hour by hour, moment by moment, the fatal explosion was delayed. Thus the day wore away, and thus darkness found us.

By this time the Confederate plans were completely uncovered, and orders were at once issued by General Schofield for the withdrawal of our entire army, as soon as it was dark enough to conceal the movements. Stanley was to hold his ground at Spring Hill; Cox, with the 23d Corps, was to withdraw first from Columbia, followed by General Wood's Division of our own Corps, and as these forces passed, our Division fell in the rear, the entire command marching left in front, ready to form for action at a moment's warning. Rapidly, silently, the National army pushed on in its flight, our flag fluttering even in the leaden darkness of that November night. The sensations of the hour were peculiar; to our continual surprise we were permitted to move on, and on, and on. As we neared Spring Hill, the Confederate camp fires seemed to be on the pike itself, but as we came nearer the space became wider, and a way of escape was opened, narrow and dangerous, to be sure, but possible. As we came still nearer we were hushed into dead silence, we were passing the front of our powerful enemy, almost within range of his infantry lines—asleep surely, now, but dreaming of the easy victory awaiting them in the morning. Stealthily, rapidly we moved on, expecting momentarily that the crash of battle would end our good fortune, and that we would be plunged into the midst of the indescribable horrors of a battle in the dark. Some of our officers were actually accosted by Confederate officers with "Who goes there?" "What command," and the like, to which evasive replies, born of the awful necessities of the hour, were given, and we moved on, nor stopped until we were in position at Spring Hill, between the enemy and our homes. How thankful we felt! It was more than we could understand, more than I can understand to this day, except as we recognize the hand of a good Providence. The thankfulness of some found expression in words more or less profane; others in abuse of "Old Hood;" others with broader views, ascribed to God the praise. One brave fellow said, "Well, boys, there's some hard work ahead of us, or the good Lord wouldn't have got us out of this." And he was right.

It was just after midnight, but we had accomplished wonders. Huddled together in some confusion, but wonderfully clear under all the circumstances, it was necessary that our whole army should at once flee, but the slumbering giant awoke and again put us in peril. General Cox's Corps was moved out and put upon its best gait for Franklin, with orders to take position and guard the bridges over the Harpeth for the crossing of the train and the remainder of the army as it came up. This force was followed by the train with suitable guards, and back of the train, Stanley. Our cavalry was on our right as we fell back. Like a great dragon our immense train, enveloped in the mysterious darkness of that eventful night, urged its way with whip and lash and spur toward greater safety. Did a mule so much as attempt to lift up his voice in protest, the stinging "snake" cut short his story. Thus on and on with discouraged flop of ear, neglected wag of tail, except in recognition of the lash; with back so straight it bent decidedly upward; with rattling chains, and clucking wheels, and vicious tramp, and thoughts we knew not of, our good but awfully tried friend, the mule, brought the unwilling train back to the banks of the Harpeth, and there breathed and brayed until the bridges were repaired.

But we were not to go in peace. About 2 o'clock in the morning the Confederate cavalry assaulted our train, destroyed several wagons, and threatened serious disaster. General Kirby was immediately called upon to disperse them—"Clear the road and keep it clear." The Brigade was off in a moment, headed by our own good Regiment. Short work was made of the troopers, and the whole command again moved on. Thus the night wore away, morning dawned, the hours fled, but not till afternoon did we reach the little town in the suburbs of which within three hours would fall the shock of fiercest battle.

CHAPTER XXVI.

THE BATTLE OF FRANKLIN.

Great was the disappointment and bitter were the recriminations among the Confederate Commanders next morning, November 30th, when it was learned that the little army which they were that day to crush and destroy, had escaped unhurt. General Hood laid the chief blame on Cheatham, but included Cleburne and several others. The fault was his own. He was on the field and was responsible. The fact is, he had lost his head the day before, the 29th, and had missed the golden opportunity of his life. One of his impetuous charges made on our nervous columns as we passed under the very muzzles of his guns, would surely have broken our lines and scattered our forces. But, thanks be to God, the assault was not made, and we escaped.

These recriminations were not loud, but they were exceeding bitter, and very deep. That Hood was angry and stubborn was shown in every act and word. His sullen and haughty air served only to intensify the bitterness that rankled in the bosom of his corps commanders, who had felt the sting of his rebuke. Nevertheless, his word was law, and the Confederate hosts were soon in motion, the spirit animating the leaders boding no good to the Union army, with which, before the set of sun, they were to engage. As Cheatham, Cleburne, Brown and others rode along that day, they nursed their wrath and resolved to wreak vengeance on the loyal boys in blue, whose marvellous escape the night before had been the immediate cause of their injured pride.

It had not been the intention either of Thomas or of Schofield to accept battle at Franklin unless compelled to do so by circumstances which they could not control. It was

LIEUTENANT W. R. DAVIS,
COMPANY E.
From photograph taken in 1894.

necessary, however, to delay Hood as long as possible at the crossing of the Harpeth, in order to gain time to complete the organization of Thomas's army at Nashville. Troops were rapidly arriving in the latter city, the defenses were being greatly strengthened, and every effort was being put forth to be ready at the earliest possible moment for the Confederate assault, which, like the coming of a great storm, could be clearly discovered in the distance. The fragment of an army under Schofield could not hope long to delay the attack of the enemy. When the head of our army reached Franklin, just before daylight on the 30th, it was discovered that the bridges were in such condition that neither trains nor artillery could cross, a discovery that would, under all the circumstances, paralyze the arm of any but the most desperately determined commander. It made it necessary to accept battle right there, with all the odds against us, unless the bridges could be repaired in time to withdraw before the enemy should assault, which was by no means probable. The pioneers at once began the reconstruction of the bridges, and by noon had a crossing prepared.

The hours of that eventful November day were full of intense interest. All the morning long, as the troops arrived, they were assigned their position in the line of battle and ordered to intrench. Picks and spades and shovels were used to excellent advantage, and soon the entire front of the Twenty-third Corps, extending from the river east of the town to the Carter's Creek road, was strongly intrenched. In the meantime our great wagon train rolled in through an opening left for the purpose in the line, and awaited the completion of the bridges. The head of Stanley's Corps arrived shortly after 11 o'clock, but our Division and Brigade did not get in till full 12 o'clock.

It was soon found that the Twenty-third Corps could not defend the entire front. Kimball's Division was therefore ordered into line on the right, our front extending from the Carter's Creek road to the river. General Wood's Division was sent to the north side of the river to act as emergency might require, and General Wagner's Division being in the rear, was halted a half mile out on the pike, Opdyke's Brigade only being brought within the lines and stationed as a reserve force near the Columbia pike. Whitaker's Brigade was on the extreme right of our line, and Kirby's next on his left. The space allotted us did not give room for all in the main line. Our Regiment and the Eighty-first Indiana, having seen the severest service during the night and on the entire march from Columbia, were placed in reserve—a novel experience for the 101st when a fight was on. Stacking their arms, the boys soon had their front lines well intrenched, after which, completely overcome with sleep, they lay around as best they could, awaiting the bursting of the storm, which was gathering in the hills just south of the town.

It was 3 o'clock in the afternoon. Our lines had been fully established; our intrenchments were completed; the musket and sword had again been substituted for the pick and shovel; half a mile out in our front, astride the Columbia pike, two Brigades of Wagner's Division were posted to observe the enemy's movements and to check his cavalry and skirmishers, and everywhere from left to right, from river above to river below the town, our grand old Flag, never more beautiful, waved and flaunted defiance at the foe, while beneath its inspiring folds loyal boys in blue stood ready to meet the enemy, nor feared the terrible odds against them. Back of us the bridges were practically clear; our trains were rapidly rolling toward Nashville; Wood's Division was over the river, and so posted as to meet promptly any emergency; the artillery of the 23d Corps was in position north of the river, part on the heights and part in Fort Granger, ready to rake the enemy front and flank—in short, the National army was ready and waiting, though we were under orders to withdraw as soon as darkness would permit, if by that time Hood should not attack.

At 3:30 o'clock a messenger from the front brought word that the enemy were forming for the assault, and a few minutes later their columns emerged from the woods and came into full view. Instantly our lines became as iron. Every man looked again to his arms and settled himself for desperate work. Batteries were shotted and cannoneers stood to their guns. Officers urged their men to deliberate and deadly aim. Should an armed enemy by any chance get within our lines, he was to be doomed to instant death. Hood would doubtless hurl column after column upon us, but we were to repel them every one with merciless slaughter. But our boys needed no special urging, for everywhere along that loyal line each man in blue seemed to have resolved to vie with the bravest of his comrades in deeds of heroic daring. Wagner's two Brigades, Lane's and Conrad's, were again ordered to fall back upon the approach of the Confederate main line, and under no circumstances were they to attempt to hold the position except against cavalry and skirmishers.

From the position of our Regiment on the extreme right we could not see the advancing column of the enemy, and yet we were fully conscious of the impending conflict. Our Brigade skirmishers were thrown well out; our position was carefully barricaded; our batteries well posted, and here, as elsewhere, the very air seemed full of battle. Silence, deep and oppressive, similar to that which precedes the resistless hurricane, fell over all the field. In such a moment the mind turns naturally to other days and other scenes. It is no reflection upon the courage and patriotism of any boy in blue that, under such circumstances, he should think of home and the dear ones gathered there; that he should once more open the locket and gaze again upon the face of the one dearest on earth to him, nor yet that a great tear should roll down his sunbrowned cheek as the memories of by-gone days swept past.

But there was little time for such reflection. The Confederate columns were already moving upon us, in two lines everywhere and in three along the Columbia pike, with cavalry on the flanks, useless now, but ready to turn confusion into panic and disaster, should our lines break, with flags waving, banners flying and bayonets gleaming. As that splendid line of brown and gray drew momentarily nearer and nearer, a slight rustle ran through our ranks, for we comprehended more and more fully the awful storm of lead and iron and glittering steel about to burst upon us. A few of our boys were strengthening their works, but for the most part our men seemed satisfied with our defenses, and long before the rebels had come within range, had leveled their guns, measured their distance, and determined their fire. It is strange, passing strange, even to this day, that under such circumstances, with the enemy in full view, coming on at a rapid pace with arms trailed, ready on the instant to halt and deliver their fire, even while the Confederate artillery was wheeling into position to open on our outposts, our boys found time and inclination to joke and be merry. But so it was, and so it had been on other fields, and doubtless so it was in the magnificent columns rushing upon us. Never before had we been able to see so much of the field of conflict—never before had the advancing foe been so long in sight. Our line extended in a crude semi-circle from the railroad and river above to the river below the town, along the crest of a slight rise of ground sloping gently to the hills and woods in which the enemy had just formed. The extreme left of our line was held by General Stiles, then Casement, then Reilly, to the Columbia pike; then Strickland and Moore to the Carter's Creek pike, then Kimball's Division to the river.

The oppressive silence, which for some time seemed to have fallen over all the field, was suddenly broken by a volley from the battery with Wagner's men out on the Columbia pike. To this the Confederates seemed to give no heed, except to increase their pace. A moment later their guns were again empty. By this time the Confederates were within range. Wagner's men delivered their first fire, without so much as checking the rebel host. Again Wagner's front blazed; this time staggering the front of the Confederate triple line, but eliciting no response. At this moment a rebel battery galloped forward to open on Wagner's battery, which, according to orders, trotted leisurely to the rear, and a little later was doing heroic service on our main line. To the surprise and consternation of the Federal commander, Wagner's men showed no signs of falling back, though orders to that effect had twice been repeated; but, on the contrary, they were evidently preparing to resist the main Confederate column, now wholly uncovered and advancing in magnificent style. Halting only one moment, the rebel fringe of glittering steel came down to a charge, and our little force astride the pike was doomed to utter rout. The failure to fall back as ordered was fatal. The slight halt to form for charge, had allowed the rebels to pass both flanks of the Union outposts, so that when the charge came a scene of indescribable confusion followed. Rushing out of their works in mad panic, Wagner's men made their way as best they could toward our main lines, distant nearly half a mile. The Confederate charging column was now ablaze. The artillery on the left of the Union line sent shot and shell into the ranks of the brown and gray on that front. But the batteries on the right and left of the Columbia pike, the very key to the whole position, were necessarily silent. The confused mass of friend and foe came surging along the pike, the Confederates yelling, firing, smiting, as they crowded on the very heels of our fleeing comrades. The track of this dreadful storm, this epic of death, was marked from beginning to end with the bodies of Union dead and wounded. It was a scene to which the boys in the National army were utter strangers, nothing in all their experience affording a parallel. They were fairly palsied, not on account of the destruction of Wagner's men, which was, indeed, terrible, but with loaded muskets, fixed bayonets and cannon double shotted, they were helpless to render assistance on account of the presence of Wagner's men in the immediate front of the charging enemy. As the yelling, struggling mass drew nearer and nearer, the intensity of the situation became almost unbearable, and taken in connection with the tumult of battle, now in full roar on both flanks, the scene beggars all description. Nearing our position, the Confederates naturally halted a moment to adjust their lines for the supreme effort of the hour. Madly the fugitive boys climbed and clambered over our works, followed closely by the rebel line now on them again, and following so closely as to carry everything before them. Our main line gave way, on both sides of the Columbia pike, for the distance of more than two regimental fronts, and the victorious enemy forced themselves nearly one hundred yards within our works before they were brought to a halt. The disaster seemed appalling. Our lines were cut in two—crushed at the Columbia pike, involving Reilly's right and Strickland's left. Unless the break could be promptly restored, our forces would be doubled back by superior numbers and the disaster made permanent.

It was at the moment of this terrible crash, this giving way of our lines, that our good Regiment, though battered and hammered and scorched in half a hundred battles, was ordered from the right to the Center to aid in restoring our lost position. Promptly and with great enthusiasm the boys responded to this new and terrible test of their courage and loyalty. Moving at first at a quick step, then at a double quick, we soon reached the field of disaster. Our feelings on nearing the scene of tumultuous battle cannot be described, nor can they be appreciated by any except those who have been similarly situated. The almost unbroken roar of musketry along our entire front; the hideous yells of the infuriated Confederates as column after column charged; the equally unearthly yells of Opdycke's men as they rushed upon the exultant enemy within our lines near the Carter house; the almost incessant crash of artillery from left to right; the shrieking of shot, the bursting of shell, the whiz and bing and sickening thud of the minie; the wounded making their way to the rear, and the indescribable din of general battle—all had a direct tendency to lessen enthusiasm, dampen ardor, and check the spirit of assault. Not so on this occasion.

How strange it seems, after the lapse of thirty years, to look back upon these awful scenes. Strange beyond comprehension that men would deliberately, aye, enthusiastically, plunge headlong into the very thickest of the fight, where with sword and musket, and club and bayonet, each took savage delight in slaying his antagonist. Courage, manhood, patriotism, duty and loyalty, all were concentrated in the strong right arm, and, consumed with the intense excitement of the moment, the desire to wreak vengeance in merciless slaughter took such entire control of every man as to dull the sense of fear, banish the presence of danger, and stir the heart to deeds of heroic daring.

Reaching the field of carnage almost at the very moment that Opdycke's men rushed to the rescue, we formed near the right of that redoubtable Brigade, and, fixing bayonets, plunged into the thickest of the fray. Our first volley was delivered at close range and was terribly fatal in its results, but not a few of our own boys went down under the galling return fire of the enemy. Then the bayonet! No pen of mine can describe the scene that followed. With a wild yell that rings in our ears to this day, we rushed upon the enemy who met us in countercharge, and for a time the scale of victory seemed to hang in even balance. We made many captures, and hurried them to the rear, but their places seemed to be taken by others, and the fight went furiously on. During a slight lull in the conflict, our lines were readjusted, and again, with Opdycke and others, we charged the enemy, smote them hip and thigh, and cast them out, just as a fresh Confederate column came charging upon our front, meeting us at our breastworks. The struggle for the possession of this barricade was exceedingly fierce, but most fortunately for us, many of the troops that at the first terrible onset had been carried back to the rear, now came to our assistance, and we soon compelled the Confederates to seek shelter in the ditch at the foot of our works. Our line, with the accessions referred to, was four deep. Those in the rear loaded their guns and passed them forward to the front line, and thus we were able to keep up a very rapid and accurate fire. Several of the boys, prominent among them Lieutenant W. R. Davis, formerly of Company E, but then commanding Company K, secured positions covering the crouching lines of brown and gray, and did most effective work. Thus the fight continued with us till night. Elsewhere along the line the struggle seemed to be exceedingly fierce. Opdycke had restored the line on our left and bravely held it, though most viciously assailed time and again. Still further toward our left, brave Jack Casement had fairly piled his front full of rebel dead, and on our right, with equal bravery, General Sherwood held to his position with a tenacity that baffled every effort of the desperate foe to force him back. Not an inch did the brave boys of the 111th Ohio yield. Like a great stone wall they held the left of Rugers' unbroken line. Further to the right and near the Carter's Creek road, the Confederates hurled one column after another upon the Federal lines, only to be broken and rolled back in merciless slaughter. Still further to the right, Kimball's guns were in full roar, and everywhere the mighty contest raged. Our lines blazed from river to river; the artillery at the front, supplemented by that on the heights and in Fort Wagner, poured shot and shell and grape and canister into the struggling Confederate masses which, despite the awful slaughter, kept up the mad assault. A Federal battery wheeled into position east of the river, and, having an enfilading fire, plowed great furrows in the ranks of the enemy. But, nothing daunted, they renewed the struggle at every point. Thus till night—till long after dark, when repulsed everywhere, with not a vestige of victory which they could claim, Hood's great army lapsed into dogged silence, beaten, broken, bleeding and disappointed.

Scarcely a breath of air stirred during the contest, and a peculiar state of the atmosphere caused the smoke of the battle, which grew more and more dense as the conflict progressed, to settle over all the field, so that long before night it was almost impossible to distinguish friend from foe at any considerable distance. But beneath this great sulphurous canopy the battle raged and roared incessantly.

But darkness, deep and mysterious, covered the field. In our own front, at least three separate squads of rebel soldiers sought to deliver themselves into our hands during the evening. But they had guns in their hands and we opened on them at sight. "For God's sake, don't fire, don't fire; we want to surrender," but many had already fallen.

CAPT. LEN. D. SMITH,
COMPANY C.
From photograph taken in 1882.

"Throw down your guns!" cried Lieutenant Davis, but though this was complied with, he feared trickery and covered the squad with muskets at an aim until they were prisoners within our lines. To Comrade Knott Crockett and a guard they were committed to be taken to headquarters. In due time Crockett returned, and soon another squad of rebels sought to come to us. Again our muskets blazed, and more than half the twenty-five fell; the remainder, throwing away their guns, reached our lines and were conducted by Crockett to headquarters. Within an hour, still another squad made the same attempt and met with the same fortune. It was on his return from delivering this third detachment that the brave Crockett fell.

At length, about 10 o'clock, the field became quiet, and General Schofield ordered the immediate withdrawal of our army to the north side of the Harpeth. The 101st was at once withdrawn from the front line and returned to its place in the Brigade. An accidental fire in the town made it so light that the order to withdraw had to be delayed until it could be extinguished, so that not till 12 o'clock, midnight, did our troops begin to cross. A strong picket line was left in our front, both to deceive the enemy and to give the alarm should they attempt to assault, while the remainder of the army hurriedly and as quickly as possible crossed the river and at once took up the line of march for Nashville, whither our trains had gone, some hours before, under a strong cavalry escort. Our own Division (Kimball's) should have been the first to cross according to orders, but other troops moving too early, blocked the way so that we were the last to leave the field. While waiting our chance to cross, word was brought General Kirby that the picket line left in our Brigade front had by some mistake been withdrawn. He at once took a small force, went again to the front, re-established the line and returned in time to cross with the Division. Our pickets were safely withdrawn later and our entire army was on the wing for Nashville.

Some time before daylight the Confederates discovered that our works in front of them were empty, and soon the news seemed to have spread throughout the town. The people came out from their hiding places, and with torch and lantern began to search the field. They were joined by hundreds of the boys in gray, who sought to learn the fate of missing comrades. The sight from the north bank of the river is said to have been very beautiful and touching. A thousand lights moving here and there over that silent field, among the dead and wounded, now halting to identify an upturned face; now ministering to the wants of the wounded, now bearing off a friend for better treatment, now grouping around some object of special interest, but soon scattering to continue the search. All this in the grim darkness and dead silence of the night made an impression on the beholders that can never be removed. The withdrawal of our army was necessarily sudden, and so hurried that we could not bring off our dead and badly wounded, though our splendid ambulance corps did most excellent service, removing all the wounded that could bear transportation.

Our march to Nashville was orderly and regular, but hurried. It was generally believed that Hood had been so severely handled that he would make no serious attempt to cut us off. Indeed, his army was in no shape to take the offensive for some days, though at daylight his lines were formed, and a forward movement was ordered.

Arriving at Nashville about 9 A.M., more dead than alive, having had neither rest nor sleep for more than two days and two nights, with a battle thrown in, we were deployed in line and allowed to rest, a privilege we all embraced with alacrity. How sweet, how refreshing was sleep even on the cold, wet ground that raw December day!

CHAPTER XXVII.

THE BATTLE OF NASHVILLE.

Next morning, December 2nd, we were assigned our regular position in line, and in the evening, the enemy having made their appearance, we were ordered to intrench. This we accomplished in time to get some sleep before morning. The line held by our Corps was about one and a half miles south of the city, the left, our Division, resting across the Granny White pike and extending westward until it joined General A. J. Smith's lines.

Daylight revealed the fact that the enemy had made a decided advance during the night, and that they were strongly intrenched in front of our Corps on a ridge parallel with the one we occupied. Skirmishers were well out on both sides, and again the old rattle and bang, so familiar on the Atlanta Campaign, greeted our ears. Our artillery at once opened in fine style, but were not able to provoke a response for three days, and then only two or three pieces replied. They were short of ammunition. The enemy made no attempt to assault us or otherwise molest us, and we soon grew to regard their presence with indifference, and yet we often cast our eyes southward, and wondered when and what next. On the 8th the enemy extended their lines further toward our left, thus securing and holding the hills which cost us so dear a few days later. Hood was stubbornly quiet, but he was doing some good work in the way of intrenching. Rumors were current in camp on the 8th to the effect that our Corps would assault within a day or two—as soon as the troops could be got into position to defend the whole line, if our advance should result in general battle. About 2 o'clock the same day, the 8th, the Confederates pushed their picket lines forward with heavy supports, and forced our skirmish line back a short distance on our Division front, extending also some distance along the front of the Twenty-third Corps. General Kimball soon sent a force forward and restored the line to its old position. Later in the evening word was received that a general assault would be made on the 10th. But this was not to be. On the 9th a severe storm of sleet and snow and rain, set in, soon covering the whole face of the country with a glare of hard, slippery ice. This made it necessary to recall the order to assault on the morning of the 10th. The storm and excessive cold weather continued for three days, the men of both armies suffering severely. The morning of the 14th found the weather much modified, the ice mostly gone, but the ground very muddy, and the air so densely foggy that the rebel works could not be seen. At 3 o'clock in the afternoon a council of Corps Commanders met with General Thomas and decided to attack early next morning, if the weather would permit.

While all this was transpiring, another play, hidden from public view, was being enacted. The effort was being made by the authorities at Washington, and also by General Grant, to compel General Thomas to move upon the enemy regardless of the impassable condition of the whole face of the country. There was ice everywhere, hard, slippery, glaring ice, upon which neither man nor beast could stand with any assurance, much less move with any certainty. To attempt to move under such circumstances would have been the height of folly and absurdity, and yet Thomas had received positive orders to do so—but he refused. He was threatened with dismissal if he did not obey, but he still refused, and finally Gen. John A. Logan was sent to Nashville with instructions to relieve General Thomas unless on his arrival he should find the army in motion. Of this last measure General Thomas knew nothing for a long time, General Logan wisely saying nothing about it when he came to understand the circumstances. But the assault was in progress when he reached Nashville.

The afternoon of the 14th was a busy time for Army, Corps and Division Commanders. The details of the great battle were being arranged as far as such uncertain things can be arranged; troops were being assigned to positions, definite instructions were being prepared for this and that Corps and Division, ammunition was being distributed, rations prepared, and, equally important, the strength of the enemy was carefully considered, the weak places in his lines discussed, his probable mode of defense, and his next point of rally after being driven off, and a thousand and one other things now wholly lost to the memory of a man who has not seen an army for thirty years. Everything was taken into account, and 6 o'clock on the morning of the 15th set for the hour of attack. In the assault to be made no thought was given to the idea of failure—we were to succeed, no matter what the opposition, no matter what the odds. The National army was to go forward, and forward only—the enemies of the Flag were to be crushed; Hood's army was to be annihilated. This was the inspiration, this the purpose.

Skirmishing had been especially heavy all day of the 14th, and now and then the deep toned artillery gave tongue to its wrath. The belief seemed quite general that another crisis had been reached, and that a battle was likely to occur at any moment. When the order came to be ready to move at daylight next morning, we boys in the ranks put our affairs in order, prepared our rations, examined our arms and sat down to write to the dear folks at home, after which we turned in for a sound sleep before entering upon the dangers of a day of battle. Of course, we were not posted as to the details—we simply knew that we were to be ready to move at daylight, and anybody could guess the rest.

Reveille sounded at 4 o'clock next morning, the 15th, and at once our great army was astir. A hasty breakfast was prepared, and at daylight we were ready for the work of the day. A heavy fog hung over the field, making it quite impossible to form the line for assault, but we soon moved out toward our position, and about 9 o'clock were in position ready to attack. The troops on our right had a much longer march to make, a long swing of their extreme flank before they could strike the enemy's left, and they were hindered by several Confederate outposts, all of which, however, fell into Union hands. To enable our Cavalry to gain the Confederate left-rear, General Schofield was transferred to the right and ordered to move into position beyond Smith. At length our Center and Right were close up to the enemy, and our lines were on the point of moving to the attack. In the meantime, General Steedman had moved out before 6 o'clock under cover of the fog, and had fallen so heavily upon Hood's right that the Confederate general began to look for serious trouble on that flank. Steedman played his part splendidly and held on like grim death. While Hood was looking for a general assault on his right, our lines were coming into shape on his left, as faintly outlined above. But the Confederate Commander soon discovered his mistake, and at once made dispositions to meet our Center and Right. By this time the fog had lifted and the day was clear. From our front the enemy could be clearly seen in their works; they were evidently expecting us. Beatty's Division on our left was the first to be ordered forward. Post's Brigade of that Division charged Montgomery Hill, strongly held by the enemy and gallantly carried it, the Confederates falling back in some confusion to their main line. This was 1 o'clock in the afternoon. Far to our

THE BATTLE OF NASHVILLE.
"Kirby, Take that Hill."—Kimball.

right there seemed to be heavy fighting, judging from the frequent discharge of artillery in that direction. The lines were also tightening along the Confederate center and left. Three redouts had already been captured and two strong outposts had been driven in. A Confederate battery in our front on a ridge strongly held by the enemy, was pouring shot and shell into our lines, and General Elliott was twice ordered to take the hill, but he preferred to await the further advance of General Smith on his right, before venturing to assault. The situation, however, soon became very serious, and General Kimball was ordered to make the attack. Acting upon the instant, he ordered Kirby's Brigade to charge the position. "Take that hill, Kirby!" he said. "I'll do it!" was the laconic reply of our brave Commander, as he saluted. We were already in line, and waiting only to fix bayonets, moved briskly forward, then charged impetuously. After a severe struggle the hill was carried, the enemy driven, and our main line in this quarter advanced. With the loss of Montgomery Hill, and the eminence just referred to, the Confederates abandoned their advanced position and fell back on their main line, the northwest angle of which was a short distance in our front. This part of the Confederate line was considered by them to be exceedingly strong. It was protected not only by a heavy stone wall along the Hillsboro' pike, but also by three redouts, strongly constructed and commanding the approaches from the west, the north, and the northwest. These works were defended by the men of Stewart's command, who had been ordered on no account to yield the position.

No sooner had Kirby succeeded in gaining the hill last referred to than were we subjected to a terrible fire from this same main line. The practiced eye of our Commander at once detected a safer position a short distance further to the front, and immediately the command was moved forward. This brought us under the shelter of a sunken road, and afforded great advantage.

Meanwhile, the troops on the extreme right had been crowding the Confederates at every point—had wrested from them one or two detached redouts, and had compelled them to abandon a portion of their main line. Almost at the same instant that Kirby moved forward to the sunken road, the battle along Smith's front took on tremendous proportions, resulting in the capture of a portion of the stone wall near its southern extremity. Taking advantage of this great gain, the Union line formed at once to roll the Confederates back toward the angle in the greatest possible confusion. The crisis on this part of the field had arrived; the moment for supreme effort was at hand. With a wild rush and a yell Kimball's men charged impetuously up the hill in their front, striking the enemy at the angle on the Hillsboro pike, and for some distance to the left of it, and at the same moment Smith's men assailed them from the break further south, the two forces carrying terror and dismay to the hearts of rebel defenders of that strong line. Smith made headway and gained the rear of the stone wall, threatening a portion of this line with capture. Kimball assaulted point blank in front, and with such viciousness as soon to break over their works. The battery in their northern redout attempted to enfilade our lines as we charged, but we at once came so close to the rebel works that their firing of necessity ceased. Widening the breach and pouring within their works, Kirby and others took the Confederate host in reverse, spreading disaster and confusion on every hand. Their batteries were powerless; portions of their line were in panic; there was safety only in flight, and to this they at once resorted, leaving us in complete possession of their works, including the four-gun battery stationed in the redout referred to and many small arms. How we cheered and yelled and sent showers of lead after the retreating foe. Our part in the day's great battle had been most important, for we, with others, had completely broken the Confederate center, and rolled their lines back right and left.

The main body of the Confederates fell back toward their right, and soon became sullen and stubborn. Orders were at once issued for our Corps to press forward toward the Franklin pike, and, if possible, to form across it, facing south. But darkness prevented this, and our line was formed some distance west of that pike and parallel with it, the Confederates holding the road in strong force. Here we slept, resting on our arms. The night was an uncomfortable one, on account of the rawness of the weather and the wet, muddy condition of the ground. Fires were not allowed, and we nibbled dry hard-tack and cold bacon. The successes of the day augured well for the morrow. We thought if Hood could not hold the positions he had deliberly chosen, there was little doubt but that we could route him next day from the positions we had compelled him to take. During the night, however, he made good use of his time. Spades were again trump, and every boy in gray did his best to render his position as nearly invulnerable as possible. Along the crest of Overton's Hill on his right, and of what is since known as Shy's Hill on his left, Hood constructed very strong defensive works, and connected them with an intrenched line well chosen and easy of defense. In front of this he had also established a strong advanced line, also intrenched, into which he threw a fresh force from his right. His line was much shorter than it had been and gave some promise that it might be defended successfully. All this kept the Confederate army busy most of the night.

With the earliest dawn we were in line, tired and sleepy, to be sure, but awake to the demands and exactions of another day of battle. The enemy were soon discovered to be in considerable force in our front, near the Franklin pike, toward which, driving their stubborn skirmishers before us, we steadily advanced, until about 8 o'clock, when, by a determined charge, we forced their position, and sent them on the run down the pike, southward. In thus advancing, our Division took everything clean, leaving nothing to be guarded or strengthened. At first it was thought that Hood had fallen back into the Brentwood Hills, and that he would then offer battle again. Turning to the southward, our Division moved cautiously down the Franklin pike, and coming close up to the Confederate position, we went into line, our Division in reserve. We, some of us at least, thought that we might be able to see a part of this fight without having to take an active part. But in this we were greatly mistaken. A reconnoissance revealed the enemy present in full force, ready to stake the issues of the campaign on the result. General Smith, on our extreme right, had been able to make progress very slowly—Shy's Hill, and the approaches to it had offered very strong opposition, so that, not arriving in our vicinity at the time expected, there was a break of nearly half a mile on the right of our line. Into this Kimball's Division was promptly thrown, and our dream of simply witnessing the battle went glimmering. We forced ourselves close up to the enemy, who was strongly intrenched. Off to the right—indeed, away round to the rear of the enemy's left, the tell-tale artillery reported something of the progress of the battle in that quarter, and as it grew in violence and came nearer, we felt sure that we were bound to win. At the same time, the heavy discharges of artillery on our left, both from our own guns, and the crashing response of the Confederate guns from the hills and ridges held by them, showed that the battle was again joined, and that the crisis of the conflict must soon be reached. It was now between 3 o'clock and 4 o'clock in the afternoon. Steedman had forced

O. J. BENHAM,
QUARTERMASTER.

his way against all opposition, and now was in line ready for action east of the Overton Hill, on which the enemy's right rested behind strong works. Joining Steedman's right was our Corps (Woods), our Division being on the right of that command. On our right, and bending slightly back in conformity to the enemy's strong works, was Smith; and on Smith's right, Schofield and our cavalry well around to the enemy's rear. Everywhere the Old Flag, grand and beautiful as ever, waved and snapped in the afternoon breeze. In front of us were rebel flags and banners without number, many of which were destined to fall into better hands before the coming of night. All this time the artillery of both sides was very busy, and the boys on the skirmish line fought incessantly over the narrow space that separated them. When, at 3:40 o'clock, General Smith carried the rebel position at the angle in his front, the gathered storm burst all along our splendid line in measureless fury. The cheers and yells of Smith's veterans as they thronged over the enemy's works, were caught up by the men of Kimball's command, as our own Brigade and Regiment led in the assault upon the Confederates in our front, nor stayed until we had routed the enemy, horse, foot and dragoon, and had them on the run for safer quarters. The Division on our left charged a few minutes later, catching the left of the rebel line where we had broken it off, and rolling it back in promiscuous rout, held the line and formed for work against the strong works on the hill. Off to our right the Confederates on Shy's Hill were in hard luck. Their friends on their left had been driven from the field, and Smith's men were now where the lines of gray had been; Schofield was hard upon their left, his artillery plowing their ranks savagely; and still further on their left indeed, on the rear of their position, Wilson's cavalry, now dismounted, was about to close in upon them. The game was up, safety could be secured only in flight—the word was given, the retreat began, soon to be turned into panic, by Smith's guns and pursuit by our cavalry. The darkness which soon settled over the field covered the wild flight of the enemy as they rushed pell-mell, helter-skelter, every fellow for himself, for the shelter of the hills of Brentwood.

On the right of their line matters were little better. The knowledge of the crushing of their left fell like a pall upon the enthusiasm of the brave fellows who were still defending their right. There was no hope of success—half their army was already gone, the plain and hillsides in front and on both flanks were full of Union troops flushed—wild with visions of completest victory—and still the gray lines held on, but not long. Steedman came thundering up on their right, Kimball swung in on their left, and Beatty came at them directly in front, while Elliott worked well around toward their rear and threatened to cut off their retreat; artillery and musketry on every hand, and charging columns concentrating from right and left and front—here, too, the game was up, the Confederates let go, and rushed madly southward along the Franklin pike, thankful for nothing but the falling darkness. If the left of their line had fled in utter rout, the right was now no better. Following up our advantage, the National Army kept at their heels till darkness prevented further efforts. We had on other occasions followed the retreat of this same great army; we had passed through their camps soon after they had left them, but never had we witnessed such a scene as was here presented. For some distance on both sides of the pike the ground was strewn with guns, bayonets, belts, cartridge boxes, knapsacks, canteens, camp kettles, clothing, and almost every other article that made up the individual and "mess" outfit, and also broken-down and overturned wagons, artillery caissons, cannon, and abandoned war material of every description. Their dead and seriously wounded were left on the field, and everything that could hinder their flight seemed to have been flung away. The confusion of that dreadful night was greatly intensified by the rain which began to fall just at dusk, and which continued till nearly morning. The darkness was intense. As the Confederate teamsters attempted to cross over from the Granny White and Hillsboro' pikes to the Franklin pike to avoid Willson's cavalry, many of them became entangled in the woods, and in their desperation cut loose from their wagons and rode rapidly forward for safety.

And thus, all night long, what had been the great Confederate Army of the Tennessee; the rival of Lee's Army of Virginia; the magnificent army that had opposed Sherman all the way from Chattanooga to Atlanta and Lovejoy; the army that by a brave flank movement had carried Sherman and his Grand Army back almost to the Tennessee; the army that had forced Schofield out of Pulaski, Columbia, and Franklin back to Nashville; the army that had spread alarm and consternation throughout all the northwest; the army that thirty hours before had flung defiance into the faces of the loyal hosts in line of battle along its front—that army was now in tumultuous flight, shorn of dignity, bereft of courage, and robbed of power. It was supposed that Hood would halt in the Hills of Brentwood and again offer battle. But the Confederate hosts were not in condition to halt nor in humor to fight. Leaving their dead, neglecting their wounded, abandoning everything that could hamper or hinder rapid flight, the rebel army pushed on in disorganized mass, nor stopped till the boiling Harpeth was placed between them and the National army, and then only to take a few hours' rest, and to organize for greater safety in retreat.

Following up our great success, we pushed on after the

JESSE H. HALL,
COMPANY I.
COLOR-BEARER AT NASHVILLE.

retreating enemy, but darkness soon settled over the field and we were compelled to go into camp about one mile north of the village of Brentwood. The muddy ground, the raw, cold wind, the incessant rain, all tended to make our situation one of discomfort. But the thought of our great victory, the crushing defeat of the enemy, the possibility of annihilating the rebel army, counteracted the discomfort, and rolling up in our rubber blankets, we lay down in the driest places we could find to dream, perchance of home and friends.

Reveille sounded at 4 o'clock next morning, and at daylight we took up the line of march, our Division in advance. We were preceded by a strong cavalry force, which during the forenoon sent back many prisoners. Nothing else of moment occurred, except that on every hand there was the most positive proof of the utter haste in which Hood's army had fled. Evidently it was not a retreat—it was a flight. Reaching Franklin soon after noon, we went into camp, awaiting the construction of bridges over the Harpeth. The recent rains had greatly swollen the stream and it could not be forded. At 7 next morning we resumed our march, going into camp three miles south of Spring Hill. There had been more or less skirmishing all day, but the resistance of the enemy was without heart. Our cavalry made strenuous efforts to cut off and capture portions of the Confederate rear, but the Brownies were down to their best gait, and too many of them got away. The recent rains had rendered the roads almost impassable; even the pike was cut up and broken to such a degree that our trains and artillery could scarcely move. Pick our way as best we could, the mud and water was often ankle deep, filling our shoes with grit and sand to such an extent that our sufferings were often intense. The incessant rains soaked us, and there was nothing pleasant about the business. Our Division trains were close behind us with ten days' rations and a hundred rounds of ammunition for each man. The swollen condition of Rutherford Creek made it exceedingly difficult to construct bridges, even foot bridges, over that stream, but by the morning of the 20th we were able to cross, and at once our Division moved out as rapidly as the condition of the roads would allow. Another serious delay occurred at the crossing of Duck River, and while waiting we were sent foraging for the animals of the pontoon train. While thus remembering the animals, we by no means forgot ourselves. But the river was at last bridged, and on the night of the 22nd we crossed over and went into camp a mile south of Columbia, the Confederates giving us all the room we needed. Early next morning the advance was again taken up, but the enemy had so much the start of the Union army that it was impossible to overtake them. Our army, however, moved on more or less leisurely, passing through Lynnville on the 24th, celebrating Christmas next day by marching through many miles of mud and going into camp at night three miles south of Pulaski, tired, wet and hungry. By the 28th we were near Lexington, Alabama, reaching Athens on the 3rd and Huntsville on the 5th. This ended the pursuit and placed our Corps in quarters more or less permanent. The roads over which, or rather through which, we had been obliged to march, were as bad as the world ever saw.

CHAPTER XXVIII.

IN CAMP AT HUNTSVILLE.

The retreat and pursuit were at last ended. Hood's army, badly broken and terribly discouraged, was at Tupelo, in northeastern Mississippi. Our own Corps was at Huntsville, Alabama; Steedman was at Decatur on the Tennessee; Smith and Wilson were at Eastpoint, and Cox at Columbia. Schofield was soon transferred to the eastern army, and Smith, a little later, was ordered south to aid General Canby in the reduction of Mobile.

In our own vicinity, however, and doubtless elsewhere also, bushwhackers, guerrillas, and other roving bands of cowardly assassins, kept the saddle and committed many outrages. Guard and picket duty were strictly maintained, and frequent scouting and forage parties were sent out. When these expeditions were well guarded they were seldom molested, but with a small guard they usually had trouble.

The inclemency of the weather made it quite necessary to fix up our camp at once in as comfortable shape as possible. Beauty of architecture, however, gave way to means and comfort. Shanties, huts and nondescript affairs of various kinds, covered or supplemented with tents, sprang up in their proper places and served to shield us against the bitter cold and the driving rain. The building of these affairs caused no little amusement. Each "mess" was the "architect of its own fortune." If the chimney stood on its head and drew down instead of up, that was no one's else business, though many a tear was shed in consequence of the error. If the shanty had no chimney, whose business was it but the proprietors'? If General Kirby's chimney blew down in a storm and another chimney blew up about the same time, what relation necessarily existed between the two events! The thermometer sank very low sometimes, and the boys kept well indoors. The high wind that prevailed so much of the time only made things worse. On pleasant days, of which there were many later on, the boys came out to sun themselves, and when the weather would permit they pitched quoits, played ball and had many a rough and tumble time of it.

WILLIAM A. KINNEY,
COMPANY C.
From a recent photograph.

Soon after going into winter quarters our little church organization was revived, our library hunted up and again put in circulation, and regular Sunday services maintained. The little chapel in which we held our services had a remarkable growth. We had been discussing the desirableness of such a structure, but not until the news of the fall of Sumter was received did we resolve to erect it. In less than forty-eight hours—less than thirty, I think—the building was ready for occupancy, and immediately, even before the last nail was driven, the boys began to gather for the service. System, hard work, and any number of willing hands did it. Chaplain Crevath conducted the service, but was sometimes assisted by the chaplains of other Regiments. Postal communications with the North were soon established, and we managed to keep fairly well posted as to events elsewhere, particularly in the east.

A distressing affair occurred on the 20th of January. Lieutenant E. J. Squire, of Company D, was detailed to command a small foraging expedition into the country, to a particular place, to bring in certain supplies known to be there. He objected on the score that the guard was insufficient, but was ordered to proceed. The story of his adventures and what came of it is graphically told in his prison experience elsewhere in this volume.

Camp life at Huntsville was about the same it had been a year before at Ooltewah, and two years before at Murfreesboro'. The boys read everything they could get, discussed everything they knew, and a good deal more; planned campaigns for the immediate close of the war, reviewed our former marches and battles, and expressed freely their opinion of "the blamed Southern country." They also laid plans for home work after the war; ran farms, built mills, laid out railroads, went into the dry goods and grocery business, ran for office, planned to mob every copperhead that

E. W. CUNNINGHAM,
COMPANY D.
From a recent photograph.

could be found, and, in a general way, fixed up almost everything. But even after all this, much time hung on our hands. Singing, whistling, and joking more or less practical, all had their turns; but euchre, muggins, old sledge, and especially among the officers, poker, held the boards all the time, and never seemed to become tiresome. Later on, when pleasant weather came, the boys were out, and played all manner of out-door games. There were no feuds, no old sores, no grudges, but all were good natured and rolicky—frisky as lambs, (with the understanding that the lambs were pretty badly crippled with corns, bunions, and rheumatism.)

It was known in camp that our old Commander, Sherman, had captured Savannah, and that stopping for nothing, he was pushing his way northward through the Carolinas. Many a shout went up from our camp when the news of success by our eastern army reached us. In the early days of the war his army would have waited for the roads to dry—but at this stage of the great conflict nothing seemed to be impossible to the Union forces. In the midst of winter General Sherman put his entire army in motion carrying everything before him. The march through the Carolinas though not as poetical as that "through Georgia," was quite as difficult and equally graphic. The letters and papers which we received from the North, gave us to understand that Lee could not succeed; that affairs at Mobile were in a satisfactory condition, and we felt abundantly able to take care of Hood any day he might wake up. It did seem to us as though the Confederacy would soon go to smash. But the enemy was still in the field, and much work remained yet to be done.

We learned also that a portion of Hood's army, under Cheatham and Lee, was being transferred to the east, that other portions had moved further south, and, naturally, we

EXPEDITION INTO NORTH CAROLINA.

wondered how all this would affect us. Grant was hanging on to Richmond and Petersburg with his characteristic tenacity, and rumor had it that Lee would be compelled either to surrender or run. Such rumors became quite current the latter part of February, and early in March General Stoneman was ordered into North and South Carolina on a tour of destruction, and most graphically did he perform the duty assigned him. About the same time, General Wilson was sent south, in support of General Canby, who was operating against Mobile.

Fearing that Lee might attempt to withdraw from Petersburg, by way of Lynchburg and Knoxville, our Corps (Stanley's) was ordered by rail to the latter city, to receive the Confederates, should they come that way. The news of this move was hailed with great joy by all the boys. Preparations were at once made, and on the morning of the 13th of March, our tents were struck and we fell in with as much boyish glee as we did when we first went into camp at Monroeville. In due time we took up our line of march through the city to the depot. While waiting for the train we learned of the fall of Charleston, and that the old Flag again floated over Sumter. The boys were wild with delight, and anxious to be off for our new field. At 5 P.M. the train moved. Passing through Stevenson, Bridgeport, Chattanooga, and Ooltewah, all familiar to us, we reached Knoxville next evening at 5 o'clock, and next day proceeded to Strawberry Plains, where we remained until the 19th, when we advanced to New Market. On the 26th the Division moved forward to Bull's Gap, taking up a strong position. Here many deserters from the rebel armies joined us, and not a few of our men who had been prisoners of war. We were ordered forward next day, and went into camp beyond Lick Creek. Here we remained until April 3rd. The depredations of guerrillas, bushwhackers and similar assassins, had become so serious that it was decided to send a force into northwestern North Carolina, to intimidate, and, if necessary, punish them.

The expedition as planned was peculiar. No blood was to be shed unless it became absolutely necessary, and yet the expedition was to move through a very dangerous gap, and into the very nest of the marauders in the mountains of North Carolina. To find a man cool, brave and judicious enough to conduct such a campaign was no easy task. General Kirby and his Brigade were, however, promptly selected, and at once ordered forward. With some misgivings, but no hesitation, the General put his troops in motion at 2 o'clock the same day, April 3rd, and in due time reached Warm Springs, on the French Broad River. Here every report indicated the hazardous character of the undertaking. But dangers had no terrors, and though the way was narrow and rough, though the road was reported to be blockaded at many points, General Kirby decided to go ahead. He, however, divided his command, leaving a part at and near Warm Springs, while with the remainder he pushed on toward Ashville. Passing through Marshall, he soon met the enemy in light force. They kept at a good distance, firing upon us from trees, stumps, rocks, etc., but doing no especial harm. Our progress was greatly hindered by the trees that had been felled across the road, and by stumps and logs and rocks that had been rolled down from the hill-sides. Soon after passing Alexander's bridge, the opposition became more serious, and as we approached Ashville, it became quite warm. The rebels used artillery, and at times the roar of musketry and the scream of shell reminded us of other days. The contest went on most of the afternoon, with no great casualties, but as soon as darkness began to fall, the enemy withdrew.

Having reached the limit to which we were to go, and

JAY C. SMITH.
COMPANY B.
From a recent photograph.

having accomplished the task set us, General Kirby began the homeward march, halting a short time near Alexander's bridge, but resuming the march at 2 o'clock in the morning and reaching Marshall at 9 the same forenoon. From this point our march was deliberate. Passing through Warm Springs, we reached Greenville on the 10th in safety. General Kirby and his command were warmly commended for their pluck and success.

Could we have been transported beyond the mountains, we should have beheld sights that would have filled our hearts with gladness. The very day before we started on the Ashville campaign, the citizens of Richmond were wild with terror, fleeing in every direction for safety from the coming Union army. Lee had been compelled to leave his defenses in front of Petersburg, and Richmond could no longer be defended. Jeff Davis and all the officials of the Confederate government took to instant flight, followed by the terrified populace. Wagons, carriages, carts, everything that could be utilized for carrying goods in bundles, boxes and bags was impressed. Negroes were loaded down like pack mules, and everyone went with a bundle, a box or a package under his arm. It was Sunday, but such a Sunday! The banks were open, and men were rapidly withdrawing their specie and greenback deposits; bankers were securing their balances; store keepers were vainly trying to save the most precious of their goods—all were frantic. The city council met and ordered the destruction of all liquors, that the terror of the hour might not be increased by the howl and vandalism of the drunkard. The streets ran with whisky and other liquors, and many a wretch scooped it up from the gutters and got drunk despite the council. The tobacco houses were fired, and from this the flames spread wildly, fanned by a high wind, until a large part of the city lay in ashes. Thus during the long, dreadful night. The Union troops were soon on hand and did much to stay the flames. But Richmond had fallen!

Arriving at Greenville we learned of the fall of the rebel capital, and at once the boys went wild. What enthusiasm! What cheering! We all shouted and yelled ourselves hoarse; saluted the Old Flag; called each other names, shook hands, danced and sang until we were tired out. The bands played, bugles sounded, drums beat,—the army was wild—drunk with delight. And again on the 14th, when we learned that Grant had trapped Lee, and compelled him to surrender, the whole scene was repeated, only this time we had sense enough left to join most heartily—many of us reverently—in a great thanksgiving service to the Most High, for these signal and concluding victories. The exercises were under the direction of Chaplain Cravath, and though he always preached well, he never before did so well, and when we all joined in singing America, the whole country seemed to spread the echoes until the mysterious mountains seemed to brighten up and join the universal song. Every face beamed, every step was young—patriotism and enthusiasm fairly sizzled.

"And now," cried the boys, "for home!" And from that moment no other thought found lodgement. But the rejoicings of the army, like those of all loyal people, were turned to deepest sadness when the news of the assassination of President Lincoln came to us. Involuntarily, and from force of habit, the boys looked to their arms, and towering with rage, were once more ready to face southward. But the war was ended. Sherman received the surrender of Johnston, the enemy had sunk from view, and we were now to head homeward.

Moving to Bull's Gap, we soon took the train and in due time reached Nashville, and went into camp five miles out on the Charlotte pike, in what was known as Camp Harker.

Here we remained for some time awaiting the closing up of affairs preceding the muster-out of the army. Time hung heavily. Even euchre and seven-up lost their charms. While the officers were busily engaged in preparing the muster-out rolls, we employed our time variously—visiting friends in other regiments, receiving visits of the same kind, getting up candle and torch processions, some of which were very pretty, and in many other ways now forgotten. Generals Kimball and Stanley paid us one or two visits, and the boys took great delight in honoring them. A grand review of the Division was planned and carried out. It was a very fine affair—one long to be remembered, probably the last we shall ever see.

At last the details were all completed. Government stores and munitions of every kind had been turned over, the hour of departure had come, again the Regiment—O, how small as compared with what it had been—was in line —only 329 of us, all told—this time to be mustered out of the service. What memories thronged for recognition! What tender thoughts went out after the dear boys who, lying beneath the sod of many a field, could never return to home and dear ones, as we were about to do!

It was the 12th of June, 1865. Boarding the cars at Nashville, we gladly said good-bye to the South, and with light hearts, noisy tongues, and enthusiasm that absolutely knew no bounds, we started for "God's Country," proud of our record, proud of the old Flag, though tattered and torn, which we had followed through half a hundred fights, and which we were now returning without one stain of dishonor. That old Flag! Always bright, always encouraging, always inviting to duty, always an inspiration, especially in hours of greatest peril. That old Flag! It had often been the center of conflict, yet never had it been brought to the ground by an armed enemy. Even when the brave boys who carried it were one after another shot down, other and equally brave hands took it up and bore it forward. At the front in the fray, with the first over the enemy's parapets, leading in the charge, "Old Glory" always led us aright. The flight of years only deepens and intensifies the halo of glory that crowns that dear old emblem of liberty. Often at our annual reunions have I seen eyes that are now dim fill with tears at sight of the Flag while memory was busy on the fields of the past. Could it but speak, how gloriously thrilling would be its story!

Rapidly as our train bore us homeward those bright June days, our thoughts were ever far in the advance. Who can describe our feelings as we moved rapidly away from the scenes of strife and bloodshed with which, per force, we had become familiar and came again into the peaceful and quiet North. No pen of mine shall attempt such a task. At last we reached the City of Cleveland, where we were to receive our final pay, and where we were to break ranks forever. The fraternal ties formed and cemented on so many fields were not easily broken, but the pains of final leave-taking were dulled by the inexpressible joy of meeting the dear ones at the old home.

Prison Experiences.

I.

CAPTAIN GEORGE W. HALE.

Lieutenant George W. Hale was severely wounded in the Battle of Chickamauga, captured with many others of his company, and kept a prisoner many months. The ball which wounded Comrade Hale entered the left thigh, passed around the bone and into and through the right thigh making two dangerous wounds. All the rest of the afternoon and all night long, the Lieutenant lay wounded on the battle-field among the dead, dying and severely wounded. His experience was something terrible. Some of the boys were in the throes of death; some were moaning and crying for help; some were praying and some were swearing; some were calling for loved ones at home, and some cursing the day they were born; a few, like Lieutenant Hale, quietly endured their intense suffering, and waited for morning. The night was clear and cold, and to our suffering comrade it seemed endless. At 9 o'clock on Sunday morning two Confederate soldiers bore Comrade Hale on a stretcher back some distance and laid him down beside a fire. He was very weak from the loss of blood, and chilled to the marrow. The neglect of his wounds and the effect of the cold were such as to contract the muscles so as to draw his limbs out of shape for several weeks. There seemed, indeed, no chance for our comrade's life. But he had pluck and endurance, and is with us to this day.

For three weeks, he and other severely wounded were kept in this field-hospital without shelter from the hot sun, the pouring rain or the cold nights. Food was scarce, coarse and poorly prepared. The officer in charge of this hospital was a drunken wretch, through whose neglect the severely wounded were not exchanged, as they were at the other hospitals. Each day this wretch told the poor fellows "to-day you will be exchanged." Wistfully the boys looked for our ambulance which never came.

A rebel surgeon examined Comrade Hale's wounds the second day after he was captured, and told him that with proper care he might get well, and promised to see him again, but he never returned. Our comrade was obliged to dress his own wounds. His limbs were entirely helpless— he could not move them. Propping himself up on one elbow, he cut open his trouser-legs with the other hand, and thus dressed his wounds. A wounded comrade near by gave him a handkerchief, which he tore into bandages for both legs. He paid a rebel wretch five dollars for a canteen of water with which to wash his wounds. Later on, other wounded comrades who were able to walk a little, brought water from a spring near by. He kept his wounds moist day and night. About one week after he was wounded, a piece of blue cloth, nearly as large as a half-dollar, worked out. It had been driven in by the ball. So poorly were his wounds dressed—so scant the bandages, that it required constant effort to keep the wounds from the flies that swarmed by the thousand.

This continued for three weeks, when they were all loaded into great army wagons, and removed to Ringold. The journey was one never to be forgotten. Several poor fellows whose limbs had been amputated the day before starting, were loaded in with the rest and left without care or assistance. A ride in an army wagon over the mountains is as much as a well man cares to endure. How these poor fellows lived through it is a mystery. The Confederate Surgeons, having no anesthetics, had tied each of these same poor fellows to the table when the amputation was being made. Such things seem to-day impossible. But this is not all. Arriving at Ringold they were at once loaded into box freight cars and sent to Atlanta. One of the poor boys, who had had a leg amputated just before starting, died on the way—bled to death. No surgeon accompanied them, nor was there a soul to render any assistance—except guards! At Atlanta they were placed in sheds on the ground. Here there were a few nurses and waiters.

At the end of three weeks it was announced that all who could walk to the depot would be taken to Richmond and exchanged. Our comrade, though he had not yet been off his back, gave his name as one who would go. He paid five dollars for a pair of crutches and prepared to move. He pulled himself into an upright position by clinging to the studding, but he could not bear his weight on either foot—he was helpless. He kept on trying, and by the third day—the time set for starting—he was able to hobble very slowly. He fell behind the rest on the way to the depot and was roundly cursed by the guards who threatened to bayonet him if he did not hurry along. He finally reached the train. All were loaded into box cars and started. Arriving at Richmond, they found to their sorrow that they were not to be exchanged. The stronger ones were sent to Belle Isle, the officers to Libby, and the severely wounded to the hospital. All this time Lieutenant Hale had been considered dead—killed at Chickamauga. He was for some time so carried on the muster rolls.

After several months, his wounds had so healed that he was removed from the hospital and sent to Libby Prison.

The rebel surgeons in Libby who looked after the wounded, dressed all wounds from the same pan, with the same water and same sponge. The cases of gangrene were doubtless more numerous than they would have been had these surgeons exercised ordinary care.

The food furnished the prisoners in Libby was simply abominable—consisting at first, so far as Lieutenant Hale and those with him were concerned, of a very limited amount of corn bread and mule meat; then of corn bread and rice soup made of mules' jaws, as they knew, for they often found mule teeth in the soup. These they kept as "souvenirs." Soon white peas took the place of soup, but these were so full of worms that the stench which arose when they were being cooked made it next to impossible to eat the stuff, yet hunger compelled them to do so. Finally the rations were reduced to a small piece of corn bread of miserable quality.

Lieutenant-Colonel McDonald, of our Regiment, who was captured at Chickamauga, was confined in Libby at the same time. Lieutenant Hale met him, and it was arranged that Hale should be one of the officers who were to escape through the tunnel then being constructed under the direction, mainly, of Colonel McDonald. It is only proper to say here that the credit of this brave and successful undertaking is due Lieutenant-Colonel McDonald, and not to Colonel Straight, as reported at the time and subsequently. Straight knew nothing of it until invited by McDonald and two or three of his friends to join them in the flight. Comrade Hale was to be one of the number, but through a misunderstanding of the countersign, he was not able to pass the sentinel who guarded the entrance to the hole.

The excitement in Richmond next morning after the escape was intense. When the rebel officers called the roll, or, rather, counted the men—they found one hundred and nine too few. They were excited, and counted again. They then went to other rooms and came back. Soon they left and rode to headquarters. In a twinkling, church bells were ringing, cavalrymen were out with horns blaring, and all hounds obtainable were yelping. The excitement was at white-heat. The cavalry and hounds started in every direction. The prison guards were all arrested, charged with bribery. All day long they hunted and quizzed to find out where and how the prisoners had escaped. Our men had made good use of their time. But at night-fall the searchers brought in one poor fellow who had been re-captured. They took him to headquarters and placing a pistol to his head, swore they would shoot him if he did not instantly tell when and how they escaped. He finally yielded. The story of the enterprise can not be repeated here, though it is intensely interesting from start to finish.

The prisoners spent their time variously. It must have been a serio-comic sight to see Generals, Colonels, Majors, Captains and Lieutenants all stark naked sitting around the room searching in the seams of their clothes for the familiar gray-back. The day was usually started off in this way, the time devoted to it depending upon the amount of game in sight. After this, some would read, if there was anything to read; others would do fancy bone whittling, if the bones could be had; others would play cards, or chess, or checkers. Some would tell stories and play practical jokes. Mock trials, theatricals, elections, initiations into improvised secret societies—all these and many more—made up the day.

When Colonel Dahlgren made his raid upon Richmond, the excitement ran high in Libby. Arrangements were made, by which, if he succeeded in entering the city, they were to arise, strike down the guards and "break" for liberty. But poor Dahlgren was not to succeed. He was killed and his forces scattered.

Lieutenant Hale, Captain Bowers, of a Connecticut regiment, and Alonzo Robbins of the 123rd Ohio, planned an escape from the cars in which they were being moved from Richmond to Macon soon after Colonel Dahlgren's raid. Comrade Hale had a case knife, the back of which had been filed into a rude saw. Their plan was to saw a hole in the bottom of the car, and then at night to drop through and make their escape. The plan failed through the lack of nerve on the part of the Connecticut man. Our comrade made the attempt, but was chased in great shape around a large tobacco house, and among cars until he finally had to surrender. He was lucky not to be shot. The failure of Captain Bowers revealed our comrade's whereabouts. The prisoners were placed in a stockade at Macon, where they were kept three months. At the expiration of this time they were—six hundred of them—taken out to be held in Charleston as hostages to prevent our gunboats from firing upon that city. With the announcement of this intention, they organized themselves into a secret band fully officered, the sole intention and purpose of which was to capture the train that should carry them. This was to be done before reaching Savannah, and while comparatively near our gunboats. Colonel Sherman was in command of the whole force. He had a lantern made of red paper, which he was to hold out, when they were to arise and seize everything, burn the train, take the guards prisoners, and make for our gunboats. But, although every possible detail had been looked after, Colonel Sherman failed to give the signal, and nothing was done. The Confederates admitted later that there was but one company that they would have had trouble with—they would have succeeded.

On arriving at Charleston, they were distributed about the city, Comrade Hale being sent to the county jail for a time. In the fall of 1864, Comrade Hale and many others captured at Chickamauga, including very many of the men in Andersonville who had been taken prisoners in the same battle, were sent to Macon for exchange. But on arrival there, it was said, and truly, that General Sherman would not exchange prisoners. They were then returned to prison at Columbia, and the poor fellows from Andersonville were sent back there to starve and die. The winter was spent by our comrade at Columbia, S. C., with many others, in a field, well guarded. Twice during the winter he made his escape. The first time while they were cutting wood for camp use. It was customary to detail a number of prisoners for this duty. The guard had become accustomed to it, and Comrade Hale, one day, instead of going upon duty, went too far, past the lines, and hid in a brush heap. Here he found two or three other officers. That night they started for our lines, only about four hundred miles away. After wandering in the woods and making long marches, they were recaptured on the fifth day and returned to Columbia. His next attempt was some weeks later, when the boys were gathering wood at the other side of the prison. One of the men had made an outlandish wagon, with which he had just brought in a load of wood. It excited a great deal of mirth, and in the midst of the jollity, Lieutenant Hale slipped away, accompanied by Captain Love of the 8th Kansas. They were captured and brought back the next day, nearly dead, having made a forced march of forty miles. When Sherman came threateningly near Columbia, the Macon prisoners were hurried off to Raleigh, N. C., and not long after to Goldsboro', where they signed exchange papers. Very soon after, they passed into our lines near Wilmington, N. C., wild with joy. They could scarcely contain themselves, nor could they realize that they were really free. Comrade Hale had been a prisoner for nearly eighteen months. They were sent by steamer first to Baltimore, then to Columbus, then home for a thirty-day visit. At the expiration of this time, Lieutenant Hale was returned to his command, where he met a royal welcome and also a Captain's commission. He remained with the boys until the Regiment was mustered out at Camp Harker, Tenn., June 12, 1865.

II.

LIEUTENANT E. J. SQUIRE.

On the morning of the 17th of January, 1865, while the Regiment was in camp at Huntsville, Alabama, Lieutenant (since Captain) E. J. Squire, of Company D, was placed in charge of a small foraging party sent out on the order of Lieutenant-Colonel McDonald, commanding the Regiment, to secure subsistance for the headquarters animals. The expedition was made up as follows: One army wagon drawn by six mules; two teamsters, Jake Adams, of Company C, and Jacob Rohrer, of Company H; two "loaders," Theodore Rebadue, of Company B, and James P. Sparks, of Company H; and one guard, Adam Dilling, of Company K, all under the command of Lieutenant Squire. The Lieutenant urged a much stronger guard, but his requests were not granted. The forage which they were to bring in was in Canamore Cove, in the hills about eight miles from camp. It was loaded all right. Lieutenant Squire had just given the usual voucher, and started back, when he was met by twenty-five or thirty men who ordered him to surrender. Many of them were in Federal uniform, and Comrade Squire supposed them to be our own men, accompanied by a few citizens out on a "lark," and acted accordingly. He soon found his mistake. They claimed to belong to General

LIEUTENANT E. J. SQUIRE,
COMPANY D.
From photograph taken in 1894.

Roddy's command, though they were doubtless operating largely on their own account. One of the teamsters, Jake Adams, made good his escape, in some way, and gave information of the capture in camp that same evening. All the rest were taken prisoners. Instantly Colonel McDonald set about effecting their recapture. The country was scoured in every direction, but to no purpose. Four other men, two of the 90th Ohio, and two of the 125th Ohio, were captured soon after Lieutenant Squire had been taken.

The whole company was immediately marched to the rear about two miles, where they encamped for the night, resuming the journey next morning. In the evening the rebel force was considerably augmented. Comrade Squire and his associates were drawn up in line to be executed, but better counsels prevailed and they were spared. Excited citizens reported that the 101st Ohio were burning and destroying everything on account of the capture of some of their men. The little company was hurried along as fast as possible, so as to get away from the "avengers." That night definite plans for escape were made. It was after night when they reached camp. In passing through a piece of woods, Comrade Sparks, who was mounted behind a 90th Ohio man, managed to slide off and escape. This came near costing the 90th man his life. He, however, paid no attention to their threats, but kept up his howl about the fellow having stolen his blanket. Sparks hid near by, and the rest, in order to give him a chance, gave their word that they would not try to escape until they reached camp if they would move on. This was agreed to, and Sparks got away, reaching camp a few days later. The extreme vigilance of the guard prevented any escape that night. Moving back into the woods they rested all next day, and after midnight crossed to the south side of the Tennessee River. A Mr. Canamore was marching with them. He had been warned by his brother-in-law, who was guide to the 101st in their retaliatory work around Huntsville.

On the night of the 22d, while stopping at the house of one Johnson, three of the boys—Theodore Rebadue of the 101st, and Crittenden and Wallace of the 125th, made a break for liberty. This was a terrible mistake, as they were soon captured, brought back to camp, and two of them, Rebadue and Crittenden, were hung for the offense. Wallace was spared by the entreaties of the citizens, who feared the vengeance of the Union army. After this they were much more strictly guarded, and all chance of escape seemed shut off. They finally reached Gadsden, where they were turned over to the Home Guard. Tired and hungry they were locked up in the court house, supperless and blanketless.

Early next morning, without breakfast, except a little flour and water, they were started on a foot march of thirty miles, to Blue Mountain. On the way Comrade Squire was permitted to purchase a dozen eggs on condition that the guard should cook them on "shares," each party to have half a dozen. The guard cooked and ate all of them. At Blue mountain they were sent by rail to Selma, Ala. At Selma they were imprisoned with other Union soldiers, who greeted them with "Fresh fish, fresh fish." This prison was without a chimney; the windows were boarded up tight; the fire was built on a quantity of earth in the middle of the room. The smoke was awful. The poor fellows at times could breathe only as they lay flat upon the floor. After a stay of two days they were sent by steamer to Cahawba, where there was a prison pen in which some three thousand Union men were confined. Comrade Squire, being an officer, was assigned to another building, with the privilege of conversing with citizens for the purpose of barter. He was permitted to visit the prison office to make inquiries, and also to mess with a number of 115th Ohio men who were doing carpentry work for the prison. The prison at Cahawba was largely "run" by Union men. As stated, the 115th Ohio boys did the carpentry work, the 18th Michigan Band (captured almost entire), furnished the music for guard-mount and dress parade, and two of the clerks in the office were Union prisoners. At one time Lieutenant Squire was called upon to inspect the prison books. This was one of the exceedingly well conducted prisons in the whole south. Even this was bad enough. During a freshet, the prison was overflowed and the boys had to stand in water two feet deep for nearly three days. Soon after this, word was received that they were to be exchanged. The prisoners were arranged in three divisions and sent forward at intervals of a few days. Lieutenant Squire was in the third division. From Cahawba they were taken to Selma, then to Meridian, Dunopolis, Jackson, Clinton and to Big Black River, on the opposite side of which they caught sight of the old Flag, the sight of which set them nearly wild. Some of the men really wept for joy. Uncle Sam sent them rations of coffee and hard bread, but they were obliged to spend the night in the mud and rain as best they could, cheered with the thought of the morning. The next morning they were taken across the river to "Camp Parole," four miles from Vicksburg, where they were detained for some time under a rebel commission, but "fed by the United States."

On the 23rd day of April, the prisoners belonging to Indiana, Ohio, Kentucky, and Tennessee regiments, were placed on board the ill-fated steamer Sultana and started north. The boat was greatly overloaded, there being about twenty-three hundred souls on board—two thousand of whom were Union soldiers. The river was extremely high, spreading out for miles in many places.

At night it was almost impossible to move about the decks on account of the many sleepers scattered everywhere. Memphis was reached on the 26th (April, 1865). Taking on wood and water, the steamer resumed the journey about 1:30 at night. The terrible scenes that followed are graphically described by Comrade Squire:

"I was aroused from slumber by a shudder that seemed to go through the vessel. The air was full of the odor of steam and ashes. Rubbish was falling everywhere, all over the deck. The lights were all out, it was intensely dark, and the cries and shrieks of the frightened passengers were terrible. I crawled upon my hands and knees through the rubbish and confusion until I came out upon an open space just back of the ladies' cabin, where a solitary lamp was still burning. The floor was literally covered with pieces of furniture, glass, etc., including blinds, doors, chairs, cots and tables. The statement was instantly circulated that the boiler had exploded, but that if no fire occurred we should be saved. A moment later a bright flame shot up in the front part of the cabin. Lieutenant McDonald, of the 4th Tennessee, had joined me, but was greatly excited. When the fire burst out he made a rush and probably jumped overboard and was drowned. I found my way back to where my cot had been, and put on my clothes. On the opposite side of the cabin lay an officer of the 6th Kentucky, unconscious, with a wound in his head. Near him was Lieutenant McCord, of the 111th Ohio, appealing for help to remove the poor fellow, so that he need not burn. I helped to lift him to the edge of the boat, from which, should he become conscious, he could roll off into the water, if he chose. As we were about to pass out of the cabin door, a lady passenger rushed in, crying 'Save me! save me!' We tried to pacify her, giving her assurance that we would do all we could. Frenzied with fear, she rushed, shrieking, into the flames. One poor crazed man rushed to the edge of the boat, crying 'I shall drown!' then back toward the fire, saying 'I shall burn!' then again to the edge of the boat, repeating the cry. Again he rushed toward the fire, and crying 'I would rather burn than drown!' he leaped into the flames and perished. Lieutenant McCord and myself were the last to leave the cabin deck. As I stood on the outside, I could see the passengers going over the side of the boat like a flock of sheep through a gap in the fence. The water was filled with a struggling, shouting, praying, screaming mass of humanity. It was the most terrible scene I ever witnessed.

No artist's brush, no word painting could depict the horrors of that night. I had by no means recovered from my prison experience, and, in my weakened condition, had no hope of escape. This fact, instead of exciting me, made me calm, so that I was able to take advantage of every favorable circumstance that occurred. Nearly everything that would float had been cast overboard, in many cases upon the heads of those struggling in the water. Finding a chair, I stripped off all my clothing except my undershirt, drawers and socks, and as soon as the water was clear of heads near where I stood, I climbed down the railing into the water, went under, came up, seized the chair, but soon relinquished it for a shutter that came my way, and endeavored to move out. I got a few rods from the boat and found that I was too much exhausted ever to reach the shore. Looking back, I saw a number of men clinging to the wheel of the boat. Having read of persons being saved in this way, I determined to return and cling to the wheel. Just before reaching the wheel my strength failed me and I gave up. Sinking rapidly, my foot came in contact with something, the bottom of the river or a drowned body, when I suddenly resolved to try once more. I came up directly under the wheel and caught hold of one of its arms. I tried to pull myself up, but I could not. Quite a number of men were clinging to them. This excessive weight on one side caused the wheel to make a partial revolution. This carried me well up out of the water, but the poor fellows on the other side were submerged and the wheel stopped, leaving me well up toward the top. I swung over and stood up on one of the paddles. Here I rested a few moments, removing more of my clothing. I feared the fire would soon cause the wheel and wheel house to fall from the boat and sink. I determined to reach the outer edge, but at that instant they broke from the boat and sank into the water. The rush of water broke my hold, and I was carried along, nearly drowned. The wheel house, in falling, had floated with the side next to the boat uppermost. I had been caught in it as in an inverted box. Floating on my back in this prison, I discovered a small hole at the top, burned through by the fire. This I enlarged by breaking away the charred parts, and finally got out. Portions of the wheel house were still burning, and the heat of the steamer was such as to make it necessary for me to let myself down into the water to prevent roasting. The rubbish upon which I was floating was not yet entirely clear of the boat, and appeared to be slowly sinking. The hull of the steamer afforded relief from the heat after the upper works were consumed. I secured a window blind to use when the boat and the wreckage upon which I floated should sink, which was liable to occur at any moment. In a short time a rowboat came to the rescue of a few men still clinging to the boat. Several, by means of chains flung over the iron railing of the vessel, had held on for dear life. These were now being taken off. In a little time a couple of mules which had been swimming around in a circle came up to the steamer and tried to climb on, endangering some men who were still clinging to the hull.

The mules were driven off. They swam between one pile of rubbish and the hull, separating the two. I floated quite a distance down the stream and was then picked up by the guard or picket boat Pocahontas, and taken to Memphis. I was in the water probably five hours."

This was probably one of the most appalling disasters that ever occurred on any of our inland waters. Of the 2,300 persons on board nearly 1,500 perished at the time, and many others subsequently died of injuries and exposure. Eighteen of the thirty-four commissioned officers perished. Of seven men with whom Lieutenant Squire messed in prison only two escaped. Of the four 101st men on board, Captain Taggart, Lieutenant Squire and Jacob Rohrer were saved. From Memphis they were sent to Camp Chase and mustered out May 15, 1865.

III.

JOHN P. GESTENSLAGER.

Comrade J. P. Gestenslager, of Company G, tells the story of his prison life in a most entertaining manner:

"I was wounded at Chickamauga, and while making my way to the rear, was struck by a limb of a tree which had been lopped off by a cannon ball, and knocked out of time. When I came to, I was in the enemy's lines. There were a good many others there, too. My wounds hurt terribly, but I had to stand it. We were sent in a gunboat of a wagon to Ringold. The next day we were joined by some more Yankees, among them some 101sters. There were Colonel McDonald (then a Major), Sergeants David Allison and James Herndon, and Privates Sam Wagner, John Base, Chris. Funk and Enos Lewis. There were others, but I don't remember their names. We were put on the cars for

Richmond, but we were unloaded at Atlanta and driven into a bull-pen to stay all night. We were reloaded next morning, and again unloaded at Raleigh, N. C. Here we saw some flinty hard-tack. While I was washing my wounds, Major McDonald said to me: "It's hard, but I guess it's honest." We were hustled off again and did not stop until we reached Richmond. The officers were sent to Libby and the enlisted men to the Pamperton building. We were sent in a day or two over to Belle Isle, where we were kept eleven days with no shelter of any kind. There were a few Bell tents, but they were full before we got there. We suffered from cold and hunger. Here I first learned to "spoon" and turn over by word of command, and here I traded off my shoes for eighteen loaves of bread, and Sam Wagner and I sat down and ate the whole eighteen. Then Sam traded his shoes for more bread, which we ate for breakfast, and felt as though we had had a square meal. Each loaf was about the size of your fist. We were sent to Danville on the 23d of November. It rained and blew up cold, and we barefooted! They finally put us in an old tobacco house which they called Prison No. 4. We had no blankets; a few of the boys had half "pup-tents," but many had no covers at all. Our ration was a chunk of corn bread about $2 \times 4 \times 1\frac{1}{2}$ inches, a half pint of rice or pea soup, or, as we called it, "bug soup," and occasionally a small bit of meat. We had a Head or House Sergeant, a Floor Sergeant for each floor, and a Mess Sergeant for each mess. The House Sergeant would receive the rations from the rebels and divide them among the three Floor Sergeants, and they gave to each Mess Sergeant, who dealt out to the mess directly. We were here at New Year's, when it was so intensely cold. There were seventeen of us in a little office on the lower floor. We had no wood, so we fell to splitting up some of the joists. In some way the boys got a few pine knots. We built a fire on a tin pan and huddled around it all night. The smallpox broke out among us here, causing many deaths. I took care of John Base while he had it, but I did not take it. In March the prisoners in Prison No. 4 were sent to Andersonville. Just before starting I was detailed to do baking for the hospitals. I remained here until I concluded to take "French leave." So one night I and three others—Coburn, Mac and Williams of the 18th Regulars—started for God's country without any permission. After being out eleven days we were recaptured and taken to Saulsbury, N. C. Here I was taken sick and sent to the hospital; my friends were sent I don't know where. In a short time I was sent to Andersonville, from Andersonville to Danville, from Danville to Richmond. During all this time I was sick. Here we were finally exchanged and sent to Annapolis. At sight of the Stars and Stripes, many of the boys broke down and cried for joy. I know I did. Several died just before reaching Annapolis. I visited my home on furlough, and rejoined the Regiment at Huntsville, Ala., January 14, 1865. I found a few humane officers among the rebels, but they were very scarce."

IV.

GEORGE MANN.

Comrade George Mann, of Company F, was captured at Chickamauga, September 19, 1863. He and many other prisoners were taken to Atlanta, Georgia, where they were stripped of their outer clothing and all valuables. From Atlanta they were removed to Richmond, where they remained three months. The latter part of December they were transferred to Belle Isle, where they remained two months longer. Here they suffered intensely from cold. They were very insufficiently clothed, had few blankets, and often had to lie in the snow with no fire at hand. "Spooning" under the few blankets they had was the only means of keeping half warm. From Belle Isle they were taken to Danville. Located on the first floor, they immediately began to plan an escape. Comrade Mann had succeeded in "cribbing" a case knife, with which a hole was cut in the floor. They at once began tunneling, using the knife and half canteens for the purpose. They carried their tunnel under the street, opening it in a hollow a little distance beyond. But they were detected, and eleven hundred of them were then huddled together on the upper floors— so crowded that there was scarcely standing room. They were kept in this condition for a month. From here they were sent to Andersonville. The prisoners had received permission to dig a well near the two trees in the prison. It was twenty-two feet deep. A plan of escape was at once put into execution. Ten feet below the top of the well they began tunneling, throwing the dirt back into the well. This was removed during the day. They tunneled a distance of six hundred feet, which brought them outside the outer stockade. At the moment when everything was ready for them to make their escape, a rebel Sergeant accidentally stepped upon the thin crust of earth over the opening, which revealed their plan and prevented their escape. Later many of them were taken to Charleston for two months and then to Florence, where they remained. Comrade Mann was detailed to cut wood for the prisoners. He received a pint of corn meal for each cord of wood he cut. He dug a hole in the ground to stay in at night, for his clothing was nearly gone. He escaped while cutting wood, about January 1, 1864. In attempting to reach Sherman's army he was compelled to cross a large swamp, having to swim some distance. Soon after crossing, the hounds treed him and kept him there until the rebel cavalry came up. He was taken back and placed one whole night and part of a day in a pen nearly sixteen feet high, the bottom of which was almost entirely covered with water. This in January! Mosby came along next day and ordered him out of this place back into prison. He returned to his hole in the ground, and was soon after taken sick. He was not able to walk again until within our own lines. At length they were to be taken north for exchange. The well ones were ordered out, and the sick ones left. Two guards came back for Comrade Mann and dragged him by his heels about six hundred yards, and threw him, with others, into a wagon and hauled him to the depot. He was very roughly handled and thrown into a car. At Williamstown they crossed the Pedee river. Here he was again dragged up the hill and left lying on the ground all day, too sick to help himself at all. At sundown all were put aboard the train again. Seventy-two sick and wounded ones were piled into one box car—corded up, as it were, like wood, and taken to Goldsboro', at which place they were pitched out again, the living on one side, the dead on the other, for many had died on the way. Loaded into a mule wagon, they were run two miles into the woods, where they remained three or four weeks. From this point they were sent into our own lines, much more dead than alive. While at Andersonville it was quite customary to allow the prisoners to carry out the dead bodies of their comrades and exchange them for logs of wood. On one occasion, Comrade Mann and another prisoner found a dead body lying near them. Gathering up the remains, they presented themselves with their burden at the door. They carried it under guard to the ridge indicated to them, and there found three rows of bodies in all stages of decomposition, from the bare bones to the freshly deposited body—

a sight too horrible to describe. They deposited the body of their dead comrade, secured their log of wood, and hastened from the revolting scene.

V.

JOHN H. CRAWFORD.

The experiences given in the preceding pages would seem to cover all the points of prison life, and yet, in a series of most interesting articles published some time since by Comrade John H. Crawford, still other forms of refined cruelty are brought out with great distinctness.

Chief among these was the ever ready and ever delusive promise of exchange. Next to the supply of daily food, the question of "exchange" was the most important to the poor fellows in prison. Rumors were constantly in circulation, and hopes were fanned into life only to die in the gloaming. Did the Confederate authorities desire to remove a portion of the prisoners to some other prison, they were quite sure to hold out the promise of immediate exchange. Under such an inspiration the men were much more easily handled. An example will illustrate: It had been decided to transfer a large number of prisoners from Danville to Andersonville, a change which, if known to the boys, would have been resisted fiercely. Comrade Crawford and many others were called into line one evening and informed that they were next day to be taken to Petersburg for exchange. The announcement had been made in such earnestness and apparent candor that the boys believed the statement, especially when the news was confirmed a little later by a fresh rumor. Early next morning the statements were reiterated, including many of the details. Hope ran high, and many a poor fellow whose name was not included in the list envied his comrades their good fortune and bemoaned his own bad luck. At last, when the hour came, the poor fellows fell in with great alacrity, forgetting their troubles; forgetting their weakness; forgetting that on many other occasions they had been made the victims of misplaced confidence. But this time the guards and overseers seemed so honest and open-faced about the matter, so candid and so earnest, that they placed implicit confidence in their statements, and bidding good-bye to those who were to remain, they moved out of the prison and across to the train with an animation born only of hope. But they were doomed to disappointment, deep and bitter.

When the poor, half-dead fellows realized that they had again been duped, that they were actually headed in the wrong direction, the cry went up from many a heart: "My God! are we going to Andersonville?" Such, indeed, was their destination, and into the horrors of that vile prison they were soon forced, many never to emerge alive.

Wounded and captured in the great Battle of Chickamauga, September 19, 1863, Comrade Crawford was imprisoned at many places. He records the fact that some of the prison keepers were not as bad as others, although the best one he knew put him and several others in a dungeon for seventy-two hours without food or water as a punishment for having attempted to escape. At length, after eighteen months of prison life, the day of exchange finally came. On the 26th of February, 1865, Comrade Crawford and many of his fellow prisoners were permitted to greet the old Flag again, and once more to breathe the air of freedom. The rejoicings of these liberated boys can never be fully appreciated by those of us who were so fortunate as to escape capture, nor can we join in their memories of one feature of our great struggle concerning which, would to God, there had never been occasion to write.

DEATH OF COLONEL STEM.

Colonel Leander Stem, of Green Springs, was commissioned Colonel of the 101st Ohio by the Governor of the State, August 14, 1862, in which capacity he was serving the Regiment at the time he fell mortally wounded at the Battle of Stone's River, December 31st, 1862. A man of great personal worth and sterling character, he was greatly beloved by all the men, and more especially by those who knew him most intimately.

Naturally, he was the reverse of a belligerant, but when the call of the Nation was made for strong and willing defenders, none, of all the thousands who responded, gave themselves more freely or more unreservedly than he. A man who had led a quiet, unobtrusive life, he was not one who had sought offices of public trust and responsibility; indeed, he often questioned his ability to command the Regiment. Without ostentation, he ruled with a firm, even, and just hand. Without a military education, and devoid of any particular military ambition, it was feared by some that in the crisis of battle he would be found wanting. Not so. Brave almost to rashness, so far as he was personally concerned, he was always cool and collected—a model of soldierly bearing under the most trying circumstances. On the afternoon of December 30, '62, while we were supporting our battery in the development of the Confederate position in the thickets of Stone's River, he stood at his horse's head, patting the animal's neck and stroking his

THE STEM MONUMENT,
Green Springs, Ohio.

nose, but was constantly on the alert for a rush or a surprise by the enemy. Otherwise he seemed unconscious of the surrounding dangers.

Next morning he was at the head of the Regiment, nor hesitated until he fell mortally wounded, about 8 o'clock. When the first terrible assault was made by the Confederates, he was observed to draw his hat down slightly over his eyes and cringe as one does in facing a driving hail storm, but with the first crash he was all life and animation —but not excitement. On the recommendation of General Carlin he had not mounted, but was commanding the Regiment on foot. We had repelled two vicious assaults of the enemy, and had just moved the Regiment some little distance, by a kind of side step to the left, when, the enemy having again charged, he fell utterly helpless and mortally wounded.

His last command was "Stand by the colors, boys!" He fell, sword in hand, and in the thickest of the fight. The exigencies of the battle soon compelled us to retire from this position, leaving our friend and Commander in the hands of the enemy. In this connection I take pleasure in transcribing a letter received from Surgeon John M. Johnson, of General Pat. Cleburne's Staff, in response to a letter of inquiry. The doctor is in error as to the cause or source of our Colonel's death, for he surely fell with the enemy close in front, shot by them, and not by our own men. Following is the letter:

"DEAR SIR: * * * I found Colonel Stem near the front of the Federal lines. He must have fallen on your extreme right, early on Wednesday morning, the 31st. He had not moved a foot from where he fell, nor was he able to do so. It was about 9 o'clock in the morning when I found him. I had just met one of our most pious Chaplains who had been assisting in the removal of our wounded, and who, finding Colonel Stem, asked for an ambulance in which to remove him. He went to get it while I went in search of your friend, and soon found him. He told me who he was. The conveyance soon came, and the driver, the Chaplain (Rev. Mr. Kimball) and myself with difficulty got him into the ambulance. He was a heavy man. There were no others of the killed or wounded near us, and I think he was killed by a stray shot, and as like as any way the bullet came from the Federal lines. I was General Pat. Cleburne's Division Surgeon at that time, and he accompanied the extreme left of the command, which did not reach as far as to where Colonel Stem was found. * * * He was shot, I think, through the kidneys, probably an oblique shot, wounding the spine. He was the most patient and uncomplaining man I ever saw. He did not utter one single word of complaint. When I found him he was lying on his face— he could not lie in any other way. In handling him he preferred to face down. When I reached the hospital in Murfreesboro', to which he had been sent, I found him in the same position on a poor little pallet of straw. His wounds had been very carefully dressed by the best surgeon I had, and who kept charge of him until he died, January 4th. He was furnished as good a bed, pillows and blankets, as could be had. * * * The lower half of his body, including the extremities, were completely paralyzed.

"He did not talk like a dying man, but like one just ready to get up and go to duty. I never saw a braver man. I was ordered to be ready to retreat on Thursday, the day he died, and having a great deal to do, I could not attend to burying him, or I might be able to point out his grave. Such are the duties of a Medical Director, that during a fight, a retreat or a forward movement, he has his hands full. This was my condition. I got the impression from my conversation with Colonel Stem that he was a preacher.

"I am seventy-four years old, and my memory is not good, or I might say much more about your friend. His patience under the greatest trials; his fortitude with face of death; his deep piety, and his religious faith and confidence assure me that I shall scarcely see his like again. I write this with great pleasure.

"I am, very truly yours,

"JOHN M. JOHNSON.

"Atlanta, Ga., December 19, 1885."

In due time the body of Colonel Stem was removed to his native State and buried with appropriate honors in the beautiful cemetery at Green Springs. At the close of the war arrangements were made for the erection of a monument to his memory. A shaft of beautiful proportions was erected, and on the 11th day of July, 1866, the monument was solemnly dedicated in the presence of a very large concourse of people. Gen. W. H. Gibson, a personal friend, a valiant soldier, and brave defender of the Republic, delivered an eloquent address, every sentence of which was teeming full of patriotism:

"Cold, lifeless granite that it is, it has all the glow which inspiration excites, and awakens all our sympathies and emotions. That monument, the production of a generous patriotism, is not alone for this day, nor this year, but for all time. And may it there stand as the cycles of time pass on, continuing to excite and attract the admiration, interest and enthusiasm of generations yet to come. That monument stands for the unborn centuries. August Future, take it and keep it, and safely through an hundred centuries preserve it. Take our memorial tribute and preserve it for all time, so that long—long after we have moldered to our native dust, our children's children, and the children of all our race who have hearts to be inspired by principles of liberty and justice shall drop tears at this tomb, and regard it as a precious heritage given them by noble ancestors."

DEATH OF LIEUT.-COL. WOOSTER.

Answering the first call for troops, Colonel Wooster entered the service of his country at the very beginning of the war. Later he became Adjutant of the 24th Ohio, and still later was promoted to the Captaincy of Company I, that regiment. Resigning this position, he was commissioned and mustered Major of the 101st, which position he held until October 14th, 1862, when, on the resignation of Lieutenant-Colonel Franz, he became Lieutenant-Colonel of the Regiment. Indeed, he had for some time been in the discharge of the duties of that position, Lieutenant-Colonel Franz not being able for duty.

Active and earnest, he was a great help to Colonel Stem in the long march of the Regiment from Crab Orchard to Nashville, and especially in the advance upon Murfreesboro'. At the Battle of Knob Gap he was constantly on duty—ready, willing, and capable. In developing the enemy's lines along Stone's River, on the 30th of December, he showed great skill and bravery, and was an inspiration to the boys in these trying hours. Alert until after midnight of the 30th, he was at his post long before the dawn next morning. His cheerful face, prompt act and brave bearing, carried a feeling of confidence and determination to the heart of many a boy as the lowering clouds of that dreadful day began to gather. The history of the unequal struggle is told in its proper place in the preceding pages. The great storm which had been gathering since Perryville had burst on the extreme right of the National line, with results disastrous to the Union cause. The enemy had fallen heavily upon our own Brigade and Regimental front, but we had gallantly repulsed them, not once, but twice, and we were in excellent spirits though scores of our brave fellows were down—some dead, some dreadfully wounded. Colonel Stem, on the order of General Carlin, had moved the Regiment by the left flank a short distance when again the Confederates assaulted, brave Colonel Stem going down in the storm, wounded unto death. Rushing to his side, a few words passed between them and Wooster took the command of the Regiment. With a fury that my pen is powerless to portray, the battle raged and swayed and grew into enormous proportions, in the midst of the din and inexpressible savage-ness of which Lieutenant-Colonel Wooster, like his chief, Colonel Stem, was laid low, and must soon be numbered with the dead. An effort was made to bear him from the field, but the exigencies of the battle—the unfortunate yielding of our right—made it necessary for us to withdraw, and he could not be taken far. "Put me down, boys," said the brave man, "and go, defend the colors. I am wounded and can be of no further service." The necessity was upon them, and he, with a number of others also wounded, fell into Confederate hands. To stay the flow of blood he had tied his sword strap tightly around his leg just above the wound, but before he was taken to the field hospital, at the Griscom house, he had become weak and cold from the loss of blood. The Confederates administered stimulants and restoratives, but all to no purpose. Comrade Edward Lepper, who was wounded and captured at the same time, remained with him, ministering to his wants in every possible way until death ended his sufferings, January 2, 1863.

A few weeks after the battle, his remains were removed to his home in the North for more suitable interment. His last resting-place is in the beautiful cemetery at Norwalk, O. Thus was another noble victim added to the long list of sacrifices so freely made for home and country.

ROSTER.

FIELD AND STAFF.

COLONEL LEANDER STEM — Enrolled at Tiffin and mustered at Monroeville, August 14, 1862. Mortally wounded while in command of his Regiment in Battle of Stone's River, December 31, 1862. Died at Murfreesboro', January 4, 1863, in the hands of the enemy. (See Death of Colonel Stem.)

GENERAL ISAAC M. KIRBY—Mustered as Captain of Company F, at Columbus, July 30, 1862. Promoted to Major, October 14, 1863. Ordered by General Carlin to command the Regiment upon the fall of Colonels Stem and Wooster, at Battle of Stone's River, December 31, 1862. Promoted to Colonel at Murfreesboro', February 14, 1863. Commissioned Brevet Brigadier-General, January 30, 1865, by the President. Mustered out with the Regiment.

LIEUTENANT-COLONEL JOHN FRANZ—Enrolled at Bucyrus and mustered as Lieutenant-Colonel at Monroeville, August 9, 1862. Resigned, October 14, 1862, on account of disability. Died at Bucyrus, O., November 14, 1870.

LIEUTENANT-COLONEL MOSES F. WOOSTER — Formerly Captain of Company I, 24th Ohio Infantry, was mustered as Major of the Regiment on commission issued by the Governor. Promoted to Lieutenant-Colonel, October 14, 1862. Mortally wounded at Battle of Stone's River, December 31, 1862. Died in hospital on the field of battle, January 2, 1863. (See Death of Col. Wooster.)

LIEUTENANT-COLONEL JOHN MESSER—Enrolled at Berlin and mustered as Captain of Company G, July 30, 1862.

Promoted to Lieutenant-Colonel, February 14, 1863. Wounded at Battle of Stone's River, December 31, 1862, and twice wounded at Battle of Chickamauga, September 19, 1863, but valiantly carried the colors, refusing to leave the field until wounded a second time. Resigned, January 7, 1864, on account of wounds. Died in Chicago, January 6, 1874.

LIEUTENANT-COLONEL BEDAN B. MCDONALD—Enrolled at Sulphur Springs, and mustered as Captain of Company C, July 23, 1862. Promoted to Major, February 14, 1863. Taken prisoner at Battle of Chickamauga, September 20, 1863. Imprisoned at Libby. Escaped, and rejoined the Regiment at Ooltewah, in February, 1864. Promoted to Lieutenant-Colonel, February 26, 1864. Wounded in Battle of Franklin, November 30, 1864. Mustered out with the Regiment. Died at Denver, Colo., December 21, 1879. For a full and most interesting account of the escape of Comrade McDonald and others, see the Century Magazine for March, 1888.

MAJOR DANIEL H. FOX—Enrolled at New London and mustered as Second Lieutenant of Company A, July 28, 1862. Promoted to First Lieutenant, December 19, 1862; to Captain, January 4, 1863, and to Major, February 18, 1864. Resigned, September 28, 1864, on account of disability. Died, May 26, 1894, at Norwalk, O. After the war, Comrade Fox became very prominent in legal and financial circles, having served as Judge of Probate for fifteen years, and at the close of that time having been chosen President of the Huron County Banking Company, which position he held at the time of his death.

SURGEON THOMAS M. COOK—Enrolled and mustered as Surgeon at Monroeville, August 12, 1861. Appointed Brigade Surgeon, in September, 1862, at Covington, Ky. Served during the war, and was mustered out with the Regiment.

ASSISTANT SURGEON GEORGE S. YINGLING—Enrolled at Tiffin, August 13, 1862. Resigned, January 15, 1863, on account of disability.

ASSISTANT SURGEON WALTER CASWELL—Enrolled at Castalia, August 17, 1862. Resigned, July 28, 1863, on account of disability.

ASSISTANT SURGEON HENRY T. LACY—Appointed from civil life, July 28, 1863. Enrolled at Winchester, August 16, 1863. Resigned, November 26, 1864.

ASSISTANT SURGEON HIRAM H. RUSSELL.— Appointed from civil life, November 26, 1864. Enrolled at Shield's Mills, Tenn., April 7, 1865. Mustered out with Regiment.

CHAPLAIN OLIVER KENNEDY—Enrolled at Monroeville, September 4, 1862. Resigned, November 17, 1863,. to enter the work of the Christian Commission, in which he continued to the end of the war. A man of great energy, sterling character, and boundless faith, he accomplished great good, not only during his connection with the army, but later, in the years of peace that succeeded the great storm. He died at Bellefontaine, Ohio, March 23, 1889, loved and mourned by all who knew him.

CHAPLAIN ERASTUS M. CRAVATH—Enrolled at Columbus, January 6, 1864, as a private in Co. G. Promoted to Chaplain and transferred to Field and Staff, January 7, 1864. Mustered out with the Regiment, June 12, 1865.

ADJUTANT LEONARD D. SMITH — Enrolled at Sandusky, August 4, 1862, as Lieutenant and Adjutant. Promoted to Captain and assigned to Company C, May 2, 1863. M. O. R.

CAPTAIN JAMES I. NEFF—Enrolled at Monroeville, August 11, 1862. Mustered with Regiment. Commissioned Second Lieutenant, Company H, September 15, 1862. Promoted to First Lieutenant and transferred to Field and Staff, as Adjutant, May 28, 1863, in which capacity he served to the end of the war. Was constantly on duty with the Regiment from muster in to muster out, participating in all its marches, campaigns, skirmishes, and battles. Was commissioned Captain Company A, November 3, 1864, and mustered as such April 27, 1865. Occupation since the war, attorney-at-law, Freeport, Ill. Died, September 14, 1893, at Chicago, Ill.

QUARTERMASTER GEORGE E. SENEY—Enrolled at Tiffin, July 28, 1862. Mustered as Quartermaster. Resigned, November 22, 1864.

QUARTERMASTER O. J. BENHAM—Enrolled at Crestline, August 11, 1862, as Quartermaster Sergeant. Promoted to extra First Lieutenant and Regimental Quartermaster, December 2, 1864. Mustered out with Regiment. Died at Cleveland, O., June 11, 1893. The very excellent condition of the Department under Quartermaster Seney was fully sustained by Comrade Benham during the trying times incident to the dying throes of the Confederacy, including the battles of Franklin and Nashville, the pursuit of Hood, the expedition into North Carolina, and the final settlement of the affairs of the Regiment at the time of muster out, June 12, 1865.

NON-COMMISSIONED STAFF.

BEER, WILLIAM N.—Enrolled at Bucyrus, August 14, 1862. Mustered as Sergeant Major and assigned to Non-Commissioned Staff. Promoted to First Lieutenant and assigned to Company C, January 2, 1863. Promoted to Captain and assigned to Company H, May 19, 1864. Mustered out with the Regiment. Died in September, 1874, at Valparaiso, Ind.

SMITH, JAY C.—Enrolled at Sandusky, August 5, 1862, as private in Company B. Promoted to Sergeant Major and assigned to Non-Commissioned Staff, February 14, 1863. Discharged to accept commission as First Lieutenant in Company I, December 18, 1864, to date September 28, 1864. Mustered out with Regiment.

LEE, MONROE—Enrolled at Tiffin, August 15, 1862, in Company K. Wounded in the Battle of Stone's River, December 31, 1862. Promoted to Corporal, April 1, 1863; to Sergeant Major and assigned to Non-Commissioned Staff, May 10, 1864. Mustered out with Regiment.

SHUMAN, JOHN—Enrolled at Tiffin, August 13, 1862, in Company K. Promoted to Sergeant, April 1, 1863; to First Sergeant, May 24, 1863. Wounded in the Battle of Chickamauga, September 19, 1863. Appointed Quartermaster Sergeant and assigned to Non-Commissioned Staff, December 2, 1864. Mustered out with Regiment.

PIERCE, GEORGE W.—Enrolled at Crestline, August 12, 1862. Mustered as Commissary Sergeant. Discharged, March 24, 1863, Columbus, O., on account of disability.

DAVIS, WILLIAM R.—Enrolled at Galion, August 16, 1862. Mustered as Corporal Company E. Promoted to Commissary Sergeant and transferred to Non-Commissioned Staff, March 17, 1863. Received commission as Second Lieutenant, but was not mustered. Discharged to accept commission as First Lieutenant Company K, December 18, 1864, to date July 30, 1864. Assigned to duty in Company A, August 11, 1864; to command of Companies A and F, September 29, 1864. Commanded Company K in the Battle of Franklin. Mustered out with Regiment.

HOMER, J. R.—Enrolled at Galion, August 6, 1862. Mustered as Corporal Company E. Promoted to Sergeant, January 27, 1863; to Commissary Sergeant, and transferred to Non-Commissioned Staff, September 29, 1864. Discharged to accept commission as First Lieutenant Company C, February 25, 1865, to date November 3, 1864. Mustered out with Regiment.

WHITEMAN, MARQUIS D. L.—Enrolled at Republic, August 11, 1862, as private in Company H. Promoted to Sergeant, September 19, 1863. Carried the flag, after Kenesaw, to Jonesboro'. Promoted to Commissary Sergeant and transferred to Non-Commissioned Staff, February 18, 1865. Mustered out with Regiment.

LATHROP, L. B.—Enrolled at Monroeville, August 15, 1862. Mustered as Hospital Steward. Discharged at Louisville, Ky., April 14, 1863, on account of disability.

MATTHEWS, J. E.—Enrolled at Sandusky, August 5, 1862, as private in Company B. Promoted to Hospital Steward and transferred to Non-Commissioned Staff, May 15, 1863. Mustered out with Regiment.

COMPANY A.

Mustered in at Monroeville, August 30, 1862.
Mustered out at Camp Harker, Tenn., June 12, 1865.

CAPTAIN CHARLES CALIGAN—Enrolled at Monroeville, July 15, 1862. Mustered as Captain. Resigned, December 10, 1852, on account of disability.

CAPTAIN DANIEL H. FOX—Enrolled at New London, July 28, 1862. See Field and Staff.

LIEUTENANT ASA R. HILLYER—Enrolled at Norwalk, July 15, 1862. Mustered as First Lieutenant. Died in rebel hospital at Murfreesboro', January 4, 1863, of wounds received in the Battle of Stone's River. December 31, 1862, while defending our second position in the cotton field.

LIEUTENANT BENJAMIN F. BRYANT—Enrolled at Norwalk, August 9, 1862. Mustered as Fifth Sergeant. Promoted to First Lieutenant, January 27, 1863, and to Captain, March 19, 1864. Mustered out with Company. At the Battle of Chickamauga all the men of this Company except four, were either killed, wounded or captured. These four were Comrades Bryant, Knapp, Whitney and Brady.

LIEUTENANT ALEXANDER C. HOSMER—Enrolled at Sandusky, July 22, 1862, in Company B. Appointed Second Lieutenant and assigned to Company A, February 1, 1863. Commanded Company B for a time after the Battle of Chickamauga, September 20, 1862. Died on the cars near Chattanooga, May 13, 1864, of wounds received at Rocky Face Ridge, May 11, 1864. Comrade Hosmer received his mortal wound in the famous assault made by the Regiment upon Buzzard Roost. Brave and capable, he fell in the thickest of the fight.

ATKINSON, DELMER—Enrolled at Ridgefield, July 30, 1862. Discharged at Murfreesboro', May 2, 1863, on account of disability. Deceased.

ALLEN, JAMES—Enrolled at Norwalk, August 9, 1862. Discharged at Camp Dennison, April 3, 1865, on account of disability.

AUSTIN, JULIUS—Enrolled at Townsend, August 9, 1862. Transferred to Company F, 7th Regiment, Veteran Reserve Corps, November 20, 1863. Mustered out June 28, 1865, at Washington.

BASE, JOHN—Enrolled at Norwalk, August 11, 1862. Promoted to Corporal, August 1, 1863. Wounded and taken prisoner in the Battle of Chickamauga, September 20, 1863. Perished by burning of steamer General Lyon off coast of Cape Hatteras, N. C., March 31, 1865.

BRADY, PATRICK W.—Enrolled at Lyme, August 6, 1862. Promoted to Corporal, May 1, 1865. Mustered out with Company. One of the four not injured at Chickamauga. (See Captain Bryant.)

BARKER, NEWBURY—Enrolled at New London, August, 9, 1862. Died at Nashville, December 1, 1862, of fever.

BRISOCK, JUSTUS F.—Enrolled at New London, August 11, 1862. Mustered as Sergeant. Discharged at Louisville, December 31, 1862, on account of disability. Died in Denver, Col.

BUCK, JOHN—Enrolled at Norwalk, August 5, 1862. Detailed as wagoner. Discharged at Nashville, March 7, 1863, on account of disability.

BLANKS, ROBERT A.—Enrolled at Lima, for a year, March 31, 1865. Discharged at Columbus, May 16, 1865.

BRADLEY, WARREN—Enrolled at New London, July 30, 1862. Discharged September 2, 1863, at Cleveland, O., on account of disability. Died in New London, O., May 27, 1882.

BARRETT, RANSOM—Enrolled at New London, August 6, 1862. Discharged at New Albany, Ind., December 4, 1862, on account of disability. Deceased.

BRADY, TRANEN—Enrolled at ———, July 30, 1862. No record after muster in.

CARTWRIGHT, CHARLES E.—Enrolled at Norwalk, August 6, 1862. Died at Camp Dennison, August 12, 1864, of disease.

COLEMAN, GEORGE P.—Enrolled at New London, July 30, 1862. Severely wounded and captured in Battle of

Chickamauga, September 20, 1863. Died in Andersonville prison, April 26, 1864, of disease and wounds. Was left without proper care for several days after Chickamauga. (See prison sketch of Captain Hale.)

CHOLLAR, LUCIUS A.—Enrolled at Norwalk, August 9, 1862. Died at Danville, Ky., November 16, 1862, of disease.

CHANCE, LEONARD—Enrolled at Peru, August 12, 1862. Died at Murfreesboro', May 30, 1863, of fever.

CHOLLAR, JAMES A.—Enrolled at Norwalk, August 5, 1862.

CARTWRIGHT, MILES E.—Enrolled at Norwalk, August 5, 1862. Dicharged, January 1, 1863.

CLEVELAND, WILLIAM P.—Enrolled at Norwalk, August 5, 1862. Discharged at Nashville, Tenn., February 12, 1863, on account of disability.

CARR, CHESTER S.—Enrolled at Ridgefield, September 4, 1862. Transferred as Quartermaster, 1st United States Veteran Volunteer Engineers. Discharged at Columbus, March 27, 1863, on account of disability.

CLOCK, ANDREW—Enrolled at Ridgefield, August 11, 1862. Transferred to Company K, 5th Regiment, Veteran Reserve Corps, March 15, 1864.

DISBRO, HIRAM C.—Enrolled at New London, August 11, 1862. Never mustered.

ERNSBERGER, HENRY—Enrolled at Hartland, August 12, 1862. Died in Green County, Ky., November 4, 1862, of fever.

EVANS, ANDREW—Enrolled at New London, August 6, 1862. Discharged at Cincinnati, March 21, 1863, on account of disability. Died in New London in 1877.

EARL, THOMAS—Enrolled at Ridgefield, August 9, 1862. Transferred to 43rd Company, 2nd Battallion, Veteran Reserve Corps, November 26, 1863. Mustered out, June 28, 1865, at Camp Dennison. Deceased.

ELLS, JAMES E.—Enrolled at New London, August 18, 1862. Appointed Corporal. No record after muster in.

FISH, HENRY—Enrolled at Clarksfield, August 8, 1862. Died of typhoid fever and congestion of the brain, April 25, 1863, at Murfreesboro', Tenn.

GRIFFIN, JOHN R.—Enrolled at Wakeman, August 11, 1862. Left sick at Nashville, December 26, 1862. Rejoined the Regiment at Murfreesboro'. Promoted to Corporal, February 1, 1863. Severely wounded in the arm and shoulder in the Battle of Chickamauga, September 19, 1863, but rejoined the Regiment in time for Atlanta and subsequent campaigns. Mustered out with Company.

GREEN, CHARLES R.—Enrolled at Clarksfield, August 8, 1862. Wounded in the Battle of Chickamauga, September 19, 1863. Mustered out with Company.

GREGORY, NORMAN—Enrolled at Ridgefield, August 9, 1862. Killed, May 30, 1864, near Dallas, Ga.

GREEN, THOMAS—Enrolled at Townsend, August 4, 1862. Discharged at Murfreesboro', July 1, 1863, on account of disability.

GASTON, HARMON—Enrolled at Sandusky, March 1, 1865. Transferred to Company A, 51st Ohio Volunteer Infantry, June 10, 1865. Mustered out, July 12, 1865, at Camp Dennison.

GREEN, LEVI—Enrolled at Sandusky, February 28, 1865. Transferred to 51st Ohio Veteran Infantry, June 10, 1865.

HALLER, FREDERICK J.—Enrolled at East Townsend, August 4, 1862. Severely wounded in the Battle of Chickamauga, September 19, 1863, the ball entering just below the left eye, and, passing through the head, came out at the back of the neck. Lay all night on the battlefield, unconscious. A rebel soldier gave him a drink in the morning and covered him with a tent cloth. Captured and kept in an open field with others for ten days. A prisoner for fifteen months in Richmond, Danville, Andersonville and Florence. Parolled in December, 1864. Rejoined the Regiment. Mustered out with Company.

HARDER, CORNELIUS F.—Enrolled at Lyme, August 7, 1862. Wounded at Nashville, December 15, 1864. Mustered out with Company. Deceased.

HARRIMAN, JOHN—Enrolled at Norwalk, July 26, 1862. Was detailed as gardener at the field hospital at Murfreesboro', in the spring and summer of 1863. Mustered out, June 30, 1865, at Murfreesboro'.

HARRIS, CHARLES—Enrolled at Ridgefield, August 18, 1862. Deceased.

HILLYER, A. WARD—Enrolled at Ridgefield, July 26, 1862. Mustered as Sergeant. Discharged at Columbus, December 19, 1862, on account of disability. Deceased.

HILL, ALBERT R.—Enrolled at Wakeman, August 9, 1862. Promoted to Corporal, September 14, 1862. Discharged at Louisville, Ky., January 31, 1863, on account of disability.

HENLEY, PHILIP F.—Enrolled at Norwalk, July 31, 1862. Discharged at Murfreesboro', March 3, 1863, on account of disability.

HASBROOK, JOHN W.—Enrolled at Wakeman, August 9, 1862. Left sick at Covington. Discharged, November 26, 1862, at Louisville, Ky., on account of disability. Died at Wakeman, O., January 5, 1864.

HILL, HORACE—Enrolled at Ridgefield, July 28, 1862. Discharged at Louisville, Ky., January 6, 1863, on account of disability. Died at Swanton, O., March 10, 1893.

HOFF, SIDNEY—Enrolled at Townsend, August 4, 1862. Wounded in Battle of Stone's River, December 31, 1862. Shot through right hand. Transferred to Company B, Second Regiment, Veteran Reserve Corps, November 17, 1864. Mustered out, July 15, 1865, at Cairo, Ill. Died at Townsend, O., February 5, 1881.

INMAN, ABRAM—Enrolled at Norwalk, August 9, 1862. Mortally wounded and captured in the Battle of Chickamauga, September 19, 1863. Died in the rebel hospital on the field of battle, October 5, 1863.

JACKSON, ANDREW A.—Enrolled at Norwalk, July 26, 1862. Mustered as Corporal. Promoted to Sergeant, December 1, 1862; to First Sergeant, May 12, 1864. Wounded in the Battle of Stone's River, December 31, 1862, but assisted in bearing Lieutenant Colonel Wooster from the field. Mustered out with Company.

JEFFERSON, FREDERICK F.—Enrolled at Ridgefield, August 11, 1862. Mustered as Corporal. Promoted to Sergeant, January 4, 1863. Promoted to First Sergeant, November 1, 1863. Killed at Rocky Face Ridge, May 11, 1864.

KNAPP, ABEL—Enrolled at New London, August 11, 1862. Promoted to Corporal, July 1, 1863. Promoted to Sergeant, November 1, 1863. Color Bearer last half of first day at Chickamauga and until March, 1864, when the old Color Bearer, wounded in the Battle of Chickamauga, September 19, 1863, came up. Mustered out with Company. One of the four left after Chickamauga. (See Captain Bryant.)

KING, JOHN—Enrolled at Norwalk, August 10, 1862. Promoted to Sergeant May 1, 1865. Mustered out with Company. Deceased.

KINGSLEY, HENRY—Enrolled at Ridgefield, August 6, 1862. Mustered as Corporal. Discharged at Nashville, March 10, 1863, on account of disability. Died, March 4, 1891, at Monroeville.

KINGSLEY, WILBUR B.—Enrolled at Ridgefield, August 9, 1862. Transferred to Veteran Reserve Corps, August 1, 1863. Deceased.

KILBURN, ENOCH H.—Enrolled at Wakeman, August 9, 1862. One of the first to reach the captured guns at Knob Gap. Severely wounded, and captured at Stone's River, December 31, 1862. Parolled at Richmond, May 3, 1863. Transferred to Veteran Reserve Corps, March 7, 1864. Mustered out, August 15, 1865.

LAMERAUX, GEO.—Enrolled at Ridgefield, August 7, 1862. Killed, Sept. 19, 1863, in the Battle of Chickamauga.

LOWE, ALPHA, JR.—Enrolled at Townsend, August 4, 1862. Died, June 14, 1864, of disease.

LEWIS, JOHN—Enrolled at Lyme, September 4, 1862. Died of typhoid fever, January 19, 1863, at Nashville.

MARTIN, HARMON H.—Enrolled at Wakeman, August 9, 1862. Detailed to drive ambulance. Captured in the Battle of Chickamauga, September 20, 1863. A prisoner fifteen months. Confined in Libby and Andersonville prisons. Exchanged, and mustered out, June 9, 1865, at Camp Chase, Ohio.

MARTIN, ELWOOD—Enrolled at Wakeman, September 4, 1862. Left sick at Nashville, December 26, 1862, at which place he died, January 23, 1863, of typhoid fever.

McPHERSON, WILLIAM L.—Enrolled at Norwalk, August 4, 1862. Died at Nashville, October 13, 1863, of wounds received in the Battle of Chickamauga, September 20, 1863.

McGRAW, JOHN—Enrolled at Clarksfield, August 6, 1862. Wounded in the Battle of Chickamauga, September 19, 1863. Discharged, July 14, 1864, at Camp Dennison, on account of disability. Died at Fitchville, O., March 25, 1884.

MINER, WILLIAM M.—Enrolled at Ridgefield, August 16, 1862. Transferred to 1st United States Veteran Volunteer Engineer Corps, August 7, 1864. Mustered out, June 30, 1865.

MOODY, JAMES S.—Enrolled at Norwich, August 5, 1862.

MARKS, JAMES—Enrolled at Wakeman, August 11, 1862.

PIKE, SAMUEL A.—Enrolled at Ridgefield, August 7, 1862. Died at Covington, Ky., October 10, 1862, of inflammatory rheumatism.

PROSSER, CYRUS B.—Enrolled at New London, July 30, 1862. Died January 12, 1863, on transport steamer at Louisville, Ky., of wounds received in the Battle of Stone's River, December 31, 1862.

POLLY, AMOS W.—Enrolled at Lyme, August 6, 1862. Discharged at Murfreesboro', May 17, 1863, on account of disability.

PARK, MATTHEW—Enrolled at Bronson, August 11, 1862. Mustered out at Nashville, May 16, 1865. Died in Missouri in 1879.

RUNYAN, EDWIN—Enrolled at New London, August 13, 1862. Killed in the Battle of Stone's River, December 31, 1862.

RIGGS, JOHN L.—Enrolled at Norwalk, August 5, 1862. Died at New Albany, Ind., January —, 1863, of disease.

RAIDART, GEORGE P.—Enrolled at Norwalk, August 9, 1862. Appointed Corporal. No record after March 30, 1863.

ROBBINS, WILLARD E.—Enrolled at Wakeman, August 7, 1862. Mustered as Corporal. Discharged at Nashville, April 29, 1863, on account of disability.

RYAN, VANRENSSALAER M.—Enrolled at Townsend, August 4, 1862. Appointed Corporal, August 30, 1862. Discharged at Columbus, April 24, 1863, on account of disability.

RUSSELL, WILLIAM H.—Enrolled at Wakeman, August 11, 1862. Wounded in the Battle of Chickamauga, September 19, 1863. Transferred to United States Navy, April 15, 1864.

SEARL, JOEL—Enrolled at Hartland, August 4, 1862. Died at Hartland, April 2, 1863, of fever.

STEWART, GEORGE A.—Enrolled at Lyme, August 4, 1862. Never mustered, too old. Died in Fall of 1862.

SMITH, DAVID W.—Enrolled at Ridgeville, August 4, 1862. Mustered as First Sergeant. Discharged at Columbus, March 6, 1863, on account of disability.

STRONG, BENJAMIN T.—Enrolled at Wakeman, August 11, 1862. Promoted to Sergeant, Feb. 1, 1863. Wounded and captured at Battle of Chickamauga, September 20, 1863. Discharged at Camp Chase, May 5, 1864, on account of gunshot wound in the left fore arm, both bones fractured. In prison for two months.

SMITH, JOHN—Enrolled at Ridgefield, August 11, 1862. Discharged at Camp Dennison, January 4, 1864, on account of wounds received in the Battle of Stone's River, December 31, 1862. Deceased.

SHANGER, WILLIAM W.—Enrolled at Peru, August 12, 1862. Transferred to 1st United States Veteran Volunteer Engineer Corps, August 7, 1864. Mustered out, June 30, 1865. Deceased.

SPRINGER, OLIVER H. P.—Enrolled at Norwalk, August 5, 1862. Transferred to Vetearn Reserve Corps, March 1, 1864.

STEVENS, MARQUIS D.—Enrolled at New London, August 11, 1862. Transferred to Veteran Reserve Corps, January 5, 1864.

STIMPSON, JOHN—Enrolled at Ridgefield, August 9, 1862. Shot through the right lung in the Battle of Stone's River, December 31, 1862. Transferred to Veteran Reserve Corps, January 14, 1864.

SIMMONS, LOVELL R.—Enrolled at Wakeman, August 9, 1862. No record after muster in.

STAUNTON, GERSHAM R.—Enrolled at Townsend, August 9, 1862. No record after muster in.

SCOTT, JOSEPH.—Enrolled at Ridgefield, July 28, 1862. No record after muster in.

TURNER, CHARLES A.—Enrolled at Ridegfield, July 29, 1862. Transferred to Mississippi Marine Brigade, January, 1863. Deceased.

VOSBURGH, ISAAC—Enrolled at New London, August 4, 1862. Discharged at Louisville, Ky., January 1, 1863, on account of disability.

VANSCOY, VANRENSSALAER—Enrolled at New London, August 13, 1862. Discharged at New Albany, January 17, 1863, on account of wounds received in the Battle of Stone's River, December 31, 1862. Killed accidentally, near Clinton, Wis.

WHITNEY, ALBERT—Enrolled at New London, August 4, 1862. Promoted to Corporal, May 1, 1865. Mustered out with Company. One of the four survivors at the Battle of Chickamauga, September 20, 1863. See Capt. Bryant.

WHALEY, JOHN—Enrolled at Ridgefield, September 4, 1862. Mustered out with Company.

WILSON, SAMUEL W.—Enrolled at Wakeman, August 9, 1862. Left sick at Bowling Green, Ky., October 3, 1862. Rejoined Regiment at Murfreesboro', Tenn., in April, 1863. Mortally wounded in a charge at Chickamauga, and died in the hands of the enemy. Body never identified.

WEBSTER, DANIEL—Enrolled at Ridgeville, August 6, 1862. Died at Murfreesboro', February 3, 1863, of typhoid fever.

WOODIN, MARVIN W.—Enrolled at Townsend, August 12, 1862. Died at Huntsville, Ala., January 12, 1865, of disease.

WEBB, GIDEON D.—Enrolled at Wakeman, August 9, 1862, as Corporal. Left sick at Bardstown, Ky. Rejoined Regiment after Chickamauga. Severely wounded at Kenesaw Mountain, June 23, 1864. Discharged at Columbus, March 27, 1865, on account of disability. Died at Wakeman, October 15, 1871.

WILLIAMS, JOHN—Enrolled at Fitchville, August 12, 1862. Discharged at Camp Dennison, June 16, 1863, on account of wounds received in the Battle of Stone's River, December 31, 1862. Died in 1886 in California.

WELCH, ALPHEUS W.—Enrolled at Wakeman, August 9, 1862, as drummer. Left sick at Monroeville. Discharged at Columbus, November 19, 1862. Died October 2, 1872, at Wakeman, O., of typhoid fever.

WEBSTER, HERMAN G.—Enrolled at Ridgefield, August 5, 1862. Transferred to Veteran Reserve Corps, November 28, 1863.

YOUNG, GEORGE A.—Enrolled at Ridgefield, August 9, 1862. Discharged March 11, 1863, at St. Louis, Mo., to enlist in Mississippi Marine Brigade. Deceased.

COMPANY B.

CAPTAIN THOMAS C. FERNALD—Enrolled at Columbus, July 19, 1862. Mustered as Captain at Columbus, July 19, 1852. Resigned at Nashville, Tenn., January 25, 1863, on account of physical disability. Died in 1890.

CAPTAIN STEPHEN P. BECKWITH—Enrolled August 8, 1862. Mustered as First Lieutenant, August 30, 1862. Promoted to Captain, January 25, 1863. Resigned, November 14, 1864, at Pulaski, Tenn., on account of disability. Died at Jackson, Mich.

CAPTAIN JAY C. BUTLER—Enrolled at Sandusky, July 22, 1862. Mustered as Sergeant. Promoted to Second Lieutenant, January 25, 1863; to First Lieutenant, March 19, 1864; to Captain, February 10, 1865. Wounded in Battle of Nashville, December 15, 1864. Mustered out with the Company, June 12, 1865.

LIEUTENANT JOHN M. BUTLER—Enrolled at Sandusky, July 22, 1862. Mustered as First Sergeant; promoted to First Lieutenant, January 25, 1863. Captured at Battle of Stone's River, December 31, 1862. Confined in Libby prison. Paroled. Exchanged. Resigned, December 27, 1864, on account of disability.

LIEUTENANT CHARLES MORFOOT—Enrolled at Bucyrus, August 9, 1862. Mustered as Corporal. Promoted to First Sergeant, August 1, 1863; to First Lieutenant, November 3, 1864, and assigned from Company C. Mustered out with the Company, June 12, 1865.

LIEUTENANT OTIS L. PECK—Enrolled at Sandusky, August 20, 1862. Mustered as Second Lieutenant. Discharged at Murfreesboro', Tenn., March 1, 1863.

ARMSTRONG, EDWARD G.—Enrolled at Berlin, February 29, 1864. Wounded at Kingston, May 18, 1864. Mustered out, August 7, 1865, at Nashville, Tenn.

AUSTIN, HARPER—Enrolled at Sandusky, August 5, 1862. Mustered out with the Company, June 12, 1865. Deceased.

BARTOW, WILLIAM P.—Enrolled at Sandusky, August 8, 1862. Wagoner. Mustered out with Company. Died at Milan, O., July 8, 1872.

BURRELL, WILLIAM—Enrolled at Milan, August 6, 1862. Wounded at Battle of Stone's River, December 31, 1862. Died at Nashville, Tenn., January 28, 1863, of disease.

BECKSTED, PHILIP—Enrolled at Sandusky, August 8, 1862. No record after December 31, 1862.

BLY, HENRY J.—Enrolled at Sandusky, August 7, 1862. Mustered as Corporal. Discharged at Nashville, February 17, 1863, on account of wounds received in Battle of Stone's River, December 31, 1862.

BAILEY, THOMAS—Enrolled at Milan, February 29, 1864. Transferred to Company A, 51st Ohio Veteran Volunteer Infantry, June 10, 1865.

BEARDSLEY, HOMER—Enrolled at Berlin, February 20, 1864. Transferred to Company A, 51st Ohio Veteran Volunteer Infantry, June 10, 1865. Deceased.

BARTOW, SETH A.—Enrolled at Sandusky, August 6, 1862. Wounded three times at Battle of Chickamauga, Tenn., September 19, 1863. Also captured, but escaped. Transferred to Company H, 19th Regiment Veteran Reserve Corps, January 4, 1864. Mustered out at Elmira, N. Y., July 13, 1865.

WILBUR F. COWLES—Enrolled at Sandusky, August 8, 1862. Promoted to First Sergeant, January 25, 1863. Taken prisoner at Battle of Stone's River, December 31, 1862, and confined in Libby prison. Paroled; exchanged. Captured at Battle of Chickaamauga, September 20, 1863, and imprisoned at Richmond, Danville, Andersonville, Charlotte, and Florence. Mustered out, June 9, 1865, at Camp Chase.

CURRAN, ALLEN M.—Enrolled at Sandusky, August 5, 1862. Promoted to Sergeant, January 25, 1863. Captured at Battle of Stone's River, December 31, 1862. Exchanged. In Pioneer Corps on Atlanta campaign. Mustered out, May 30, 1865, at Cleveland.

CULLEN, ROBERT—Enrolled at Sandusky, August 7, 1862. Mustered out with Company.

CARPENTER, WILLIAM H.—Enrolled at Sandusky, August 1, 1862. Discharged at Nashville, Tenn., January 15, 1863, on account of disability.

CLAFLIN, EDWIN—Enrolled at Sandusky, August 6, 1862. Mustered out at Nashville, May 13, 1865, on account of accidental wound received at Ayersville, N. C., April 5, 1865.

CORELL, WILLIAM H.—Enrolled at Sandusky, August 8, 1862. Transferred to Marine Service, May 3, 1863.

CAMPBELL, JAMES—Enrolled at Milan, February 29, 1864. Wounded near Kingston, Ga., May 19, 1864. Transferred to Company A, 51st Ohio Veteran Volunteer Infantry, June 10, 1865. Deceased.

DOUGLASS, ANSON B.—Enrolled at Sandusky, July 29, 1862. Promoted to Corporal, March 1, 1865. Mustered out with Company. Deceased.

DENNIS, CHARLES B.—Enrolled at Sandusky, August 7, 1862. Wounded and captured at Battle of Stone's River, December 31, 1862. Exchanged. Detailed as clerk at General Davis' headquarters, January 30, 1863. Mustered out, June 13, 1865, at Nashville.

DODGE, MILTON C.—Enrolled at Sandusky, August 6, 1862. Killed at Battle of Chickamauga, September 20, 1863.

DRURY, JEROME—Enrolled at Berlin, February 23, 1864. Died at Jeffersonville, Ind., June 23, 1864, of disease.

DAVIS, JOSHUA B.—Enrolled at Sandusky, August 6, 1862. Mustered as Corporal. Transferred to 1st Regiment United States Engineers, and promoted to Sergeant-Major, July 29, 1864. Mustered out, June 30, 1865, at Nashville, Tenn.

DODGE, JOHN W.—Enrolled at Sandusky, August 6, 1862. Transferred to 120th Company, 2nd Battalion, Veteran Reserve Corps, January 4, 1864. Mustered out, June 29, 1865, at Evansville, Ind. Deceased.

DAVIS, SIMEON A.—Enrolled at Sandusky, August 7, 1862. Wounded at Battle of Stone's River, December 31, 1862. Transferred to Veteran Reserve Corps, May 2, 1864.

DAVISON, GEORGE—Enrolled at Sandusky, February 26, 1864. Transferred to Company A, 51st Ohio Volunteer Infantry, June 10, 1865.

ELWOOD, HENRY M.—Enrolled at Sandusky, August 21, 1862. Discharged at Nashville, December 20, 1862, on account of disability. Deceased.

EGGLESTON, JOSIAH—Enrolled at Berlin, February 29, 1864. Discharged at Louisville, Ky., May 18, 1865.

FORD, THEODORE—Enrolled at Sandusky, August 21, 1862. Wounded at Battle of Chickamauga, September 19, 1863. Transferred to Company B, 15th Regiment, Veteran Reserve Corps. Mustered out at Springfield, Ill., July 7, 1865. Died of wounds, after discharge.

FAXON, SIDNEY—Enrolled at Sandusky, August 6, 1862. Discharged at Louisville, Ky., January 28, 1863, on account of disability.

FITCH, JAMES C.—Enrolled at Sandusky, August 6, 1862. Mustered out at Chattanooga, May 29, 1865.

FOREMAN, ALFRED—Enrolled at Sandusky, August 8, 1862. Discharged at Nashville, January 14, 1863, on account of disability.

FOX, AMOS W.—Enrolled at Sandusky, August 21, 1862. Transferred to Company F, 2d Regiment, Veteran Reserve Corps, July 1, 1863.

GLENN, JAMES—Enrolled at Sandusky, August 6, 1862. Died at Danville, Ky., November 5, 1862, of disease.

GORDON, JAMES—Enrolled at Sandusky, August 5, 1862. Mustered as Sergeant. Discharged at Danville, Ky., March 8, 1863, on account of disability.

GRANT, ALFRED—Enrolled at Sandusky, August 28, 1862. Discharged at Bowling Green, Ky., February 24, 1863, on account of disability.

GAY, LEONARD—Enrolled at Sandusky, August 6, 1862. Discharged at Nashville, January 10, 1863, on account of disability.

GLASIER, GEORGE H.—Enrolled at Berlin, February 28, 1864. Mustered out, May 18, 1865, at Nashville.

GROSS, CHARLES—Enrolled at Sandusky, August 8, 1862. Wounded in the Battle of Chickamauga, September 20, 1863. Transferred to Company H, 19th Regiment, Veteran Reserve Corps. Mustered out, July 13, 1865, at Elmira, N.Y.

HILL, JAMES L.—Enrolled at Sandusky, August 6, 1862. Mustered out at Camp Cleveland, June 20, 1865.

HUNTINGTON, SIMON—Enrolled at Sandusky, August 5, 1862. Mustered as Sergeant. Mortally wounded in the Battle of Stone's River, December 31, 1862. Died, January 19, 1863, at Nashville.

HILL, GEORGE W.—Enrolled at Sandusky, August 5, 1862. Detailed as Musician. Died at Perryville, Ky., November 12, 1862, of disease.

HOLLY, JEROME—Enrolled at Sandusky, August 5, 1862. Died at Murfreesboro', May 8, 1863, of disease.

HAMMOND, HARRISON J.—Enrolled at Sandusky, August 5, 1862. Died at Murfreesboro', February 14, 1863, of disease.

HOLLY, ORLANDO—Enrolled at Sandusky, August 7, 1862. Died at Danville, Ky., Nov. 8, 1862, of disease.

HUTTON, WILLIAM L.—Enrolled at Sandusky, August 5, 1862. Discharged at Nashville, October 7, 1863, on account of disability.

HINMAN, ALBERT—Enrolled at Sandusky, August 6, 1862. Discharged at Louisville, Ky., October 10, 1863, on account of wounds received in the Battle of Stone's River, December 31, 1862. Died in 1890.

HARRINGTON, SMITH—Enrolled at Sandusky, August 8, 1862. Discharged at Bowling Green, Ky., February 24, 1863, on account of disability.

HOLBROOK, OLIVER—Enrolled at Sandusky, August 8, 1862. Discharged at Nashville, March 10, 1863, on account of disability.

HOSMER, ALEXANDER C.—Enrolled at Sandusky, July 22, 1862. Promoted to Second Lieutenant and assigned to Company A, January 4, 1863.

HOUSMAN, FRANCIS—Enrolled at Sandusky, August 5, 1862. Transferred to 139th Company, 2d Battalion, Veteran Reserve Corps, March 18, 1864. Mustered out, June 30, 1865, at Nashville. Died at Wauseon, O., April 15, 1888.

HINDS, DAVID—Enrolled at Sandusky, August 6, 1862. Transferred to 139th Company, 2nd Battalion, Veteran Reserve Corps, March 18, 1864. Mustered out at Nashville, Tenn., June 30, 1865. Died in 1890.

INGLES, MARTIN—Enrolled at Sandusky, August 21, 1862. Died at Bridgeport, Ala,, December 9, 1863, of disease.

JUNG, JACOB—Enrolled at Sandusky, August 11, 1862. Wounded in the Battle of Stone's River, December 31, 1862. Promoted to Corporal, March 1, 1865. Mustered out with Company. Deceased.

JOHNSON, THOMAS—Enrolled at Sandusky, August 2, 1862. No record after September 4, 1862.

KUNZ, PHILIP, JR.—Enrolled at Sandusky, August 7, 1862. Promoted to Corporal, March 1, 1863. Detailed to carry Division battle flag, and received same from General Stanley with a little speech. Carried same through several battles. Placed in command of Division Orderlies. Acted as aid to General Kimball. Mustered out with the Company.

KILBURN, JOSIAH W.—Enrolled in Erie County, March 30, 1864. Mustered out at Camp Dennison, May 25, 1865, on account of disability.

LADD, GEORGE W.—Enrolled at Sandusky, August 5, 1862. Promoted to Sergeant, January 25, 1863. Mustered out June 20, 1865, at Camp Cleveland.

LUHRS, JUSTUS—Enrolled at Sandusky, August 7, 1862. Promoted to Corporal. June 1, 1864. Mustered out with Company. Died in New York City in 1878.

LITTLETON, GEORGE W.—Enrolled at Sandusky, August 6, 1862. Mustered out with Company.

LADEN, JAMES H.—Enrolled at Sandusky, August 7, 1862. Discharged at Nashville, April 7, 1863, on account of disability.

LINCOLN, EMMETT—Enrolled at Sandusky, August 6, 1862. Transferred to Marine Service. Deceased.

MEACHAM, WILLIAM—Enrolled at Sandusky, August 5, 1862. Wounded at Buzzard's Roost, May 11, 1864. Mustered out with Company.

MERKLEY, JACOB—Enrolled at Sandusky, August 7, 1862. Mustered out with Company.

MEEKER, ROLLA—Enrolled at Monroeville, September 3, 1862. Wounded in the Battle near Atlanta, Ga., July 22, 1864. Mustered out at Louisville, May 22, 1865, on account of gunshot wound in right hand.

MULLEN, DENNIS—Enrolled at Sandusky, August 5, 1862. Detailed in Pioneer Corps, October 19, 1862. Returned to Company, March —, 1864. Wounded at Kenesaw, June 23, 1864. Mustered out with Company. Deceased.

MILLER, JOHN F.—Enrolled at Sandusky, August 5, 1862. Died at Nashville, Tenn., May 26, 1864, from accidental wound received May 8, 1864.

MARSHALL, JOSEPH T.—Enrolled at Sandusky, August 5, 1862. Discharged at Louisville, April 18, 1863, on account of wounds received in the Battle of Stone's River, December 31, 1862.

McGATTIGAN, CHARLES—Enrolled at Sandusky, August 5, 1862. Transferred to Veteran Reserve Corps, May 3, 1864. Deceased.

MATTHEWS, EDWARD J.—See Non-Commission Staff.

MUNSON, FRANK—Enrolled at Berlin, February 29, 1864. Transferred to Veteran Reserve Corps, January 16, 1865.

MILLS, MYRON—Enrolled at Berlin, February 25, 1864. Transferred to Company F, 51st Ohio Veteran Volunteer Infantry, June 10, 1865. Mustered out at Camp Dennison, July 10, 1865. Deceased.

PIRTSCHMAN, OSCAR—Enrolled at Sandusky, August 5, 1862. Promoted to Corporal, March 1, 1865. Mustered out with Company. Died at Franklin, Tenn.

POMEROY, EDWIN C.—Enrolled at Sandusky, August 5, 1862. Died at Chattanooga, June 30, 1864, of wounds received June 21, 1864, at Kenesaw Mountain.

PAGE, JAMES—Enrolled in Erie County, March 30, 1864. Died at Pulaski, Tenn, January 17, 1865, of disease.

PIERCE, CHARLES D.—Enrolled at Sandusky, August 5, 1862. Discharged at Louisville, Ky., June 11, 1863, on account of disability. Deceased.

PENFIELD, HENRY B.—Enrolled at Sandusky, August 5, 1862. Discharged at Bridgeport, Ala., December 30, 1863, on account of disability.

POPE, WILLIAM H.—Enrolled at Sandusky, August 6, 1862. Discharged, March 12, 1864, on account of wounds received in the Battle of Chickamauga, September 19, 1863.

PEASE, FRANCIS L.—Enrolled at Sandusky, August 5, 1862. Mustered as Corporal. Transferred to 148th Company, 2nd Battalion, Veteran Reserve Corps, April 6, 1864. Mustered out, June 30, 1865, at Nashville, Tenn.

RICE, WILLIAM B.—Enrolled at Sandusky, July 29, 1862. Mustered as Corporal. Promoted to Sergeant, January 25, 1863. Captured at Stone's River, December 31, 1862, and confined in Libby prison. Parolled. Exchanged. Detailed as Clerk at Division Headquarters, January 19, 1865. Mustered out with Company.

RICE, ADEN O.—Enrolled at Sandusky, August 6, 1862. Wounded and captured in Battle of Stone's River, December 31, 1862. Returned to Company in November, 1863. Detailed as Clerk at Corps Headquarters. Mustered out, June 13, 1865, at Nashville.

REBADUE, THEODORE—Enrolled at Sandusky, August 5, 1862. Taken prisoner near Huntsville, Ala., January 17, 1865. Hanged by guerrillas for attempting to escape. (See Lieutenant Squire's account of prison experience.)

REED, HIRAM—Enrolled at Sandusky, March 28, 1864. Mustered out, July 6, 1865, at Louisville, Ky.

REED, LOUIS C.—Enrolled at Sandusky, March 28, 1864. No further record.

SHUPE, CHARLES—Enrolled at Milan, August 6, 1862. Captured in Battle of Chickamauga, September 20, 1863. Imprisoned at Andersonville, Charlotte and Florence. Exchanged at Wilmington. Mustered out at Camp Chase, June 16, 1865. Died, August 29, 1891, at Milan, O.

SCHELB, ROBERT—Enrolled at Sandusky, August 8, 1862. Wounded in Battle of Chickamauga, September 20, 1863. Mustered out with Company.

SEVERY, BRADFORD J.—Enrolled at Sandusky, August 5, 1862. Mustered out with Company.

SANKEY, ROBERT—Enrolled at Sandusky, August 7, 1862. Died at Nashville, March 28, 1863, of disease.

SHAY, THEODORE—Enrolled at Sandusky, August 6, 1862. Captured at the Battle of Stone's River, December 31, 1862. Parolled.

SMITH, CHARLES E.—Enrolled at Sandusky, July 22, 1862. Mustered as Sergeant. Discharged at Murfreesboro', February 14, 1863, on account of disability.

SHARP, ALONZO R.—Enrolled at Sandusky, August 6, 1862. Mustered as Corporal. Discharged at Louisville, June 1, 1863, on account of disability.

SEAMANS, ORANGE—Enrolled at Sandusky, August 8, 1862. Discharged at Bowling Green, January 9, 1863, on account of disability.

SMITH, JAY C.—See Non-Commissioned Staff.

SEARS, AMOS—Enrolled at Berlin, February 29, 1864. Transferred to Company A, 51st Ohio Volunteer Infantry, June 10, 1865.

TAYLOR, WILLIAM D.—Enrolled at Sandusky, August 6, 1862. Mustered as Corporal. Promoted to Sergeant, January 25, 1864. Mustered out with Company.

TERRILL, JOSEPH—Enrolled at Sandusky, August 8, 1862. Captured in Battle of Chickamauga, September 20, 1863. Imprisoned at Richmond, Danville, Andersonville, Florence and Charlotte. Exchanged at Wilmington, April 1, 1865, but died a few days later at Annapolis.

TAYLOR, RALPH E.—Enrolled at Sandusky, August 5, 1862. Discharged at Murfreesboro', October 9, 1863, on account of disability.

TUCKER, ROYAL H.—Enrolled at Sandusky, August 8, 1862. Wounded near Murfreesboro' while on picket. Mustered out at Chattanooga, May 29, 1865, on account of disability.

THOMPSON, DANIEL W.—Enrolled at Sandusky, August 5, 1862. Promoted to Corporal. Transferred to Veteran Reserve Corps, September 20, 1863.

TUCKER, JOHN—Enrolled at Berlin, February 29, 1864. Transferred to Company A, 51st Ohio Volunteer Infantry, June 10, 1865.

WALL, CHRISTOPHER—Enrolled at Sandusky, August 5, 1862. No record after August 31, 1862.

WARD, JOHN—Enrolled at Sandusky, August 5, 1862. Mustered as Corporal. Discharged at Nashville, April 7, 1863, on account of disability. Deceased.

WRIGHT, SAMUEL G.—Enrolled at Sandusky, August 8, 1862. Discharged at Bridgeport, Ala., December 30, 1863, on account of disability.

WOOLVERTON, JOEL S.—Enrolled at Sandusky, August 5, 1862. Discharged at Bowling Green, Ky., December 30, 1862, on account of disability. Deceased.

WOOD, DANIEL.—Enrolled at Sandusky, August 6, 1862. Discharged at Nashville, January 7, 1864, on account of disability.

WOOD, MICHAEL — Enrolled at Milan, August 5, 1862. Wounded at Perryville, Ky., October 8, 1862, also in the Battle of Stone's River, December 31, 1862. Discharged at Nashville, December 30, 1863, on account of disability.

WENCK, ANTON—Enrolled at Sandusky, August 8, 1862. Discharged at Bridgeport, Ala., December 30, 1863, on account of disability.

WRIGHT, HENRY O.—Enrolled at Sandusky, August 8, 1862. Transferred to Veteran Reserve Corps. Re-enlisted in 23rd Illinois Veteran Volunteers, and mustered out at Richmond, Va., August 5, 1865.

WASHBURN, DUSTIN—Enrolled at Milan, August 8, 1862. Transferred to 1st United States Engineer Corps, August 29, 1864. Mustered out, June 30, 1865, at Nashville, Tenn.

ZIMMERMAN, JACOB M.—Enrolled at Sandusky, August 5, 1862. Appointed Sergeant, January 1, 1863. Wounded and captured in Battle of Chickamauga, Sept. 20, '63. Imprisoned at Richmond, where he died, January 9, 1864.

COMPANY C.

CAPTAIN B. B. MCDONALD—See Field and Staff.

CAPTAIN LEONARD D. SMITH—Enrolled and mustered at Sandusky, August 4, 1862, as Lieutenant and Adjutant. Promoted to Captain and assigned to Company C, May 2, 1863. Mustered out with the Company at Camp Harker, Tenn., June 12, 1865.

LIEUTENANT ISAAC ANDERSON—Enrolled at Bucyrus, July 29, 1862. Discharged at Nashville, Tenn., January 2, 1863, on account of disability.

LIEUTENANT WILLIAM N. BEER—See Non-Commissioned Staff.

LIEUTENANT JAMES M. ROBERTS—See Company K.

LIEUTENANT JAMES R. HOMER—Enrolled at Galion, August 6, 1862. See Non-Commissioned Staff.

LIEUTENANT JOHN B. BIDDLE—Enrolled at Sulphur Springs, July 23, 1862. Mustered as Second Lieutenant. Killed in Battle of Stone's River, December 31, 1862. He was instantly killed while the Regiment was making its third stand, at the northern edge of the cotton field. At the moment of his death he was waving his sword and encouraging his men to stand firm, no matter what the odds. Brave, generous, noble-hearted, he was greatly loved by all the boys who knew him.

ADAMS, JACOB—Enrolled at Bucyrus, August 9, 1862. Wounded, captured and recaptured in Battle of Stone's River, December 31, 1862. Captured near Huntsville, Ala., January 17, 1865, but made his escape. See Prison Experience of Lieutenant Squire. Mustered out with Company.

AYRES, MATSON—Enrolled at Bucyrus, August 8, 1862. Mustered as Corporal. Died at Nashville, Tenn., February 9, 1863, of disease.

ANDREWS, HARVEY—Enrolled at Bucyrus, August 8, 1862. Died at Nashville, Tenn., February 10, 1863, of disease.

BAKER, EPHRIAM H.—Enrolled at Sulphur Springs, August 9, 1862. Ambulance driver and stretcher-bearer for one year. Mustered out with Company.

BECKER, SAMUEL W.—Enrolled at Bucyrus, August 6, 1862. Detailed as wagon master after the Battle of Chickamauga, September 19-20, 1863. Wounded at Battle of Nashville, Tenn., December 15, 1864, ball passing through the body. Mustered out, June 3, 1865, at Detroit.

BECKER, HENRY W.—Enrolled at Bucyrus, August 6, 1862. Mustered out with Company.

BIRK, JOHN—Enrolled at Bucyrus, August 9, 1862. Mustered out with Company.

BRESSLER, EDWARD—Enrolled at Bucyrus, August 6, 1862. Wounded at Battle of Jonesboro', September 1, 1864. Mustered out with Company.

BRETZ, EDWIN W.—Enrolled at Bucyrus, August 8, 1862. Wounded, May 14, 1864, in Battle of Resaca, Ga. Mustered out with Company.

BURWELL, FINIS S.—Enrolled at Bucyrus, August 5, 1862. Appointed Sergeant, August 29, 1862. Discharged at Murfreesboro', May 31, 1863, on account of disability.

BEACH, JOHN P.—Enrolled at Bucyrus, August 1, 1862. Mustered as Sergeant. Wounded in Battle of Stone's River, December 31, 1862. Transferred to Veteran Reserve Corps.

CARNAHAN, WILLIAM R.—Enrolled at Bucyrus, July 24, 1862. Appointed Sergeant, August 29, 1802. Captured at Battle of Perryville, October 8, 1862. In hospital, exchanged, and rejoined the Regiment. Mustered out with Company.

CRALL, SAMUEL—Enrolled at Sulphur Springs, August 11, 1862. Mustered out, May 12, 1865, at Louisville, Ky.

CLAPPER, HENRY E.—Enrolled at Bucyrus, August 8, 1862. Wounded, July 4, 1864, in action near Ruff's Station. Mustered out with Company.

CHARLTON, JONAS J.—Enrolled at Sulphur Springs, August 5, 1862. Wounded at Huntsville, Ala. On detached duty with 2nd Minnesota Battery as forager. Mustered out with Company.

CRALL, David—Enrolled at Bucyrus, August 8, 1862. Captured in Battle of Chickamauga, September 19, 1863. Died in prison at Danville, Va., May 24, 1864, of disease.

CHAMBERS, AARON J.—Enrolled at Sulphur Springs, August 11, 1862. Discharged at Nashville, March 8, 1863, on account of disability.

CRALL, SIMON—Enrolled at Bucyrus, August 7, 1862. Wounded in right leg in Battle of Chickamauga, September 19, 1863. Transferred to Company F, 15th Regiment, Veteran Reserve Corps, December 5, 1864. Mustered out, July 14, 1865, at Cairo, Ill.

DISE, MICHAEL—Enrolled at Bucyrus, August 6, 1862. Killed in the Battle of Chickamauga, September 19, 1863.

DILLINGHAM, WILLIAM—Enrolled at Sulphur Springs, August 7, 1862. No record after November 3, 1862.

EBERTH, JOHN—Enrolled at Bucyrus, August 8, 1862. Mustered out with Company.

EICHER, PETER M.—Enrolled at Sulphur Springs, August 4, 1862. Killed in the Battle of Chickamauga, September 19, 1863.

ECKIS, EZRA.—Enrolled at Monroeville, September 3, 1862. Appointed Sergeant. Dicharged at Columbus, December 23, 1862, on account of disability. Deceased.

FLOHR, OLIVER—Enrolled at Sulphur Springs, August 5, 1862. Appointed Corporal, March 1, 1865. Mustered out with Company.

FRY, OBEDIAH—Enrolled at Sulphur Springs, August 11, 1862. Appointed Corporal. No record after November 3, 1862.

FORTNEY, DAVID—Enrolled at Sulphur Springs, August 5, 1862. Wounded in the Battle of Stone's River, December 31, 1862. Sent to Camp Chase, March 31 1863. Enlisted in Company E, 14th Ohio Volunteer Infantry, March 6, 1864, from which mustered out as Corporal, July 11, 1865.

FORSYTHE, CHARLES A.—Enrolled at Bucyrus, August 15, 1862. Discharged at Louisville, Ky., June 12, 1863, on account of disability.

FREEBURN, CHARLES A.—Enrolled at Bucyrus, August 8, 1862. Transferred to Marine Brigade, June 13, 1863, at Louisville, Ky.

FLICKINGER, JOSEPH—Enrotled at Bucyrus, August 6, 1862. Transferred to Company H, 12th Regiment, Veteran Reserve Corps, at Louisville, Ky , August 1, 1863. Mustered out, June 5, 1865, at Washington, D. C.

FAGAN, WALKER V.—Enrolled at Bucyrus, August 8, 1862. Transferred to Veteran Reserve Corps, August 10, 1864.

GEORGE, WILLIAM—Enrolled at Sulphur Springs, August 11, 1862. Mustered out with Company.

GRASS, ADAM—Enrolled at Bucyrus, August 8, 1862. Transferred to Veteran Reserve Corps, December 1, 1863. Deceased.

HALLER, JOHN—Enrolled at Bucyrus, August 14, 1862. Mustered out with Company.

HOLSAPLE, JAMES—Enrolled at Sulphur Springs, August 2, 1852. Mustered out with Company.

HUND, JOSEPH—Enrolled at Bucyrus, August 5, 1862. Appointed Corporal, June —, 1863. Killed in the Battle of Chickamauga, September, 19, 1863.

HUTCHINSON, WILLIAM H.—Enrolled at Bucyrus, August 9, 1862. Appointed Corporal, January 9, 1863. Killed instantly in charge at Battle of Franklin, November 30, 1864.

HARMON, JONATHAN—Enrolled at Sulphur Springs, August 5, 1862. Deceased.

HALL, GILBERT—Enrolled at Bucyrus, August 1, 1862. Discharged at Murfreesboro', February 9, 1863, on account of disability. Deceased.

HOLMES, ELISHA—Enrolled at Bucyrus, August 8, 1862. Transferred to Mississippi Marine Brigade, May 11, 1863. Deceased.

HOLLINGER, JASON—Enrolled at Bucyrus, August 5, 1862. Transferred to 43rd Company, 2nd Battalion, Veteran Reserve Corps, August 31, 1863. Mustered out, August 30, 1865, at Camp Dennison, O.

JOHNSON, FRANK—Enrolled at Bucyrus, August 6, 1862. Discharged at Bowling Green, Ky., February 16, 1863, on account of disability.

KINTZEL, FREDERICK E.—Enrolled at Bucyrus August 5, 1862. Appointed Corporal, December 3, 1862. Promoted to Sergeant, May 1, 1864. Mustered out with Company.

KANZLEITER, FREDERICK—Enrolled at Bucyrus, August 8, 1862. Wounded in Battle of Chickamauga, September 19, 1863. Mustered out with Company.

KINNEY, WILLIAM A.—Enrolled at Oceola, August 7, 1862. Wounded and captured in Battle of Stone's River, December, 31, 1862. Confined in Libby Prison. Exchanged. Mustered out with Company.

KIES, EMANUEL— Enrolled at Bucyrus, August 14, 1862. Wounded in Battle of Chickamauga, September 20, 1863; also in Rocky Face, Ga., May 11, 1864. Mustered out with Company.

KILE, HENRY — Enrolled at Bucyrus, August 8, 1862. Killed in Battle of Stone's River, December 31, 1862.

KIMMICK, FELIX—Enrolled at Bucyrus, August 5, 1862. Died, September 23, 1863, of wounds received in Battle of Chickamauga, September 19th, 1863.

KELLER, WILLIAM H.—Enrolled at Sulphur Springs, August 9, 1862. Transferred to 43rd Company, 2nd Battalion. Veteran Reserve Corps, August 31, 1863. Mustered out, June 28, at Camp Dennison.

KIMBLE, NICHOLAS—Enrolled at Bucyrus, August 6, 1862. Wounded and captured in Battle of Chickamauga, September 19, 1863. Transferred to Veteran Reserve Corps, April 10, 1864.

LASH, PETER B —Enrolled at Sulphur Springs, August 9, 1862. Wounded in left wrist while on picket. Discharged at Columbus, December 23, 1862, on account of disability.

McCULLOUGH, HARVEY—Enrolled at Sulphur Springs, August 11, 1862. Appointed Corporal, January 9, 1863. Wounded at Liberty Gap, June 25, 1863. Promoted to First Sergeant, March 16, 1865. Mustered out with Company.

MOLLENKOPF, GEORGE—Enrolled at Bucyrus, August 6, 1862. Wounded in the Battle of Chickamauga, September 20, 1863. Mustered out with Company.

McBRIDE, JOHN — Enrolled at Bucyrus, August 5, 1862. Captured in Battle of Chickamauga, September 20, 1863. Mustered out at Camp Chase, June 26, 1865.

MYERS, JOHN H.—Enrolled at Bucyrus, August 8, 1862. Detailed as teamster. Captured and recaptured at La Vergne, December 3, 1862. Mustered out with Company.

MOORE, JOHN J.—Enrolled at Bucyrus, August 7, 1862. Killed in Battle of Stone's River, December 31, 1862.

MILLER, HENRY W.—Enrolled at Sulphur Springs, August 9, 1862. Mortally wounded in Battle of Chickamauga, September 19, 1863. Died in the hands of the enemy.

MYERS, JACOB B—Enrolled at Bucyrus, August 7, 1862. Mustered as Corporal. Died of rheumatism of the heart, December 7, 1862, at Bowling Green.

MOORE, ROBERT F.—Enrolled at Bucyrus, August 6, 1862. Captured in Battle of Chickamauga, September 19, 1863. Died in prison at Andersonville, November 15, 1864, of disease.

MORFOOT, CHARLES—See Company B.

MILLER, JACOB—Enrolled at Bucyrus, August 7, 1862. Discharged at Bowling Green, June 12, 1863, on account of disability.

MODDERWELL, HIRAM C.—Enrolled at Bucyrus, August 8, 1862. Discharged at Columbus, April 10, 1863, on account of dssability.

MCCONNELL, CHARLES—Enrolled at Sulphur Springs, August 9, 1862. Discharged at Louisville, Ky., May 22, 1863, on account of disability.

MILLER, ISAAC L.—Enrolled at Oceola, August 7, 1862. Transferred to 149th Company, 2nd Battalion, Veteran Reserve Corps, April 10, 1864. Mustered out as Sergeant, June 30, 1865, at Nashville, Tenn.

MILLER, ANANNIAS—Enrolled at Bucyrus, August 6, 1862. Transferred to Company K, 1st Regiment, United States Veteran Volunteer Engineer Corps, August 7, 1864. Mustered out, June 30, 1865, at Nashville, Tenn.

NEWELL, GILBERT M.—Enrolled at Oceola, August 7, 1862. Appointed Corporal, January 9, 1863. Wounded in the Battle of Chickamauga, September 19, 1863, while carrying the flag. Promoted to Sergeant, March 16, 1865. Mustered out with Company.

ROSTER. 391

OMWIG, JACOB— Enrolled at Sulphur Springs, August 9, 1862. Wounded in the left thigh in the Battle of Stone's River, December 31, 1862; in the right arm in the Battle of Chickamauga, September 20, 1863; in the right hip at Resaca, May 14, 1864. Mustered out, June 19, 1865, at Camp Chase.

POUNSTONE, ALVIN—Enrolled at Bucyrus, August 4, 1862. Appointed Corporal, August 29, 1862. Discharged to receive appointment as Hospital Steward, November 28, 1863, in Regular Army.

PORTER, GEORGE A.—Enrolled at Bucyrus, August 4, 1862. Transferred to 148th Company, 2nd Battalion, Veteran Reserve Corps, April 10, 1864. Mustered out, June 30, 1865, at Nashville, Tenn.

POWER, WILLIAM H. H.—Enrolled at Bucyrus, August 7, 1862. Transferred to Company K, 1st Regiment, United States Veteran Volunteer Engineers, August 7, 1864. Mustered out, June 30, 1865, at Nashville, Tenn.

QUAINTANCE, AARON J.—Enrolled at Bucyrus, August 9, 1862. Appointed Corporal, January 9, 1863. Wounded and rendered unconscious in Battle of Chickamauga, September 19, 1863. Captured at the same time. Said to have been wounded by the same shot that killed his brother, and J. Hund.

QUAINTANCE, TILLEY E.—Enrolled at Bucyrus, August 7, 1862. Killed in Battle of Chickamauga, September 19, 1863.

RICE, JACOB—Enrolled at Bucyrus, August 7, 1862. Appointed Corporal, March 1, 1865. Captured in the Battle of Stone's River, December 31, 1862. Confined in Montgomery, Pemberton and Libby Prisons. Parolled and sent to Annapolis. Transferred to Camp Chase. Rejoined the Regiment at Bridgeport. Mustered out with Company.

RESH, AUGUSTUS — Enrolled at Bucyrus, August 8, 1862. Transferred from Company E. Mustered out with Company.

ROBERTS, JOHN A.—Enrolled at Bucyrus, August 5, 1862. Mustered as Sergeant. Discharged at Cincinnati, September 23, 1863, on account of disability. Severely wounded in Battle of Stone's River, December 31, 1862.

ROBERTS, SAMUEL.—Enrolled at Bucyrus, August 5, 1862. Appointed Corporal, January 9, 1863. Transferred to Veteran Reserve Corps, September 1, 1863.

RUPERSBERGER, HENRY—Enrolled at Bucyrus, August 8, 1862. Wounded at Rocky Face, Ga., May 11, 1864. Discharged at Nashville, May 30, 1865.

SIMS, JOSEPH—Enrolled at Sulphur Springs, August 9, 1862. Appointed Corporal, July 4, 1863. Mustered out with Company.

STONER, ALMON H.—Enrolled at Bucyrus, August 2, 1862. Wounded in the Battle of Chickamauga, September 19, 1863. Mustered out with Company.

SOWERS, WILLIAM A.—Enrolled at Sulphur Springs, August 9, 1862. Died at Murfreesboro', August 6, 1863, of disease.

SHRADER, WILLIAM A. Enrolled at Bucyrus, August 5, 1862. Appointed Corporal, August 29, 1862. Captured at Battle of Stone's River, December 31, 1862, but escaped. Discharged at Murfreesboro', February 14, 1863, on account of disability.

SHONG, SAMUEL.—Enrolled at Sulphur Springs, August 7, 1862. Transferred to Company B, 15th Regiment, Veteran Reserve Corps, September 1, 1863, at Louisville. Mustered out, June 6, 1865, at Springfield, Ill.

TAYLOR, EPHRAIM—Enrolled at Bucyrus, August 5, 1862. Appointed Corporal, March 1, 1865. Mustered out with Company. Deceased.

TAYLOR, JOSEPH N.—Enrolled at Bucyrus, August 6, 1862. Wounded in the Battle of Stone's River, December 31, 1862. Transferred to Veteran Reserve Corps, December 15, 1863, at Louisville, Ky.

UNDERWOOD, ABRAM A.—Enrolled at Bucyrus, August 5, 1862. Appointed Corporal, August 30, 1862. Discharged at Louisville, Ky., December 24, 1862, on account of disability.

WILLIAMS, WILLIAM H.—Enrolled at Oceola, August 7, 1862. Appointed Sergeant, January 9, 1863. Died at Murfreesboro', April 24, 1863, of typhoid pneumonia.

WINGERT, FREDERICK—Enrolled at Bucyrus, August 20, 1862. Wounded in Battle of Stone's River, December 31, 1862. Sent to Camp Chase, April 24, 1863.

WILLIAMS, HENRY—Enrolled at Bucyrus, August 18, 1862. Transferred to Veteran Reserve Corps, August 31, 1853.

WOLF, JOHN—Enrolled at Bucyrus, August 8, 1862. Transferred to Company I, 17th Regiment, Veteran Reserve Corps, August 31, 1863. Mustered out, June 30, 1865, at Indianapolis, Ind.

WOLF, EMANUEL—Enrolled at Sulphur Springs, August 9, 1862. Captured, September 20, 1863, at Chickamauga. Mustered out at Columbus, June 7, 1865.

YOST, DAVID J.—Enrolled at Bucyrus, August 9, 1862. Transferred to 20th Company, 2d Battalion Veteran Reserve Corps, September 1, 1863. Mustered out at Madison, Ind., June 30, 1865. Deceased.

YARNELL, MARTIN—Enrolled at Sulphur Springs, August 9, 1862. Mustered as Corporal. Promoted to Sergeant, April 26, 1863. Died at Chattanooga, September 23, 1864, of disease.

COMPANY D.

CAPTAIN HENRY G. SHELDON—Enrolled at Greenwich, July 8, 1862. Mustered as Captain. Resigned, January 28, 1863, at Nashville, on account of disability. Died at Delaware, O., April 12, 1889.

CAPTAIN JOHN M. LATIMER, JR.—Enrolled July 23, 1862. Mustered as Second Lieutenant. Promoted to First Lieutenant, January 28, 1863; to Captain, March 21, 1863, to date January 28, 1863; to Major, May 30, 1865, but not mustered. Mustered out with Company.

LIEUTENANT J. B. CURTIS—Enrolled at Fairfield, August 5, 1862. Resigned, January 2, 1863, at Nashville, on account of disability. Died in Illinois.

LIEUTENANT IRA B. READ—See Company E.

LIEUTENANT ELBERT J. SQUIRE—Enrolled at Ridgefield, August 9, 1862. Mustered as Corporal. Promoted to Sergeant, November 14, 1862; to Second Lieutenant, January 28, 1863; to First Lieutenant, March 19, 1864. Captured at Huntsville, January 17, 1865. Wounded in Battle of Chickamauga. Commanded Company F from December 5, 1863, to August 19, 1864; commanded Company A, in connection with Company F, May 12, 1864, to August 19, 1864, when he was relieved of both Companies by Lieutenant Milliman. Commanded Company I from December 1, 1864, to January 17, 1865, when he was captured. Mustered out, May 16, 1865. See prison experience, given elsewhere.

ABBOTT, JACOB M.—Enrolled at Fitchville, August 5, 1862. Died at Nashville, January 25, 1863, of typhoid pneumonia.

AMSDEN, LUZERNE—Enrolled at Norwich, August 4, 1862. Discharged at Ooltewah, March 23, 1864, on account of disability.

AUSTIN, DUANE—Enrolled at Fitchville, August 5, 1862. Transferred to Veteran Reserve Corps, August 10, 1864.

BROWN, JUSTUS N.—Enrolled at Ripley, July 29, 1862. Transferred to Veteran Reserve Corps, June, 1863. Mustered out, June 21, 1865, at Camp Cleveland.

BLAIR, JOHN D.—Enrolled at Norwalk, July 29, 1862. Wounded in Battle of Stone's River, December 31, 1862. Killed in Battle of Chickamauga, September 19, 1863.

BARBER, CLARK—Enrolled at Clarksfield, August 11, 1862. Died, July 7, 1863, at Louisville, Ky., of typhoid pneumonia.

BURGESS, EGBERT M.—Enrolled at Greenwich, August 9, 1862. Died, December 3, 1862, at Louisville, Ky., of disease.

BACON, CHARLES C.—Enrolled at Ripley, August 7, 1862. Died, January 1, 1863, at Nashville, of typhoid pneumonia.

BRIGGS, WILLIAM M.—Enrolled at Greenwich, August 8, 1862.

BRIGGS, CHARLES M.—Enrolled at Greenwich, August 8, 1862.

BREWSTER, CHARLES F.—Enrolled at Norwalk, August 4, 1862. Discharged at Nashville, April 25, 1863, on account of wounds received in Battle of Stone's River, December 31, 1862. Deceased.

BELL, WILLIAM R.—Enrolled at Ripley, August 8, 1862. Discharged at Cincinnati, March 13, 1863, on account of disability.

BELL, JESSE W.—Enrolled at Ripley, August 8, 1862. Discharged at Louisville, February 7, 1863, on account of disability.

BROWN, FREDERICK G.—Enrolled at Monroeville, July 30, 1862. Discharged at Tyner's Station, February 3, 1864, on account of disability. Died, July 7, 1893, at Waverley, Tenn.

BISHOP, ALONZO T.—Enrolled at Norwich, August 1, 1862. Discharged at Columbus, April 27, 1865, on account of wounds received in Battle of Franklin, November 30, 1864.

BISHOP, DELOS—Enrolled at Norwich, August 5, 1862. Transferred to Veteran Reserve Corps, August 1, 1863.

BISHOP, JOSEPH L.—Enrolled at Norwich, August 5, 1862. Transferred to Veteran Reserve Corps, November 1, 1863. Deceased.

CRAWFORD, JOHN H.—Enrolled at Ripley, July 28, 1862. Wounded and captured in Battle of Chickamauga, September 19, 1863. A prisoner at Belle Isle, Libby, Danville, Andersonville, Charleston, and Florence. (See prison experience.) Exchanged at Wilmington, N. C., February 26, 1865. Returned to Company, February 28, 1865. Mustered out, June 9, 1865, at Camp Chase.

CURTIS, JOTHAM A.—Enrolled at Fitchville, July 28, 1862. Died at Nashville, August 15, 1864, of wounds received in the storming of Kenesaw Mountain, Ga., June 27, 1864.

CONOVER, WILLIAM N.—Enrolled at Fairfield, August 9, 1862. Discharged at Bowling Green, February 3, 1863, on account of disability.

COLE, ENOCH P.—Enrolled at Greenfield, August 8, 1862. Mustered out at Nashville, May 16, 1865, on account of disability.

CURTIS, GEORGE W.—Enrolled at Fairfield, August 9, 1862. Discharged at Bowling Green, January 13, 1863, on account of disability.

CUNNINGHAM, EDWIN W.—Enrolled at Clarksfield, August 1, 1862. Discharged at Lebanon, Ky., June 22, 1863, to accept Hospital Stewardship in Regular Army.

CARPENTER, CHESTER H.—Enrolled at Fairfield, August 11, 1862. Transferred to Company F, 15th Regiment, Veteran Reserve Corps, January 15, 1864. Mustered out, July 14, 1865, at Cairo, Illinois.

CRANE, JOEL R.—Enrolled at Norwalk, February 2, 1864. Transferred to Company A, 51st Ohio Volunteer Infantry, June 10, 1865.

DICKINSON, WILLIAM L.—Enrolled at Fairfield, August 9, 1862. Died at Louisville, December 12, 1862, of disease.

DENTON, WILLIAM S.—Enrolled at Fitchville, August 5, 1862. Died at Chattanooga, June 26, 1864, of typhoid pneumonia.

DRAKE, GEORGE F.—Enrolled at Ridgefield, August 8, 1862. Discharged at Winchester, Tenn., July 15, 1863, on account of disability.

DILLS, HENRY G.—Enrolled at Greenwich, August 9, 1862. Transferred to Company F, 7th Regiment, Veteran Reserve Corps, September 30, 1863. Mustered out, June 28, 1865, at Washington, D. C.

FOWLER, EDWARD P.—Enrolled at Ripley, August 7, 1862. Wounded at Atlanta, August 3, 1864. Mustered out with Company. Died at St. Barnardino, Cal., September 9, 1889.

FRANK, CONSTANTINE—Enrolled at Peru, July 28, 1862. Died at Murfreesboro', May 31, 1863, of typhoid pneumonia.

FISH, GEORGE W.—Enrolled at Fairfield, August 9, 1862. Died at Nashville, January 5, 1863, of typhoid pneumonia.

FURLONG, MYRON G.—Enrolled at Clarksfield, August 8, 1862. Discharged at Nashville, February 10, 1863, on account of disability.

GOWDY, CHARLES A.—Enrolled at Ridgefield, August 9, 1862. Died at Bardstown, Ky., December 8, 1862, of disease.

GIBSON, JEROME G.—Enrolled at Greenwich, July 28, 1862. Appointed Corporal, August 9, 1862. Discharged at Nashville, January 7, 1863, on account of disability.

GUTHRIE, LEROY L.—Enrolled at Greenfield; July 26, 1862. Mustered out at Nashville, May 15, 1865. Deceased.

GOODMAN, GEORGE W.—Enrolled at Norwalk, August 9, 1862. Discharged at Nashville, February 6, 1863, on account of disability. Deceased.

HUBBELL, GEORGE N.—Enrolled at Ridgefield, August 9, 1862. Appointed Sergeant, May 1, 1863. Promoted to First Sergeant, September 20, 1863. Wounded in Battle of Chickamauga, September 20, 1863. Mustered out with Company.

HOLLOWAY, JAMES—Enrolled at Peru, July 26, 1862. Mustered out with Company.

HOPKINS, WILLIAM W.—Enrolled at Greenwich, August 8, 1862. Mustered out with Company.

HANKS, EUGENE F.—Enrolled at Norwalk, August 11, 1862. Captured in Battle of Chickamauga. Mustered out at Camp Chase, June 9, 1865.

HOPKINS, JAMES H.—Enrolled at Ripley, August 12, 1862. Died at Bowling Green, December 4, 1862, of disease.

HOPKINS, JOHN N.—Enrolled at Ripley, August 12, 1862. Died at Murfreesboro', June 15, 1863, of disease.

HAMILTON, WILSON—Enrolled at Norwich, August 4, 1862. Appointed Corporal, May 1, 1863. Discharged at Camp Chase, August 24, 1864, on account of wounds received in the Battle of Chickamauga, September 20, 1863.

HUNT, GEORGE—Enrolled at Ridgefield, August 9, 1862. Discharged at Nashville, February 9, 1863, on account of disability. Deceased.

HACKETT, THADDEUS W.—Enrolled at Fairfield, August 9, 1862. Discharged at Ooltewah, March 25, 1864, on account of disability.

HUME, EDWARD M.—Enrolled at Norwalk, August 4, 1862. Discharged at Nashville, February 9, 1863, on account of wounds received in the Battle of Stone's River, December 31, 1862.

JONES, FLAVEL B.—Enrolled at Ripley, August 8, 1862. Killed in the Battle of Chickamauga, September 20, 1863.

JOHNSON, JOHN W.—Enrolled at Ripley, August 7, 1862. Mustered out at Nashville, May 17, 1865. Deceased.

JONES, DUTTON—Enrolled at Fairfield, August 8, 1862. Appointed Sergeant, August 9, 1862. Discharged at Louisville, Ky., September 9, 1863, on account of disability.

KINGSBURY, CORYDON—Enrolled at Fairfield, August 9, 1862. Appointed Corporal, January 1, 1864. Promoted to Sergeant, March 1, 1864. Mustered out with Company.

KEELER, GEORGE N.—Enrolled at Fairfield, August 6, 1862. Mustered out with Company.

KINSEY, SIMEON W.—Enrolled at Ripley, August 9, 1862. Mustered out with Company.

LEAK, WILLIAM—Enrolled at Fairfield, August 11, 1862. Mustered out with Company.

LAWRENCE, GEORGE A.—Enrolled at Bronson, August 11, 1862. Mustered out with Company.

LOWE, WILLARD W.—Enrolled at Fitchville, August 9, 1862. Mustered out, May 16, 1865, at Elmira, N.Y.

LYON, ERWIN E.—Enrolled at Fitchville, July 28, 1862. Discharged at Columbus, December 13, 1863, on account of disability.

LAWRENCE, GEORGE—Enrolled at Norwalk, August 11, 1862. Transferred to Company I, 16th Regiment, Veteran Reserve Corps, April 29, 1864. Mustered out at Harrisburg, June 28, 1865.

MATTOON, GEORGE E.—Enrolled at Greenwich, August 9, 1862. Mustered out, June 12, 1865, at Louisville, Ky.

MAYNARD, ALANSON W.—Enrolled at Monroeville, August 30, 1862. Captured at Resaca. Imprisoned at Atlanta, Macon, Andersonville, Charleston and Florence. Exchanged. Mustered out with Company.

MERRITT, WILLIAM F.—Enrolled at Greenwich, August 9, 1862. Died at Danville, Ky., November 12, 1862, of disease.

MARSH, CHARLES E.—Enrolled at Norwalk, August 11, 1862. Mustered as Corporal. Discharged at Nashville, December 28, 1862, on account of disability.

MARSH, ENOS L.—Enrolled at Ripley, August 7, 1862. Mustered as Corporal. Discharged at Columbus, May 9, 1863, on account of wounds received in the Battle of Stone's River, December 31, 1862.

MEAD, CHARLES H.—Enrolled at Bronson, August 11, 1862. Appointed Sergeant, March 1, 1864. Transferred to First United States Veteran Volunteer Engineers, July 27, 1864. Promoted to Sergeant Major, July 9, 1865. Mustered out, September 26, 1865, at Nashville, Tenn.

MEAD, GEORGE N.—Enrolled at Fitchville, August 7, 1862. Mustered as Corporal. Wounded in the Battle of Stone's River, December 31, 1862. Transferred to 79th Company, 2nd Battalion, Veteran Reserve Corps, February 15, 1864. Mustered out as Sergeant, May 23, 1865, at Lexington, Ky., on account of disability.

MINOR, LAWRENCE—Enrolled at Bronson, August 11, 1862. Mustered as Corporal. Discharged at Camp Dennison, March 28, 1863, on account of disability.

NEWTON, HENRY M.—Enrolled at Norwalk, July 29, 1862. Appointed Corporal, September 3, 1862. Promoted to Sergeant, May 1, 1863. Mustered out with Company.

PALMER, ALBERT—Enrolled at Fitchville, August 5, 1862. Mustered out at Cleveland, June 21, 1865.

PETERSON, JOB—Enrolled at Ripley, August 7, 1862. Mustered out with Company.

PICKENS, CHARLES — Enrolled at Ridgefield, August 11, 1862. Died near Murfreesboro', January 1, 1863, of wounds received in the Battle of Stone's River, December 31, 1862.

PAYNE, GEORGE W.—Enrolled at Ripley, August 7, 1862. Mustered as Sergeant. Discharged at Columbus, March 28, 1863, on account of disability.

PENFIELD, CHARLES — Enrolled at Fitchville, August 9, 1862. Discharged at Louisville, May 4, 1863, on account of wounds received in the Battle of Stone's River, December 31, 1862. Deceased.

PALMER, DARWIN G.—Enrolled at Fitchville, August 5, 1862. Mustered out at Chattanooga, May 22, 1865.

PERKINS, JONAS R.—Enrolled at Norwalk, January 28, 1864. Transferred to Company G, 8th Regiment, Veteran Reserve Corps, June 10, 1865. Mustered out, August 28, 1865, at Springfield, Ill.

ROSE, CHARLES B.—Enrolled at Fairfield, August 7, 1862. Wounded in the Battle of Stone's River, December 31, 1862, while attempting to care for Colonel Stem after he was wounded. Mustered out with Company.

RICKEY, JOHN H.—Enrolled at Peru, August 9, 1862. Died at Big Shanty, Ga., June 23, 1864, of wounds received in action near Kenesaw Mountain, Ga., June 23, 1864.

ROWLAND, WATSON W.—Enrolled at Clarksfield, August 11, 1862. Died at Nashville, January 31, 1863, of typhoid pneumonia.

RUSSELL, ERASTUS E.—Enrolled at Fitchville, August 8, 1862. Discharged at Nashville, February 14, 1863, on account of disability. Deceased.

ROWLAND, LEVI O.—Enrolled at Clarksfield, August 11, 1862. Discharged at Camp Dennison, February 15, 1864, on account of wounds received in the Battle of Stone's River, December 31, 1862.

REED, IRA B.—See Company E.

SAUERS, GEORGE H.—Enrolled at Fairfield, August 9, 1862. Wounded and captured in Battle of Stone's River, December 31, 1862. Appointed Corporal, March 1, 1864. Promoted to Sergeant, May 1, 1864. Wounded at Rocky Face Ridge, Ga., May 11, 1864.

SUTTON, ORRIN S.—Enrolled at Greenwich, August 9, 1862. Mustered out with Company.

SCOTT, CHARLES—Enrolled at Fitchville, July 28, 1862. Killed, May 19, 1864, in action near Kingston, Ga.

SNYDER, WILLIAM H.—Enrolled at Bronson, August 9, 1862. Discharged at Bowling Green, December 18, 1862, on account of disability.

SPRAGUE, JOHN C.—Enrolled at Fitchville, August 5, 1862. Discharged at Nashville, February 14, 1863, on account of disability. Deceased.

SLOCUM, MANFRED D.—Enrolled at Fairfield, August 6, 1862. Mustered as First Sergeant. Transferred to Veteran Reserve Corps, August 1, 1863.

SMITH, SAMUEL L.—Enrolled at Norwich, August 1, 1862. Transferred to Company I, 5th Regiment, Veteran Reserve Corps, January 10, 1865. Mustered out, June 13, 1865, at Indianapolis.

SCOTT, BYRON—Enrolled, July 28, 1862. Never mustered.

TOWNSEND, HIRAM W.—Enrolled at New London, July 31, 1862. Discharged at Columbus, March 7, 1863, on account of wounds received in the Battle of Stone's River, December 31, 1862.

TREMBLY, WILLIAM H.—Enrolled at Ripley, August 8, 1862. Discharged at Nashville, March 8, 1863, on account of disability.

TRUXELL, JACOB W.—Enrolled at Ripley, August 8, 1862. Discharged at Louisville, December 12, 1863, on account of disability.

TRUXELL, HOMER—Enrolled at Ripley, August 9, 1862. Discharged at Nashville, February 14, 1863, on account of disability.

- TERRY, LUTHER L.—Enrolled at Fairfield, August 7, 1862. Transferred to 151st Company, 2nd Battalion, Veteran Reserve Corps, February 5, 1864. Mustered out, June 30, 1865, at Nashville, Tenn.
- TERRY, JAMES E.—Enrolled at Fairfield, August 11, 1862. Transferred to Company I, 5th Regiment, Veteran Reserve Corps, February 15, 1864. Mustered out, July 5, 1865, at Indianapolis, Ind.
- WICKS, W. C.—Enrolled at Fairfield, August 7, 1862. Appointed Corporal, May 1, 1864. Mustered out with Company.
- WHITE, SAMUEL C.—Enrolled at Ripley, August 7, 1862. Killed at Chickamauga.
- WYCKOFF, MERRIT—Enrolled at Ridgefield, July 31, 1862. Discharged at Bowling Green, January 10, 1863, on account of disability.
- WASHBURN, WILLIAM I.—Enrolled at Greenwich, August 8, 1862. Transferred to Veteran Reserve Corps, September 30, 1863.
- WOOD, LEMUEL—Enrolled at Fitchville, August 9, 1862. Transferred to 87th Company, 2nd Battalion, Veteran Reserve Corps, January 15, 1864. Mustered out at Cincinnati, June 26, 1865.

COMPANY E.

- CAPTAIN W. C. PARSONS—Enrolled and mustered as Captain at Columbus, July 24, 1862. Taken sick on the march. Died at Louisville, Ky., November 3, 1862.
- CAPTAIN LYMAN PARCHER—Enrolled and mustered as First Lieutenant, July 24, 1862, at Columbus. Promoted to Captain, November 15, 1862. Resigned at Murfreesboro', Tenn., February 26, 1863, on account of wounds received in Battle of Pea Ridge, Mo., March 7, 1862. Afterwards raised a Company in the 179th Ohio; was commissioned Captain, and served to the end of the war. Died at Marysville, Mo., August 28, 1893.

CAPTAIN ROBERT D. LORD—Enrolled and mustered as Second Lieutenant at Crestline, July 29, 1862. Promoted to First Lieutenant, November 15, 1862; to Captain, February 16, 1863. Resigned on account of disability, August 12, 1863. Died at Cleveland.

CAPTAIN IRA B. READ—Enrolled at Norwalk, August 2, 1862. Mustered as Sergeant, Company D. Promoted to First Lieutenant of same Company, March 13, 1863, to date January 28, 1863. Promoted to Captain and assigned to Company E, March 19, 1864. Wounded at Chickamauga. Served as Assistant Inspector General during last six months of service. Mustered out with Company.

LIEUTENANT CHARLES McGRAW—Enrolled at Crestline, July 23, 1862. Mustered as First Sergeant. Promoted to Second Lieutenant, November 15, 1862; to First Lieutenant, February 26, 1863. Killed at Battle of Chickamauga, September 20, 1863.

LIEUTENANT JOHN L. MILLIMAN—Enrolled at Berlin, August 4, 1862. Mustered as First Sergeant of Company G. Promoted to Second Lieutenant, May 28, 1863; promoted to First Lieutenant and assigned to Company E, March 19, 1864. Wounded and captured at Battle of Stone's River, December 31, 1862. In Libby Prison four months. Mustered out with Company.

LIEUTENANT SAMUEL S. BLOWERS—Enrolled at Bucyrus, August 9, 1862. Mustered as Sergeant. Promoted to Second Lieutenant, February 26, 1863. Resigned, January 9, 1864, on account of disability. Several months in hospital at Nashville. Died at his home near Bucyrus, Ohio, February 17, 1884.

ALBRIGHT, JACOB—Enrolled at Galion, August 11, 1862. Died at Perryville, October 29, 1862, of typhoid fever.

BEAL, CYRUS H.—Enrolled at Bucyrus, August 9, 1862. Died at Lebanon, Ky., February 6, 1863, of consumption.

BERNARD, AMER W.—Enrolled at Bucyrus, August 2, 1862. Deceased.

BERNARD, PERRY W.—Enrolled at Bucyrus, August 2, 1862. Deceased.

BABCOCK, WILLIAM—Enrolled at Bucyrus, August 6, 1862. Discharged, October 31, 1862, at Columbus, Ohio.

BOOR, JOSIAH F.—Enrolled at Crestline, August 7, 1862. Appointed Corporal, September 20, 1862. Discharged at Bowling Green, February 16, 1863, on account of disability.

BURGET, ANDREW J.—Enrolled at Crestline, August 11, 1862. Discharged at Louisville, November 24, 1862, on account of disability. Deceased.

CROW, JOHN—Enrolled at Crestline, September 3, 1862. Appointed Corporal, January 1, 1865. Mustered out with Company.

CURRIE, WILLIAM—Enrolled at Crestline, August 5, 1862. Deceased.

CIRTS, ELIAS—Enrolled at Crestline, August 4, 1862. No record after October 14, 1862.

COVILL, LAFAYETTE—Enrolled at Galion, August 7, 1862. Discharged at Tyner's Station, February 2, 1864, on account of disability.

COX, WILLIAM—Enrolled at Crestline, August 11, 1862. Discharged at Columbus, February 26, 1865, on account of wounds received at Kenesaw Mountain, June 23, 1864. Died at Soldiers' Home, Dayton, May 15, 1887.

COFFY, ANDREW—Enrolled at Crestline, August 14, 1862. Discharged at Louisville, August 22, 1863, on account of disability. Killed near New Washington, O., by the running away of his team.

CASSELL, DANIEL O.—Enrolled at Galion, August 4, 1862. Captured and recaptured in Battle of Stone's River, December 31, 1862. Wounded in left leg and left arm in Battle of Chickamauga, September 20, 1863. Mustered out at Plattsburg, N, Y., July 20, 1865.

CARPENTER, JEREMIAH J.—Enrolled at Crestline, August 4, 1862. Transferred to Pioneer Corps in November, 1862. Mustered out, July 3, 1865, at Nashville, Tenn.

DEWALT, WILLIAM—Enrolled at Leesville, August 6, 1862. Wounded in calf of leg, knee and thigh in the Battle of Chickamauga, September 19, 1863. In the hospital at Chattanooga and Stevenson, Tenn, two months. Appointed Corporal, January 1, 1864; Sergeant, January 1, 1865. Mustered out with Company.

DARGITZ, HARRISON—Enrolled at Galion, August 6, 1862. Wounded in the Battle of Chickamauga, September 19, 1863. Appointed Corporal, January 1, 1865. Mustered out with Company.

DYCHE, VALENTINE—Enrolled at Crestline, August 11, 1862. Mustered as Sergeant. Discharged at Nashville, February 22, 1863, on account of disability. Died at Chicago, Ill., February 13, 1885.

DAVIS, WILLIAM R.—Enrolled at Galion, August 6, 1862. See Non-Commissioned Staff.

DAY, LEWIS W.—Enrolled at Galion, August 6, 1862. Mustered as Corporal. Promoted to Sergeant, January 1, 1863. Detailed as Topographical Engineer, and assigned to Brigade Headquarters. Discharged at Nashville, December 17, 1863, on account of disability.

DICE, JOHN—Enrolled at Galion, August 7, 1862. Wounded in Battle of Stone's River, December 31, 1862. Transferred to Company H, 8th Regiment, Veteran Reserve Corps, July 1, 1863. Mustered out, July 2, 1865, at Chicago, Ill.

DOTY, WILLIAM—Enrolled at Crestline, August 4, 1862. Wounded in the Battle of Stone's River, December 31, 1862. Transferred to Company C, 5th Regiment, Veteran Reserve Corps. Mustered out, July 21, 1865, at Indianapolis, Ind.

FARNSWORTH, ISAAC—Enrolled at Crestline, August 6, 1862. Killed in the Battle of Stone's River, December 31, 1862.

FLOHR, JOHN—Enrolled at Sulphur Springs, August 6, 1862. Taken prisoner in the Battle of Chickamauga, September 19, 1863. In Andersonville Prison thirteen months, where he died in October, 1864.

Fox, Solomon—Enrolled at Galion, August 19, 1862. Discharged, June 8, 1863, at Murfreesboro', on account of disability. Died, near Crestline, July 28, 1863.

Fisher, Louis—Enrolled at Crestline, August 6, 1862. Discharged at Bowling Green, February 10, 1863, on account of disability.

Furlong, James—Enrolled at Crestline, August 9, 1862. Discharged at Louisville, Ky., August 10, 1863, on account of disability. Died, March 25, 1879, at Crestline, O.

Genter, John H.—Enrolled at Adrian, O., August 20, 1862. Discharged at Nashville, May 30, 1863, on account of disability. Musician.

Geiger, George E.—Enrolled at Galion, August 7, 1862. Mustered out with company.

Good, Jacob Y.—Enrolled at Monroeville, August 21, 1862. Wounded and taken prisoner in the Battle of Chickamauga, September 20, 1863. Exchanged. Mustered out with Company.

Gibler, Isaac—Enrolled at Galion, August 11, 1862. Transferred to 7th Regiment, Veteran Reserve Corps, September 30, 1863. Mustered out, June 29, 1865, as Commissary Sergeant, at Washington, D. C.

Harvey, James H.—Enrolled at Bucyrus, August 9, 1862. Wounded in the Battle of Stone's River, December 31, 1862. Appointed Sergeant, January 1, 1864. Mustered out with Company.

Heis, George—Enrolled at Leesville, August 5, 1862. Wounded in Battle of Chickamauga, September 20, 1863. Mustered out with Company. Died at Leesville, in October, 1871, of consumption.

Hillficker, David—Enrolled at Crestline, August 6, 1862. Wounded and captured in Battle of Chickamauga, September 20, 1863. Died in hands of the enemy.

Halliwell, James—Enrolled at Bucyrus, August 5, 1862. Wounded in foot in the Battle of Stone's River, December 31, 1862. Appointed Corporal, March 1, 1864. Died in Nashville, January 3, 1865, of wounds received in Battle of Nashville, December 15, 1864.

- HANLEY, JOHN—Enrolled at Crestline, August 11, 1862. Discharged at Nashville, August 1, 1863, on account of wounds received in Battle of Stone's River, December 31, 1862. Died at Upper Sandusky, O.
- HUHN, CHRISTIAN—Enrolled at Crestline, August 12, 1862. Discharged at Bridgeport, Ala., January 12, 1864, on account of disability. Died at Louisville, November 24, 1882, of heart disease.
- HOMER, JAMES R.—See Non-Commissioned Staff.
- HARRINGTON, NATHANIEL.—Enrolled at Crestline, August 6, 1862. Transferred to Company H, 8th Regiment, Veteran Reserve Corps, July 2, 1863.
- HANDLIN, DAVID—Enrolled at Galion, August 6, 1862. Wounded in Battle of Nolensville, December 26, 1862, and at Franklin, March 12, 1863, while on picket duty. Transferred to Veteran Reserve Corps, September 30, 1863.
- HAKE, CORDON—Enrolled at Crestline, August 7, 1862. Transferred to Veteran Reserve Corps, November 13, 1863.
- HOWENSTEIN, JOHN P.—Enrolled at Galion, December 28, 1863. Transferred to 51st Ohio Volunteer Infantry, June 10, 1865, to date May 14, 1865.
- HILLGENDORFF, CHARLES C. J.—Enrolled at Galion, February 27, 1864. Wounded in Battle of Kenesaw Mountain, June 23, 1864. Transferred to Company A, 51st Ohio Volunteer Infantry, June 10, 1865.
- JACKSON, WILLIAM—Enrolled at Crestline, August 5, 1862. Discharged at Louisville, November 24, 1862, on account of disability. Died, February 18, 1885, at Crestline, O.
- KIRKLAND, ANDREW J.—Enrolled at Bucyrus, August 7, 1862. Wounded in Battle of Stone's River, December 31, 1862. Detached as Provost Guard. Mustered out with Company.
- KIRTZ, CHRISTIAN—Enrolled at Galion, August 7, 1862. Wounded at Buzzard Roost, May 11, 1864, and at Nashville, December 15, 1864. Transferred to Company G, 16th Regiment, Veteran Reserve Corps. Mustered out, July 14, 1865, at Cleveland, O.

KROHN, WILLIAM—Enrolled at Galion, August 7, 1862. Appointed Corporal, April 12, 1863. Died at Chattanooga, November 23, 1863, of disease.

LEYMAN, HENRY T.—Enrolled at Crestline, August 5, 1862. Mustered as Corporal. Promoted to Sergeant, February 26, 1863. Wounded at Kenesaw, June 23, 1864. On detached service at Corps headquarters for a time. Rejoined the Regiment at Ooltewah. Mustered out with Company.

LEWIS, ENOS B.—Enrolled at Crestline, August 15, 1862. Promoted to Corporal, January 1, 1863. Captured at Battle of Chickamauga, September 19, 1863. Confined in Libby Prison. Promoted to Sergeant, January 1, 1864. Mustered out with Company. Died at Marion, O., 1890.

LOWE, LEWIS S.—Enrolled at Galion, August 5, 1862. Mortally wounded and taken prisoner in the Battle of Stone's River, December 31, 1862. Paroled on account of wounds. Died at Nashville, March 13, 1863.

LANGADAFFER, FRANK—Enrolled at Galion, August 6, 1862. Discharged at Columbus, O., April 20, 1863, on account of wounds received in the Battle of Stone's River, December 31, 1862, where he was taken prisoner and exchanged.

LINDSEY, SAMUEL—Enrolled at Crestline, August 6, 1862. Transferred to 34th Company, Veteran Reserve Corps, September 30, 1863. Mustered out July 18, 1865, at Mound City, Ill.

LOEBENTHAL, LEO—Enrolled at Galion, December 24, 1863. Transferred to Company D, 22d Regiment, Veteran Reserve Corps, April 21, 1865. Mustered out at Camp Chase, O., July 19, 1865.

McKEE, GEO. S.—Enrolled at Crestline, August 14, 1862. Wounded in the Battle of Stone's River, December 31, 1862, and at Resaca, May 14, 1864. Promoted to Corporal, January 1, 1865. Mustered out with Company.

McLAIN, SAMUEL—Enrolled at Bucyrus, August 6, 1862. Died near Lebanon, October, 1862, of disease.

McMICHAEL, JOHN A.—Enrolled at Bucyrus, August 9, 1862. Detailed as teamster. Discharged at Nashville, December 26, 1862, on account of disability. Injured in a smash up.

NICHOLS, W. H. W.—Enrolled at Galion, August 6, 1862. Mustered as Corporal. Accidentally wounded at Edgefield Junction, November 10, 1862. Transferred, December 24, 1862, to the 20th Company, 2nd Battalion, Veteran Reserve Corps, and promoted to Sergeant Major, on duty at Madison Barracks, Ind. Mustered out, January 6, 1865.

OSTENBERGER, JOHN—Enrolled at Galion, August 8, 1862. Wounded and taken prisoner in Battle of Stone's River, December 31, 1862. Wounded at Rocky Face, Ga., May 11, 1864. In hospital at Cleveland. Mustered out at Cleveland, May 30, 1865.

PARCHER, HENRY C.—Enrolled at Bucyrus, July 26, 1862. Mustered out, June 8, 1865, at Camp Dennison, O. Deceased.

PAYNE, MILES C.—Enrolled at Galion, August 7, 1862. Mustered out with Company.

POTH, PHILIP—Enrolled at Crestline, August 7, 1862. Detailed first as teamster; then as orderly at Division Headquarters. Mustered out with Company.

POTH, GEORGE—Enrolled at Crestline, August 7, 1862. Detailed as teamster. Mustered out with Company.

POTH, ADAM—Enrolled at Crestline, August 7, 1862. Discharged at Camp Dennison, September 22, 1863, on account of disability.

PECK, QUINBY—Enrolled at Bucyrus, August 6, 1862. Transferred to Mississippi Marine Brigade.

RITTER, JEREMIAH C.—Enrolled at Galion, August 2, 1862. Wounded at Kenesaw Mountain, June 23, 1864. Mustered out with Company.

RESH, AUGUSTUS—Enrolled at Bucyrus, August 8, 1862. Transferred to Company C.

RECK, JACOB — Enrolled at Galion, August 11, 1862. Wounded at Rocky Face, Ga., May 11, 1864. Mustered out with Company.

RUTH, HENRY F.—Enrolled at Galion, August 11, 1862. Left in charge of knapsacks at the Battle of Stone's River, December 31, 1862, but could not hold them against the entire rebel Left. Discharged at Nashville, March 29, 1863, on account of disability.

REYNOLDS, WM. H.—Enrolled at Galion, August 4, 1862. Discharged at Columbus, April 18, 1863, on account of wounds received at the Battle of Stone's River, December 31, 1862, where he was taken prisoner and exchanged.

STOVER, JAMES H. — Enrolled at Galion, July 18, 1862. Mustered as Sergeant. Appointed First Sergeant, November 15, 1862. Taken prisoner at Battle of Stone's River, December 31, 1862. Confined in Libby and Castle Thunder Prisons. Paroled in March, 1863. Exchanged in July, 1863. Mustered out, June 19, 1865, at Columbus.

SNIDER, HENRY L.—Enrolled at Bucyrus, August 9, 1862. Appointed Corporal, January 1, 1865. Mustered out with Company.

SHERER, WILLIAM—Enrolled at Galion, August 11, 1862. Wounded at Huntsville. Promoted to Corporal, March 1, 1865. Mustered out with Company.

SNYDER, PETER—Enrolled at Crestline, August 10, 1862. Mustered as Sergeant. Wounded and taken prisoner at the Battle of Stone's River December 31, 1862. Died in hands of the enemy, January 2, 1863. Snyder Post, G. A. R., of Crestline is named in memory of our comrade.

SHERER, ADAM — Enrolled at Galion, August 11, 1862. Killed at the Battle of Stone's River, December 31, 1862. Comrade Sherer was among the first to respond to Col. Stem's call for volunteers to silence the murderous fire of the enemy's sharpshooters on the morning of the battle.

SMALLEY, JOHN—Enrolled at Bucyrus, August 2, 1862. Mustered as Corporal. Promoted to Sergeant, November 1, 1862. Died at Murfreesboro', January 27, 1863, of disease.

SCHNURR, ANDREW J.—Enrolled at Galion, August 11, 1862. Appointed Corporal, September 20, 1862. Died at Murfreesboro', May 3, 1863, of fever.

SMITH, HENRY W.—Enrolled at Galion, August 7, 1862. Wounded and taken prisoner at the Battle of Stone's River, December 31, 1862. Starved in Libby Prison. Died December 1, 1863, while at home on furlough.

SHERER, MICHAEL.—Enrolled at Galion, August 11, 1862. Died November 17, 1862, at Edgefield Junction of disease.

SHERER, HENRY—Enrolled at Galion, August 11, 1862. Died at Bridgeport, Ala., December 7, 1863, of disease.

STEVENS, DAVID W.—Enrolled at Galion, December 24, 1863. Wounded near Atlanta.

SWONGER, AMER L.—Enrolled at Bucyrus, August 9, 1862. Detailed as teamster. Discharged at Murfreesboro', March 3, 1863, on account of disability from wounds received in an accident to his wagon.

STERNER, FRANCIS—Enrolled at Bucyrus, August 9, 1862. Discharged at Louisville, November 8, 1862, on account of disability.

SLORP, JOSHUA—Enrolled at Galion, August 5, 1862. Wounded in Battle of Chickamauga, September 20, 1863. Discharged at Columbus, January 27, 1865, on account of disability.

SMITH, SAMUEL.—Enrolled at Galion, August 5, 1862. Discharged at Louisville, January 7, 1863, on account of disability.

STAHLE, WALLACE—Enrolled at Crestline, August 7, 1862. Wounded and taken prisoner in Battle of Stone's River, December 31, 1862. In Libby Prison two months. Exchanged. Discharged at Columbus, April 14, 1863, on account of wounds.

SMITH, JOHN G.—Enrolled at Galion, August 6, 1862. Discharged at Nashville, January 27, 1863, on account of disability.

SPRAW, JACOB—Enrolled at Crestline, Aug. 7, 1862. Transferred to Company K, 1st Regiment, Veteran Reserve Corps. Mustered out, June 30, 1865, at Nashville, Tenn.

SNYDER, VALENTINE—Enrolled at Crestline, August 9, 1862. Transferred to Mississippi Marine Brigade.

TAYLOR, NATHANIEL—Enrolled at Leesville, August 6, 1862. Mustered out with Company. Deceased.

TAYLOR, WILLIAM M.—Enrolled at Crestline, August 5, 1862. Mustered out with Company.

WILLIAMS, ISAAC M.—Enrolled at Bucyrus, August 9, 1862. Captured in Battle of Stone's River. In Libby Prison four months. Exchanged. Mustered out with Company. Died at Soldiers' Home in Dayton, July 20, 1878, from injuries received while marching to Richmond.

WARDEN, WILLIAM P.—Enrolled at Bucyrus, August 6, 1862. Mustered as Corporal. Wounded in Battle of Stone's River, December 31, 1862. Transferred to Veteran Reserve Corps, November 13, 1863. Mustered out July 2, 1865, at Chicago, Ill. Deceased.

WEST, HENRY J. F.—Enrolled at Bucyrus, August 6, 1862. Transferred to Mississippi Marine Brigade.

ZINK, SAMUEL, JR.—Enrolled at Crestline, August 10, 1862. On detached service at Columbus after March 11, 1864. Mustered out at Columbus, June 15, 1865.

COMPANY F.

CAPTAIN I. M. KIRBY—See Field and Staff.

CAPTAIN WILLIAM H. KILMER—Enrolled August 9, 1862. Promoted to First Lieutenant, October 14, 1862; to Captain, January 28, 1863. Wounded in Battle of Stone's River. Killed in the Battle of Chickamauga; shot through the shoulder while gallantly leading a charge upon the enemy's lines.

CAPTAIN GEORGE W. HALE—Enrolled at Upper Sandusky, August 9, 1862. Promoted to Second Lieutenant from First Sergeant, December 23, 1862; to First Lieutenant, February 17, 1863. Wounded in both legs and captured, September 19, 1863, in the Battle of Chickamauga. A prisoner for eighteen months. Promoted to Captain, November 3, 1864. Mustered out with Company. (See Prison Experience.)

LIEUTENANT FRANKLIN POPE — Enrolled at Columbus, August 10, 1862. Mustered as First Lieutenant. Promoted to Captain, October 14, 1862, but not mustered. Resigned at Nashville, Tenn., January 28, 1863.

LIEUTENANT JACOB NEWHARD — Enrolled at Columbus, August 4, 1862. Mustered as Second Lieutenant. Promoted to First Lieutenant, October 14, 1862, but not mustered. Resigned at Nashville, Tenn., December 22, 1862.

ANDERSON, JOSEPH—Enrolled at Upper Sandusky, August 9, 1862. Mustered as Corporal. Killed at Rocky Face, May 11, 1864.

ALLISON, DAVID—Enrolled at Upper Sandusky, August 9, 1862. Mustered as Corporal. Promoted to Sergeant February 17, 1863. Taken prisoner in Battle of Chickamauga, September 19, 1863. Promoted to First Lieutenant, February 21, 1865, but not mustered. Mustered out at Cincinnati, June 20, 1865, close of war. Died at Columbus, O., in 1870.

BIXBY, HERBERT — Enrolled at Carey, August 5, 1862. Mustered out with the Company.

BRIGGS, JAMES M.—Enrolled at Carey, August 6, 1862. Taken prisoner November 29, 1864, at Spring Hill, Tenn. Mustered out at Camp Chase, O., June 16, 1865.

BOLANDER, OLIVER—Enrolled at Upper Sandusky, August 9, 1862. Died at Nashville, Tenn., January 15, 1863, of wounds received in Battle of Stone's River, December 31, 1862.

BARKER, JAMES E.—Enrolled at Upper Sandusky, August 9, 1862. Discharged at Louisville, Ky., May 29, 1865, on account of disability.

BROWN, SOVEREIGN H.—Enrolled at Carey, August 8, 1862. Killed in Battle of Chickamauga, September 19, 1863.

CORNING, JAS. H.—Enrolled at Upper Sandusky, August 9, 1862. Wounded in the Battle of Chickamauga, September 19, 1863, and at Rocky Face Ridge, Ga., May 11, 1864. On detached duty at Brigade Headquarters after April 13, 1865. Mustered out with Company.

CULVER, FRANK—Enrolled at Upper Sandusky, August 9, 1862. Wounded in the leg and captured at the Battle of Chickamauga, September 19, 1863. Mustered out with Company.

CARNEY, DAVID E.—Enrolled at Carey, August 5, 1862. No record after December 17, 1862.

CARNEY, WILLIAM J.—Enrolled at Carey, August 5, 1862. No record after December 17, 1862.

CAROTHERS, WILLIAM H.—Enrolled at Carey, August 8, 1862. Discharged, December 13, 1862, at Bowling Green, Ky., on account of disability.

CARMICHAEL, WILLIAM—Enrolled at Upper Sandusky, August 9, 1862. Discharged at Bowling Green, Ky., January 13, 1863, on account of disability.

CLARK, THOMAS A.—Enrolled at Upper Sandusky, August 9, 1862. Discharged at Bridgeport, Ala., January 8, 1864, on account of disability.

CUTLER, CALVIN P.—Enrolled at Upper Sandusky, August 9, 1862. Discharged at Bridgeport, Ala., January 23, 1864, on account of disability.

DEWITT, ALFRED J.—Enrolled at Carey, August 6, 1862. Mustered as Corporal. Died at Nashville, Tenn., March 8, 1863, of wounds received in the Battle of Stone's River, December 31, 1862. He was a great favorite.

DIXON, HENRY H.—Enrolled at Upper Sandusky, August 9, 1862. Seriously injured at Rolling Fork, Ky. Discharged at Bowling Green, Ky., February 7, 1863, on account of disability.

FOYER, WALTER—Enrolled at Upper Sandusky, August 9, 1862. Mustered out with Company.

FLICKINGER, JACOB H.—Enrolled at Upper Sandusky, August 14, 1862.

GESTENSLAGER, JOHN P. — Enrolled at Upper Sandusky, August 9, 1862. Wounded in the arm and taken prisoner at the Battle of Chickamauga. Imprisoned at Richmond, Danville and Andersonville. Appointed Corporal, May 1, 1865. Mustered out with Company. (See Prison Experience.)

GOOD, WILLIAM—Enrolled at Upper Sandusky, August 9, 1862. Wounded at Jonesboro, September 1, 1864. Mustered out with Company.

GOOD, DAVID—Enrolled at Upper Sandusky, August 9, 1862. Wounded in the Battle of Chickamauga, September 20, 1863, and in Battle of Resaca, May 14, 1864. Mustered out with Company.

GOOD, DANIEL.—Enrolled at Upper Sandusky, August 9, 1862. Discharged, January 7, 1863, at Nashville, Tenn., on account of disability. Died at Nevada, O., November 29, 1892.

GLASSER, CHRISTIAN H.—Enrolled at Upper Sandusky, August 9, 1862 Killed in the Battle of Chickamauga, September 19, 1863.

GOULD, THEOPHILUS D.—Enrolled at Carey, August 5, 1862. Killed in Battle of Rocky Face, Ga., May 11, 1864.

GROSSELL, JOHN—Enrolled at Carey, August 14. 1862. Mustered as Sergeant. No record after October 28, 1862.

GOLDSBY, GEORGE—Enrolled at Upper Sandusky, August 9, 1862. No record after September 27, 1862.

HERNDEN, JAMES W.—Enrolled at Carey, August 9, 1862. Mustered as Corporal. Promoted to Sergeant, February 17, 1863. Was wounded and captured in Battle of Stone's River, December 31, 1862, but made his escape. Wounded and taken prisoner in the Battle of Chickamauga, September 19, 1863. Promoted to First Sergeant, May 22, 1865. Mustered out with the Company.

HOLLENSHEAD, THOMAS—Enrolled at Upper Sandusky, August 9, 1862. Wounded and captured at Battle of Stone's River, December 31, 1862. Died in the hands of the enemy.

HILL, FIRMAN G.—Enrolled at Upper Sandusky, August 9, 1862. Mustered as Corporal. Promoted to Sergeant, February 17, 1863. Captured in Battle of Chickamauga, September 19, 1862. Died March 28, 1865, at Wharton, O., of typhoid fever.

HALE, DAVID E.—Enrolled at Upper Sandusky, August 9, 1862. Mustered as Sergeant. Discharged January 27, 1863, at Nashville, Tenn., on account of disability.

HALLIWELL, WILLIAM—Enrolled at Upper Sandusky, August 9, 1862. Wounded in the Battle of Stone's River, December 31, 1862, while carrying a wounded comrade from the field. Appointed Corporal, February 17, 1863. Mustered out May 18, 1865, at Nashville.

HELLER, PHILIP—Enrolled at Upper Sandusky, August 9, 1862. Discharged at Quincy, Ill., May 11, 1863, on account of disability.

HUTTON, JOHN—Enrolled at Upper Sandusky, August 9, 1862. Wounded in Battle of Stone's River, December 31, 1862. Discharged June 20, 1863, at Camp Chase, O., on account of disability.

HARSH, JOSEPH—Enrolled at Upper Sandusky, August 9, 1862. Color Guard in Battle of Stone's River, December 31, 1862. Transferred to 1st United States Veteran Volunteer Engineers, July 7, 1864. Mustered out June 30, 1865. Deceased.

HARRIS, CHARLES J.—Enrolled at Carey, August 5, 1862, Appointed Corporal, May 22, 1865. Mustered out with Company. Died at Carey, O.

KRIDER, JOHN— Enrolled at Upper Sandusky, August 9, 1862. Mustered out with the Company.

KERR, JOHN A.—Enrolled at Upper Sandusky, August 9, 1862. Mustered as Corporal. Promoted to Sergeant, November 1, 1862. Killed in the Battle of Stone's River, December 31, 1862.

LICKFELT, AUGUST—Enrolled at Upper Sandusky, August 9, 1862. Promoted to Corporal, May 1, 1865. Mustered out with the Company.

- LINK, SHIPLEY H.—Enrolled at Upper Sandusky, August 9, 1862. Wounded in the Battle of Chickamauga, September 19, 1863, and at Rocky Face Ridge, May 11, 1864. Mustered out with Company.
- LOWELL, MARCUS L.—Enrolled at Upper Sandusky, August 13, 1862. Mustered out with Company.
- LUDWIG, FREDERICK—Enrolled at Carey, August 5, 1862. Taken prisoner in the Battle of Chickamauga, September 20, 1863. Mustered out with Company.
- LAUGHLIN, JOHN M.—Enrolled at Carey, August 9, 1862. Detailed as Teamster. Mustered out with the Company.
- LAWRENCE, GEORGE—Enrolled at Upper Sandusky, August 9, 1862. Killed in Battle of Chickamauga, Tenn., September 19, 1863.
- LAWRENCE, WASHINGTON—Enrolled at Upper Sandusky, August 9, 1863. Died at Bowling Green, Ky., December 16, 1862, of disease.
- LACY, HARMON H.—Enrolled at Upper Sandusky, August 9, 1862. Mustered as Sergeant. Died at Camp Dennison, O., January 2, 1863, of disease.
- LILES, JOHN—Enrolled at Upper Sandusky, August 9, 1862. Died at Danville, Ky., December 2, 1862, of disease.
- LOUDERMILCH, JOSEPH—Enrolled at Upper Sandusky, August 9, 1862. Discharged, January 8, 1864, at Bridgeport, Ala., on account of disability.
- MARTIN, CLAUDIUS—Enrolled at Upper Sandusky, August 9, 1862. Mustered as Corporal. Promoted to Sergeant, February 7, 1863. Taken prisoner in Battle of Chickamauga, September 20, 1863. Paroled. Exchanged. Mustered out with Company.
- MYERS, GEORGE S.—Enrolled at Carey, August 7, 1862. Appointed Corporal, July 7, 1864. Wounded in the arm while carrying the Colors at Chickamauga. Received medal of honor for service at Chickamauga. Promoted to Sergeant, May 1, 1865. Mustered out with Company.

MANN, GEORGE—Enrolled at Upper Sandusky, August 9, 1862. Mustered as Corporal. Promoted to Sergeant, March 9, 1863. Wounded and taken prisoner in the Battle of Chickamauga, September 20, 1863. Imprisoned at Andersonville, Libby, Belle Isle, Danville and Goldsboro'. Mustered out at Columbus, June 12, 1865. (See extract from Prison Life.)

McELWAIN, ANDREW—Enrolled at Upper Sandusky, August 9, 1862. Appointed Corporal, February 17, 1863. Shell wound in the right shoulder in the Battle of Chickamauga, September 19, 1863. Mustered out June 15, 1865, at Columbus, O. Died, April 6, 1891, at Lafayette.

MYERS, SKILES R.—Enrolled at Upper Sandusky, August 9, 1862. Mustered out with the Company.

MARTIN, SAMUEL—Enrolled at Upper Sandusky, August 9, 1862. Died at Nashville, Tenn., January 17, 1863, of wounds received in the Battle of Stone's River, December 31, 1862. Color Guard.

MILLER, CHARLES—Enrolled at Upper Sandusky, March 1, 1865. Transferred to Company A, 51st Ohio Volunteer Infantry, June 10, 1865.

MILLER, DAVID—Enrolled at Upper Sandusky, August 9, 1862. Killed in the Battle of Stone's River, December 31, 1862.

NORTON, JOHN W.—Enrolled at Upper Sandusky, August 9, 1862. Transferred to 43rd Company, 2nd Battalion, Veteran Reserve Corps. Mustered out June 28, 1865, at Camp Dennison, O.

NYE, EDWIN—Enrolled at Carey, August 5, 1862.

NICHOLS, WILLIAM—Enrolled at Upper Sandusky, August 9, 1862. Wounded in the Battle of Chickamauga, September 19, 1863. Transferred to Veteran Reserve Corps, January 5, 1864.

PARKS, R. H.—Enrolled at Upper Sandusky, August 9, 1862. Wounded and captured in the Battle of Stone's River, December 31, 1862. Exchanged. Appointed Corporal, February 17, 1863. Detached as Blacksmith, May 24, 1863. Promoted to Sergeant, May 22, 1865. Mustered out with Company.

PRICE, LEVI—Enrolled at Richland, August 7, 1862. Shot through the lung and taken prisoner in the Battle of Chickamauga, September 20, 1863. Appointed Corporal, May 1, 1865. Mustered out with Company.

QUAINTANCE, GEORGE—Enrolled at Upper Sandusky, August 14, 1862. Died at Nashville, January 8, 1863, of fever.

REAM, BENJAMIN—Enrolled at Upper Sandusky, August 9, 1862. Appointed Corporal, September 12, 1864. Mustered out with Company.

REEVES, JAMES—Enrolled at Upper Sandusky, August 9, 1862. Transferred to Company E, 34th Ohio Volunteer Infantry, September 1, 1862.

REX, JOHN D.—Enrolled at Upper Sandusky, August 9, 1862. Transferred to Company H, 15th Regiment, Veteran Reserve Corps, July 1, 1863. Mustered out July 15, 1865, at Cairo, Ill.

STEWART, JAMES A.—Enrolled at Upper Sandusky, August 9, 1862. Appointed Corporal, February 17, 1863. Wounded in the right shoulder in the Battle of Chickamauga, September 20, 1863. Detailed as Clerk at General Thomas' Headquarters at the time of the Battle of Franklin on account of the wound. Mustered out June 26, 1865, at Cleveland, O.

SHADE, AMOS K.—Enrolled at Carey, August 5, 1862. Wounded and captured in Battle of Chickamauga, Sept. 19, 1863. Nurse in Hospital at Chattanooga, October 8, 1863. Mustered out with Company.

SIBERTS, CORNELIUS J.—Enrolled at Upper Sandusky, August 9, 1862. Wounded at Resaca, May 15, 1864. Mustered out with Company.

SHEPARD, RUSSELL—Enrolled at Upper Sandusky, August 9, 1862. Mustered out with Company.

SPAFFORD, ADELBERT A.—Enrolled at Upper Sandusky, August 9, 1862. Mustered out with Company.

SHIVELY, AARON C.—Enrolled at Carey, August 5, 1862. Killed in Battle of Stone's River, December 31, 1862.

SCOTT, JOHN—Enrolled at Upper Sandusky, August 9, 1862. Killed in the Battle of Stone's River, December 31, 1862.

STEVENS, WILLIAM—Enrolled at Upper Sandusky, August 9, 1862. Died at Murfreesboro', February 7, 1863, of disease.

STERLING, FRANCIS M.—Enrolled at Carey, August 7, 1862. Died in the hands of the enemy at Richmond, Va., February 20, 1863, of wounds received in the Battle of Stone's River, where he was captured.

SPAFFORD, GEORGE F.—Enrolled at Upper Sandusky, August 9, 1862. Died at New Albany, Ind., October 28, 1862.

SIPES, PETER—Enrolled at Carey, August 7, 1862. Died near Atlanta, August 29, 1864, of disease.

SHAW, EDWARD W.—Enrolled at Carey, August 6, 1862. Discharged at Louisville, January 26, 1863, on account of disability.

SHOEMAKER, LEVI—Enrolled at Upper Sandusky, August 6, 1862. Discharged at Murfreesboro', January 15, 1863, on account of disability.

SMITH, JACOB W.—Enrolled at Upper Sandusky, August 9, 1862. Discharged at Cincinnati, February 9, 1865, on account of disability. Detailed as Musician.

SWEARINGER, WILLIAM—Enrolled at Upper Sandusky, August 9, 1862. Detailed as Musician. Discharged, May 11, 1865, at Nashville, Tenn., on account of disability. Died at Forest, O., September 10, 1880, of heart disease, following rheumatism and effects of gunshot wound in the face, received at La Vergne, Tenn., September 1, 1864.

SHEPHERD, JOHN E.—Enrolled at Upper Sandusky, August 9, 1802. Appointed Corporal, March 9, 1863. Transferred to Veteran Reserve Corps, March 15, 1864. Mustered out, June 28, 1865, at Camp Dennison, O.

STUMP, MICHAEL—Enrolled at Carey, August 7, 1862. Wounded in the foot at Kenesaw Mountain, June 23, 1864. Transferred to Company C, 8th Regiment, Veteran Reserve Corps. Mustered out, July 12, 1865, at Chicago. Died, March 7, 1890, at Whartonburg, O.

ROSTER. 421

SHAFFSTALL, JOSIAH—Enrolled at Upper Sandusky, August 9, 1862. Wounded and taken prisoner at Battle of Chickamauga, September 19, 1863. Transferred to Veteran Reserve Corps, March 11, 1864.

SWARTZ, LEVI—Enrolled at Upper Sandusky, August 9, 1862. Transferred to Company G, 15th Regiment, Veteran Reserve Corps. Mustered out July 8, 1865, at Springfield, Ill.

STRYCHER, AMOS—Enrolled at Carey, August 7, 1862. Wounded and taken prisoner in the Battle of Chickamauga, September 19, 1863. Transferred to Veteran Reserve Corps, November 19, 1864.

STIRM, NOAH—Enrolled at Carey, August 7, 1862. Transferred to 8th Regiment, Veteran Reserve Corps, November 15, 1863. Mustered out June 30, 1865, at Chicago.

SHELL, WILLIAM—Enrolled at Carey, August 6, 1862. Transferred to 8th Regiment, Veteran Reserve Corps, November 15, 1863. Mustered out July 5, 1865, at Detroit, Mich. Deceased.

TURNER, ALBERT H.—Enrolled at Carey, August 5, 1862. Mustered out with Company. Deceased.

TAYLOR, GARRETT—Enrolled at Upper Sandusky, August 9, 1862. Killed in the Battle of Stone's River, December 31, 1862.

TROUP, SAMUEL—Enrolled at Upper Sandusky, August 9, 1862. Transferred to 1st United States Veteran Volunteer Engineer Corps, July 20, 1864. Mustered out June 30, 1865.

VRENDENBURG, C. J.—Enrolled at Carey, August 5, 1862. Captured November 29, 1864, at Spring Hill, Tenn. Mustered out with Company.

VROMAN, HENRY D.—Enrolled at Upper Sandusky, August 9, 1862. Died at Nashville, January 18, 1863, of fever.

WELTER, WILLIAM H.—Enrolled at Carey, August 7, 1862. Appointed Corporal, May 1, 1865. Mustered out with Company. Deceased.

WAGNER, SAMUEL S.—Enrolled at Upper Sandusky, August 9, 1863. Taken prisoner at Chickamauga, September. Confined at Belle Island, Danville, Andersonville and Florence. Mustered out with Company. Killed in accident, November 1887, in Kansas.

WELLS, JOHN A.—Enrolled at Carey, August 5, 1862. Mustered out with Company.

WHITE, ELIJAH—Enrolled at Upper Sandusky, August 9, 1862. Appointed Corporal, March 9, 1863. Killed in the Battle of Chattahoochee River, July 7, 1864.

WISE, AUGUST—Enrolled at Upper Sandusky, August 9, 1862. Discharged at Huntsville, Ala., February 15, 1865, on account of disability.

COMPANY G.

CAPTAIN JOHN MESSER—See Field and Staff.

CAPTAIN JOHN P. FLEMING—Enrolled August 1, 1862. Mustered as First Lieutenant, August 30, 1862. Wounded through the arm and taken prisoner in Battle of Stone's River, December 31, 1862. Promoted to Captain, January 3, 1863. Mustered out with Company.

LIEUTENANT HORACE D. OLDS—Enrolled August 7, 1862. Mustered as Second Lieutenant, August 9, 1862. Promoted to First Lieutenant, January 3, 1863, and transferred to Pioneer Brigade. Discharged, December 25, 1864, to accept commission in Company B., 1st Regiment, United States Veteran Volunteer Engineers. Mustered out, September 28, 1865.

LIEUTENANT JOSEPH F. WEBSTER—Enrolled at Berlin, January 31, 1862. Mustered as Corporal. Promoted to First Sergeant, May 28, 1863. Detached on recruiting service, December 4, 1863. Promoted to First Lieutenant, July 30, 1864. Mustered out with Company. Died in April, 1887.

LIEUTENANT JOHN L. MILLIMAN—See Company E.

ROSTER.

ANDREWS, FRANKLIN—Enrolled at Berlin, August 6, 1862, as private. Promoted to Corporal, March 1, 1865. Mustered out with Company.

ANDREWS, EMERSON—Enrolled at Berlin, August 9, 1862. Wounded in Battle of Stone's River, December 31, 1862. Detached as teamster, at Division Headquarters, December 9, 1863. Mustered out with Company.

ABBOTT, SQUIRE—Enrolled at Groton, August 7, 1862. Wounded and captured in Battle of Stone's River, December 31, 1862. Mustered out at Columbus, O., June 9, 1865.

AMES, WILLIAM H.—Enrolled at Berlin, February 2, 1865. Mustered out at Trenton, N.J., June 14, 1865.

BUTLER, SQUIRE A.—Enrolled at Berlin, August 4, 1862. Appointed Corporal. Captured in Battle of Stone's River, December 21, 1862. Exchanged. Wounded in the Battle of Chickamauga, September 19, 1863. Promoted to Sergeant, November 1, 1863. Mustered out with Company.

BLAIR, ALBERT A.—Enrolled at Florence, August 7, 1862. Detailed in Ambulance Corps, May 7, 1864. Mustered out with Company.

BEARDSLEY, WALTER C.—Enrolled at Florence, August 9, 1862. Captured in Battle of Chickamauga, September 19, 1863. Mustered out at Cleveland, O., May 30, 1865.

BUTLER, OLIVER H.—Enrolled at Berlin, August 11, 1862. Mustered out with Company.

BENSCHOTTEN, OLIVER W.—Enrolled at Berlin, August 7, 1862. Died at Nashville, December 28, 1862, of disease.

BALDWIN, ISAAC—Enrolled at Berlin, August 4, 1862. Died at Chattanooga, June 12, 1863, of disease.

BRADLEY, ANDREW—Enrolled at Monroeville, August 30, 1862. Captured at Chickamauga, September 19, 1863. Died in Andersonville Prison, September 24, 1864, of disease.

BUDD, JAMES H.—Enrolled at Groton, January 2, 1864. Discharged at Camp Dennison, May 25, 1865.

BARBER, DAVID S.—Enrolled at Groton, August 7, 1862. Discharged at Murfreesboro', February 21, 1863, on account of disability.

BURNHAM, HENRY E.—Enrolled at Berlin, August 7, 1862. Discharged at Louisville, Ky., February 25, 1863, on account of disability.

BURKHOLDER, JAMES C.—Enrolled at Groton, August 8, 1862. Transferred to Company H, 7th Regiment, Veteran Reserve Corps, May 27, 1864. Mustered out, June 29, 1865. Died at Wamego, Kan., January 1, 1888.

CRANNELL, MARCUS—Enrolled at Groton, August 6, 1862. Wounded in the Battle of Nashville, Tenn., December 15, 1864. Mustered out at Louisville, June 12, 1865.

CESSEN, ISAAC C.—Enrolled at Berlin, July 31, 1862. Appointed Corporal. Promoted to Sergeant, May 4, 1863. Killed in the Battle of Chickamauga, September 19, 1863.

COOK, JONATHAN—Enrolled at Berlin, July 31, 1862. Transferred to 1st United States Veteran Volunteer Enggineer Corps, November 20, 1864. Mustered out at Nashville, Tenn., September 26, 1865.

CURTIS, WILLIAM—Enrolled at Berlin, December 28, 1863. Transferred to Company A, 51st Ohio Volunteer Infantry, June 10, 1865.

CRAVATH, E. M.—See Field and Staff.

DRAKE, HEZEKIAH S.—Enrolled at Groton, August 7, 1862. Appointed Corporal, March 1, 1865. Wounded and captured in Battle of Stone's River, December 31, 1862. Mustered out with Company.

DWIGHT, HENRY E.—Enrolled at Groton, August 6, 1862. Captured in Battle of Stone's River, December 31, 1862. Mustered out with Company.

DENMAN, AMBROSE B. C.—Enrolled at Florence, August 7, 1862. Appointed Sergeant. Captured in Battle of Chickamauga, September 19, 1863. Mustered out at Cleveland, June 19, 1865.

DUNHAM, WILLIAM—Enrolled at Groton, August 6, 1862. Killed in front of Kenesaw Mountain, Ga., June, 25, 1864.

DALZELL, FLORON—Enrolled at Berlin, August 7, 1862. Died at Nashville, January 28, 1863, of disease.

DANIELS, JOHN—Enrolled at Berlin, July 31, 1862. Died at Nashville, February 19, 1863, of disease.

DUNNING, JOHN J.—Enrolled at Groton, August 1, 1862. Discharged at Louisville, Ky., July 16, 1863, on account of disability.

DEVGO, ALLEN H.—Enrolled at Monroeville, September 3, 1862. Discharged at Bridgeport, Ala., January 8, 1864, on account of disability.

DWIGHT, OSCAR — Enrolled at Groton, January 5, 1864. Transferred to Company A, 51st Ohio Veteran Infantry, June 10, 1865.

FOWLER, GEORGE L.—Enrolled at Berlin, August 11, 1862. Appointed Corporal, September 15, 1862; to Sergeant, July 1, 1864. Mustered out with Company. Deceased.

FISHER, HENRY D.—Enrolled at Berlin, August 3, 1862. Mustered out with Company.

FULLER, RALPH G.—Enrolled at Berlin, August 11, 1862. Mustered out with Company.

FLEMING, HIRAM P.—Enrolled at Groton, January 2, 1864. Died at Nashville, July 10, 1864, of disease.

FLEMING, GEORGE W. — Enrolled at Groton, August 6, 1862. Discharged, March 4, 1863, on account of disability.

FORD, ALFRED—Enrolled at Groton, August 8, 1862. Wounded in the Battle of Chickamauga, September 19, 1863. Appointed Corporal, November 1, 1863. Discharged, May 13, 1865, on account of wounds received, December 15, 1864, in the Battle of Nashville.

FALLEY, ALPHA B.—Enrolled at Groton, August 7, 1862. Discharged at Louisville, Ky., June 23, 1863, on account of disability.

FORD, JAMES—Enrolled at Groton, August 11, 1862. Transferred to Mississippi Marine Brigade, March 11, 1863. Deceased.

GARDNER, OLIVER—Enrolled at Berlin, August 8, 1862. Mustered out with Company.

GARMON, JAMES M.—Enrolled at Groton, August 8, 1862. Killed, September 19, 1863, in Battle of Chickamauga.

GREINER, PETER—Enrolled at Berlin, August 10, 1862. Wounded and taken prisoner in the Battle of Stone's River. Recaptured. Transferred to Signal Corps, October 22, 1863.

GREEN, ALVIN—Enrolled at Berlin, January 2, 1864. Transferred to Company A, 51st Ohio Volunteer Infantry, June 10, 1865.

GRANT, JOHN W.—Enrolled at Berlin, December 23, 1863. Transferred to Company A, 51st Ohio Volunteer Infantry, June 10, 1865.

HOOVER, GEORGE—Enrolled at Groton, August 7, 1862. Mustered out with Company.

HOUCK, FREDERICK—Enrolled at Groton, August 7, 1862. Mustered out with Company.

HOWEY, ALBA—Enrolled at Groton, August 11, 1862. Mustered out with Company.

HOWELL, JOHN—Enrolled at Groton, August 11, 1862. Wounded in the arm in the Battle of Stone's River, December 31, 1862. Mustered out with Company.

HARRIS, DANIEL W.—Enrolled at Berlin, July 30, 1862. Mustered out with Company.

HIGGINS, DANIEL B.—Enrolled at Berlin, August 9, 1862. Mustered out with Company.

HUTCHINSON, WILLIAM—Enrolled at Florence, August 8, 1862. Killed in the Battle of Nashville, December 15, 1864.

HEWITT, GEORGE—Enrolled at Groton, August 6, 1862. Killed in the Battle of Stone's River, December 31, 1862.

HODGE, MARTIN—Enrolled at Berlin, December 23, 1863. Died at Bridgeport, February 22, 1864, of disease.

HALE, MILES E.—Enrolled at Florence, August 9, 1862. Discharged at Columbus, O., January 31, 1863, on account of disability.

HUMPHREY, MALACHI G.—Enrolled at Berlin, August 8, 1862. Wounded in the Battle of Stone's River, December 31, 1862. Discharged at Camp Dennison, O., May 25, 1865, on account of wounds received in the Battle of Nashville, December 15, 1864. Died at Bellevue, Ohio, October 22, 1893.

HOWEY, JOHN—Enrolled at Groton, August 11, 1862. Wounded in the Battle of Stone's River, December 31, 1862. Transferred to 120th Company, 2nd Battalion, Veteran Reserve Corps. Mustered out, June 29, 1865, at Evansville, Ind. Deceased.

HORN, EDGAR F.—Enrolled at Florence, August 9, 1862. Transferred to Company K, 15th Regiment, Veteran Reserve Corps. Mustered out, May 8, 1865, at Springfield, Ill.

HOWSER, MARTIN W.—Enrolled at Groton, January 2, 1864. Transferred to Company A, 51st Ohio Volunteer Infantry, June 10, 1865.

HUMPHREY, CHARLES—Enrolled at Groton, January 2, 1864. Mustered out, May 30, 1865, at Cleveland, O.

HAY, JACOB—Enrolled at Berlin, August 8, 1862. Transferred to Veteran Reserve Corps, May 3, 1864. Mustered out at Louisville, June 12, 1865.

JONES, BENJAMIN F.—Enrolled at Groton, August 6, 1862. Mustered out with Company.

JOHNSON, PHILIP—Enrolled, February 15, 1864. Transferred to Company A, June 10, 1865.

JOHNSON, GEORGE—Enrolled at Berlin, January 2, 1864. Died at New Albany, Ind., February 28, 1865, of disease.

KEITH, WILLIAM M.—Enrolled at Berlin, December 28, 1863. Died at Chattanooga, July 18, 1864, of disease.

LONG, CHARLES—Enrolled at Groton, August 11, 1862. Detached as Blacksmith, September 29, 1863. Mustered out with Company.

LEWIS, ALEXANDER—Enrolled at Berlin, July 31, 1862. Died at Lebanon, Ky., December 2, 1862, of disease.

LOWRY, LABAN D.—Enrolled at Berlin, August 11, 1862. Discharged at Madison, Ind., December 11, 1863, on account of disability.

LANDIN, PETER—Enrolled at Berlin, August 8, 1862. Discharged at Bowling Green, Ky., February 7, 1863, on account of disability.

MORDOFF, GEORGE—Enrolled at Florence, August 7, 1862. Mustered as Corporal. Promoted to Sergeant, July 2, 1864. Mustered out with Company.

MORSE, GEORGE B.—Enrolled at Florence, August 8, 1862. Promoted to Corporal, January 1, 1863. Mustered out with Company.

MILLER, ANDREW J.—Enrolled at Florence, August 7, 1862. Promoted to Corporal, March 1, 1865. Mustered out with Company.

MYERS, DANIEL—Enrolled at Florence, August 7, 1862. Mustered out with Company.

McKESSON, ANDREW D.—Enrolled at Groton, August 6, 1862. Mustered out with Company.

MULLENIX, CURTIS B.—Enrolled at Berlin, July 31, 1862. Killed in Battle of Stone's River, January 1, 1863.

MEIKLE, ANDREW—Enrolled at Groton, August 6, 1862. Killed in the Battle of Stone's River, January 2, 1863.

MILLER, JOHN—Enrolled at Florence, December 15, 1893. Transferred to Company A, 51st Ohio Volunteer Infantry, June 10, 1865, as Jacob Miller.

MYRES, NICHOLAS—Enrolled at Berlin, August 7, 1862. Killed in assault upon Bald Knob, in front of Kenesaw Mountain, June 20, 1864.

MULLENIX, LEROY—Enrolled at Berlin, August 10, 1862. Promoted to Corporal, November 1, 1863. Died, July 25, 1864, in Field Hospital, near Kenesaw Mountain, of wounds received, July 4, 1864, in action at Ruff's Station, near Marietta.

MILLER, FRANCIS M.—Enrolled at Florence, August 9, 1862. Discharged, October 17, 1862, on account of disability.

MOREHOUSE, CHARLES D.—Enrolled at Berlin, July 31, 1862. Discharged at Ooltewah, February 28, 1864, on account of wounds received in Battle of Stone's River, December 31, 1862. Deceased.

MILLER, LAFAYETTE—Enrolled at Florence, August 7, 1862. Transferred to Company K, 1st United States Veteran Volunteer Engineer Corps, August 7, 1864. Mustered out, June 30, 1865.

MAGILL, ALFRED—Enrolled at Groton, January 2, 1864. Transferred to Company A, 51st Ohio Volunteer Infantry, June 10, 1865.

MAGILL, FRANCIS—Enrolled at Groton, August 6, 1862. Transferred to Company H, 12th Regiment, Veteran Reserve Corps. Mustered out, June 29, 1865, at Washington, D. C.

MUNSON, WILLIAM—Enrolled at Florence, August 7, 1862. Transferred to Veteran Reserve Corps, April 10, 1864.

MANNING, GEORGE—Enrolled at Berlin, January 5, 1864. Transferred to Company I, 6th Regiment, Veteran Reserve Corps, March 29, 1865. Mustered out July 11, 1865, at Cincinnati.

MORTON, PHILIP—Enrolled at Berlin, December 28, 1863. Mustered out at Chattanooga, May 31, 1865.

OSBORN, LEWIS—Enrolled at Berlin, July 30, 1862. Taken prisoner in the Battle of Chickamauga, September 19, 1863. Died in rebel prison at Richmond, Va., December 14, 1863, of disease.

OSTERHOUT, HENRY C.—Enrolled at Berlin, December 28, 1863. Transferred to Company I, 22nd Regiment, Veteran Reserve Corps. Mustered out, July 12, 1865, at Cleveland, O.

PAXTON, STEPHAN Z.—Enrolled at Groton, August 6, 1862. Promoted to Corporal, May 10, 1863. Wounded and captured at Battle of Chickamauga, September 19, 1863. Mustered out with Company.

PLUE, DAVID—Enrolled at Berlin, August 6, 1862. Promoted to Corporal, July 1, 1864. Wounded in the Battle of Chickamauga, September 19, 1863. Wounded at Jonesboro', September 1, 1864. Mustered out with Company.

PIKE, JAMES J.—Enrolled at Florence, August 7, 1862. Discharged, January 6, 1864, at Bridgeport, on account of disability.

PHELPS, ISAAC — Enrolled at Berlin, January 5, 1864. Transferred to Company F, 51st Ohio Volunteer Infantry, June 10, 1865.

RAY, GILES W.— Enrolled at Groton, August 7, 1862. Wounded in the Battle of Chickamauga, September 19, 1863. Appointed Corporal, July 1, 1864. Mustered out with Company.

RUSSET, JOHN—Enrolled at Berlin, August 4, 1862. Mustered out with Company.

RUSSETT, CHARLES—Enrolled at Berlin, August 4, 1862. Wounded in leg in the Battle of Chickamauga, September 19, 1863. Mustered out with Company.

RUSSELL, LYMAN B.—Enrolled at Florence, August 8, 1862. Appointed Corporal, November 1, 1863. Mustered out with Company.

RAMSDELL, HORACE V.—Enrolled at Groton, August 6, 1862. Discharged, March 11, 1863, on account of wounds received in Battle of Stone's River, December 31, 1862.

RUSSELL, RODERICK—Enrolled at Florence, August 7, 1862. Detailed as Musician. Discharged, March 26, 1883, at Columbus, on account of disability.

SHERMAN, ALMON—Enrolled at Berlin, August 3, 1862. Mustered out with Company.

SUTTON, ALFRED—Enrolled at Berlin, August 11, 1862. Detached on Gunboat "Newsboy," July 20, 1863. Mustered out at Columbus, June 30, 1865.

SMITH, ESBON W.—Enrolled at Groton, January 2, 1864. Killed in the Battle of Jonesboro', Ga., September 1, 1864.

SMITH, GEORGE L.—Enrolled at Florence, August 7, 1862. Died at Nashville, December 4, 1862, of disease.

SHAFER, GEORGE W.—Enrolled at Florence, August 7, 1862. Died at Chattanooga, June 19, 1864, of disease.

SAUNDERS, RUSSELL—Enrolled at Florence, August 7, 1862. Discharged at Camp Dennison, August 15, 1863, on account of disability.

SMITH, ELISHA D.—Enrolled at Groton, August 6, 1862. Wounded in the Battle of Stone's River, December 31, 1862. Discharged at Madison, Ind., June 4, 1864, on account of wounds received in the Battle of Chickamauga, September 20, 1863.

SHERMAN, CHARLES—Enrolled at Berlin, December 26, 1863. Transferred to Company F, 51st Ohio Volunteer Infantry, June 10, 1865.

THOMPSON, DEWITT C.—Enrolled at Groton, August 6, 1862. Mustered out with Company.

VAN NESS, WILLIAM H.—Enrolled at Groton, August 7, 1862. Mustered as Sergeant. Discharged, October 26, 1863, on account of disability.

WHITE, JOHN—Enrolled at Groton, August 6, 1862. Mustered as Corporal. Wounded and captured in the Battle of Stone's River, December 31, 1862. Promoted to Sergeant, October 15, 1863. Mustered out with Company. Deceased.

WHEAT, JOHN D.—Enrolled at Groton, August 6, 1862. Detached in Brigade Band, July 5, 1864. Mustered out with Company.

WILBUR, MARTIN V.—Enrolled at Florence, August 1, 1862. Discharged, March 27, 1865, on account of wounds received in action at Ruff's Station, near Kenesaw.

WOLCOTT, LAFAYETTE—Enrolled at Groton, February 22, 1864. Transferred to Company F, 51st Ohio Volunteer Infantry, June 10, 1865.

WEATHERLOW, DANIEL R.—Enrolled at Berlin, December 26, 1863. Transferred to Company F, 51st Ohio Volunteer Infantry, June 10, 1865. Deceased.

WILSON, JOHN—Enrolled at Sandusky, February 13, 1865. Transferred to Company F, 51st Ohio Volunteer Infantry, June 10, 1865.

WELLS, MADISON E.—Enrolled at Berlin, August 8, 1862. Promoted to Corporal, May 10, 1863; to Sergeant, July 1, 1864. Wounded, September 1, 1864, in the Battle of Jonesboro', Ga. Mustered out with Company.

WHEAT, GEORGE W.—Enrolled, August 11, 1862. Discharged, February 4, 1863, at Bowling Green, Ky., on account of disability. Deceased.

COMPANY H.

CAPTAIN JESSE SHRIVER—Enrolled at Tiffin. Mustered as Captain, at Monroeville, August 1, 1862. Resigned, April 8, 1863, at Columbus, on account of disability. Died in Tiffin, July 12, 1870.

CAPTAIN LEONARD D. SMITH—See Field and Staff and Company C.

CAPTAIN WILLIAM N. BEER—Enrolled at Bucyrus, August 14, 1862. See Non-Commissioned Staff.

LIEUTENANT HERBERT G. OGDEN—Enrolled at Monroeville, August 15, 1862. Mustered as First Lieutenant. Resigned, February 17, 1863.

LIEUTENANT WILLIAM P. MYERS—Enrolled at Republic, O. Mustered as First Sergeant, August 11, 1862. Promoted to Second Lieutenant, February 17, 1863; to First Lieutenant, at Ooltewah, March 19, 1864. Resigned, May 12, 1865.

LIEUTENANT JAMES I. NEFF—Enrolled, August 11, 1862. Mustered as Second Lieutenant. Promoted to extra First Lieutenant and Adjutant and transferred to Field and Staff, May 30, 1863. Mustered out to accept commission as Captain of Company A, April 27, 1865, to date February 24, 1865. Mustered out as Captain by reason of strength of Company not allowing muster until further orders were received from War Department, May 10, 1865. Mustered out with Company.

ANDERS, DAVID B. Enrolled at Tiffin, August 13, 1862. Wounded in the Battle of Stone's River, December 31, 1862. Promoted to Sergeant, February 23, 1864. Mustered out with the Company.

ANWAY, SILAS B.—Enrolled at Republic, August 7, 1862. Mustered out with the Company.

ANWAY, JOHN E.—Enrolled at Republic, August 9, 1862. Mustered out with the Company.

AMES, JAMES S.—Enrolled at Tiffin, August 9, 1862. Died at Nashville, Tenn., February 25, 1863, of wounds received in the Battle of Stone's River, December 31, 1862.

BELL, CHARLES W.—Enrolled at Tiffin, August 9, 1862. Promoted to Corporal, February 28, 1865. Wounded in the Battle of Stone's River. Mustered out with Company.

BURNS, WILLIAM J.—Enrolled in Seneca County, August 11, 1862. Wounded in the Battle of Resaca, May 14, 1864. Discharged at Madison, Ind., January 13, 1865, on account of disability.

BOROFF, WILLIAM C.—Enrolled in Seneca County, August 9, 1862. Died at Murfreesboro', Tenn., January 24, 1863, of disease.

BOWLAND, JAMES A.—Enrolled at Tiffin, August 11, 1862. Died at Louisville, Ky., January 23, 1863, of disease.

BELL, BENJAMIN F.—Enrolled at Tiffin, August 9, 1862. Discharged, May 30, 1863, at Camp Dennison, O., on account of wounds received in the Battle of Stone's River, December 31, 1862.

BARGER, JOHN—Enrolled at Tiffin, August 11, 1862. Transferred to Company F, 7th Regiment, Veteran Reserve Corps, September 30, 1863. Mustered out, June 28, 1865, at Washington, D.C.

BESSEY, JACOB—Enrolled in Seneca County, August 9, 1862. Wounded in the Battle of Stone's River, December 31, 1862. Transferred to Company B, 23rd Regiment, Veteran Reserve Corps, November 1, 1863. Mustered out at Clinton, Ia., July 13, 1865.

BEAVER, M. A.—Enrolled, August 11, 1862, in Seneca County. Mustered out with the Company,

COLE, LEONARD G.—Enrolled at Tiffin, August 2, 1862. Promoted to Corporal, June 30, 1863. Wounded in the Battle of Chickamauga, September 19, 1863. Wounded in the Battle of Resaca, May 14, 1864. Mustered out with Company.

COOK, JOHN H.—Enrolled at Republic, August 7, 1862. Captured in the Battle of Stone's River, December 31, 1862. Mustered out with the Company.

CRUM, WILLIAM — Enrolled at Tiffin, August 2, 1862. Mustered out with the Company. Deceased.

CHAFFEE, GEORGE W.—Enrolled at Tiffin, August 7, 1862. Died at Danville, Ky., October 31, 1862, of typhoid fever.

CROSS, HAMILTON J.—Enrolled at Tiffin, August 9, 1862. Discharged, August 30, 1863, at Camp Chase, O., on account of disability.

CURRIGAN, EDWARD W.— Enrolled at Tiffin, August 8, 1862. Discharged at Nashville, May 6, 1863, on account of wounds in the shoulder, received in the Battle of Stone's River; also, wounded at La Vergne, Tenn., on the way to Nashville, by bushwhackers. Re-enlisted at Tiffin, February 5, 1865, in Company B, 195th Ohio Volunteer Infantry. Appointed Sergeant. Promoted to Brevet-Lieutenant, but refused to accept commission. Mustered out, December 22, 1865.

CROSS, HENRY C. — Enrolled at Tiffin, August 9, 1862. Transferred to Company K, 1st Regiment, United States Veteran Volunteer Engineers, August 7, 1864. Mustered out, June 30, 1865.

DIBBLE, HENRY — Enrolled at Tiffin, August 11, 1862. Wounded in the Battle of Chickamauga, September 20, 1863. Mustered out with Company.

DIBBLE, CHARLES — Enrolled at Tiffin, August 11, 1862. Mustered out with Company. Deceased.

DIBBLE, FREDERICK—Enrolled at Tiffin, August 11, 1862. Died in Andersonville Prison, October 9, 1864, having been wounded and captured in the Battle of Chickamauga, September 19, 1863.

DENSON, DAVID B.—Enrolled at Tiffin, August 11, 1862. Died of brain fever, at Nashville, Tenn., January 4, 1863. Detailed as teamster. His wagon was in the train captured at Murfreesboro'—overheated himself in making his escape—took brain fever and died.

ECKMAN, LEANDER—Enrolled at Tiffin, August 7, 1862. Discharged at Bowling Green, Ky., March 14, 1863, on account of disability.

EATON, ALEXANDER H.—Enrolled at Republic, August 9, 1862. Discharged, April 7, 1863, at Nashville, Tenn., on account of wounds received at Stone's River, December 31, 1862.

ECKLEBERRY, PETER—Enrolled at Bloomville, August 9, 1862. Wounded in Battle of Stone's River, December 31, 1862. Discharged at Nashville, Tenn., March 5, 1863, on account of disability.

FOX, CHARLES C.—Enrolled at Republic, August 11, 1862. Promoted to Corporal, October 31, 1862; to Sergeant, December 1, 1864. Mustered out with Company.

FOX, JAMES B.—Enrolled at Republic, August 11, 1862. Wounded in the Battle of Stone's River, December 31, 1862. Transferred to Company G, 21st Regiment, Veteran Reserve Corps, February 16, 1864. Mustered out as Sergeant, July 6, 1865.

FISER, JOHN S.—Enrolled at Tiffin, August 11, 1862. Died in camp at Murfreesboro', Tenn., March 3, 1863, of pneumonia.

FROST, JOSIAH B.—Enrolled at Tiffin, August 11, 1862. Discharged, February 14, 1863, at Nashville, Tenn.

FLINN, BENJAMIN D.—Enrolled at Tiffin, August 12, 1862. Discharged, September 19, 1863, at Louisville, Ky., on account of disability.

GUIESBERT, SAMUEL—Enrolled at Tiffin, August 11, 1862. Promoted to Corporal, October 31, 1862. Wounded in the Battle of Stone's River, December 31, 1862. Wounded and captured by Forrest, on the boat, between Nashville and Louisville. Paroled. Exchanged. Rejoined the Regiment at Chattanooga. Promoted to Sergeant.

February 28, 1865. Mustered out with Company. Died in Seneca County, Ohio, in 1869.

GREEN, TIMOTHY M.—Enrolled at Republic, August 7, 1862. Mustered out with Company.

GREEN, OWEN R.—Enrolled at Republic, August 7, 1862. Mustered out with Company.

GUIESBERT, DANIEL.—Enrolled at Tiffin, August 11, 1862. Wounded in the Battle of Stone's River, December 31, 1862. Transferred to Company H, 15th Regiment, Veteran Reserve Corps, December 3, 1863. Mustered out, July 15, 1865, at Cairo, Ill.

HULET, CHESTER—Enrolled at Tiffin, August 9, 1862. Mustered out with Company, June 12, 1865.

HEILMAN, EDWARD—Enrolled at Republic, August 9, 1862. Discharged, December 11, 1862, at Louisville, Ky., on account of disability.

HILL, JEREMIAH B.—Enrolled at Tiffin, August 9, 1862. Discharged, April 7, 1863, at Louisville, Ky., on account of disability.

HEWETT, CECIL C.—Enrolled at Tiffin, August 11, 1862. Discharged, February 24, 1864, at Columbus, O., having furnished an accepted substitute.

HOWLAND, STEPHEN M.—Enrolled at Republic, August 13, 1862. Promoted to Corporal, October 31, 1862. Wounded in the Battle of Chickamauga, September 20, 1863. Promoted to Sergeant, October 31, 1863. Transferred to 148th Company, 2nd Battalion, Veteran Reserve Corps, March 15, 1865. Mustered out, June 30, 1865, at Nashville, Tenn.

HADE, DALLAS W.—Enrolled at Tiffin, August 10, 1862. Mustered as Sergeant. Died at Nashville, Tenn., February 1, 1863, of wounds received in the Battle of Stone's River, December 31, 1862.

JENKINS, BENJAMIN F.—Enrolled at Tiffin, August 11, 1862. Mustered out with the Company.

KOLLER, HENRY C.—Enrolled at Tiffin, August 11, 1862. Wounded at Battle of Stone's River, December 31, 1862. Mustered out with the Company.

- Koch, John L.— Enrolled at Tiffin, August 9, 1862. Wounded at Chickamauga, September 19, 1863. Mustered out with Company.
- Kent, Henry W.—Enrolled at Republic, August 7, 1862. Transferred, August 7, 1864, to Company K, United States Veteran Volunteer Engineer Corps. Mustered out, June 30, 1865, at Nashville.
- Keller, Joseph—Enrolled at Tiffin, August 5, 1862. Mustered as Sergeant. Died at Camp Dennison, O., February 9, 1864, of wounds received in the Battle of Chickamauga, September 19, 1863.
- Long, Samuel.—Enrolled at Tiffin, August 9, 1862. Mustered out with the Company. Deceased.
- Lapham, Egbert—Enrolled at Republic, August 7, 1862. Died, April 21, 1863, in Field Hospital at Murfreesboro', Tenn., of disease.
- Lanning, Isaac — Enrolled at Tiffin, August 7, 1862. Died, June 9, 1863, in Field Hospital at Murfreesboro', Tenn., of disease.
- Leonard, Jaraway—Enrolled at Republic, August 7, 1862. Died, April 5, 1863, of disease, while at home in Republic on furlough.
- Lapham, Joseph C.— Enrolled at Republic, August 13, 1862. Died on the field, May 16, 1864, of wounds received in the Battle of Resaca, Ga., May 14, 1864.
- Leffler, John H.—Enrolled in Seneca County, August 8, 1862. Captured at Stone's River, December 31, 1862. Paroled prior to March 7, 1863.
- Lamberson, Virgil L. — Enrolled at Tiffin, August 12, 1862. Transferred, March 21, 1863, to Mississippi Marine Brigade.
- Miller, Austin W.—Enrolled at Tiffin, August 10, 1862. Mustered as Sergeant. Promoted to First Sergeant, June 30, 1863. Mustered out with Company. Died at Kenton, O., February 15, 1880. Editor of Kenton Republican after the war.
- Miller, Henry C.—Enrolled at Tiffin, August 7, 1862. Mustered out with Company.

MILLER, WILLIAM H.—Enrolled at Tiffin, August 12, 1862. Transferred to 154th Company, 2nd Battalion, Veteran Reserve Corps. Mustered out, June 30, 1865, at Nashville, Tenn.

MUNDWILER, WILLIAM—Enrolled at Tiffin, August 11, 1862. Wounded, December 15, 1864, in Battle of Nashville, Tenn. Mustered out with Company.

MUNDWILER, JACOB—Enrolled at Tiffin, August 11, 1862. Musician. Mustered out, June 16, 1865, at Columbus, O.

METLER, WILLIAM C.—Enrolled at Republic, August 7, 1862. Taken prisoner in the Battle of Chickamauga, September 19, 1863. Taken to Atlanta and to Richmond in cattle cars. In Pemberton Prison three months; in Danville five months, in an old tobacco house, called Prison No. 2. "Our suffering for food can never be told. Many a time I have arisen from the hard floor at 3 o'clock in the morning and sat until 7 o'clock in hopes of getting a crust of corn bread, often thrown in to see the 'Yanks' struggle for it." Exchanged. M. O. C.

McMELLEN, LEGRAND—Enrolled at Tiffin, August 13, 1862. Died of disease, at Nashville, Tenn., January 17, 1863.

NONEMAN, JACOB F.—Enrolled at Tiffin, August 11, 1862. Wounded in the Battle of Chickamauga, September 19, 1863; also at Franklin, November 30, 1864. Mustered out with Company.

NORRIS, CHARLES P.—Enrolled at Tiffin, August 16, 1862. Died at Louisville, Ky., November 25, 1862, of disease.

PETTYS, GILBERT W.—Enrolled at Republic, August 7, 1862. Mustered as Corporal. Died in Field Hospital at Murfreesboro', March 29, 1863, of disease.

PAYNE, MARTIN V.—Enrolled at Tiffin, August 14, 1862. Discharged at Louisville, Ky., May 25, 1863, on account of disability. Deceased.

RICHEY, HENDERSON D.—Enrolled at Tiffin, August 7, 1862. Discharged at Ooltewah, March 23, 1864, on account of disability.

ROHRER, JACOB T.—Enrolled in Seneca County, August 7, 1862. Mustered out, May 20, 1865, at Columbus, as a paroled prisoner, having been captured near Huntsville, Ala., while with forage train. Was on the "Sultana" at time of disaster. See prison experience of Lieut. Squire.

SMITH, LEONARD D.—See Field and Staff.

STEWART, JAMES R.—Enrolled at Tiffin, August 9, 1862. Mustered out with Company.

SPARKS, GEORGE W.—Enrolled at Republic, August 11, 1862. Wounded, captured and paroled in the Battle of Chickamauga, September 19, 1863. Exchanged. Mustered out with Company.

STONER, JOHN C.—Enrolled at Tiffin, August 11, 1862. Detailed for a time in Quartermaster's Department. Mustered out with Company.

STEPHENS, ALFRED—Enrolled at Tiffin, August 11, 1862. Mustered out with Company.

SWEITZER, WILLIAM—Enrolled at Tiffin, August 9, 1862. Taken prisoner at Chickamauga, September 19, 1863. Mustered out, June 9, 1865, at Camp Chase, O. Deceased.

STINCHCOMB, FRANCIS A.—Enrolled at Tiffin, August 5, 1862. Mustered as Corporal. Promoted to Sergeant, April 30, 1863. Died, September 1, 1864, in Andersonville Prison, having been captured in Battle of Chickamauga, September 19, 1863.

SNYDER, SAMUEL—Enrolled at Tiffin, August 11, 1862. Died at Nashville, Tenn., January 14, 1863, of disease.

STEPHENS, GEORGE W.—Enrolled at Tiffin, August 12, 1862. Died, August 12, 1864, in Andersonville Prison, having been captured in the Battle of Chickamauga, September 19, 1863.

SHUFELT, HENRY—Enrolled at Tiffin, August 11, 1862. Captured in the Battle of Stone's River, December 31, 1862. Confined in Libby and Andersonville Prisons. Paroled, March 25, 1863. Exchanged, September 4, 1863. Transferred, April 29, 1864, to Veteran Reserve Corps. Mustered out, July 6, 1865, at Nashville, Tenn.

SPENCE, THOMAS P.—Enrolled at Tiffin, August 5, 1862. Transferred, March 21, 1863, to the Mississippi Marine Brigade. Died in Hancock County, O., November 8, 1878.

SPARKS, JAMES P.—Enrolled at Republic, August 11, 1862. Transferred, December 10, 1863, to the Veteran Reserve Corps.

SHUFELT, ABRAHAM—Enrolled at Tontogany, Wood County, December 16, 1863. Captured in the Battle of Franklin, November 30, 1864. Confined in Andersonville Prison. Mustered out, June 16, 1865, at Camp Chase.

SHUFELT, AMBROSE—Enrolled at Tiffin, August 8, 1862. Captured and paroled in Battle of Stone's River, December 31, 1862. Wounded at Bermuda. Enrolled in a New York Regiment.

STRAYER, SYLVANUS—Enrolled at Tiffin, August 5, 1862. Discharged, June 10, 1863, at Nashville, Tenn., on account of disability. Died on way home from Hospital.

SEARLES, IRVING W.—Enrolled at Tiffin, August 9, 1862. Discharged, February 13, 1863, at Gallipolis, O., on account of disability.

SNEATH, WILLIAM C.—Enrolled at Tiffin, August 2, 1862. Discharged, March 17, 1863, at Nashville, on account of disability. Deceased.

SHARP, HENRY J.—Enrolled at Tiffin, August 11, 1862. Discharged, January 23, 1863, at Bowling Green, Ky., on account of disability.

STRAYER, JOSEPH—Enrolled in Seneca County, August 5, 1862. Discharged, January 10, 1865, at Camp Dennison, O., on account of disability. Wagonmaster until after Chickamauga.

STEWART, JAMES H.—Enrolled at Tiffin, August 11, 1863. Wounded in the Battle of Stone's River, December 31, 1862. Discharged, October 1, 1864, at Camp Dennison, O., on account of disability.

SELLNER, TILGHMAN—Enrolled at Columbus, O., February 24, 1864. Mustered out, July 6, 1865, at Nashville, Tenn.

SHAFER, AMBROSE—Enrolled, August 9, 1862.

THOMPSON, JOHN — Enrolled at Tiffin, August 5, 1862. Discharged, March 16, 1863, at Louisville, Ky., on account of wounds received in the Battle of Stone's River, December 31, 1862. Died at Tiffin, O., June 18, 1880.

TRAXER, PETER — Enrolled at Tiffin, August 9, 1862. Wounded and captured at Chickamauga, September 19, 1862. Paroled. Promoted to Corporal, February 28, 1865. Mustered out with Company. Deceased.

VANDENBERG, GEORGE W.—Enrolled at Republic, August 7, 1862. Mustered as Sergeant. Died, July 3, 1863, of gunshot wounds received accidentally at the hands of a comrade, at Manchester, Tenn., June 29, 1863.

WHITEMAN, WILLIAM H.—Enrolled at Tiffin, August 11, 1862. Died, January 7, 1865, of wounds received in the Battle of Nashville, December 15, 1864, in the charge near Montgomery Hill. The remains were brought home for interment.

WHITMIRE, GEORGE W. — Enrolled at Tiffin, August 7, 1862. Died, February 16, 1863, at Bowling Green, Ky., of disease.

WHITEMAN, MARQUIS D. L.—See Non-Commissioned Staff.

WITTER, JONATHAN—Enrolled at Republic, August 11, 1862. Discharged, May 7, 1863, at Louisville, Ky., on account of disability. Died, April 14, 1894, at Toledo, O.

WILLIAMS, JOHN—Enrolled at Tiffin, August 9, 1862. Discharged, August 30, 1863, at Stevenson, Ala., on account of disability. Deceased.

WHITEMAN, HARMON—Enrolled at Tiffin, August 12, 1862. Transferred to Company B, 23rd Regiment, Veteran Reserve Corps, December 3, 1864. Mustered out, July 15, 1865, at Cairo, Ill. Deceased.

WERNER, SAMUEL—Enrolled at Tiffin, February 10, 1865. Transferred to Company F, 51st Ohio Volunteer Infantry, June 10, 1865. Joined Regiment at Huntsville, Ala.

WERNER, JACOB—Enrolled at Tiffin, February 10, 1865. Transferred to Company F, 51st Ohio Volunteer Infantry, June 10, 1865.

YEAGER, JACOB F.—Enrolled at Tiffin, August 11, 1862. Wounded in the left leg in the Battle of Stone's River. Wounded at Resaca, May 14, 1864. Transferred to 153rd Company, 2nd Battalion, Veteran Reserve Corps, March 15, 1865. Mustered out, June 29, 1865, at Nashville, Tenn.

YOUNG, JEREMIAH R.—Enrolled at Tiffin, August 13, 1862. Promoted to Corporal. Taken prisoner in the Battle of Stone's River, December 31, 1863. Paroled.

YEAGER, JACOB C.—Enrolled at Tiffin, August 9, 1862. Promoted to Corporal, June 30, 1863. Wounded in the Battle of Chickamauga, September 19, 1863. Mustered out with Company.

COMPANY I.

CAPTAIN NEWCOMB M. BARNES—Enrolled at Tiffin, August 2, 1862. Mustered as Captain. Resignation accepted, January 13, 1864. Died, December 1, 1874, at Tiffin, O.

CAPTAIN HENRY A. TAGGART—Enrolled at Tiffin, August 1, 1862. Mustered as Second Lieutenant. Promoted to First Lieutenant, January 25, 1863. Promoted to Captain, March 19, 1864. Taken prisoner in the Battle of Franklin, November 30, 1864. Mustered out, May 15, 1865. One of the survivors of the ill-fated Sultana. Died at the Soldiers' Home, Dayton, O., July 12, 1876.

LIEUTENANT ROBERT LYSLE, JR.—Enrolled at Tiffin, August 11, 1862. Mustered as First Lieutenant. Resignation accepted, February 19, 1863. Deceased.

LIEUTENANT JAY C. SMITH—Enrolled at Sandusky, August 5, 1862. See Non-Commissioned Staff.

LIEUTENANT ISAAC P. RULE—Enrolled at Tiffin, August 12, 1862. Mustered as First Sergeant. Promoted to Second Lieutenant, January 25, 1863. Died, September 20, 1863, of wounds received in the Battle of Chickamauga, September 19, 1863. Lieutenant Rule was mortally wounded about 3 o'clock Saturday afternoon; was carried to the rear by Comrade Raymond and another, and placed in a hospital some two miles back. This hospital fell into the hands of the enemy next day, and all were made prisoners.

ARNDT, SAMUEL F.—Enrolled at Tiffin, August 9, 1862. Died, January 2, 1863, of wounds received in the Battle of Stone's River, December 31, 1862, in the Field Hospital, Murfreesboro', Tenn.

ARMSTRONG, THOMAS—Enrolled at Tiffin, March 30, 1864. Died, June 9, 1864, at Chattanooga, of disease.

BONNELL, JOHN—Enrolled at Tiffin, August 12, 1862. Wounded in the Battle of Stone's River, December 31, 1862. Detailed in Quartermaster's Department. Mustered out with Company.

BROCK, ABRAHAM—Enrolled at Tiffin, August 12, 1862. Mustered out with Company.

BEMISDORFER, SIMON P.—Enrolled at Tiffin, August 12, 1862. Captured in the Battle of Chickamauga, September 20, 1863. Confined in Belle Isle, Libby, Danville, Andersonville, Charleston, and Florence Prisons. Paroled December 10, 1864; sent to Annapolis; furloughed and sent to hospital. Rejoined the Regiment at Camp Harker in May, 1865. Mustered out with Company.

BRADY, JACOB H.—Enrolled at Tiffin, August 13, 1862. Mustered as Corporal. Wounded in the Battle of Stone's River, December 31, 1862. Captured on Cumberland River, January 18, 1863. Died, October 31, 1864, at Chattanooga, of wounds received in the Battle of Jonesboro,' September 1, 1864.

BIRDSALL, WILLIAM—Enrolled at Tiffin, August 8, 1862. Died at Nashville, November 29, 1862, of disease.

BROSHIER, NICHOLAS—Enrolled at Louisville, April 15, 1864. Died at Chattanooga, July 6, 1864, of wounds received at Kenesaw, June 27, 1864.

BROWN, PETER—Enrolled at Tiffin, January 18, 1864. No further record.

BONNELL, RICHARD W. — Enrolled at Tiffin, August 9, 1862. Discharged at Nashville, February 5, 1863, on account of disability. Died on day of discharge, February 5, 1863.

CRONKITE, TUNIS — Enrolled at Tiffin, August 12, 1862. Wounded and captured in the Battle of Stone's River, December 31, 1862. Escaped the same day. Promoted to Corporal, March 5, 1865. Mustered out with Company.

CRABBS, CHARLES — Enrolled at Tiffin, August 12, 1862. Died, September 3, 1864, in Field Hospital, of wounds received at Jonesboro', September 1, 1864.

CARL, JONAS H.—Enrolled at Tiffin, August 3, 1862. No record after October 7, 1862.

CARR, JOHN—Enrolled at Tiffin, February 15, 1864. Transferred to Company F, 51st Ohio Volunteer Infantry, June 10, 1865.

DEWITT, PETER J.—Enrolled at Tiffin, August 12, 1862. Twice wounded in the Battle of Jonesboro', September 1, 1864, once while carrying Sergeant Wood from the field. Mustered out with Company.

DOUGHERTY, JOHN—Enrolled at Tiffin, August 12, 1862. Wounded in the Battle of Stone's River, December 31, 1862. Detailed in Quartermaster's Department for a time. Mustered out with Company.

DONDORE, ADAM—Enrolled at Tiffin, August 12, 1862. Died at Danville, November 12, 1862, of disease.

DELLGEIT, ANTHONY—Enrolled at Tiffin, August 11, 1862. Died at Nashville, January 9, 1863, of wounds received in the Battle of Stone's River, December 31, 1862.

DAVEY, HENRY C.—Enrolled in Wyandot County, December 28, 1863. Died at Ooltewah, Tenn., April 11, 1864, of disease.

DAYWALT, WALLACE P.—Enrolled at Tiffin, August 12, 1862. Mustered out at Camp Denison, May 25, 1865. Died at Watson, O., November 3, 1885.

EMERSON, JOHN H.—Enrolled at Tiffin, August 9, 1862. Mustered out with Company. Died at Tiffin, November 6, 1867.

ELLIS, WILLIAM I.—Enrolled at Tiffin, August 12, 1862. Mustered out with Company.

EGBERT, NORMAN D.—Enrolled at Tiffin, August 12, 1862. Discharged at Nashville, February 9, 1863, on account of disability.

FUNK, CHRISTIAN M.—Enrolled at Tiffin, August 14, 1862. Promoted to Corporal, February 28, 1863. Color Guard in the Battle of Chickamauga. Captured in the Battle of Chickamauga, September 20, 1863, by the 29th Alabama. Escaped from Danville Prison after seven months confinement. Reached Union lines at Little Washington, N. C. Mustered out with Company.

FRAVOR, JOHN—Enrolled at Tiffin, August 11, 1862.—Wounded in the Battle of Stone's River, December 31, 1862. Shot in right arm, ball passing from wrist to elbow. Captured, but on retreat was left in hospital. Wounded in the Battle of Franklin, November 30, 1864, in left shoulder. Mustered out with Company.

FAHNESTOCK, LEANDER H.—Enrolled at Tiffin, August 12, 1862. Mustered out with Company.

FRANKS, FREDERICK—Enrolled at Tiffin, August 11, 1862. Killed in the Battle of Stone's River, December 31, 1862.

FRARY, JUSTIN—Enrolled at Tiffin, August 11, 1862. Captured at Chickamauga, September 20, 1863. Died at Danville, Va., December 27, 1863, of disease.

FRANKS, WILLIAM—Enrolled at Tiffin, August 11, 1862.

FRAZER, JAMES—Enrolled at Tiffin, January 25, 1864. No further record.

FUNK, JOSEPH—Enrolled at Tiffin, August 12, 1862. Discharged at Covington, October 3, 1862, on account of accidental wounds received, September 19, 1862, at Camp Mitchell, Ky.

FUNK, DAVID R.—Enrolled at Tiffin, August 12, 1862. Discharged at Louisville, July 20, 1863, on account of disability. Died at Bascom, O., April 26, 1881.

FAHNESTOCK, EZRA, A.—Enrolled in Erie County, March 31, 1864. Transferred to Company A, 51st, Ohio Volunteer Infantry, June 10, 1865. Died at Springfield, O.

GOETCHINS, DUDLEY—Enrolled at Tiffin, August 12, 1862. Wounded and captured in the Battle of Chickamauga, September 19, 1863. Confined in Belle Isle, Libby, Danville, Andersonville, and other prisons for eighteen months. Mustered out, May 22, 1865, at Columbus.

GITTENGER, GEORGE W.—Enrolled at Tiffin, August 12, 1862. Died in the Field Hospital, January 2, 1863, of wounds received in the Battle of Stone's River, December 31, 1862.

GEORGE, OLIVER — Enrolled at Tiffin, August 13, 1862. Discharged, March 11, 1863. Died at Beta, Fulton County, September 9, 1880.

HALL, JESSE H.—Enrolled at Covington, Ky., September 18, 1862. Promoted to Corporal, January 1, 1863. Promoted to Sergeant, March 1, 1863. Transferred to Veteran Reserve Corps, August 1, 1863. Re-transferred at his own request, August 15, 1864. Color Bearer at Battle of Nashville. Mustered out with Company.

HUBER, URIAH—Enrolled at Tiffin, August 12, 1862. Mustered as Sergeant. Taken prisoner in the Battle of Stone's River, December 31, 1862. Confined in Libby and other prisons. Taken prisoner a second time, in front of Atlanta, Ga. Mustered out, June 9, 1865, at Camp Chase.

HOLMAN, WILLIAM R.—Enrolled at Tiffin, August 12, 1862. Promoted to Corporal, February 29, 1864. Mustered out with Company. Died at Sioux City, March 7, 1887.

HERRIG, MATTHIAS—Enrolled at Tiffin, August 11, 1862. Wounded in the Battle of Stone's River, December 31, 1862. Also wounded in the Battle of Rocky Face, Ga., May 11, 1864. Promoted to Corporal, March 5, 1865. Mustered out with Company.

HUBER, DANIEL—Enrolled at Tiffin, August 11, 1862. Wounded in the Battle of Kenesaw Mountain, June 23, 1864. Mustered out with Company.

HISKY, HARRISON W.—Enrolled at Tiffin, February 15, 1864. Died at Jeffersonville, July 11, 1864, of disease.

HOLTZ, WILLIAM—Enrolled at Tiffin, August 9, 1862. Captured at Chickamauga, September 20, 1863. Died in Andersonville Prison, March 8, 1865, of disease.

HICKMAN, PETER P.—Enrolled at Tiffin, August 13. 1862. Died at Louisville, October 21, 1862, of disease.

HOYT, WILLIAM McK.—Enrolled at Tiffin, August 9, 1862. Mustered as Corporal. Promoted to Sergeant, March 1, 1863. Discharged, March 25, 1864, on account of disability.

HERRIN, DAVID—Enrolled at Tiffin, August 5, 1862. Discharged at Nashville, February 22, 1863, on account of disability.

HUBER, HENRY W.—Enrolled in Seneca County, January 21, 1864. Discharged at Columbus, March 20, 1865, on account of wounds received at Jonesboro', September 1, 1864.

HERALD, WILLIAM—Enrolled at Tiffin, August 13, 1862. Transferred to Company K, 1st Regiment, United States Veteran Volunteer Engineers, August 7, 1864. Mustered out, June 30, 1865.

JORDAN, WILLIAM J.—Enrolled at Tiffin, August 12, 1862. Mustered out with Company. Died, March 23, 1872, at Tiffin, O.

JACKSON, JOHN—Enrolled at Tiffin, December 15, 1863.

JORDAN, PHILIP W.—Enrolled at Tiffin, August 12, 1862. Taken prisoner in the Battle of Stone's River, December 31, 1862. Discharged at Nashville, October 10, 1863, on account of disability. Deceased.

JORDAN, ALONZO—Enrolled at Tiffin, August 12, 1862. Discharged at Columbus, November 17, 1863, on account of disability.

JOHNSON, PHILIP—Enrolled at Tiffin, February 15, 1864. Transferred to Company A, 51st Ohio Volunteer Infantry, June 10, 1865.

KNOTT, CROCKETT—Enrolled at Tiffin, August 12, 1862. Mustered as Third Corporal. Promoted to Sergeant, August 30, 1864. Killed in Battle of Franklin, November 30, 1864. Mention of this brave Comrade will be found in the Battle of Franklin, page 300.

KIPKE, FRANGOTT—Enrolled at Tiffin, August 12, 1862. Promoted to Corporal, February 29, 1864. Discharged, November 15, 1864, on account of disability.

KAUP, THOMAS A—Enrolled at Tiffin, August 11, 1862. Mustered as Eighth Corporal. Discharged at Louisville, Ky., June 6, 1863, on account of wounds received in the Battle of Stone's River, December 31, 1862. Died at Tiffin, O., October 1, 1876.

KUNSMAN, JOHN G.—Enrolled at Tiffin, January 27, 1864. Transferred to Company A, 51st Ohio Volunteer Infantry, June 10, 1865. Died at Green Springs, O., in 1886.

KERSHNER, JOSEPH—Enrolled at Tiffin, August 11, 1862. Transferred to Company G, 12th Regiment, Veteran Reserve Corps, April 29, 1864. Mustered out, June 29, 1865, at Washington, D. C.

KISSINGER, JAMES A.—Enrolled at Tiffin, August 12, 1862. Wounded in the Battle of Stone's River, December 31. 1862. Transferred to Company B, 123rd Regiment, Veteran Reserve Corps, September 30, 1864. Mustered out, July 13, 1865, at Clinton, Iowa.

LUTZ, SCOT, McD.—Enrolled at Tiffin, August 12, 1862. Died at Nashville, Tenn., December 30, 1862, of disease.

LEE, WILBUR D.—Enrolled at Tiffin, August 12, 1862. Discharged, May 22, 1863, at Louisville, Ky., on account of disability. Died, December 19, 1890, at Attica, O.

LEPPER, EDWARD—Enrolled at Tiffin, August 11, 1862. Discharged, December 27, 1862, at Nashville, on account of disability.

LOWE, GEORGE W.—Enrolled at Tiffin, August 12, 1862. Captured in the Battle of Stone's River, December 31, 1862. Transferred to United States Navy, June 16, 1864. Deceased.

LAUX, JOSEPH—Enrolled at Tiffin, August 11, 1862. Wounded in the Battle of Chickamauga, September 20, 1863. Transferred to Veteran Reserve Corps, March 15, 1864. Mustered out, June 28, 1865, at Camp Dennison.

ROSTER. 449

MEALY, MILTON C.—Enrolled at Tiffin, August 5, 1862. Promoted to Corporal, March 5, 1865. Mustered out with the Company.

MESSER, W. L.—Enrolled at Tiffin, August 8, 1862. Mustered out with the Company.

MORRIS, SAMUEL—Enrolled at Tiffin, August 6, 1862. Taken prisoner in the Battle of Stone's River, December 31, 1862. Confined in Castle Thunder and Libby Prisons. Exchanged. Mustered out with Company.

MILLER, ADEN W.—Enrolled at Tiffin, August 12, 1862. Killed in Battle of Chickamauga, September 19, 1863.

McMEEN, ROBERT—Enrolled at Tiffin, August 13, 1862. Died at Nashville, Tenn., January 19, 1863, of wounds received in Battle of Stone's River, December 31, 1862.

MYERS, FREDERICK—Enrolled at Tiffin, August 12, 1862. Discharged, October 18, 1863, at Nashville, Tenn., on account of wounds received in Battle of Stone's River, December 31, 1862. In hands of the enemy until they retreated.

MILLER, JACOB—Enrolled at Tiffin, December 15, 1863. Transferred to Company A, 51st Ohio Volunteer Infantry, June 10, 1865. Deceased.

MEHAN, ANDREW—Enrolled at Tiffin, January 27, 1864. Transferred to Company F, 51st Ohio Volunteer Infantry, June 10, 1865. Died at Marine City, Mich.

MYERS, GEORGE—Enrolled at Tiffin, February 15, 1864. Transferred to Company A, 51st Ohio Voluntner Infantry, June 10, 1865. Mustered out, November 3, 1865, at Columbus, O.

MYERS, JOSEPH P.—Enrolled at Tiffin, January 5, 1864. Wounded at Marietta, Ga., on Atlanta campaign. Transferred to Company A, 51st Ohio Volunteer Infantry, June 18, 1865.

MINER, ANTHONY—Enrolled at Tiffin, January 4, 1864. Transferred to Company F, 51st Ohio Volunteer Infantry, June 18, 1865. Deceased.

McCleary, Joseph W.—Enrolled at Sandusky, January 28, 1864. Transferred to Company A, 51st Ohio Volunteer Infantry, June 10, 1865.

Moore, William—Enrolled at Tiffin, August 12, 1862. Killed in the Battle of Chickamauga, September 19, 1863.

Orwig, John B.—Enrolled at Tiffin, August 12, 1862. Died in Andersonville Prison, Ga., April 18, 1865, of disease, having been captured in the Battle of Chickamauga, September 20, 1863.

Omwake, Jeremiah—Enrolled at Tiffin, August 12, 1862. Discharged, October 29, 1863, at Louisville, Ky., on account of disability. Deceased.

O'Connell, Michael—Enrolled at Tiffin, August 12, 1862. Transferred to Veteran Reserve Corps, September 30, 1863. Died at Tiffin, September 29, 1880.

Price, William—Enrolled at Tiffin, August 12, 1862. Wounded in the Battle of Chickamauga, September 19, 1863. Promoted to Corporal, February 29, 1864. Promoted to Sergeant, March 5, 1865. Mustered out with Company.

Pittenger, Henry C,—Enrolled at Tiffin, August 12, 1862. Wounded at Atlanta, June 23, 1864. Mustered out with the Company.

Park, Robert F.—Enrolled at Tiffin, August 12, 1862. Mustered as Sergeant. Died at Nashville, Tenn., February 2, 1863, of disease.

Peck, David G.—Enrolled at Tiffin, August 12, 1862.

Patten, Austin H.—Enrolled at Tiffin, January 27, 1864. Transferred to Company F, 51st Ohio Volunteer Infantry, June 10, 1865.

Quinn, David—Enrolled at Tiffin, January 27, 1864. Wounded at Buzzard's Roost, May 11, 1864. Transferred to Company F, 51st Ohio Volunteer Infantry, June 10, 1865.

Reinbolt, Michael—Enrolled at Tiffin, August 12, 1862. Mustered out with the Company.

Richards, Albert—Enrolled at Tiffin, January 17, 1864.

RAYMOND, JOSEPH M.—Enrolled at Tiffin, August 13, 1862. Mustered as Sixth Corporal. Wounded and captured in the Battle of Chickamauga, September 19, 1863. Ten days in field hospital. Promoted to Sergeant, January 20, 1864. Promoted to First Sergeant, January 1, 1865. Mustered out with Company.

REINBOLT, JOSEPH—Enrolled at Tiffin, January 5, 1864. Transferred to Company F, 51st Ohio Volunteer Infantry, June 10, 1865.

SCHNOOR, JOHN T.—Enrolled at Tiffin, August 12, 1862. Mustered out with the Company.

SELLERS, JACOB—Enrolled at Tiffin, August 12, 1862. Died at Bowling Green, Ky., November 10, 1862, of disease.

SHRIVER, EZRA C.—Enrolled at Tiffin, August 12, 1862. Died at Nashville, Tenn., December 12, 1862, of disease.

SHRIVER, EMANUEL J.—Enrolled at Tiffin, August 12, 1862. Died at Nashville, Tenn., January 13, 1863, of disease.

SEITZ, JACOB—Enrolled at Tiffin, August 12, 1862. Died at Covington, Ky., October 3, 1862, of disease. First death in the Regiment.

SHUMAKER, WILLIAM H.—Enrolled at Tiffin, August 12, 1862. Died at Bowling Green, Ky., December 29, 1862, of disease.

SNOOK, JAMES H.—Enrolled at Tiffin, January 4, 1864. Died at Washington, March 11, 1865, of disease.

SNYDER, SIMON—Enrolled at Tiffin, August 12, 1862. Mustered as Third Sergeant. Promoted to First Sergeant, March 1, 1863. Discharged, June 23, 1864, on account of disability.

SHAFER, JOHN A.—Enrolled at Tiffin, August 12, 1862. Captured in the Battle of Chickamauga, September 20, 1863. Confined in Andersonville. Exchanged. Sultana survivor. Mustered out, May 22, 1865, at Columbus, O.

SHEETS, JACOB—Enrolled at Tiffin, August 8, 1862.— Wounded in the Battle of Stone's River, December 31, 1862. Mustered as Seventh Corporal. Transferred to Veteran Reserve Corps, September 30, 1863. Mustered out, June 20, 1865, at Chicago, Ill.

SOMERS, GEORGE — Enrolled at Tiffin, January 18, 1864. Wounded at Rocky Face Ridge, May 11, 1864. Transferred to 107th Company, 2nd Battalion, Veteran Reserve Corps, March 15, 1865. Mustered out, November 11, 1865, at Springfield, Ill.

SCHMIDT, JOHN — Enrolled at Tiffin, August 6, 1862. Transferred to Company K, 1st Regiment, United States Veteran Volunteer Engineers, August 7, 1864. Mustered out, June 30, 1865.

SMITH, LEWIS E. — Enrolled at Tiffin, August 12, 1862. Promoted to Corporal, December 1, 1864. Mustered out with Company.

TREXLER, ALFRED J. — Enrolled at Tiffin, August 13, 1862. Promoted to Corporal, March 5, 1865. Mustered out with Company. Died, April 28, 1880.

TREXLER, JOHN J. — Enrolled at Tiffin, August 13, 1862. Transferred to Veteran Reserve Corps, December 15, 1863. Mustered out, August 18, 1865, at Louisville.

TAYLOR, HENRY L. — Enrolled at Tiffin, August 11, 1862. Discharged, May 17, 1864, at Columbus, O. Died at Republic, O., January, 1894.

VAN NEST, JOSEPH — Enrolled at Tiffin, August 11, 1862. Wounded three times in the Battle of Stone's River. December 31, 1862. Taken prisoner, January 18, 1863, at Harfish Sholes, on the Cumberland River. Wounded in knee in Battle of Resaca, Ga., May 14, 1864. Color Guard on the Atlanta Campaign until wounded.

WERNER, UPTON S. — Enrolled at Tiffin, August 12, 1862. Promoted to Corporal, March 5, 1865. Mustered out with Company,

WHITMAN, WILLIAM — Enrolled at Tiffin, August 13, 1862. Mustered out with the Company. Died at Tiffin. O., March 4, 1878.

WISE, LEVI — Enrolled at Tiffin, August 11, 1862. Mustered out with the Company.

WEITZ, LAWRENCE — Enrolled at Tiffin, August 11, 1862. Mustered out with the Company.

WEISBECKER, VALENTINE—Enrolled at Tiffin, August 12, 1862. Wounded and captured in the Battle of Chickamauga, September 20, 1862. Mustered out with Company. Died at Carey, O.

WAGAMAN, DANIEL—Enrolled at Tiffin, August 18, 1862. Mortally wounded in the Battle of Chickamauga, September 19, 1863. Died, September 21, 1863, in hands of the enemy.

WOOD, GEORGE W.— Enrolled at Tiffin, August 9, 1862. Mustered as Fourth Sergeant. Promoted to First Sergeant, June 30, 1864. Wounded in the leg in the Battle of Jonesboro', September 1, 1864. Killed in the Battle of Franklin, November 30, 1864.

WILSON, JOSEPH C.—Enrolled at Tiffin, August 9, 1862. Died at Murfreesboro', Tenn., May 2, 1863, of disease.

WEIRICK, SAMUEL T.—Enrolled at Tiffin, August 11, 1863. Discharged, January 22, 1863, at Nashville, on account of disability.

WATSON JOHN McK.—Enrolled at Tiffin, August 12, 1862. Discharged, December 12, 1862, at Nashville, Tenn., on account of disability.

WHITEMAN, DANIEL—Enrolled at Tiffin, December 28, 1863. Transferred to Company F, 51st O. V. I., June 10, 1865. Died at White Pigeon, Mich.

YINGST, CONRAD S.—Enrolled at Tiffin, August 9, 1862. Discharged, September —, 1864, at Louisville, Ky., on account of disability. Died at Tiffin, October 26, 1879.

ZINT, BERGERT—Enrolled at Tiffin, August 12, 1862. Transferred to Company H, 8th Regiment, Veteran Reserve Corps, February 15, 1864. Mustered out, July 2, 1865, at Chicago, Ill.

COMPANY K.

CAPTAIN MONTGOMERY NOBLE—Enrolled at Fostoria, August 16, 1862. Mustered as Captain. Resigned, May 30, 1863. Deceased.

Captain Milton N. Ebersole—Enrolled August 2, 1862. Mustered as First Lieutenant, August 30, 1862. Promoted to Captain, January 21, 1863. Wounded in charge at Kenesaw Mountain, June 27, 1864. Died of wounds at Chattanooga, July 12, 1864.

Captain James M. Roberts—Enrolled at Bucyrus, August 15, 1862. Color Bearer at Battles of Perryville and Stone's River. Promoted to Second Lieutenant, December 31, 1862; to First Lieutenant, March 19, 1864; to Captain and assigned to Company K, February 10, 1865. Died at Anaheim, Cal., May 7, 1886.

Lieutenant Philip F. Cline—Enrolled at Monroeville, August 2, 1862. Mustered as Second Lieutenant at Monroeville, August 30, 1862. Promoted to First Lieutenant at Murfreesboro', Tenn., January 21, 1863. Resigned, December 3, 1863.

Lieutenant John G. Petticord—Enrolled at Tiffin, August 13, 1862. Promoted to Sergeant, January 22, 1863; to First Sergeant, April 1, 1863; to Second Lieutenant, to date February 6, 1863; to First Lieutenant, March 19, 1864. Wounded at Chickamauga, September 20, 1863. Resigned, September 28, 1864.

Lieutenant William R. Davis—See Non-Commissioned Staff.

Alspaugh, George W.—Enrolled at Sandusky, May 3, 1864. Transferred to Company A, 51st Ohio Volunteer Infantry, June 10, 1865. Detailed for pioneer work for some months. Mustered out at Victoria, Texas, October 3, 1865.

Alspaugh, Michael—Enrolled at Tiffin, August 22, 1862. Discharged at Louisville, April 10, 1865, on account of disability.

Ash, Edmund R.—Enrolled at Tiffin, August 14, 1862. Discharged at Murfreesboro', June 14, 1863, on account of disability. Musician.

Ash, Valentine W.—Enrolled at Tiffin, August 16, 1862. Died at Nashville, Tenn., February 11, 1863, of disease.

ARMSTRONG, JOHN W.—Enrolled at Tiffin, August 16, 1862. Taken prisoner at Chickamauga, September 19, 1863. Mustered out, June 29, 1865, at Camp Chase, O.

BLOSSER, SAMUEL—Enrolled at Fostoria, August, 12, 1862. Transferred to 139th Company, 2nd Battalion, Veteran Reserve Corps, April 10, 1864. Mustered out at Nashville, Tenn., May 31, 1865, on account of disability. Deceased.

BEATTY, HIRAM—Enrolled at Fostoria, August 20, 1862. Promoted to Sergeant, May 24, 1863. Mustered out with the Company.

BLOSSER, DAVID—Enrolled at Fostoria, August 12, 1862. Mustered as Sergeant. Mustered out with the Company.

BLOSSER, JACOB—Enrolled at Fostoria, August 12, 1862. Killed on the picket line at Bald Knob, near Kenesaw Mountain, June 20, 1864, while advancing the line.

BLOSSER, JOHN—Enrolled at Fostoria, August 12, 1862. Wounded at Kenesaw Mountain, June 27, 1864. Mustered out with the Company.

BYERS, HENRY—Enrolled August 12, 1862. Wounded at Battle of Stone's River, December 31, 1862. Mustered out with the Company.

BEATTY, SYLVESTER—Enrolled at Fostoria, August 20, 1862. Killed in the Battle of Stone's River, Dec. 31, 1862.

BACHER, WILLIAM F.—Enrolled at Fostoria, August 15, 1862. Wounded and died in the hands of the enemy, after the Battle of Chickamauga, September 19, 1863.

BELLMAN, JAS. W.—Enrolled at Fostoria, August 18, 1862. Died of disease at Murfreesboro', March 22, 1863.

BELLMAN, GEO. W.—Enrolled at Fostoria, August 13, 1862. Discharged at Murfreesboro', Tenn., May 22, 1863, on account of disability. Deceased.

BERGER, JACOB H.—Enrolled at Fostoria, August 12, 1862. Died at Chattanooga, Tenn., Nov. 13, 1863, of disease.

BECK, DANIEL—Enrolled at Fostoria, August 18, 1862. Discharged at Murfreesboro', Tenn., May 28, 1863, on account of disability. Deceased.

BEIGHTLE, WILBUR—Enrolled at Fostoria, August 12, 1862. Discharged at Nashville, Tenn., March 12, 1863, on account of disability. Deceased.

BEIGHTLE, GEORGE F.—Enrolled at Fostoria, August 12, 1862. Transferred to Veteran Reserve Corps, January 15, 1864.

COUCH, RUFUS B.—Enrolled August 21, 1862. Mustered out with the Company.

OLUMBUS, LEWIS—Enrolled at Tiffin, August 11, 1862. Promoted to Corporal, April 1, 1863. Killed in the Battle of Chickamauga, September 19, 1863. Color Bearer for a time.

CRONE, PETER—Enrolled at Fostoria, August 16, 1862. Promoted to Corporal. Discharged at Louisville, Ky. February 11, 1863, on account of disability.

CARTWRIGHT, NORMAN S.—Enrolled at Sandusky, May 2, 1864. Transferred to Company A, 51st Ohio Volunteer Infantry, June 10, 1865.

DERN, WILLIAM— Enrolled at Fostoria, August 12, 1862. Mustered out with the Company.

DICKENS, JOHN W—Enrolled at Fostoria, August 12, 1862. Wounded and captured in the Battle of Stone's River, December 31, 1862. In Libby Prison fourteen months. Rejoined Regiment. Wounded at Kenesaw Mountain, June 27, 1864. Mustered out, May 27, 1865, at Cincinnati.

DIEHL, JACOB— Enrolled at Fostoria, August 18, 1862. Died at Nashville, Tenn., February 23, 1863, of disease.

DILLING, ADAM—Enrolled at Fostoria, August 13, 1862. Wounded in the Battle of Chickamauga, September 19, 1863. Accidentally drowned near Memphis, Tenn., April 27, 1865, in Sultana disaster.

DENNIS, GEORGE H.—Enrolled August 14, 1862. Wagoner. Discharged at Murfreesboro', Tenn., March 9, 1863, on account of disability. Deceased.

DAYS, CLARK — Enrolled at Fostoria, August 14, 1862. Discharged at Murfreesboro', Tenn., December 14, 1863, on account of disability. Deceased.

- DECKER, WILLIAM O.—Enrolled at Sandusky, May 10, 1864. Transferred to Company A, 51st Ohio Volunteer Infantry, June 10, 1865.
- ETTINGER, LEVI J. B.—Enrolled at Fostoria, August 18, 1862. Promoted to Corporal, April 1, 1863. Mustered out with the Company.
- EVERETT, JACOB—Enrolled at Fostoria, August 14, 1862. Mustered out with the Company. Deceased.
- EHRHART, DAVID—Enrolled August 16, 1862. Transferred to Company K, 1st United States Veteran Volunteer Engineers, August 4, 1864. Mustered out, June 30, 1865. Deceased.
- FRY, JEREMIAH B.—Enrolled at Fostoria, August 11, 1862. Died at Chattanooga, Tenn., November 21, 1863, of disease.
- FREESE, AMON—Enrolled at Fostoria, August 12, 1862. Transferred to Company H, 19th Regiment, Veteran Reserve Corps, March 24, 1864. Mustered out, June 13, 1865, at Elmira, N.Y.
- FEBLES, GEORGE—Enrolled at Fostoria, August 12, 1862. Transferred to Veteran Reserve Corps, April 15, 1864. Musician.
- GEORGE, HENRY—Enrolled August 2, 1862. Promoted to Corporal, September 25, 1862. Wounded and captured in the Battle of Stone's River, December 31, 1862. Promoted to Sergeant, April 1, 1863. Wounded in Battle of Franklin, Tenn., November 30, 1864. Promoted to First Sergeant, December 2, 1864. Mustered out at Louisville, Ky., May 13, 1865. Deceased.
- HEMMING, ALBERT—Enrolled at London, August 14, 1862. Mustered as Sergeant. Taken prisoner in Battle of Stone's River, December 31, 1862. Compelled to drive team from between lines. Escaped during a stampede caused by cavalry charge, and rejoined Regiment at Stevenson, Ala. Sent in the winter of 1864 to Ohio on recruiting service. Assigned to special service looking after deserters and bounty-jumpers. Mustered out, June 15, 1865, at Columbus, O.

HOOVER, JOHN A.—Enrolled at Tiffin, August, 14, 1862. Wounded and captured in the Battle of Nolensville, Tenn., December 26, 1862. Mustered out with the Company.

HULETT, GEORGE W.—Enrolled, August 14, 1862. Promoted to Corporal, November 15, 1862. Killed in Battle of Stone's River, December 31, 1862.

HUGHES, GILBERT—Enrolled at Tiffin, August 14, 1862. Wounded and captured in the Battle of Stone's River, December 31, 1862. Confined in Libby Prison. No record after April, 1863.

HORDSOCK, GEORGE W.—Enrolled at Tiffin, August 13, 1862. Discharged at Louisville, Ky., February 20, 1863, on account of disability.

HUDSON, THOMAS—Enrolled at Tiffin, August 21, 1862. Discharged at Murfreesboro', Tenn., May 17, 1863, on account of disability.

HOLLOPETER, DAVID F.—Enrolled at Fostoria, August 14, 1862. Wounded and captured in the Battle of Stone's River, December 31, 1862. Escaped during a cavalry charge. Wounded in the Battle of Chickamauga, September 20, 1863. Transferred to Veteran Reserve Corps, April 10, 1864.

ILER, JOSEPH D.—Enrolled at Tiffin, August 14, 1862. Mustered as Corporal. Discharged at Ooltewah, Tenn., April 2, 1864, on account of disability.

KNOWLTON, MARK L.—Enrolled at Fostoria, August 14, 1862. Wounded in the Battle of Stone's River, December 31, 1862. Mustered out with the Company.

KIMMEL, MICHAEL—Enrolled at Fostoria, August 16, 1862. Mustered as Corporal. Discharged at Nashville, May 2, 1863, on account of disability. Died at South Milford, Ind., of disease.

KEMPHER, GEORGE—Enrolled at Fostoria, August 12, 1862. Discharged at Annapolis, Md., May 2, 1863.

KREIGER, JACOB—Enrolled at Fostoria, August 14, 1862. Mustered out with the Company.

LONGNECKER, MICHAEL—Enrolled at Fostoria, August 14, 1862. Promoted to Corporal, May 1, 1865. Mustered out with the Company.

LEONARD, JOSEPH B.—Enrolled at Fostoria, August 14, 1862. Promoted to Corporal, May 1, 1865. Mustered out with the Company.

LANEY, LUKE H.—Enrolled at Fostoria, August 14, 1862. Mustered out at Nashville, Tenn., July 4, 1865.

LONG, LUKE A.—Enrolled at Fostoria, August 14, 1862. Died, September 22, 1863, of wounds received in the Battle of Chickamauga, September 19, 1863.

LEE, MONROE—Enrolled at Tiffin, August 15, 1862. See Non-Commissioned Staff.

MILLER, ELISHA P.—Enrolled at Sandusky, April 27, 1864. Died, March 15, 1865, at Louisville, Ky., of disease.

MOORE, GEORGE D. — Enrolled at Fostoria, August 14, 1862. Taken prisoner in the Battle of Stone's River, December 31, 1862. Paroled. No record after May, 1863.

McCLELLAN, JOSEPH—Enrolled at Tiffin, August 15, 1862. Discharged, December 26, 1862, at Bowling Green, Ky., on account of disability.

MOHLER, JOHN H.—Enrolled at Fostoria, August 15, 1862. Discharged at Cincinnati, April 14, 1863, on account of disability.

MILLER, HENRY—Enrolled at Fostoria, August 12, 1862. Transferred to 139th Company, 2nd Battalion, Veteran Reserve Corps, April 10, 1864. Mustered out, June 30, 1865, at Nashville, Tenn.

MOWRY, DAVID—Enrolled at Fostoria, August 18, 1862. Transferred to Company K, 1st Regiment, United States Veteran Volunteer Engineers, August 7, 1864. Mustered out, June 30, 1865.

MARTIN, JACOB W.—Enrolled at Fostoria, August 14, 1862. Wounded in the Battle of Chickamauga, September 19, 1863. Promoted to Corporal, August 22, 1864. Wounded in the Battle of Franklin, November 30, 1864. Mustered out with Company.

MILLER, EMANUEL—Enrolled at Fostoria, August 8, 1862. Promoted to Corporal, December 2, 1864. Mustered out with Company.

NEDERHOUSER, JOHN J.—Enrolled at Fostoria, August 14, 1862. Mustered out with the Company.

NORTON, CYRUS G.—Enrolled at Tiffin, August 12, 1862. Mustered as Corporal. On detached service at Louisville, Ky. Mustered out with Company.

NEWHOUSE, DAVID K.—Enrolled at Fostoria, August 18, 1862. Wounded at Knob Gap, December 26, 1862. Ordered to the Hospital, but rejoined Regiment in front of the enemy at Stone's River, and was killed—shot through the head, in battle, December 31, 1862.

NICKOLAS, JEREMIAH — Enrolled at Fostoria, August 13, 1862. Wounded and captured in the Battle of Stone's River, December 31, 1862. Died at Chattanooga, Tenn., November 25, 1863, of wounds received in the Battle of Chickamauga, September 19, 1863.

NEIKIRK, SAMUEL—Enrolled at Tiffin, August 15, 1862. Discharged at Nashville, Tenn., April 12, 1863, on account of disability.

NORTON, JAMES A.—Enrolled at Tiffin, August 16, 1862. Mustered as Sergeant. Discharged at Louisville, Ky., October 13, 1864, to date October 6, 1864, to accept appointment as First Lieutenant and Adjutant in 123rd United States Colored Infantry. Mustered out, October 16, 1865.

ORWIG, JAMES S.—Enrolled, August 13, 1862. Discharged at Murfreesboro', Tenn., May 15, 1863, on account of disability. Deceased.

PARKHURST, MOSES — Enrolled at Fostoria, August 12, 1862. Mustered as Corporal. Killed in the Battle of Stone's River, December 31, 1862. Mortally wounded and died a few hours later on the field where he fell.

POWELL, JOHN P.—Enrolled at Fostoria, January 20, 1864. Transferred to Company F, 51st Ohio Volunteer Infantry, June 10, 1865. Mustered out, June 13, 1865, at Nashville.

POWELL, JOSEPH—Enrolled at Fostoria, August 16, 1862. Captured in the Battle of Stone's River, December 31, 1862, but was left at Murfreesboro' when the rebels retreated. Promoted to Corporal, August 22, 1864. Died at Nashville, Tenn., January 14, 1865, of wounds received in Battle of Nashville.

REESE, JOSEPH—Enrolled at Fostoria, August 13, 1862. Wounded in right forearm at Kingston, Ga., May 19, 1864. Mustered out, July 1, 1865, at Cairo, Ill.

REESE, GIDEON H.—Enrolled at Fostoria, August 15, 1862. Discharged at Louisville, Ky., November 20, 1863, on account of disability. Died at his home, Kansas, O., April 12, 1881.

REESE, GEORGE W.—Enrolled at Fostoria, August 13, 1862. Transferred to Veteran Reserve Corps, September 1, 1863. Mustered out, 1865.

SHUMAN, THOMAS G.—Enrolled at Tiffin, August 13, 1862. Promoted to Corporal, December 2, 1864. Mustered out with Company.

SHUMAN, AMOS C.—Enrolled at Tiffin, August 11, 1862. Promoted to Corporal, May 5, 1865. Mustered out with the Company. Died at his father's home, near Kansas, Ohio, February 3, 1868.

SHUMAN, WILLIAM F.—Enrolled at Tiffin, August 13, 1862. Detailed as Bugler. Mustered out with Company.

SOLOMON, ISAIAH N.—Enrolled at Fostoria, August 16, 1862. Wounded at Rocky Face Ridge, May 11, 1864. Promoted to Corporal, May 1, 1865. Mustered out with Company.

SPROUT, SAMUEL—Enrolled at Fostoria, August 15, 1862. Mustered out with Company.

SHUMAN, JOHN—Enrolled at Tiffin, August 13, 1862. See Non-Commissioned Staff.

SHOUP, JOHN H.—Enrolled at Tiffin, August 20, 1862. Transferred to 154th Company, 2nd Battalion, Veteran Reserve Corps, April 30, 1864. Mustered out, June 30, 1865, at Nashville, Tenn. Died in 1885.

SAUM, SOLOMON—Enrolled at Fostoria, August 14, 1862. Transferred to Veteran Reserve Corps, November 11, 1863.

STRAYER, SAMUEL.—Enrolled at Sandusky, August 14, 1862. Mustered as Sergeant. Taken prisoner in the Battle of Stone's River, December 31, 1862. Died in the hands of the enemy at Atlanta, January 9, 1863. Promoted to Second Lieutenant, January 21, 1863, before notice of death was received.

STEVENS, THOMAS—Enrolled at Sandusky, August 2, 1862. Mustered as Sergeant. Died at Nashville, Tenn., January 22, 1863, of disease.

STEWART, SAMUEL H.—Enrolled at Tiffin, August 13, 1862. Died of typhoid fever, at Edgefield, Tenn., November 25, 1862. Stewart Post, G. A. R., of Bettsville, is named in honor of this excellent man.

SMITH, ALEXANDER—Enrolled at Tiffin, August 12, 1862. Died of disease, at Nashville, Tenn., December 8, 1862.

SMITH, JACOB—Enrolled at Fostoria, August 14, 1862. Taken prisoner in the Battle of Chickamauga, September 19, 1863, and died in prison at Richmond, Va., February 17, 1864.

SHUMAKER, MICHAEL W.—Enrolled at Tiffin, August 13, 1862. Died at Cincinnati, October 7, 1862, of disease.

SECKMAN, JESSE D.—Enrolled at Tiffin, August 15, 1862. Mustered as Corporal. Died of typhoid fever, at Murfreesboro', Tenn., February 26, 1863. Remains brought home and interred on the old farm.

SHRINER, JOHN H.—Enrolled at Tiffin, August 15, 1862. Taken prisoner in the Battle of Chickamauga, September 19, 1863. Died in Andersonville Prison, August 11, 1864.

SCHAULL, GEORGE W.—Enrolled at Tiffin, August 22, 1862. Mustered as Corporal. Discharged at Louisville, Ky., December 26, 1862, on account of disability.

SLAYMAKER, RUFUS H.—Enrolled at Tiffin, August 14, 1862. Wounded in the right thigh in the Battle of Perryville; also wounded at Kenesaw Mountain, Ga.

Mustered out at Nashville, Tenn., May 18, 1865, on account of wounds. First man in the Regiment wounded by the enemy.

STEWARD, WILLIAM H.—Enrolled at Fostoria, August 12, 1862. Discharged at Nashville, Tenn., March 14, 1863, on account of disability.

STRAUSBAUGH, WILLIAM G.—Enrolled at Tiffin, August 13, 1862. Discharged at Bridgeport, Ala., December 13, 1863, on account of disability.

VALENTINE, JOHN W.—Enrolled at Tiffin, August 14, 1862. Died at Murfreesboro', Tenn., February 11, 1863, of disease.

WEIKERT, GEORGE W.—Enrolled at Tiffin, August 15, 1862. Wounded and taken prisoner in the Battle of Stone's River, December 31, 1862. Promoted to Corporal, November 15, 1862; to Sergeant, December 2, 1864. Mustered out with the Company. Deceased.

WARNER, SYLVESTER—Enrolled at Fostoria, August 22, 1862. Died at Nashville, Tenn., January 29, 1863, of disease.

WELLS, WILLIAM—Enrolled at Fostoria, August 18, 1862. Discharged at Louisville, Ky., February 14, 1863, on account of disability.

WONDERLY, JOSEPH W.—Enrolled at Fostoria, August 18, 1862. Transferred to Company K, 1st Regiment, United States Veteran Volunteer Engineers, August 7, 1864. Mustered out, June 30, 1865. Deceased.

YENTER, JOHN H.—Enrolled at Tiffin, August 20, 1862. Discharged on account of disability, at Nashville, Tenn., May 30, 1863. Mustered in as John H. Bentzer. Transferred to Company E, as Musician.

www.ingramcontent.com/pod-product-compliance
Lightning Source LLC
Chambersburg PA
CBHW031955300426
44117CB00008B/764